This book would have been impossible without the help, assistance and guidance of Barrie Downer from the Barrow Submariners Associate. He kindly proof read, checked the technicalities of the craft and next to the National Archives was my main source.

Thank you Barrie.

A PLEA FROM THE AUTHOR

This is the second volume of The Suicide Club, its predecessor having been a trouble creature and withdrawn. There were in that original publication's technical issues in uploading the file, problems which even Amazon could not resolve. A 'work-around' I devised resulted unintentionally in an early draft, that had yet to be proofread being published.

The Suicide Club has now been proofread and the appendix vastly expanded. It is a huge piece of work based on over 2000 pages within the National Archives at Kew. This new edition has been proofread and checked by three people, me included. However, I am not naive enough to think it will emerge free of errors. If you find any, please do not post a bad review but drop me an email and I will correct any mistakes. This volume is the result of hundreds of hours work and a head of hair that went from brown to white during its editing. So, allow me the chance to make amendments.

THANK YOU

Andy South (andyuknaval@gmail.com)

ANDY SOUTH

THE SUICIDE CLUB

CLUB

A HISTORY OF THE ROYAL NAVY'S STEAM POWERED 'K' CLASS SUBMARINES.

CONTENTS

THE 'K' BOAT MAPS.

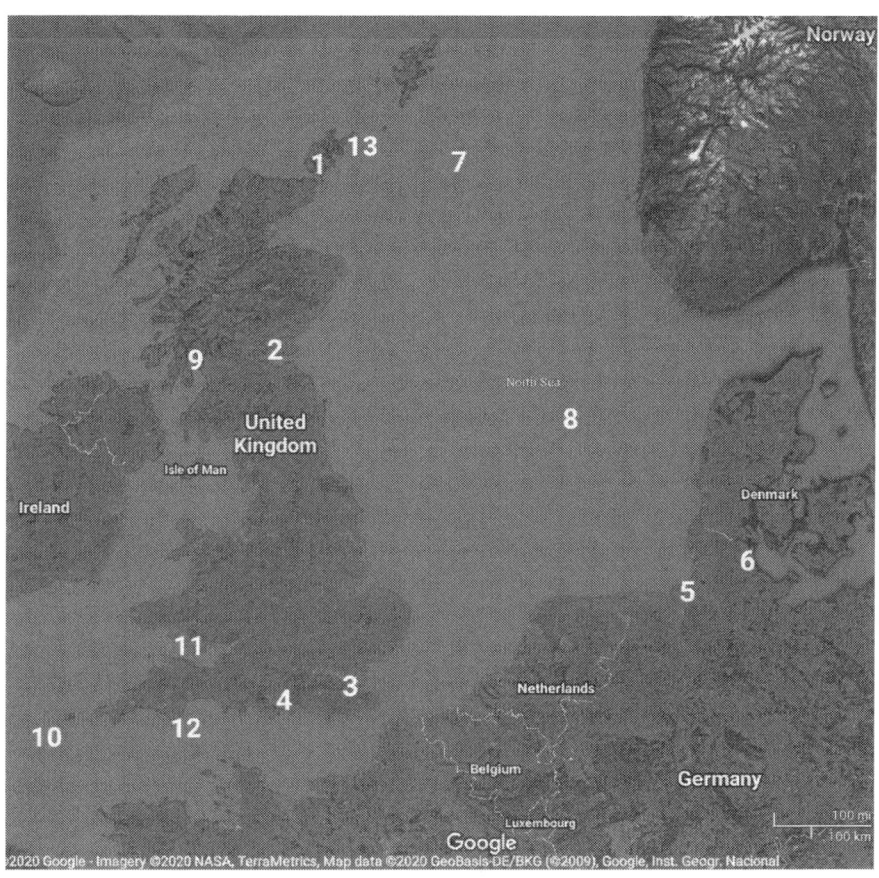

1: SCAPA FLOW, 2: ROSYTH & MAY ISLAND, 3: CHATHAM, 4: PORTSMOUTH & THE SOLENT, 5: WILHELMSHAVEN, 6: KIEL, 7: HMS K7 U-BOAT INCIDENT, 8: HMS K4 WRECK, 9: GARELOCH, 10: HMS K5 WRECK, 11: MILFORD HAVEN, 12: TOR BAY, 13: HMS K1's GROUNDING. (ALL POSITIONS ARE APPROXIMATED)

MODERN DAY PORTSMOUTH

A: THE TIDAL BASIN. THE AREA OF THE DOCKYARD WHERE HMS K15 SANK WHILE MOORED ALONGSIDE THE CRUISER, HMS CANTERBURY.

B: FOUNTAIN LAKE WHERE THE K15 WAS TOWED TO AND BEACHED AFTER SHE HAD BEEN WAS RECOVERED. THE 'LAKE' TODAY HOLDS THE ROTTED REMAINS OF TWO DESTROYERS FROM THE KAISERS HIGH SEAS FLEET AND IS THE CURRENT HOME OF THE FALKLANDS VETERAN, HMS BRISTOL.

C: PORTSMOUTH NAVAL DOCK YARD, HOME OF THE ROYAL NAVY AND ALSO THE LOCATION FOR THE CONSTRUCTION OF THE K1,K2 & K5.

D: HMB DOLPHIN, THE SHORE ESTABLISHMENT AND HOME FOR R.N SUBMARINE THE FORCE DURING THE TWO WORLD WARS.

E: STOKES BAY, WHERE NUMBER OF K BOATS EXPERIENCED DIFFICULTIES.

THE CLYDE & GARELOCH TODAY.

A: THE SITE OF THE SHIPYARD FAIRLANDS.

B: THE WHITEINCH FERRY, WHICH AS WITH A, IS NO MORE.

C: SHANDON

D: HMB FASLANE TODAY THE HOME OF THE ROYAL NAVY'S SUBMARINE FORCE.

E: AN APPROXIMATION OF THE SITE WHERE THE K13 SANK.

F: THE ROUTE OUT TO SEA.

(FROM A TO E IS AN APPROXIMATE 24 MILES OR 39 KM, WHICH IS BETWEEN 2 TO 3 HOURS AT 8 KNOTS).

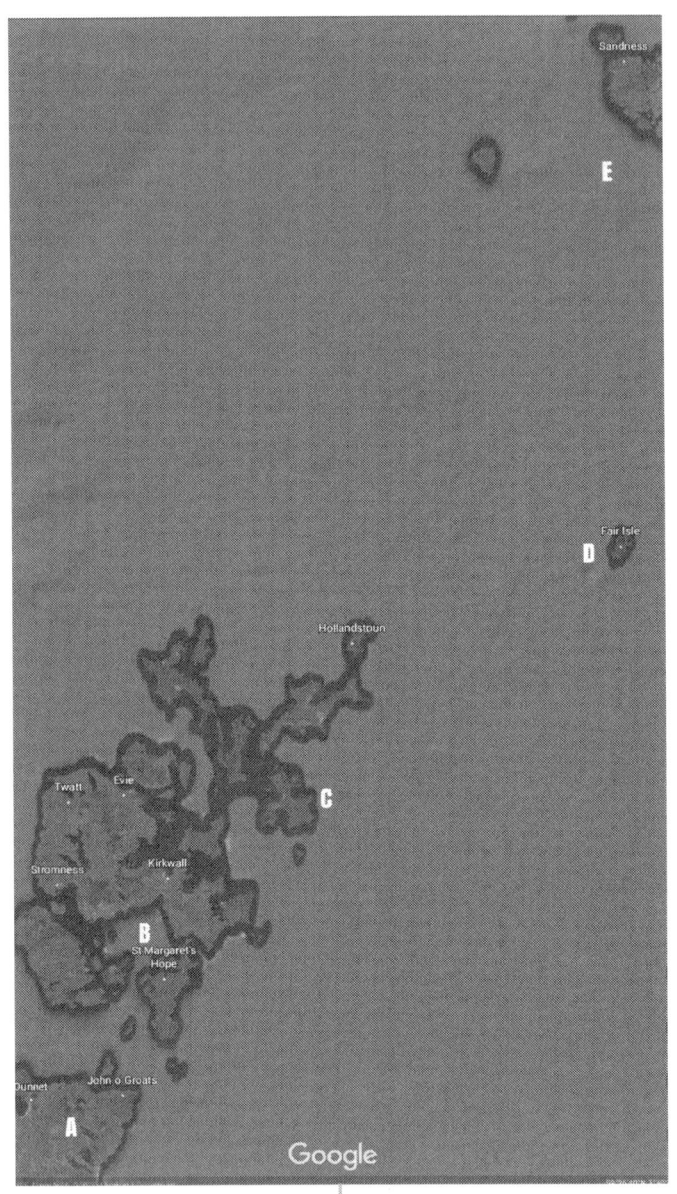

PREVIOUS PAGE
A: SCOTTISH MAINLAND B: SCAPA FLOW C: K1'S
GROUNDING D: FAIR ISLE E: SHETLAND

THE BATTLE OF MAY ISLAND
31st JANUARY 1918

A: ROSYTH, B: CEAMOND ISLE, C: INCHCOLM ISLAND, D: INCKEITH, E: ISLE OF MAY, F: K4 WRECKAGE, G: K17 WRECKAGE

INTRODUCTION

Jinx: "bad luck, or a person or thing that is believed to bring bad luck". (The Cambridge English Dictionary)

On England's southern coastline is an area known as the Solent. It is formed of a large body of water, which is framed by the isle of Wight to the south and Portsmouth (the home of the Royal Navy) to its northern boundary. The river Hamble empties into this large expanse of water, bringing with it shipping from one of England's main seaports, Southampton. The area is never devoid of shipping and in addition to those merchant and warships are the numerous ferries that ply the route between the mainland and the island. During 1916 the area was even busier than was usual, as this was a time of conflict and the Royal Navy was fighting the war, as well as escorting the crowded troopships to the French and Belgium ports.

On a cold autumnal day in October 1916 the troops bound for France and the passengers on the ferries would have seen a unique and bizarre sight, as they peered out over the deck rails of their transports. Towering over the water, leaning at a deranged angle, stood a steel spire of over a hundred feet in its height. The summit of this steeple was not marked by a weathervane or a cross, but instead by two bronze seven-foot propellers, that were spinning as if they were possessed by a demonic force.

AN IMAGE OF THE K2's FORWARD PORTION OF HER HULL. IT ALLOWS A CLEAR VIEW OF HER NEW SWAN BOW AND THE CONNING TOWER'S PROFILE. THE OPEN HATCH IN THE SUPERSTRUCTURE HOUSES THE DECK TORPEDO TUBES

Within that sea bound 'church' 'steeple was "Bertie", the future King of England and father of Queen Elizabeth II. The Prince was clinging on to the submarine's internal fittings, in a frantic effort to avoid sliding down the 'K' boats interior length. Alongside him and holding on with an equal determination was an Admiral and around them, struggling to redeem the situation, were over 50 Royal Navy officers and crew. As odd and weird as the scene appeared both on the surface and within that 'steeple it could be accepted as just another normal day in the life of the 'Jinx'. A 'curse, that seemed to both haunted and blight the commissions of the Royal Navy's giant submarines, the 'K' class.

THE STERN PORTION OF THE K2, MOST LIKELY IN THE SAME DOCKYARD AS THE PREVIOUS PHOTO.

The eighteen submersible boats are probably the worst submarines to ever have flown the White Ensign. From that October day in Southern England, they were to quickly become known for being both accident prone and killers of their own crew. The reputation was so bad that to some within the naval world the boats earned the name, the 'Suicide Club' and to others they were known as the 'Kalamity' class. By the time in 1931 when the final boat (the K26) in a saga lasting just fifteen years, hauled down her White Ensign, over two hundred men had died serving on the vessels. Of those crews many were burnt, scolded, and scarred by service on the boats. Most served within the Royal Navy, but amongst those hundreds were a small number of dockyard workers who also became ensnared by the 'jinx'.

The boats were to serve through the latter half of World War one and after hundreds of hours patrolling the North Sea, only one was to ever encounter and engage the enemy. True to the reputation of the 'K' class, that encounter started farcically with friendly fire and ended with a rapid withdraw by the British submarine. The 'K' boats were never to fight or be present in a sea battle, but in 1918 nine of them took part in the 'Battle of May' Island, where two 'K' boats were sunk, four more, (and a light cruiser) were heavily damaged. But although boats were lost and men died, no enemy were present at the 'battle'! But despite all the 'weirdness' of the class, they held one more trump card. They were something rare in the world of naval craft, they were steam powered...

PART ONE. THE CONCEPTION.

(1914-1916)

HMS K15 RUNNING AWASH ON THE SURFACE

CHAPTER ONE. THE CONCEPT OF THE FLEET-SUBMARINE

"Horrible things to have around from
[a] big ship point of view".
(Admiral Keyes)

P rior to the First World War, a study that had been
undertaken by the Royal Navy's War College, concluded that the addition of submarines working in
advance of the battle fleet, would be of a great benefit and
support of the battleships even should the enemy become
aware of their presence. That report was to be the seedling
from which developed the concept of the Fleet-submarine.

HMAS A1, the first British submarine had only entered service twelve years before the outbreak of war in 1914. As the
British and German fleets exchanged blows across the world,

the submarine was an unknown factor within the Naval world of planning and strategy. The Admirals, Captains and the 'experts' had no real evidence on which to predict the role that this new-fangled and very 'un-English' type of warship would fill. The submersible commerce raider that the Germans would refine within the waters of the Atlantic, was before 1914 all but inconceivable. If the navy must have the submarine, then it would surely stalk the unwary battleship Captain and from the depths, launch salvos of torpedoes sending the mighty dreadnought to the seabed.

The submarine would operate in direct support of the fleet's squadrons as they steamed out to confront the Kaiser's fleet. Then once the enemy had been crushed and defeated, the submarine would lie in wait and sink the battered remnants as they tried to flee home.

The inconclusive nature of the battle of Jutland brought a new urgency and life to the concept. The German High Seas Fleet had managed to escape from the jaws of defeat, but if there had been a number of submarines with a sufficient speed present, they could have launched attacks before the battleships met. Then as the big guns exchanged fire they could have slipped past the German squadrons and ambushed them on their route home. The German Admiral Scheer had his own version of a similar plan with his U-boats at Jutland. He had ordered them to be positioned along the most likely routes of the Grand Fleet as it steamed south east across the North Sea. They were to snare the unaware Grand Fleet and to whittle its superior Dreadnought numbers down. A cunning plan, that on the day was to prove to be beyond the diesel-powered U-boats capacity and was to fail. However, the British Admiralty were confident that their fleet-submarines would have a sufficient turn of speed to enable them to keep station with the fleet and be able to react to events as they unfolded. Unlike the German efforts, no prepositioning would be needed. A maximum speed of 24 knots was deemed sufficient to meet with this goal and to be flexible to the developing battle. It was envisaged by the Admirals in London that their 'K' boats be capable of maintaining a speed of between 19 and 20 knots, in weather that would force the escorting destroyers to reduce their speed to 15 knots or suffer structural damage. In September 1918 as the Grand Fleet lay hove too in heavy seas, two of the 'K' boats steamed past the battered ships, as if the weather were of little account to them. It was not mentioned that the 'K' boats would surely in turn receive damage to their own bridges and superstructure, which with their lower freeboard, were much nearer to the seas level and the impact of its pounding waves.

Once the concept of steam power had been introduced to the Navy's corridors of command, it was overlooked that the stokers would be deluged by cascades of bitterly cold sea water as it flooded down the boat's funnels and the crafts numerous vents. The invading waters would in the process extinguish the boilers, but the Admirals reasoned that (in a waterlogged and pitching boat) these would easily be relit. It was also felt that the ½ inch hull plating that was to form the 'K' boats hull, would keep the pounding seas at bay, protecting them from suffering as much damage as the thinner plating of a destroyer. The operational plan that was devised for the 'K' boats was for them to sail with the fleet, being stationed in advance of the battle squadrons and behind the fleet's scouts. Once the scouts sighted the German fleet, the submarines were to use their superior surface speed and low silhouette to achieve a position from where they could launch salvos of torpedoes at the oncoming enemy battle squadrons. The thinking was that the 21 plus knot fleet-submarine could achieve what the more traditional diesel-powered submersible could not, as the smaller craft would be secured alongside in harbour and would not arrive on the field of battle until the action was over. While there would be a few conventional submarines already out on patrol, they would lack the speed to work themselves into an attacking position. In addition to a higher speed, the fleet-submarine would require as large a number of torpedo tubes as was feasible, combined with an experienced Captain serving as the flotilla leader (on board an attached light cruiser), who had a good grasp of submarine warfare tactics.

On the occasions during the war when the 'K' boats worked in unison with the fleet, they were allocated a position 10 miles in advance of the main battle squadrons. There they were located between the bows of the battleships that lay astern of them and the screen of light forces spread out to about 25 miles in advance of them. Once the screening or scouting forces sighted the enemy their orders were to report the discovery by W/T (wireless transmission). The Captain (S) (or flotilla leader) would then manoeuvre his 'K' boats to a position from where they would lie ahead of the predicted course of the enemy battle fleet. They would also seek to be stationed slightly to the side furthest from the British heavy ships. Having manoeuvred themselves into position the boats would be allocated into pairs and within those two boat groups, they were to act independently of each other. It was reasoned that there would be at least three pairs of the fleet-submarines now laying on the surface awaiting the enemies massed fleet to appear on the horizon. The distance between the pairs of boats would vary according to the circumstances of the day, but the goal was to achieve the placement of at least two of the pairs of 'K' boats in an attacking position, even if the enemy were to make an unexpected change of course.

As the smudges of funnel smoke announcing the enemy's forces appeared on the horizon, the pairs of boats would separate until a mile of sea water lay between each individual submarine. This would permit them sufficient space to be able to operate submerged, but with no immediate fear of collisions between them. Aside from the submarine's plumes of funnel smoke, it was reasoned that the conning tower (seen from two miles and end-on) of a surfaced 'K' boat was not an easy thing to see, even in calm weather. In addition, the exchange of fire between the opposing light forces would distract the enemy's lookout's attention sufficiently, to ensure the 'K' boats would remain unobserved. Having parted the two Captains would prepare their craft for diving and as the leading enemy ships came to about four miles off the boats, they would slowly partially submerge, taking at the most five minutes. Then once a signal notifying Captain (S) that all was prepared, the 'K' boats would be trimmed down to create as lower profile as was possible in the current sea conditions to avoid being sighted. If they were threatened the 'K' boat could (in theory) reach periscope depth in four minutes, with her hull being under water in less than two minutes. But if the enemy somehow sighted the low 'K' boat hull and opened fire, the chance of a shell damaging the inner hull when the submarine was low in the water, was remote (?). At a short range the shells would burst, (or ricochet), on the water or on her outer hull. It was reasoned that the superstructure might be shot to pieces without doing more damage (again, in theory) than flooding the conning tower and funnels, which could easily be adjusted for within the trim. Maybe a slightly dubious line of thought, by the Admirals in London.

Having delayed their submergence until it was no longer safe to remain on the surface, the 'K' boats had now to surrender their main asset, speed, and submerge. They were from this point limited in their effective range of operations (and battery time) and unless the Captain (S) had succeeded to position his boats well, the enemy fleet would soon pass out of range of the craft. The submerged hunters could only give chase at seven knots, with each turn of the propellers, their batteries lives were a tiny bit more diminished and their remaining range that bit less. But if the planning and positioning had gone well, the boats would now be in the ideal position. Their scope of manoeuvrability would allow one hour of submerged existence, which should be enough to last until the battle had passed over the horizon. The Admirals reasoned how would Jutland have been concluded if swarms of torpedoes were fired from beneath the waves even before the first large calibre shell fire was exchanged? With the time required to reload the tubes, the possibility of a second salvo of torpedoes would have been all but impossible before the enemy had passed once more out of range. As the fleets gently pulled apart, the 'K' boats would now adopt the role of hunters for stragglers. Once the enemy fleet had passed over the horizon, the boats could surface and having relighted their boilers, would concentrate on a pre-arranged line off the enemy coast to intercept the defeated and battered enemy ships as it fled for the sanctuary of its home ports.

After the war a few of the class's critics derided the usefulness of even using the 'K' boats to patrol the North Sea. But it is too often forgotten that the boats were conceived, designed, and built as fleet-submarine and operating within the fleet was originally the classes primary role. In addition, the class originated largely at the request of the surface fleet admirals and not, as is so easily assumed, a product of the

Submarine Branch. They were not a type of vessel the submarine service wanted or requested.

The North Sea patrols adopted during the latter part of the war at sea were undertaken once it was realized there was unlikely to be a 'Jutland II'. The patrols served to exercise the boats, which had been found to suffer from a catalogue of minor breakdowns after a too long a period alongside in Scapa or Rosyth. Plus, with their complexity of diving, the crew's mantra had to be practice, practice, practice. While the patrols were not to be of a success in combating the enemy, it was found after a few weeks the average number of effective boats was nearly doubled.

The role of a 'K' boat on a North Sea patrol was considerably different to the other classes of submarines within the Royal Navy. When, (or if) a 'K' boat sighted the enemy her orders were to despatch a W/T report immediately. Then partially submerged they were to shadow under steam power, (and trailing a cloud of funnel smoke), all the time passing updates to the oncoming Grand Fleet. They were not there to attack the enemy, that was a role reserved for once the battleships had arrived on the scene.

To quote an optimistic Admiral Fisher to Admiral Hall on the 4th September 1913:

> *"Without any doubt whatsoever, a fast battle fleet which can always be accompanied by submarines under all circumstances would possess an overwhelming fighting advantage".*

Hindsight tells us how impossible Fisher's idea was in the early twentieth century.

CHAPTER TWO. HMS SWORDFISH

"The fleet submarine is a submarine with the speed, range, and endurance to operate as part of a navy's Battle Fleet. Examples of fleet submarines are the British K class and the American Gato class. Within the modern Royal Navy, the term is used for the British nuclear-powered attack submarines". Wikipedia

One of the first supporters of the concept for the Battle Fleet-Submarine was to be the Royal Navy's Inspector Captain of Submarines, Roger John Brownlow Keyes. In addition to the Commodores support, the Admirals John Jellicoe and David Beatty were to become champions of the idea. But in contrast an early opponent of the theory was Admiral 'Jacky' Fisher.

As the conception took on a solid form, it was deemed in the offices of the Admiralty that these craft should have the capacity to:

> *"steam at 23 knots, to dive in five minutes, to stay submerged for six hours and to be seaworthy on the high seas".*

It was also decided that they would require ten hours of submerged endurance in calm weather. Only once was the fleet-submarines final form (in the shape of the *K12)* able to exceed the 23-knot goal by 1.2 knots, (over a 72-mile stretch). The designers were also tasked with the goal of achieving a dive time of less than 24 minutes and 15 seconds! The class record was to be established by the *K8* at 3 minutes, 25 seconds. The times specified were excessive for a conventional submarine, but for work with the Fleet this was not a real disadvantage. The 'K' boats would in theory receive ample warning of the need to submerge, but no matter how much time, the Captain would still require a well-trained crew who were familiar with every detail of their complex boat.

On the 14th November 1910 Keyes had been appointed as the Royal Navy's Inspecting Captain of Submarines. Before the year was out, he was to call on the two shipbuilders, Vickers Shipbuilding and Engineering in Barrow-in-Furness and the Scotts Shipbuilding and Engineering Company Limited in Greenock on the river Clyde, to each present a design for a submarine capable of overseas service. In addition, the craft were to be capable of working with the fleet at a surfaced speed of 20 knots. The gigantic "HM Flotilla Leaders" design that was presented by Vickers to Keyes was twice the size of the largest submarine currently in service, with an estimated 5,300-mile range.

The Scott's design was for a smaller craft, but they had dismissed the Italian Fiat diesel engines which they were currently building under licence and offered instead the radical idea of installing steam turbines. Keyes loved the notion of the Scott's steam concept, but he was unsure if the scale of the engines needed to power the design was even practical within the hull of a submarine. The steam machinery would force an extraordinary width on the 'K' boats to allow the hull to be capable of containing the steam systems. But placing his concerns aside, Keyes welcomed the concept of steam as a well-tried idea and tested method of (surface) propulsion. On the 4th May 1915 the design was despatch to the Barrow-in-Furness shipyard and despite his mixed feelings, he ordered prototypes for both designs. The Scotts boat was on her completion to become *HMS Swordfish*, while Vickers was to become *HMS Nautilus.*

NAUTILUS (1)

DISPLACEMENT
1,441 TONS SURFACED, 2,026 TONS SUBMERGED.

DIMENSIONS
LENGTH 258 FT 6 INCH (78.79 MTR).

BEAM 17 FT 9 INCH (5.41 MTR).

DRAUGHT 26 FT 0 INCH (7.9 MTR).

PROPULSION
2 SHAFTS , DIESEL, 2 ELECTRIC MOTORS
3,700 BHP 1,000 SHP.

RANGE
5,300 NAUTICAL MILES (9,820 KM) AT 11 KNOTS.

CREW
42.

ARMAMENT
TORPEDO 8 X 18-INCH (457 MM) TORPEDO TUBES
(2 BOW, 4 BEAM, 2 STERN), 16 TORPEDO.

GUN: 1X 3-INCH (76MM) AA GUN.

SWORDFISH

DISPLACEMENT
932 LONG TONS SURFACED. 1,105
LONG TONS SUBMERGED.

DIMENSIONS
LENGTH 231 FT 3.5 INCH (70.49 MTR) (OVERALL.)

BEAM 22 FT 11 INCH (6.99 MTR).

DRAUGHT 14 FT 11 INCH (4.55 MTR.)

PROPULSION
2 SHAFTS, 2 GEARED STEAM TURBINES
4,000 SHP (3,000 KW) 1BOILER)), 2 ELECTRIC
MOTORS 1,400 BHP (1,000 KW).

RANGE
3,000 NAUTICAL MILES (5,600 KM;
3,500 MI) AT 8.5 KNOTS.

CREW
18

ARMAMENT
TORPEDO 2 × 21-INCH (530 MM) TORPEDO
TUBES (BOW)
4 × 18-INCH (460 MM) TORPEDO TUBES (BEAM.

GUN: 2 × 3-INCH (76 MM) GUNS.

It was to be from the *Swordfish* that the 'K' class design drew their steam DNA. The Admiralty placed an order for the Scotts boat on the 18th August 1913, but the laying down of her keel was to be delayed for six months until the 28th February the following year. Then with the outbreak of the First World War in August of that year, her progress on the slip was to be slowed even further and it was not until fourteen months later on the 18th March 1916 that the Swordfish was finally launched. She was to be commissioned just over a month later the 28th April and on the day the white ensign was first hoisted over her, she was renamed *HMS S1*.

The *S1* was to set the trend for headaches with the use of steam power within a submarine hull. She experienced complications of condensation after diving and her fuse box caught fire burning at least one seaman. In her cramped boiler room, a flash back burnt a crewman's face. In addition, the *S1* was found to roll badly whilst she was submerged. But she was not to be deemed finally ready for service until the 21st July 1916, by which time the first of the 'K' boats were already under construction and nearing their own trials. The *S1's* first Captain was to be Commander Geoffrey Layton, who was fresh from his Baltic adventures in command of *HMS E13*. The *S1's* post-completion trials were to drag on for over five months, while she was used to evaluate the feasibility of steam power within a submarines hull. A great deal was to be learnt in those long months about the operation of the navy's first steam powered submarine, which was to 'help' with the 'K' class. During her trials the *S1* proved to be an unstable craft whilst running on the surface, possibly due to the fact that having surfaced, she was unable to pump the water out of the upper part of her double hull-controlled flooding spaces quickly enough. These problems combined with the fact that she was to prove to be too slow to work with the fleet, as had been originally specified, meant it was not possible for her to be an effective warship and she was laid up after her trial's completion.

HMS SWORDFISH IN 1916

But with the demands of war, in June 1917 work was started in the conversion of the *S1* into the role of a surface patrol vessel. In July she returned to her original name and by the 24th January 1918 was ready for her new surface bound role. Her torpedo tubes and disappearing guns had been removed and she was fitted with a forecastle and a bridge. In addition, her funnel was now fixed in place and had been lengthened. She was also rearmed with two 12 pounder guns (3-inch/76 mm) and depth charges, weapons far more suited for her role as an anti-submarine patrol boat. *HMS Swordfish* finally joined the 1st Destroyer Flotilla at Portsmouth upon completion of her second set of sea trials, but nothing much is known today of her subsequent career. She was to be paid off on the 30th October 1918 and had by January 1919 been removed from the Navy List. She was sold for scrap to Poundon, of Portsmouth in July 1922, but was reported to have been resold to Hayes of Porthcawl in 1923.

Before the keel of the *Swordfish* was even laid down in February 1914, the idea of installing steam engines within the hull of a submarine had been classified as 'Strictly Secret' by the admiralty. The First Sea Lord, Admiral Fisher remained uneasy of the steam concept and in June 1913 had written:

> *"The oil engine will govern all sea fighting and all sea fighting is going to be governed by submarines and yet like damned fools we are only spending as much money on them as the Germans and we are behind them in the oil engine and so like the French we are hankering after steam engines in submarines."*

In the spring of 1913, the Director of Naval Construction Sir Eustace Tennyson-d'Eyncourt had been tasked with the production of a third design in the Admiralties quest for a fleet submarine. Keyes described the new design as an 'Ocean' Type and its displacement was to have been 1,700 tons, (2,600 submerged) on a hull of 338 feet (103.02 mtrs) in length, a beam of 29 feet (2) (8.83 mtrs)) and an 11 foot (3.35 mtrs) draught. Her machinery would be:

· Two oil fired steam boilers for the surface.

· Four electric motors for underwater

· One auxiliary diesel motor for the switch from electrical power to steam.

The geared brown-Curtis/Parsons turbines would deliver 10,000 shp, a design speed of 24 knots and a range of 3,000 miles. She was to have been armed with four 21-inch bow torpedo tubes, four 21-inch tubes on the beam and two guns. The boat's design was of a partial double-hull type of construction. A ships model of the 'Ocean' type was ordered, and it was to be tested at the tank at Haslar Creek in Gosport. But by the years end, the design had been rejected as unworkable and at a conference soon after, the Third Sea Lord and Controller of the Navy Rear-Admiral Gordon Moore, cancelled any further work on the design. His stated reasons were the substantial increase in her size over the Navy's existing boats, (1,700 tons as opposed to the 660 tons of the 'E' class boats). It was decided better to wait on the completion of the (non-steam) Nautilus (1,270 tons) which had been laid down in March 1913, before proceeding on anything larger. It was unknown at this stage of the delay in completing the *Nautilus* that her displacement would rise to 1,440 tons.

By 1st January 1915 Fisher had become concerned at the Germans rapid evolution and skill with the handling and design of their U-boats. He was to write on the same day:

> "we can't touch their submarines. We know two of them have gone 19 knots on the surface".

He duly ordered the Director of Naval Construction to waste little time and to produce a design for a 20-knot submarine. To meet Fisher's 20 knot goal d'Eyncourt raised once again the concept of steam propulsion, as the diesel engine had yet to exceed 15.5 knots in service. With the use of steam, he argued he could create a design that would easily exceed the 20-knot goal.

As to the question of steam engines, the French navy had made use of them, but only because their heavy oil engines were found to perform poorly in service. Two months earlier the French steam powered submarine *Archimède* (1911) had been attached to Admiral Keyes command. The 17th December 1914 found the French boat on a North Sea patrol in company with a force of seven British submarines. The eight submarines were laid out in a line across the Heligoland Bight, with the goal of ensnaring Hipper's battlecruiser squadron as it returned from the bombardment of the English east coast ports of Scarborough and Hartlepool.

In the evening heavy seas had washed over the *Archimède* and the force of the waves had bent one of the boat's funnels, rendering her unable to fold it down for diving. Through the night the seas grew gradually worse and the waves washed repeatedly down the offending funnel, (a failing that was to become a trademark of the 'K' class). With water filling the engine room, the crew were forced to form a chain of buckets to bail the *Archimède* out. Over the next two days the crippled submarine crawled westwards on her electric motors unable to dive and her crew bailing constantly. Fortunately for the exhausted men the storm that had doused their steam engines was to keep the German patrols tucked up in their bases. On board during the French boats patrol was a man who was to command the *K13,* Captain Herbert. He was on board in the role of a British Liaison Officer and had won the Frenchmen's praise by assisting with the bailing and by his encouraging comments. While out in the stormy North Sea a French Captain struggled to bring his boat home, the complexity of a steam submarines construction had delayed Swordfish's completion by additional months. She was already 14 months into the build and still incomplete. The French experience and the build problems with the *Swordfish* all seem to forewarn the combination of steam and submersibles were not an easy mix, but few in London were listening. One man who did pay attention was Fisher and on learning of the French patrol debacle had warned d'Eyncourt that he never wanted to hear of steam submarines again. This disillusionment was in part the reason Fisher was to order eight 'H' and twenty-eight 'J' class during January 1915. The 'J' boats were a more realistic solution for a true fleet-submarine, but despite that it was a role, (like the 'K' boats) they were to fail in.

During 1913 Keyes, (a man who was never to serve on board a submarine), remained a strong supporter of the fleet-submarine concept and he organised a joint exercise. Four diesel submarines were to be stationed in a line abreast, with a mile of sea water between each vessel, forming the forward screen of the fleet's cruisers. Keyes, (who was onboard the destroyer *HMS Swift)*, ordered the cruisers to warn him on their sighting of the 'enemy' and he would despatch his submarines to attack the opposing fleet. The entire saga was to be restricted to 14 knots, that being the best speed the participating submarines were capable of. Keyes said after the exercise's conclusion that he had:

> *"some very bad moments...watching heavy ships, cruisers and destroyers manoeuvring in all directions over the submarines and for some hours I was in mortal fear that one of the submarines had come to grief; however, she rose at last and all was well".*

Despite this and the imposed speed restriction, he confidently announced that the exercise had been a success and had proved the fleet-submarine concept. Fisher remained a believer of the diesel-powered fleet submarine and a supporter of Sydney Stewart Hall, who was to become the Royal

Navy's top submarine officer as Commodore (S), replacing Keyes. Hall was as his predecessor had been, a supporter of the Fleet-submarine concept. But after two months service in his new post he announced that the 'J' class would not be up to their envisaged fleet role. The triple-screw diesel configuration had the capacity to only allow them to make 19 knots on the surface, less than the 21 knot's envisaged that they'd need if they were to accompany the fleet, (21 knots being the design speed of *HMS Dreadnought*). The Admirals Jellicoe, Beatty and Hall had all insisted on a Fleet-submarine having a top speed of 21 knots.

Within the offices of the Admiralty and amongst the Admirals commanding at sea, there was a growing fear that Germany would soon master and develop a true fleet-submarine of their own. Vickers being aware of that school of thought, continued to advise that in their opinion only steam would proof sufficient to provide the power and speed for such a craft and submitted a supporting design. d'Eyncourt's 1913 plan was brought out once more, dusted down and compared to the Vickers design. But d'Eyncourt's concept was deemed to offer the faster surface speed and was seen for that reason as the better design. At 24 knots d'Eyncourt claimed that his boat was better than the *Archimède,* plus he had resolved the funnel and vent issues, his solution being "fool-proof". Tennyson-d'Eyncourt described his finished design as a submersible destroyer and after consideration Fisher finally relented to the pressure for a steam power submarine, but he added the rider that an auxiliary diesel engine be added to the design in order to shorten the boats dive time and getting her underway once more on having surfaced. The new steam submarines that would in time become the 'K' boats, were accordingly to have seven power units. Fisher also insisted changes be made to the boiler room design. He foresaw that once the order to dive had been given, the redundant boilers would become a hazard with their residual temperature, and they would continue to expel heat as they slowly cooled. The heat would no longer have the ability to escape through the funnels and the boiler room would become uninhabitable, a shipboard sauna! With the crew unable to tolerate the stifling heat, the boiler room could only really be sealed off behind two watertight doors, effectively cutting the boat into two. The door that separated the boiler and engine room was in the form of an airlock. Fisher insisted that the finalized design incorporate a corridor that was to run parallel to the boiler room and which would allow the crew to pass between the forward and stern portions of the hull. Fisher also had the two guns increased to three and in addition the eight 21-inch torpedo tubes were amended to ten 18-inch, due to the 18-inch being already in production and the construction time that would be saved. The deck tubes were added to the design and only then did Fisher confirmed the order for four of the finalized project.

D'Eyncourt's forwarded the completed design to Vickers requesting that a fast delivery be provided on two of the four boats. The Admiralty accepted Vickers proposed price tag of £300,000. (2017=£26,578,548) (3) which poorly compared to a 'D' class (1908) submarine with a price tag of £89,000 (average) (2017=£6,957,325)). This was a 237% increase in price over the smaller conventional craft. The 'K' class in price matched a light cruiser, for example HMAS Sydney had a comparative price tag of £334,053. But price aside, the new Fleet-Submarines were on a scale not seen before, plus in both their size and armament they were more akin to a destroyer than the navy's existing submarines (4). Whichever way the cost of a 'K' is examined, they remain expensive and for the amount of success they brought to the navy, the cost of the class £5,700,000 (approx.) (2017=

£555,180,000)) was in hindsight a waste of money. The technology was never developed beyond the original class and the money could have been used for more useful projects. The unit cost of £300,000 could have brought the navy three much needed destroyers or a light cruiser. In 1915 the contracts for *K1* and *K2* were awarded to the Portsmouth naval yard, while *K3* and *K4's* contracts went to Vickers. Then on the 27th May 1915 Fisher resigned over the Dardanelles campaign and as soon as he was gone, an additional ten 'K' boats were ordered. With the orders placed d'Eyncourt push for an even bigger 30 knot boat, but the Admirals turned the concept down.

The first of the craft to be laid down, (by the king) was the *K3*, commissioning on the 4th August 1916. The Admiralty had ordered twentyone hulls now with no working-class prototype and were committed to an expenditure of over £6,000,000 (2017=£353,953,200) on an untried concept. But the designers reassured the Admirals, telling them not to worry as the 'K' boat design could not be faulted!

1: The order was given to Vickers in 1912 and her keel was laid down in March 1913. Although launched in 1914 it took until 1917 to complete the vessel. Nautilus spent most of her life with the 1st Submarine Flotilla at Portsmouth as a depot ship and later as a battery charging vessel. She was renamed N1 in June 1917.

Following her decommissioning she was to be sold for scrap to John Cashmore Ltd on 9th June 1922 and broken up at their yard at Newport, Wales.

2: Another source list the designs length as 338ft long

3: In the Grand Fleet by D.K. Brown the price per boat is listed as £340,000 each.

4: Indeed, it might be plausible to consider the 'K' class a submersible destroyer, rather than a submarine?

PART TWO. THE NUTS & BOLTS

"SUBMARINE CRUISER K CLASS" SOURCE: CENTRAL NEWS

CHAPTER ONE. THE MECHANICS

The steam beasts specifications
"more holes than a French tart"

('K' boat stoker crewman)

I f ever there was ever a definition of a 'Heath-Robinson' or 'Steam-Punk' submersible design, the 'K' boats would be a good candidate. The process of diving was frighteningly complex, hazardous and it could with little effort, be lethal, as levers were pulled, wheels spun, and motors hummed. They were incredibly complicated machines and to appreciate both their comparatively short time in commission and the 'jinx' we need to grasp something of both their scale and complexity.

Boilers, Funnels, Holes & Vents.

The steam method of propulsion was, by the year 1916 both a tried, tested and a proven method of creating propulsive power within warships. The conversion process required four things, the first being copious amounts of air (or oxygen) to feed the boilers fire. Next water and fire were needed to boil the water and finally funnels to expel the resultant heat and smoke. The latter two being for the submariners, the biggest problem. But as tried and tested as steam propulsion was, installing both its machinery and its resultant requirements into the limited confines of a submarine hull was untried prior to 1900. Boilers are big and water is exceptionally heavy. The 'K' boats carried 10.81 tons of the liquid which could have been acceptable but for the fact they also carried oil for their diesel engines. All this equated to weight, the enemy of a machine that needed the ability to lower and raise itself through the sea's own waters. But in addition to the waters weight, the boilers, funnels, and other steam engine requirements brought a further 92.88 tons to the design. But these were problems that could be solved by engineering solutions. Tricky ones but still resolvable? The heat was without meaning to sound callous, not going to inhibit the boats process, it would 'merely' bake (or slowly roast) the men who crewed the craft. But the smoke was a problem as it needed huge holes cut into the hull through which giant tubes (or funnels) could be fitted to expel the said smoke. These two giant holes were joined by a series of vents (or more holes) to allow for the movement of air into the craft. All holes that needed to be both capable of being open to the sky but with the additional ability of being 100% water resistant to allow the hull to go beneath the waves.

To conclude, the design required an oxygen guzzling, water fed, heat generating machinery process, which in turn required a large number of holes cut into a watertight hull, a hull that needed the capacity to submerge. As attractive as the speed a steam propulsion could in theory bring to a submarine, it was both by the processes of the by-products created, as well as its requirements to function, not submarine friendly. But the engineers had grown up in the late Victorian age, an era when any problem could be solved by the Great God of Victorian ingenuity and mechanical know-how. In theory it was possible, but in practicality it was the stuff of a submariner's nightmare...   The class's source of surface propulsion was provided by two 10,500 shp (7,800 kw) oil-fired Yarrow boilers (235 lb per inch), each powering either a Brown-Curtis or Parsons geared steam turbines, (depending on the yard of construction). The boilers were of the small tube type with a forced draft (1) and which were fuelled by between 170 and 197 tons (depending on your source) of oil that the *K1* to *K17* (Group 1) carried within their tanks. Located over the boilers were six large hull openings, (or 'holes'), two of which served as the funnel's drafts (or uptakes). They were connected through the pressure hull to the boilers by a trunk and each one was fitted with a hatch top and bottom to seal the funnel watertight while the boat was submerged. The other four 'holes' were 37 inches (93.98 cm) in diameter and were used to supply fresh air to the boiler room. They were, (in theory) able to be automatically closed by motor-operated valves, but these were often not as "fool-proof" an operation as the designers had claimed it would be.

Aft of the conning tower and located on the superstructure, which ran out towards the stern, were two five-foot-tall funnels (2). Once the command "prepare to dive" had been given, two electric motors located within the turbine room tilted the hot funnels away from each other into two recesses within the superstructure. Once the funnels had descended into the 'narrow superstructure', the two upper hinged watertight doors were lowered (once more by motors) over them to seal off each of the funnel's respective openings. The 'funnel doors' were then clipped secure from the inside. The funnels and their upper or top doors (which were connected by a gearing system) could be closed in ten seconds and the lower doors operated at the faster time of between four and five seconds. The funnel doors were fitted with a method of water circulation to cool them down. In addition to the watertight doors, a draining valve was fitted at the base of each of the funnel's uptakes in case the upper funnel cover had been damaged and were no longer 100% watertight.

The complex funnel mechanics had originated with the design Scotts had developed and installed in the *Swordfish*. The earlier boats of the 'K' class had been fitted with a very similar electric funnel operating gear to the Swordfish's, but for the *K15, K16, K17,*(and most likely *K26)* Scotts were to design a hydraulic type gear to close the 'funnel door' clips. Each of these four clips were operated by a hydraulic cylinder and their design was to prove to be a great improvement on those fitted to the first 'K' boats. It allowed for the clips to be used at any time and with little problem, the action being all but instantaneous.

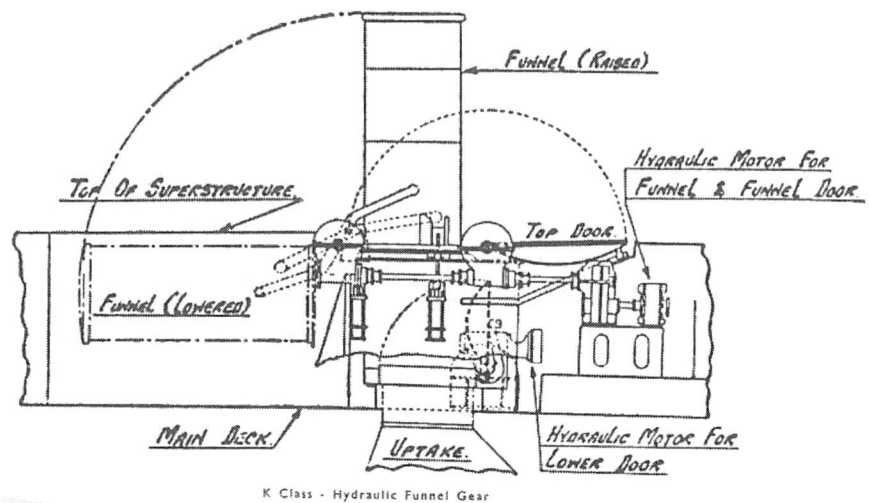

K Class - Hydraulic Funnel Gear

THE FUNNEL MECHANICS. (SOURCE BR 3043 K CLASS).

Once the funnels were lowered and all was secured, a hydraulic interlocking gear ensured that neither of the funnels (or their respective 'doors') could be moved once the clips were 'on'.

While the boats had been on the draughtsman's board, a series of ideas for covers to the air intakes had been considered, but it was finally decided to fit several telemotor (3) operated covers. These covers were also dome-shaped and with lugs located on their rims, which slid closed on vertical bars. The air intake covers could be opened by about 10 inches by the telemotor ram to allow air to enter though the intakes. The telemotor ram was also capable of applying sufficient downward pressure onto the covers to ensure they were both secure and watertight once shut. Each of these covers weighed 896 Ibs (406 kg) (4) and the weight in addition helped the rams with the closing procedure, which was a fast operation. In the event of there being a failure with the telemotor, a hand gear had been installed to allow for the intakes to be manually sealed.

THE K22's TWO FUNNELS BEING LOWERED AS SHE PREPARES TO SUBMERGE.

The air that was supplied to the stokehold was delivered by two turbofans which sat directly below the air intakes, but these were too prove not to be a success in combating the compartments overwhelming heat.

A series of electrical indicators were installed in the turbine room to enable the crew on duty to see the current position of the doors and covers. Once the indicators showed them as finally closed, word was passed to the Commanding Officer in the control room. The tragic accident to the *K13* at Gareloch was to be caused by a failure in leaving these air intakes open, even though word had been passed to the boats Captain that they were closed. The resulting disaster only to clearly showed the necessity of fitting indicators in the control room, a modification finally undertaken in all the boats post January 1917.

HMS K8'S CAPTAIN AT THE PERISCOPE IN THE CONTROL ROOM. DESPITE THERE SIZE, THE BOATS WERE CRAMPED INSIDE.

As the funnels slowly descended into their storage areas, the crew were busy blowing ballast, operating the clutches to convert the drive over to the battery powered electric motors and sealing the seemingly countless 'holes'. One other hazard the all too many hull openings brought was the risk of being occasionally jammed in a partially open position by driftwood or flotsam, or as we will see a tin of paint!

This frightening combination of the hatches, valves and 'holes' within a submarines hull was to cause the comment *"too many holes!"*, or as one stoker more eloquently put it, the 'K' boats *"have got more holes than a French tart"*.

A series of lower doors along the pressure hull were hinged

and where hemispherical (a half globe) in shape. These lacked the 'funnel door' clips to hold them shut, but they were self-adjusting to allow for any changes in their shape caused by variations in the sea's temperature.

To complicate a convoluted procedure even further, the numerous larger openings or 'holes' were located within an area of the boat (the pressure hull), that became inaccessible once the craft had commenced her dive. With such a large number of compartments within the huge vessel, any communication from the control room was by means of telephones or voice pipes. All the compartments that held hatches, ventilators and 'holes' needed to be advised to close them before diving could commence. The verbal command "prepare to dive" would be reinforced by the diving siren or klaxon (sources vary) sounding out from the bridge. Many of the 'holes' not closed correctly or failing to be 100% watertight, would be impossible to access and the sea water would flood in unchecked until (or if) the boat surfaced once more.

THE FIVE FOOT HEIGHT OF THE FUNNELS WITH A DECK GUN MOUNTED BETWEEN

46

From the moment the first command to *"dive"* was issued, the Captains found that despite their best efforts from the crews, it took on average 30 minutes to transfer from steam-powered surface propulsion to submerged electric operations. The minimum time needed to secure the main engines, transfer to the battery motors and 'crash' dive under emergency conditions was nearer 5 minutes, which was agreeably better than the 15 minutes required of the *Swordfish* 'prototype'. On the order to dive the red-hot boiler fires needed to be dampened down to avoid an accumulation of fumes whilst the boat was submerged. But even a dampened fire produces heat and consumes oxygen, neither being desirable on a submerged vessel. This operation alone required a complicated series of hydraulics, mechanical rods and levers to lower the twin funnels, one towards the stern and the other towards the bow, dropping them into a horizontal position in two wells situated within the superstructure. At the same time the hatches over the funnel uptakes needed to be shut and secured watertight. In addition, the main intake ventilators required closing, along with the sea water connections for both the condensers and boiler feeds.

Given this complexity for a normal dive, let alone one in an emergency, the service considered that with their 24 knots speed the submarines would do better to turn away and out run any threat if they were attacked on the surface. Fortunately, these were the days before the airborne threat. But this 'turn-and-run' plan was an unspoken admission that the record breaking 'crash dives' of the conventional boats was simply beyond a 'K' boat. The design basically had to many of those "damned holes", or openings in the pressure hull that required securing before a dive could even be commenced. Most of the 'holes' all served important surface operations, but on diving they were an extra level of tasks that more conventional submarine crews simply did not face. These holes and vents were to be the cause of much pain and too many deaths amongst the 'volunteer' crews of the boats over the coming.

LOOKING AFT ON THE K6 WHILE SHE IS AT FULL STEAM. NOTE THE LOW HEIGHT OF THE FUNNELS IN COMPARISON TO THE DECK GUN.

Once the dive was underway the residual heat within the boiler room made it uninhabitable and consequently inaccessible. But with the funnels folded down and the vents sealed shut, the heat had nowhere to escape too. In the national archives there is a file that records over a brief 30-minute period the temperatures within the engine and boiler rooms onboard the K1:

Engine room: 87°, 87°, 87°, 87°, 90°, 90°, 92°, 93°.

Boiler room: 82°, 88°, 86°, 90°, 90°, 89°, 90°, 90°, 70°.

A sauna on average operates at between 70° and 100 °C (158° and 212°F)! The crews would have to work in the suffocating heat and if the seas were breaking over the low superstructure's funnels, they were then clad in thick heavy waterproofs, making the heat doubly unbearable. Another note states that in rough seas the hatches had to be kept closed to keep the boats interior dry from waves breaking over the casing. True this kept the crew dry, but it left the heat from the machinery spaces with nowhere to escape and only made the crews working spaces hotter. In harbour things were easier, with the boilers only required for distilling water.

It was at this point that Fisher's foresight to order a passageway, all be it cramped and narrow, now provided the only way to bypass the boiler room and allow the crew to move between the two halves of the submarine. But a percentage of the heat from the adjacent boiler rooms would still have permeated through to the narrow passage. On a final note, the funnels were in front and behind one of the superstructure guns with the fore funnel blowing its emissions over the gun crew. The funnels stood 5 foot (1.52 mtrs) in height and the gunners were 5 to 6 foot on average. It must have created considerable problems! The funnels were both lagged with non-combustible, non-conducting materials.

In a calm sea and with maximum visibility, the conceived invisibility of the 'K' Class at six miles was surprising. If the boats were sighted it was from the funnels emissions and the sun reflecting off the salt encrusted funnels.

1: *Forced draft: When air or flue gases are maintained above atmospheric pressure. Normally it is done with the help of a forced draft fan.*

2: *K15's funnel is noted in the 1919 edition of Janes Fighting Ships as being longer than her siblings.*

3: *A hydraulic device by which the movement of the wheel on a ship's bridge operates the steering gear at the stern.*

4: *This equates to between 81 & 82 bags of domestic sugar in weight*

Trim & Buoyancy

"When a submarine is on the surface, or when it reaches a desired depth, the first objective is to attain perfect, or nearly perfect, trim, that is, a balancing of the forces. The trimming of the boat is accomplished by varying, or adjusting, the amount of water in the variable ballast tanks".

(Submarine Trim and Drain Systems - Chapter 1)

Before the boat's Captain could consider giving the order to dive, he needed to be confident his boat was accurately trimmed, to compensate for any change in the density of the sea water and the amount of fuel, ammunition, water and stores that had been consumed. If the craft was trimmed by too much, or was simply too heavy forward, the two sets of hydroplanes, (one fore and one aft) in company with the ballast tanks would provide insufficient buoyancy to return her to the surface. With nearly 200 tons of water flooding into the tanks every minute, it was all too easy to trim the boat inaccurately. A poor trim and the slightest problem or error in forcing the compressed air into the tanks would see the boat go too deep for any chance of regaining the surface. The 'K' boats needed to conduct a controlled dive, between 300 to 800 tons of sea water, according to the amount of buoyancy with which the vessel was trimmed. In addition, the current weather, the rate of knots, the urgency of the dive and the competence level of the crew, were all additional factors towards a successful dive.

A CLEAR VIEW OF A K BOATS HYDROPLANES AS SHE LAYS IN DRY DOCK
UNDERGOING ANOTHER OF THE CLASSES NUMEROUS REFITS

With water flooding the tanks and the vessel delicately trimmed, it was possible for a raw or poorly trained crew, to create or amplify the slightest hitch in getting the compressed air into a tank and then the vessel would drop to a level too deep for recovery. Once successfully submerged the boat weighed over two and a half thousand tons and had in addition the momentum of the dive pushing her ever downwards. If there was a rough sea (or even a heavy swell) it was vital to give the boat some negative buoyancy (1) to get her to dive and though the compressed air could blow one or two tanks rapidly, there was often considerable delay in stopping the crafts downward momentum.

This was also the case if the tanks into which the air was flooding were not quite full and the vessel was already getting too deep. The air had first to raise the pressure in the whole of the empty part of the tank, while the water was still being admitted and rising in pressure. Only when the air pressure exceeded this level and started to push the water out would buoyancy be gained. Even then it would be some time before the vessel was slowed in her dive and began to surface. Sea water was then admitted into the ballast tanks, which extended for about 300 feet of the submarine's length. Diving a 'K' boat was a careful, cautious, and hazardous task and was no place for an incompetent or untrained crew. A dive was never on a 'K' boat, (or any submarine) no matter how experienced the crew, to be undertaken lightly and without careful supervision.

The classes inability to conduct a dive with any rapidity is often quoted as both a design error and failing. But it is all too frequently overlooked that the craft were designed to serve with the Grand Fleet and not for the submarine service. In such an environment a slower speed of dive was no real disadvantage as the Captain would always expect to get ample warning that a dive was necessary. But no matter the amount of notice given; a highly trained crew familiar with every detail of the vessel was still required. In perfect conditions a K-boat could dive from 20 knots on the surface in about four minutes, but only with that well-trained crew. The faster the crew strove to dive their craft, the greater the risk of 'human error'. Any attempt otherwise could be highly dangerous in deep water. Crash dives for a 'K' boat were something they were not capable of and it was simpler to turn the stern towards the enemy and run.

If the boat's buoyancy (or trim), was set incorrectly the bow would slice its path through the sea and its motion would throw sheets of ice-cold sea water over both the bridges' foredeck and the superstructure. In some of the class the bridges folding canvas deck screen was replace later in their careers by a permanent rigid brass one, making life a little easier for those on the exposed bridge space. In the face of a heavy sea battering the bridge, hull and the funnels, the Captain would be faced with the choice of either diving beneath the waves (always a heart stopping moment in a 'K' boat) or decreasing the forward rate of knots. But for a 'fleet' submarine any loss of speed meant the ability to keep up with the fleet was impacted. Some Captains found through experience that by lightening the ballast carried in the bow, it would stop the forward part of the hull from sliding under the waves and the boats motion became less wild. To compound matters, as the huge submarines battled their way through the waves, the seas washing over the bow would render the forward gun as unusable. Further aft the deck torpedoes were put out of action as the water seeped into its mechanics and damage the weapon. As the hulls battered their way through the seas, they would pitch and roll badly, but with no rhythm. This reduced the boats passage into an extremely uncomfortable ride and the cold wet sea water would cascade down the conning towers hatch's, fusing the electrical switchboards. If any crewmen were to touch the ladder, they were in danger of receiving an electric shock. In the boiler room the problematic funnels and vent forced the stokers to being reduced to wearing oilskins as the seas waters came in through the vents, which as we have seen extinguished the boilers but in addition it could cause flash back and many a stoker lost his eyebrows.

1: "Negative Buoyancy. Negative buoyancy occurs when an object is denser than the fluid it displaces. The object will sink because its weight is greater than the buoyant force". www:sciencing.com

Pressure Hulls

"Most submarines have two hulls, one inside the other, to help them survive. The outer hull is waterproof, while the inner one (called the pressure hull) is much stronger and resistant to immense water".

www.explainthatstuff.com

The class has been referred to as a double-hull design, but, as with so many aspects of the 'K' boat, it was not to be that simple. The boats were not even partially double-hulled, if the term referred to a submarine with a hull comprising of an outer and inner hull. In fact, they were closer to an early Maxime Laubeuf type, (a French designer). Laubeuf had soon recognized that the stability problem of the early submarine designs was caused by their rounded pressure hulls. The hull shape was necessary to withstand the pressure at depth, but it was in turn to prove to be a poor shape for steaming once surfaced. The result of the roundness would be that the boat handled poorly on the surface and was unstable once submerged. Laubeufs's solution was for a double hull design comprised of an inner rounded and reinforced hull to resist pressure combined, with an outer boat-shaped hull to make the vessel more seaworthy. His design was a dramatic leap forward in the fledgling art of submarine design and was in time to become adopted throughout the world's navy's. Laubeufs's external hulls ran mainly parallel to the upper half of the pressure hull and the outer hull plating then merged into the pressure hull beneath the waterline.

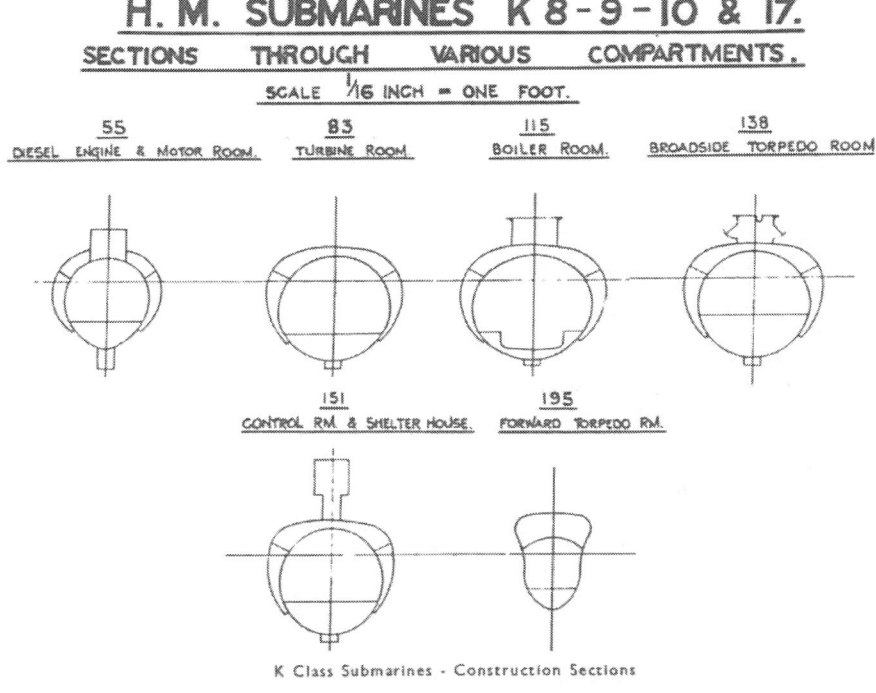

H. M. SUBMARINES K 8-9-10 & 17.

SECTIONS THROUGH VARIOUS COMPARTMENTS.

SCALE 1/16 INCH = ONE FOOT.

55	83	115	138
DIESEL ENGINE & MOTOR ROOM.	TURBINE ROOM.	BOILER ROOM.	BROADSIDE TORPEDO ROOM

151	195
CONTROL RM. & SHELTER HOUSE.	FORWARD TORPEDO RM.

K Class Submarines - Construction Sections

CROSS SECTION OF THE 'K' BOATS.

The overall shape of the hull was created with a flat top, which served to provide a good area of deck space. The flat deck was made of good use by the crews for recreational spaces. However, the sides of the outer hull had a considerable curvature and were in that sense equally unlike the hull shape of a double-hull Laubeuf boat. At the forward end of the external tanks, the top plating extended out to the bows at a steep incline and the enclosed structure it created was used as a controlled free flooding area. At the stern end the external plating continued through the controlled free flooding superstructure until it merged into the pressure hull. With this design it was possible for the bow or stern portions of the hull to be damaged, but without any real danger to the boat, in the short term. A few of the boats suffered bow collisions and yet they managed to limp back to port with no losses. At the sides the 'K' boat plates were only single-hulled.

The pressure hull itself was of an oval (or elliptical) form, except at the extreme bow and stern ends of the external hull. It was deemed that on theory the hulls shape would permit the boat structure to withstand a dive to a depth of 200 feet. But the figure was based on calculations and not on actual experience with the craft.

The Conning Tower

T he class benefitted from a fully enclosed bridge deck house built over the conning tower, allowing the men on watch to benefit from 'additional protection' during bouts of rough weather. The onning tower itself was of an oval construction and was made from a heavy brass casting. It had a length of 5 feet 6 inches (1.67 mtrs), a width of 3 feet 6 inches (1.06 mtrs) and a height of 4 feet 6 inches (1.37 mtrs). It could be accessed from the interior of the boat through a hatchway, which had a watertight hinging hatch that opened upwards into the tower. The rear portion of the roof was occupied by the exit hatch with another water- tight hatch opening upwards into the chart room.

THE K14 ALONGSIDE HER SISTER BOAT, THE K12, THE PHOTO GIVES A CLEAR INDICATION AS TO THE DESIGN OF THE CRAFTS CONNING TOWERS. THE CONNING TOWERS HAVE BY THE TIME THIS PHOTO WAS TAKEN, SUBSTITUTED THEIR CANVAS BRIDGE SCREENS FOR THE MORE SOLID METAL ONES. DESPITE MUCH RESEARCH I HAVE BEEN UNABLE TO ESTABLISH A DEFINITIVE REASON FOR THE TOWERS WHITE PAINT JOB

Each of the two hatches within the conning tower could

be opened and closed only from its underside. The forward portion of the conning towers interior rose to an additional height of 3 feet 6 inches (1.06 mtrs) in the shape of a dome, which was 2 feet 6 inches (0.81 mtrs) by 2 feet (0.60 mtrs). It was designed to carry the Projector Compass at a sufficient distance from the steelwork of the main hull so as not to affect the needle. On either side of the tower was a series of glass bull's-eyes, fitted with prisms which enabled an observer to see ahead, as well as on the beam. From the top of the dome was suspended an electric lamp and a fuel vent pipe that was one inch in diameter and leading from below it ran out through the after side of the tower, with a valve on the inside. The Projector Compass tube led down to the control room and was also fitted with a valve inside the main hull. A high-pressure air pipe led up to the siren and was likewise fitted with valves inside the main hull and within the tower. Some of the class had their conning towers raised to enable the bridge crew to see over the fitted swan bow and her forward gun relocated to the superstructure to make room for the new bow, (i.e. *K16*).

A 'K 'BOATS SIDE CONNING TOWER WINDOW DISPLAYED BY THE SUBMARINE MUSEUM AT GOSPORT, PORTSMOUTH.

Turbines & Electric Motors.

The width of the hull was dictated too (in a large degree) by the bulk of the main machinery, (the steam turbines) which filled 35% of the overall length. While the boats were in the conception stage it became evident that to obtain the level of power required for 10,000 shp it could only really be achieved by steam. To have used 'traditional' diesels each 'K' boat would have required eight of the twelve-cylinder diesels. The diesels used in the class were of the models that had originally been reserved to be installed in the 'K' classes predecessor, the 'J' Class, when steam propulsion was being considered, but it was to be rejected.

PREVIOUS PAGE: "THE WALLSEND SLIPWAY AND ENGINEERING COMPANY LIMITED-GEARED TURBINE MACHINERY AS FITTED IN A "K" CLASS SUBMARINE"

Two sets of single reduction turbines powering two shafts were to be fitted within each 'K' boat and each of the two shafts were to rotate a twin 3 bladed 7 feet 4 inch (2.13 mtrs) diameter 'Solid Admiralty Pattern Manganese Bronze brass propeller'. Between each of the propellers stood a single rudder and while the dimensions are not recorded, it was of such a size as to be marginally taller than the propellers. Each set of turbines had in addition one HP and one LP with helical gearing (1). The Vickers boats are noted in the Kew files as being able to develop 10,500 hp at a speed of 380 to 400 revolutions per minute. The remainder of the class were to be fitted with Brown-Curtis turbines. For their submersible propulsion the boats were equipped with four electric motors (1,440 hp (1,070 kw)) that were to charge the batteries. Each of the boat's batteries consisted of 336 Exide cells which were sub-divided into three sections comprising 112 cells, each being stowed within two battery tanks well forward of amidships. In 1917 K2 is noted as having 138 tons of batteries and each of the twin shafts was driven by single armature motors that worked in tandem and developed 360 bhp, each making a total of 1,440 bhp. A Helical gearing system ran from the motors to the propeller shafts, instead of the more usual method of being mounted onto the shafts themselves. The motors were also capable of acting as a limited source of propulsive power in the event of problems with the boilers. To allow the batteries to be recharged once the boat had returned to the surface, one 800 hp (600 kW) cylinder Vickers diesel generator was installed which drove a dynamo and which in turn supplied the required current to the main motors, but it was not connected to either of the shafts and consequently was not an option for propelling the boat.

The 800 hp diesel engine, (the same Vickers model as was

installed in the 'E' Class submarines) drove a 700 hp dynamo which supplied a current to the boat's main motors for use on the surface. It could propel the boat at between 9 and 10 knots and its main purpose was to provide power once the boat had surfaced and had yet to raise steam. The dynamo also allowed the turbines to be reserved for the higher speeds. In addition, it was used for the reverse purpose of propelling the boat just before she dived, while her boilers were being shut down and the turbines de-clutched. The turbines could also in addition be used for charging the batteries. It had originally been planned that the diesel engine would drive an independent shaft and propeller, but this was to be discarded during the design stage as being to inefficient.

The main electric motors were rated, over a 90-minute period at 1,440 bhp and at 2,040 bhp for 20 minutes. At the lesser rate the boats were capable (whilst submerged), of achieving just over 8 knots and its feasible that a higher rate would have produced sufficient power for 9 knots. At that speed the submerged endurances were 13.5 mile (21.72 km) and at 1.75 knots, 83 miles (133.57 km) was achieved. But the submerged endurance was considered to be disappointing and this could have been due to the unreliability of the electric generating plant when it was needed to run for any periods of length. There are in addition figures giving a rate of 8 miles (12.87 km) at 8 knots, 30 miles (48.28 km) at 4 knots and 45 miles (39.10 km) at 1.5 knots.

The 'designed' surface range for Group 1 was 960 miles (1544.97 km) at their full speed, but once they had entered service and commenced their trials, it was found to be more realistically nearer the 800 nautical mile mark (1500 km). Traveling on the surface at 10 knots (19 km) they could achieve 12,500 nautical miles (23,200 km) which equates to the distance from the southern English port of Portsmouth, via the Panama Canal to Japans port of Nagasaki. To further increase Group 1 's range, two of the amidships ballast tanks, (on either beam) were filled each with an additional 100 tons of oil. But not unsurprisingly the extra weight of the 100 tons of 'emergency' fuel cost the craft ½ knot when on the surface, due to the increased draught from the extra weight. On their entry into service the boats were found to be heavier on fuel than had been planned. At full power the steam turbines used 1.25 lbs/shp/hr, compared to 0.43 lbs/shp/hr for diesels, a difference of 190.69%.

The Admiralties 1921 report into the K5's loss noted that the 'K' boats achieved between 8 and 9 miles (12.87-14.48 km) per ton of oil and the most economical rate for the boat was 10 knots. But the report goes on to note these figures were produced by measuring equipment that was deemed to be "inaccurate"!

The craft carried two high powered compressors to charge the 2,500 lb air bottles and there were also two low powered compressors to blow the main ballast tanks empty once the 'K' boat had surfaced. In addition, there were two electric powered bilge pumps and hydraulic rams for raising both the pairs of periscopes and telescopic masts. The hydroplanes were controlled by a hydroelectric power source.

1: Helical gears are cylindrical gears with a slanted tooth trace. Compared to spur gears, they have the larger contact ratio and both quieter and suffer from less vibration as well as being able to transmit large force. A pair of helical gears has the same helix

angle but the helix hand is opposite.

Dimensions & Displacement.

T he 'K' class were true giants amongst their own kind. If the 'Holland 1' was a minnow, the arrival of the 'K's was to witness the birth of the whales! To gain a true sense as to the scale of these steam belching steel monsters, we need to compare them in their size and scale with their smaller siblings.

On the outbreak of war in August 1914 the 'D' class boats were among the latest and more 'conventional' of the Submarine Service's boats. The 8 boats (10 were laid down) of the 'D' class were 163 feet 0 inches (49.7 mtrs) in their overall length from bow to stern and the 'K' class were 339 ft (103 mtrs) in their full length. A total difference of 170 feet, or if you moored two 'D' class hulls bow to stern a single 'K' boat would still be 1 foot longer. In their beam the 'D' class were 13 foot 6 inches if measured from their widest point. The 'K' class was 26 ft 6 inches (8.08 mtrs), which once again means two 'D' boats moored side to side would be the same combined width as one 'K' class. The extraordinary scale of the 'K' boats width was due to the boilers, their girth forcing a wider beam on the hulls design. You would most likely fail to find a British World War one destroyer to either match or even to surpass a 'K' boat in length and most of the navy's pre-1900 light cruisers were only marginally longer. Finally, if you moored two 'K' boats stern to bow, alongside the Grand Fleet's Dreadnought flagship, *HMS Iron Duke,* the submarines would be 55 feet longer. They were truly big!

In 2019 the nuclear-powered *Astute* class are the pinnacle of the Royal Navy's submarine service. Yet even 100 years on, they are shorter than the 'K' class by 21 feet in the length. But in the width, they manage to surpass the K's by 10 foot 7 inches.

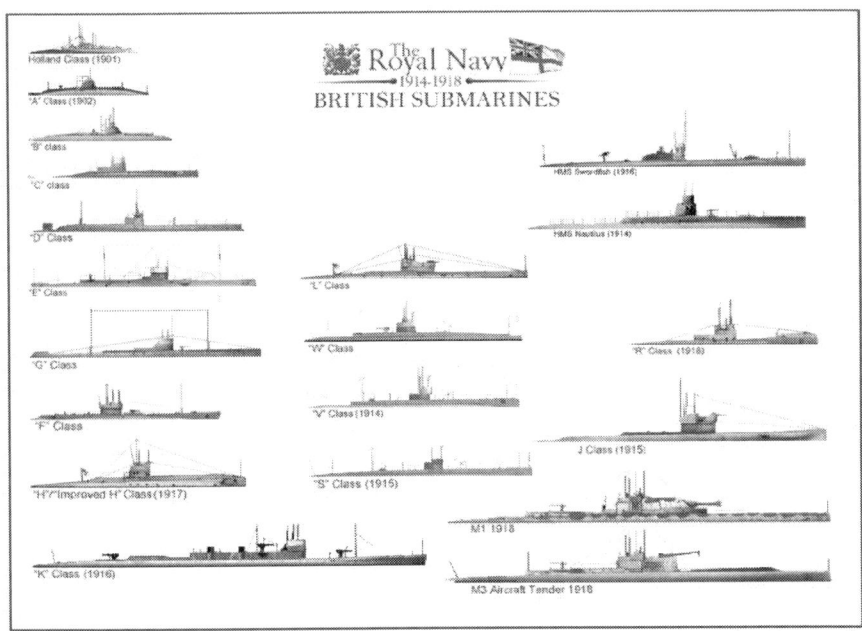

A SIZE COMPARISON OF JUST HOW BiG THE K BOATS WERE. (NAVAL ENCYCLOPEDIA.COM)

The design draft of the 'K' class, measured from their waterline to the bottom of the point where the keel joined the hull, (with the thickness of the hull included and if based on a surface displacement of about 1,880 tons) was around 16 feet (58.52 mtrs). However, with the modifications the boats underwent both on the slip way and during their careers, the final measurement from waterline to keel (or the 'Mean' draught) was about 17 feet 0 inches, (62.17 mtrs) based on a tonnage of 1,980. This gave a freeboard to the main deck of about 5 foot 3 inches (19.20 mtrs) and to the bridge deck of about 9 feet 9 inches (35.66 mtrs).

Vickers had listed the submerged displacement of the *K3* and *K4* as 2,566 tons, but that figure omits the controlled free flooding spaces which equated to a capacity of 56 tons. As originally designed the class was to have carried 531 tons of main ballast water in their external tanks and an additional 127 tons in the internal tanks. This additional 658 liquid tonnage would have resulted in a surface displacement of circa 1,908 tons. But with a 'K' boat complexity, the introduction of reserve oil fuel tanks, the internal main ballast capacity decreased to 79 tons. This would have raised the surface displacement to a figure of around 1,956 tons. But Vickers having agreed with the tank's capacity, listed a surface displacement of approximately 2,000 tons which meant that only 35 tons of internal water ballast was used.

Vickers listed the latter 'K' boats they produced as having a surface displacement of 1,976 tons, which meant that 59 tons of internal water ballast was carried. But it needs to be bourne in mind that these figures would fluctuate anyway between individual boats. But generally, the Group 1 'K' boats are listed today with a submerged displacement of 2,566 tons.

The 'Kew files' list the following weights for the *K2* on the 21st October 1916, (Seven days after her launch) and the *K1* on the 14th November 1916. While both ships design sizes are not unsurprisingly identical, there is a tiny variation in the finished products dimensions:

- Floating out: 1,228.6 tons,
- Floating: 1,228.6 tons,
- Machinery: 224.9 tons,
- Ballast: 39.54 tons,

- Weight of hull: 956.05 tons.

The same file notes her dimensions as:

DISTANCE BETWEEN PERPENDICULARS

- As designed: 335 ft 0 inches 102.10 mtrs),
- As built: 335 ft 3 inches (102.18 mtrs),
- (K1 was 1 ½ in shorter in length).

"BREATH EXTREME"

- As designed: 26 ft 5 ⅞ inches (8.10 mtrs),
- As built: 26 ft 7 1/8 inches (8.15 mtrs) (to outside plating),
- (*K1* 1-inches 2/8 shorter).

"MOULDED"

- As designed: 26 ft 5 ½ inches (8.05 mtrs),
- As built: 26 ft 8 3/4 inches (8.12 mtrs),
- (K1 was 2 3/4 inches shorter).

LENGTH FROM UNDERSIDE OF BALLAST KEEL TO UPPER SIDE OF UPPER DECK PLATING MIDSHIPS AT MIDDLE

- As designed 21 ft 8 1/4 inches (6.60 mtrs),
- As built 21 ft 8 5/8 inches (6.61 mtrs),
- K1 was 2/8 inches shorter.

LENGTH OF ENGINE ROOM (FRAME NO: 125-148)

- As designed: 34 ft 6 inches (10.36 mtrs),
- As built: 34 ft 6 ½ inches (10.37 mtrs),
- *(K1 was 1/4 inches shorter).*

BOILER ROOM (FRAME NO 101-125)

- As designed 36 ft 0 inches (10.97 mtrs),
- As built 36 ft 0 ½ inches (10.98 mtrs),
- *(K1 was ½ inches shorter).*

MOTOR ROOM (FRAME NO: 148-178)

- As designed 45 ft 0 inches (13.71 mtrs),
- As built: 45 ft 0 ½ inches (13.72 mtrs),
- *(K1 was 1/3 inches shorter).*

LEAKAGE ON FLOATING

- As designed: 0 inches,
- As built: 1 1/8 inches (2.55 cm).

DRAUGHT OF WATER

- As launched 9 ft 0 ½ - 11 ft inches fwd. (2.74 - 3.35 mtrs).13 ft 6 1/4 aft (4.11 mtrs).

KEEL PROJECTION AMIDSHIPS

- 1 ft 3 inches (38.1 cm).

POSTWAR, THE K22 LONGSIDE THE SURRENDERED COASTAL U-BOAT S.M.S. UB 28 , NOTE THE HUGE SIZE DIFFERENCE. (SOURCE LASTSTANDONZOMBIEISLAND.COM)

When the external emergency oil fuel was carried in the Number 5 and 6 port (as well as the main Starboard tanks), the amount of external main ballast water taken on was decreased by 113 tons. The surface displacement would then increase in such circumstances to 2,093 tons and the reserve of buoyancy fell to 25.3%. The reserve of buoyancy figures included the controlled free flooding spaces which totalled 56 tons. But once more, generally the Group 1 'K' boats are listed today with a surfaced displacement of 1,980 tons.

The ballast keel for both the *K3* and *K4* was recorded by Vickers as having weighed 179 tons and in the latter *K8, K9* and *K10* it had increased by an additional 23 tons to 202 tons. Both sets of figures included the two 10-ton drop keels the boats carried. Vickers was later to supply a ballast keel figure for the five boats as 235 tons which included 27 tons of lead and 56 tons of metallic 'billets'.

But to try and put it simply, the 'K' boats were to have a displacement of 1,980 tons when surfaced and 2,566 tons while submerged. The 'D' class was (when surfaced) 483 tons and once submerged 595 tons. Once more, the differences in scale were staggering.

❖ ❖ ❖

Within the Kew files is a volume that is over an inch thick in its depth. The hundreds of pages between the two hard covers detail the K boats technical data. One small group of pages give the tonnage for the K5 in minute detail, allowing us to see ton by ton, what went in to comprise the final displacement.

The pages are too faint after 100 years to include as a readable image, but the following charts are a transcribe of those pages, in the order that they appear in the volume.

DATE AND PLACE DRAUGHT TAKEN. 7/4/17 NO 3 BASIN PORTSMOUTH. DENSITY OF WATER (CUBIC FEET PER TON)35.	WEIGHT ON BOARD WHEN DRAUGHT WAS TAKEN	WEIGHT TO GO ONBOARD TO COMPLETE EQUIPMENT
DRAUGHT OF WATER fore 16'7" at 72.5 feet from fore perp		
aft 17'2" at 76.0 feet from aft perp		
DRAUGHT OF WATER	7.02	0.77
FRESH WATER IN TANKS, FILTERS & C...	0	2.55
BREAD, PROVISIONS, SPIRITS &C...	0	0
OFFICERS STORES AND SLOPS	0	0.1
OFFICERS CREW AND EFFECTS NO 50	3.13	3.12
MAST, YARDS, DERRICKS, SPARE SPARS & C...	1.11	0
RIGGING & BLOCKS	1.5	0
SAILS, AWNINGS & CANVAS FURNITURE	0.55	0
CABLES & S/W HAWSERS	3.95	0
ANCHORS	2.05	0
BOATS	0.29	0.25
NAVAL STORES 2 MONTHS	11.48	0.69
MAIN GENERATOR	10.66	0
W/T GEAR	0.81	0
GUNS, INCLUDING SMALL ARMS	2.34	0
AIR	1.3	0.41
CARRIAGE, SLIDES AND SPARE PARTS	3.41	0
ELECTRIC MOTORS	14.08	0
SHOT, SHELL & OTHER AMMUNITION	0	3.22
CORDITE, POWDER & CASES	0	0.45
GUNNERS STORES (NAVAL ORDINANCE)	0.25	0.02
TORPEDO TUBES & FITTINGS	29.85	0
TORPEDO'S & ELECTRICALS STORES INCLUDING WARHEADS	4.55	6.09
AIR COMPRESSORS, RESERVOIRS & PIPING	36.47	0
MAIN ENGINES, SHAFTING, TURBINES AND ENGINE ROOM FITTINGS AND SPARE GEAR	81.02	0
MAIN PROPELLING ELECTRIC MOTORS	22.2	0
SCREW PROPELLERS, SHAFTING AND FITTINGS	0	0
TURBINE ENGINE ROOM INCLUDING MOTOR GEARING	31.9	0
BOILERS FUNNELS & C, AND ALL FITTINGS AND SPARE GEAR IN BOILER ROOMS	92.88	0
ELECTRIC BATTERIES	138	0
WATER IN BOILERS (FULL TO CROWN)	17.8	12.07
WATER IN CONDENSERS AND PIPES	3.1	0
WATER IN FEED TANKS FULL	2.7	0
AUXILIARY MACHINERY (INC WATER)	59.79	0.2
ENGINEERS STORES INCLUDING NAVAL STORES	207.93	1.63
OIL FUEL	10.81	39.57
WATER IN RESERVE FEED TANKS	53.38	8.06
WATER IN BALLAST TANKS AND CABLE LOCKERS	1.85	0
PERMANENT BALLAST (INTERNAL)	10	0
PLANT, EXCESS PEOPLE, BILGE WATER & PIG BALLAST	17	0
HULL AND FITTINGS TO COMPLETE	0	1.83
TOTAL	885.16	81.03
TO COME OFF		91.25
NET WEIGHT TO COME OFF		10.22

The first table is detailed above and the following few lines are recorded at the foot of that table.

NOTE; THE AFT 4" GUN & AMMO HAVE SINCE BEEN REMOVED MAKING A FURTHER WEIGHT, AS FOLLOWS	
	TONS
GUN	1.31
CARRIAGE SLIDE	1.64
SHOT SHELL & C	1.38
CORDITE POWDER	0.45
TOTAL	4.78

The second page was comprised of the following series of tables.

PARTICULARS OF MAIN AND AUXILIARY MACHINERY	WEIGHT ON BOARD WHEN DRAUGHT WAS TAKEN			
MAIN ENGINES, SHAFTING, FITTINGS & SPARE GEAR IN MAIN TURBINE ENGINE ROOM	TONS	CWTS	QRS	LBS
TURBINES, GEARING, CONDENSERS &	57	6	3	0
OIL FUEL PIPES & FITTINGS IN TURBINE ROOM	1	13	1	0
MAIN AIR PUMPS	3	13	3	0
FORCED LUBE	5	10	0	0
MAIN CIRC	6	2	3	0
STEAM & EXHAUST, PIPES & FITTINGS	6	14	0	0
TOTAL	81	0	2	0

BOILERS, FUNNELS, FITTINGS & SPARE GEAR IN BOILER ROOM	TONS	CWTS	QRS	LBS
BOILERS & MOUNTINGS	62	11	3	0
FEED PUMPS, PIPES & FITTINGS	4	2	3	0
OIL FUEL PUMPS FITTINGS & C IN BOILER ROOM	6	0	0	0
TURBO FANS	4	0	2	0
STEAM & EXHT, PIPES, FITTINGS & C IN BOILER ROOM	2	0	3	0
FUNNELS, DOORS & FITTINGS	14	2	0	0
TOTAL	92	17	3	0

AUXILIARY MACHINERY	TONS	CWTS	QRS	LBS
OIL FUEL, PIPES & FITTING, MACHINERY SPARES	1	18	1	0
FORCED LUBE PUMPS & FITTINGS IN MOTOR ROOM (INC WATER)	5	10	3	0
EVAPORATOR & DISTILLING MACHINERY	1	11	2	0
WATER BALLAST, PUMPS & FITTINGS	9	3	3	0
ELECTRIC GENERATING ENG. PIPES ETC (INCLUDING CIRCULATING WATER)	30	0	0	0
STEAM & EXHAUST PIPES, OIL FUEL, STM HEATING	1	15	0	0
FIRE & BILGE PUMPS & FITTINGS	1	4	1	0
STEERING & HYDROPLANES CONTROL GEAR	4	3	3	0
ENGINE ROOM & REV TELEGRAPH GEAR	1	17	2	0
SPARE GEAR FOR AUX ENGINES & C	2	11	0	0
TOTAL	59	15	3	0

	TONS	CWTS	QRS	LBS
EVAPORATOR & DISTILLING MACHINERY	1	11	2	0
WATER BALLAST, PUMPS & FITTINGS	9	3	3	0
ELECTRIC GENERATING ENG. PIPES ETC (INCLUDING CIRCULATING WATER)	30	0	0	0
STEAM & EXHAUST PIPES, OIL FUEL, STM HEATING	1	15	0	0
FIRE & BILGE PUMPS & FITTINGS	1	4	1	0
STEERING & HYDROPLANES CONTROL GEAR	4	3	3	0
ENGINE ROOM & REV TELEGRAPH GEAR	1	17	2	0
SPARE GEAR FOR AUX ENGINES & C	2	11	0	0
TOTAL	59	15	3	0

Diving Depth & Framework

With the nature of their oversized bulk came problems with the handling and controlling of the boats. The 'cruiser' size submarines were found in service to give problems in both control and depth-keeping, particularly as an efficient telemotor control had yet to be developed. The poor handling was made worse by an estimated maximum diving depth of 200 feet (61 mtrs) (1), a difference making the hulls length 139 feet (or 69.5%) greater than the maximum diving depth. But the diving depth was only an estimate as the true figure was hard to calculate. Even with a dive of a 10-degree angle on the 339-foot hull there would be a 59-foot (18 mtrs) difference in depth of between bow and stern and 30 degrees would produce 170 feet (52 mtrs). This would result in the stern being almost on the surface while the bow would be at its maximum safe depth. If you planted the hull vertically in water to a depth of 200 feet (maximum diving depth), 139 feet would stand proud of the sea level, the seven-foot propellers spinning in the air like an 'impressionist' vision of a nautical windmill. A windmill equating to over nine two storey busses, (with a top layer of almost an entire single storey bus) stacked on top of each other!

The first groups frame numbering reverted to the usual practice of totalling the frames from the stern. But with the Group 2's K26's frames they were once more numbered from the bow. These frames were constructed from 6 ½ inch x 3-inch x 15 lb bulb angle bars and were spaced 18 inches (45.72 cm) apart, as it had been with the 'D' class.

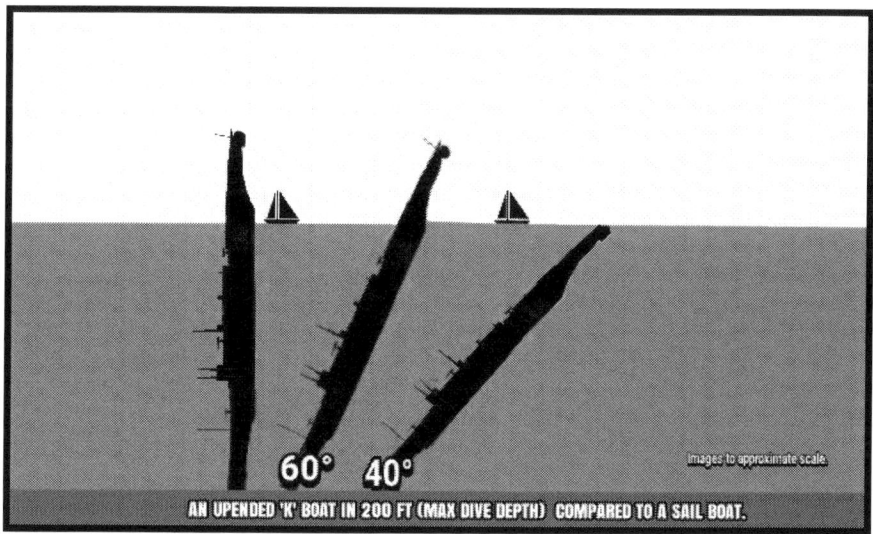

AN UPENDED 'K' BOAT IN 200 FT (MAX DIVE DEPTH) COMPARED TO A SAIL BOAT.

The boats hulls had eight main watertight bulkheads that sub-divided the craft into nine main compartments, all having been tested to a pressure of 35 lb per square inch. The hulls largest compartments were the machinery spaces, the boiler and the turbine room. Their weight, minus any machinery was 240 and 275 tons respectively. With their 500 tons plus of buoyancy whilst riding on the surface, even with the addition of the emergency oil fuel, the hulls subdivision was considered generally to be reasonably good, a fact the crews manning *K3* and *K13* would all be grateful of.

THE K9 ALONGSIDE IN AN UNKNOWN PORT. THE SIZE OF BOTH THE NEW SWAN BOW AND THE BULK OF THE VESSEL ARE CLEARLY VISIBLE WITHIN THE PHOTO.

In keeping with the bizarre theme that permeated the design, the eight internal bulkheads were calculated during the planning phase to be able to withstand a pressure equivalent of up to 70 feet (21 mtrs). This meant that at any depth exceeding 70 foot their integrity could not be guaranteed. While the boats could in theory dive to 200 feet, beyond 70 feet their bulkheads could become unreliable! To add to the Captain's problems the bows were found to lack buoyancy, even in a moderate sea. This lack of lifting buoyancy meant that the bow would not rise as it plunged through the waves.

On a final note *K16* appears in some images to show a raised bridge to permit her crew to see over her swan bow. Her guns appear to have been relocated at some stage to her superstructure to make room for the new bow. In keeping with the bizarre theme that permeated the design, the eight internal bulkheads were calculated during the planning phase to be able to withstand a pressure equivalent of up to 70 feet (21 mtrs). This meant that at any depth exceeding 70 foot their integrity could not be guaranteed. While the boats could in theory dive to 200 feet, beyond 70 feet their bulkheads could become unreliable! To add to the Captain's problems the bows were found to lack buoyancy, even in a moderate sea. This lack of lifting buoyancy meant that the bow would not rise as it plunged through the waves. On a final note K16 appears in some images to show a raised bridge to permit her crew to see over her swan bow. Her guns appear to have been relocated at some stage to her superstructure to make room for the new bow.

1: A second source states 150 feet.

The 'Tanks'

While the 'K' boat design was still on the draughtsman's board, it was intended to fit the new submarines with 'Baling Flats'. These were an area where one deck was built over a second level, but with an allowance for space of between 2 to 5 inches (5 to 10 cm) to be left between the decks. From here the seas water would drain away through a series of holes at the aft end of the deck space. Their purpose was to keep the deck free of water and in effect was to make the 'K' boats effectively controlled free flooding. But as the design developed and before the first keel was laid, changes were made to the Baling Flats. They were now to be made watertight and the

The two hulls were fitted with 20 external ballast tanks and along the bottom of the craft, (between the hulls), were additional ballast tanks. The tanks were located on both the port and starboard side and were built with a divisional bulkhead on the middle line at the top.

The class carried 156 tons of oil fuel within their sixteen internal tanks, but each tank held a varying amount of the oil's tonnage. Fourteen of the tanks held 140 tons of 'sg 0.93' oil (1) and the remaining two held 16 tons of '0.896'. In the *K8*, *K9* and *K10* the number 11 fuel tank, (which had a capacity of 4.7 tons) was converted for use as storage area, but this was to result in criticism given that it reduced the boats operational range.

In addition to the above 16 fuel tanks, two of the internal

main ballast tanks, (one on each beam for stability purposes) were adapted to serve as reserve fuel tanks. These two tanks (numbered 5 & 6) had a capacity for 44.5 tons of fuel and held 'sg 0.93', but Vickers listed the quantity carried in *K3* and *K4's* number 5 and 6 tanks as 40.2 tons. These two 'emergency' fuel tanks had an impact on the boat's buoyancy, reducing it by 7% to 25.5%. But the extra fuel increased the operational range by 50%.

But for the later *K8, K9* and *K10* Vickers quoted the figure of 41.6 tons as tanks 5 & 6 liquid capacity, but there is some speculation that these tanks were never to be completely filled with oil. The total quantity of the fuel oil carried for the "purpose of endurance" was around 197 tons in the earlier boats but as the class progressed, it was reduced to around 192 tons.

Fuel tanks aside, the boats were constructed with a few tanks for other purposes, the configuration being similar to the navy's preceding classes. But there were no compensating tanks, (2) listed as the compensating water was carried in the eight auxiliary ballast tanks with a total capacity of 56.5 tons. The 'K' boats were to be the first within the Royal Navy to be built with a Drop Keel Gear tank and the controls were installed within the turbine room and sat about 50 feet aft of amidships, being tested to a rate of 50 lb per square inch.

The boats also had a feed water tank to supply water suitable for the boilers and reserve feed water tank, both essential for a steam plant. These tanks held 23 tons of water that was pumped into the boilers to be heated and to produce the steam.

The 'K' boats of Group 1 were built with four forward internal main ballast tanks which were designated A, B, C and D, while the four aft were Q, X, Y and Z (3).

The *K6* (20/05/25 Chatham) tank contents were listed as:
- 51,850 gallons of fuel oil in external tanks   (4-7 port & starboard).
- 54,525 gallons of fuel oil in internal tanks.
- 4,700 gallons diesel oil.
- 650 gallons lubricating oil.
- 1,510 gallons fresh water.

1 'sg' is an abbreviation for specific gravity

2: Compensating tanks work to provide adjustments to the trim, the submarine may encounter once submerged. The tanks usually sit close to the centre line of the hull, were their adjustments can have a more immediate effect.

3: A full list of the K7's tanks as well as both their location and capacity are reproduced below in the appendix.

Comforts & Interior

T he Admiralty had made the decision during the class's conception, that as the 'K' boats were of a scale like a surface vessel, the crews when in port, could 'happily' stay living onboard. This was a departure from the submarine service's practice for their boat crews, who once in port exchanged the cramped living conditions of their submarine, for the comparative 'comforts' of a depot ship. Such 'luxury' was to be denied to the crews of the navy's steam powered submarines.

This would have been acceptable if the colossal boats matched the surface fleet standard of onboard accommodation, but they were cramped, damp, humid, uncomfortably hot and not a good billet to live on 24/7.

However, in May 1918 there was a move away from the 'K' boats crews living onboard full time and on the 1st January the Submarine Monthly Report No. 1 published the news that:

> "H.M.S. "ROYAL ARTHUR" had been turned over to 12th Submarine Flotilla of "K" Class to serve as a recreation hulk. While the bulk of the crew would transfer to the Royal Arthur, a Care and Maintenance Party was always retained onboard to keep steam for auxiliary purposes".

But there was a twist, the crews, due to a lack of space on their new depot ship, could only sleep on board her occasionally.

*HMS ROYAL ARTHUR (1890-1921) IN HER DAYS SERVING AS A
FIRST CLASS CRUISER OF THE EDGAR CLASS.*

The living conditions on board the navy's new Fleet-submarine (even by the standards of a World War One submersible), were poor. The officer's 'territory' was situated in line (but beneath) the forward edge of the foremost gun. The Captain had the privacy of a small cabin and the officers a comfortable bunk-wardroom. Such accommodation for officers was not usual on a submarine, but for the available space, both cabin and wardroom were spacious and well furnished. The officers even had the 'luxury' of a 4-foot (sit-in) bath which was filled by fresh water drawn from either the ships boilers or heated by electricity. Aft between the rear most steering compartment and the engine room, in an area where the hull slowly contracted towards the stern, was the crews (and N.C.O's) quarters. The Petty Officers and the Engine Room Artificers were allocated curtained messes, but these were despite the inhabitant's rank, cramped spaces. For the two groups of N.C.Os' the boilers provided heating but given the stifling heat that they generated, and which permeated through the ship, this was a redundant perk.

While the officers had a comfortable wardroom, the seaman felt as if their accommodation was squeezed into any space left over. The engine room was fitted with several bunks which were used by three crewmen in a rotation of "hot bunking", which was indicative of the crew's quarters. Later in the boats careers the crew were given a bathroom, taken from a section of the interior. But the conversion did not turn out to be permanent and after a while it was restored back to other 'non-bathing' uses.

The heat generated by the boilers was a problem never to be satisfactorily resolved, with one crewman describing the boats interior as like *"an unventilated oven"*. Following her trials and the *K3's* 'incident' off the Clyde, the Admiralty accepted that the boats interiors were made uncomfortably hot by the steam turbines and fans were duly fitted in the turbine rooms. But they were to make little real difference to the heat and humidity, just moving warm air around the interior. It was considered normal on a 'K' boat to find pools of condensation on the floor of the mess decks. The ventilation was so poor that it was not unusual to use the diesel engines to try and draw air through the interior. The humidity turned most things damp, with clothing, papers and food left unprotected soon growing a mould. Wireless Operator William Piggott who served on the K5 wrote an account of life on a 'K' boat:

"Everything was damp, every nut and bolt dripping water. You always felt damp, it's a wonder you never got rheumatism! When you opened a tin of biscuits if you left it till the next day it went mouldy. If you left bread out when you went to sea, five hours after you got out it began to go mouldy. There's forty-seven men breathing with no outlet when you're

underneath so there's no outlet, so there's damp everywhere. It was a very sparse life, it really was, a terrible life. Two heaters: one in the stokers' mess and one in the ordinary mess where I was aft. You were at your diving station and that's it you don't move, not when you're underneath. You can't go wandering about on a submarine when you're underneath - you'd tip the boat over - your just balanced. When you stood up you were always nearly bumping your head. You had a diesel engine running all the time when you were on the surface to charge the battery - there was a terrific noise all the time - you couldn't hear. The turbines were underwater. Always the smell of oil fuel - it was on the bare steel plates".

Lieutenant, Arthur Pederick's son was to write of his father's death (7th January 1918) onboard the *K7*:

"I have suffered all my life even from a by product of the 1914–18 war even if I was born after it. It is a personal fact that my father was a Lieutenant (E) serving in the disastrous K class submarines, by which the Royal Navy tried to create a Submarine which could steam on the surface at 20 knots to keep up with the Fleet, and he died of a lung infection created by the appalling conditions in such submarines....."

When ashore, the crew of a 'K' boat were easy to identify by the stench of oil and mould. Edward Whitman in 'K for Katastrophe' notes that tension amongst the crew were often high and fist fights or insults were not uncommon.

But the heat and humidity were only half the problems the crews faced. The undersides of the oil tanks were open to the sea and the fuel held in the tanks would accordingly float on the contained sea water and was extracted by pumps mounted overhead. As the oil was gradually used, sea water would seep in to replace it. This exchange served to keep the submarines weight under control and the set up worked well unless the boat was in a rough sea and the hull was rolled by the waves motion. In that event the oil and water would mix and extinguish the boiler's fire, a process that became known as *"losing suction"*. The result was that the vessel would glide to a quick and unexpected halt, with no warning to the vessel in line behind her. Another flaw with the oil tanks was that the tops were not fully sealed. As a result, the oily contents would seep out, covering the interiors decking. The floors to the mess, living spaces and passageways were often covered in a film of oily water, that had seeped up as the boat rolled and pitched.

But despite these issues, the Admirals continued to put a 'good spin' on the class, as the Naval Review, volume VII, 1919 illustrated:

> *"In a case of urgency a 'K' boat can keep up a speed*
> *of 19 to 20 knots in weather that would force des-*
> *troyers to reduce to 15 knots or break up; admittedly,*
> *damage to the bridge and superstructure must be ex-*
> *pected, the stokers in the boiler-room would suffer*
> *severe discomfort from water pouring down the air*
> *intakes and funnels, sometimes extinguishing the*
> *fires (which can very quickly be relighted), but the*
> *main point is that the ½-inch hull will not suffer*
> *from any amount of overdriving in bad weather like*
> *the thin plating of a destroyer; so unless the Com-*

mander-in-chief was willing to leave his destroyers he would never have to outpace his 'K' boats".

As the months passed and the number of 'accidents' grew within the class, the boats understandably grew a reputation of being jinxed or even worse in a crewman's eyes, cursed! The 'K' boats were quickly to become unpopular to serve in and the crews morale was to become an increasing problem.

Captains And Crew

I t would be easy to assume the accidents suffered by the 'K' class were the result of a poor quality in their appointed Captains, who in turn were not capable of training their crews to the level of experience the boats required. But from the first appointment the admiralty had recognized that such huge and 'cutting edge' vessels would require officers of proven experience and all the men in command were veterans within the service, most with many years submarine experience.

The lead boat of the class *HMS K1* was in 1917 under the Captaincy of Commander Charles Benning. Prior to his 'K' boat command he had been commended for his work in the torpedoing and damaging of the German auxiliary vessel *Schwarzwald* off the Norderney Lighthouse on the 14th April 1915. He was as a result promoted to the rank of Commander on 30th June 1915 and awarded a D.S.O for his work in command of submarines in enemy waters. His service record noted that he:

> *"...has made 16 cruises in enemy waters, during* [which] *he has repeatedly been in action with zeppelins, seaplanes & anti-submarine craft. On one occasion after torpedoing an armed auxiliary he was forced by sweepers to dive into the German minefield, when his battery was exhausted. On another occasion he was 3 hours in a minefield before sinking another armed auxiliary off Borkum."*

NOEL LAURENCE (RIGHT), COMMANDER OF E1, WITH MAX HORTON (LEFT), COMMANDER OF E9, IN THE BALTIC. LAURENCE WOULD GO ON TO COMMAND THE K2.

The *HMS K2's* Commander Noel Laurence had served with distinction in the Baltic and on the 19th August 1915, he had torpedoed and damaged the battlecruiser *Moltke* in the Gulf of Riga.

HMS K4's Captain, Commander David de B. Stocks' had taken *HMS E2* through the Dardanelles and undertaken a patrol within the Sea of Marmara, which lies surrounded by enemy territory.

LAYTON IN 1915

Lieutenant-Commander Geoffrey Layton of the *K7* was appointed to command the submarine *E13* on 2nd September
1914. The submarine was to be lost when it ran aground on
the Danish coast while trying to break through to the Baltic. Having been found by German destroyers, they sank her
by gunfire in Danish territorial waters. The officers and crew
were interned in Copenhagen, but Layton was able to escape
to Norway on 29th October. He returned to Newcastle by

the S.S Venus, arriving around 1st November 1914.

The *K10's* Commander Claude C. Dobson, was appointed in command of the submarine *C27* on 7th April 1914. On 20th July 1915, he torpedoed and sank the *U23* off Fair Island. Dobson was to be awarded the D.S.O for this sinking, being decorated by the King on the 14th October 1915 at Buckingham Palace. He would go onto earn the Victoria Cross in July 1919 when *"for most conspicuous gallantry"* when on the 18th August 1919 his *C.M.B 31BD* was credited with scoring two torpedo hits on a Russian battleship *Andrei Pervozvanny* in Kronstadt harbour during a raid that Dobson was commanding.

HMS 13/22's Captain was Lieutenant-Commander Godfrey Herbert and had been appointed in command of a Holland class submarine in January 1905 and had served in both the Holland and 'A' class boats. He had in addition commanded *A4, C36, C30, D5, E22,* and the *H8* before joining the *K13*. He had also survived a diving accident in the *A4*, the loss of the *D5* to a mine and the afore mentioned *Archimede* patrol. He also commanded the 'Q' ship *H.M.S. Antwerp* on 27th January 1915. He was also appointed in command of the 'Q' ship *Baralong* on 5 April 1915. On 19th August, Baralong was involved in the 'Baralong Incident' after sinking *U 27* in the Irish Sea. Just eight days later, Herbert was appointed in command of the *E 22*. He was then appointed to *Dolphin* on the 27th April 1916 and loaned to command the Q-ship *Carrigan Head,* also known as *Q4* in June. While some Captains submarine experience was limited, (ie Herbert), each Captain was experienced in the task of commanding a warship at sea and brought those years of knowledge to the "Kalamity" class.

THE CREW OF HMS K8. (SOURCE WIKIPEDIA).

But as experienced as these captains were, they found they had been appointed to command a new and untried class of submersible. They were greeted at the dockside by an oversized, steam powered and inordinately complex vessel, with which no one had any 'vast' experience with its operating systems or conduct at sea.

THE CREW OF HMS K14. (SOURCE CSSSLIDER, COURTESY OF STEPHEN JOHNSON)

The complement carried by a 'K' boat numbered on average 59 men, comprised of 6 officers and 53 ratings.

On the day of her loss the K4 had the following breakdown of crew members:

- Able Seaman: 15

- Chief Engine Room Artificer, (Petty Officer (PO)): 1
- Chief Stoker: 1
- Commander: 1
- Engine Room Artificer: 3
- Gunner : 1
- Leading Stoker, (PO): 6
- Leading Telegraphist: 1
- Lieutenant : 2
- Lieutenant Commander: 1
- Officer's Steward, (PO): 1
- Petty Officer: 2
- Petty Officer Telegraphist: 1
- Signalman, (PO): 1
- Stoker: 10
- Stoker (PO): 3.

The Coxswain if not having the rank of a Chief Petty Officer would often hold the rank of acting C.P.O while in the post of Coxswain. There was no Gunner on board if the boat was not equipped with a 4-inch gun, but one S.G.1 instead. The K26 had 3 G.L.2 and 3 S.G's, (S.G=seaman gunner. G.L= Gun layer)

If a commander was in command an officer's steward 1st class was posted to the boat.

One crewman was carried for "hydraulic duties".

While in 'immediate reserve' three boats shared one crew, which allocated one third of the crew per boat. In material reserve it was one full crew per ten boats, allowing one tenth of a crew per boat.

A DESIGN FOR THE HMS K14 CREST. ITS UNCLEAR IF THIS WAS AN OFFICAL
CREATION OR A DOODLE BY A CREW MEMBER.

The 'Kew' files hold with the pages of the K2's Ships Book, the following comparative break down on a 'K' boats comple-ment:

"Complements of Submarines
No deviations to be made without SPECIAL Admiralty sanction
11th April 1921"

Source: K2 ships book, National Archives	R CLASS	M CLASS	L5 CLASS	L CLASS	K CLASS	H CLASS	E&S CLASS
COMMANDER	-	0	0	0	1	0	0
LIEUT CMDR OR LIEUT	1	2 (B)	1 (B)	1(B)	1	1	1
LIEUTENANT (G)	0	1	0	0	0	0	0
LIEUTENANT (N)	0	1	0	0	1	0	0
LIEUT SUB-LIEUT, MATE & WARRANT OFFICER	2	1	2	2	1	2	2
WARRANT OFFICER	0	0	1	1	0	0	0
PETTY OFFICER	2	5 (A)	4(A)	3(A)	3(A)	2	3
LEADING SEAMAN	2	6	3	3	4	2	2
A.B OR ORD SEAMAN	6	25	8	8	13	4	5
P.O TELEGRAPHIST	0	1	1	1	1	1	0
?DG TELEGRAPHIST	0	0	1	1	1	1	1
TELEGRAPHIST	1	1	0	1	1	0	0
YEOMAN OF SIGNALS	0	0	1	1	0	0	0
?DG SIGNALMAN	0	0	-	-	1	1	1
SIGNALMAN	1	1	-	-	-	-	-

INCLUDED IN THE ABOVE							
G.M, G.L.1ST CL	-	1	-	-	-	-	-
G.L 1ST CL	-	1	-	-	-	-	-
G.L 2ND CL	-	2	2	1(C)	2(D)	-	-
RANGE TAKER 3RD CL	-	1	-	-	1	-	-
S.G	-	20	2	2(C)	4(4)	1	1
Q.O	-	1	-	-	-	-	-
T.G.M	1	1	1	1	1	1	1
T.C	-	1	-	-	1	-	-
SUB COXSWAIN	1	1	1	1	-	1	1
L.T.O	2	3	2	3	2	2	2
S.T	6	6	7	6	9	4	6
ENGR LIEUT. LIEUT OR	-	-	-	-	1	-	-
CMDR OR W.T ENGR	-	1	1	1	-	-	-
CHIEF E.R.A	-	1	-	-	1	1	1
E.R.A	2	3	4	4	5	2	3
CHIEF STOKER	-	1	1	-	1	-	-
STOKER P.O	1	1	1	1	3	1	1
LEADING SEAMAN	2	4	3	4	3	2	3
STOKER	2	8	9	9	13	3	6
ORDNANCE ARTIFICER	-	2(F)	-	-		-	-
ELECTRICAL ARTIFICER	-	1	1	-	-	-	-
OFF. STD. 2ND CL	-	1(E)	-	-	-	-	-
TOTAL	22	67	42	39	57	23	30

96

WHILE THE TOTALS GIVEN ARE 'INTERESTING', THE FIGURES AT LEAST ALLOW THE BREAKDOWN OF THE CREW TO BE SEEN. THERE IS ALSO NO KEY SUPPLIED WITHIN THE FILE FOR THE ABBREVIATIONS OR THE BRACKETED LETTERS. (SEE APPENDIX L FOR ORIGINAL DOCUMENT)

Armaments

The boats forming Group 1's main armament was comprised of four 18-inch (460 mm) torpedo tubes mounted on the beam, (one to port and one to starboard) with an additional four 18-inch seated in the bows. But the stern was to remain devoid of any torpedo tubes. The classes design had originally specified that the newly developed 21-inch torpedoes were to have been installed, but with the delay of their introduction into service, Fisher changed the specification to the current and lesser sized 18-inch torpedo. The boats carried a total of sixteen (1) 18-inch (45 cm) Mark VIII torpedoes of which 8 were reloads. The weapon had been first introduced in 1913 and at 35 knots had a range of 2,500 yards (2,286 mtrs). At 4,000 yards (3,657 mtrs) the speed was 29 knots.

THE K8's BOW TORPEDO TUBES. THE SIZE OF THE BOATS DID NOT TRANSLATE

As originally built the 'K' boats were fitted with two 18-inch swivel mounted deck tubes on the superstructure for night use. But fitted on the structure , (which with the boats general dimensions was low to the water level and with the addition of a bow throwing sheets of water over them in anything but calm seas), the weapons soon became damaged. The weight of the mounting and its torpedoes was also found to be affecting the motion of the hull, being attached to the boats uppermost surface. Following the 1917 operation 'B.B' the boats took it in turns to go into dock for the fitting of their new 'Swan' bows and the two tubes were removed during the refits. The redundant surface tubes and deck guns were then installed onto the navy's 'Q' ships.

In addition to the boat's main armament of torpedoes, on their completion the Group 1 boats carried a total of three deck guns. Two 4-inch/40 (10.2 cm) Q[uick] F[ire] Mark IV were mounted on the upper deck with one between the fore funnel and 'bridge', while the other 4-inch gun was mounted before the conning tower on the deck casing. The third gun was a single 3-inch (76 mm) anti-aircraft gun and was located on the superstructure, between the funnels. Both the K5 and K12 were to retain the gun located before the conning tower and the K17 had two 5.5"/50 (14 cm) B[reech] L[oading] Mark I in place of the 4-inch. Later in their careers one of the 4-inch guns was removed and the other placed on top of the superstructure with the 3-inch gun to make room for the swan bow. The boats magazine and deck storage (by the guns) carried 175 rounds of 4-inch and 100 rounds of 3-inch ammunition.

The 4-inch weapon had first entered service in 1908 and had a weight of 1,296 tons (1,317 kg). Its overall barrel length was of 13 feet, 10 ½ inches (4.227 mtr) and could on average fire between 6 to 8 rounds per minute. It made use of three types of shells:

1. HE: 31 lbs. (14.06 kg)
2. CPC: 31 lbs. (14.06 kg)
3. Shrapnel: 31 lbs. (14.06 kg)

The *K17's* two 5.5-inch guns were obtained by the Royal Navy when two cruisers that were being built for Greece, (*Antinavarhos Kontouriotis* and *Lambros Katsonis*) prior to the outbreak of war were taken over and renamed *HMS Birkenhead* and *HMS Chester,* respectively. The weapon was chosen by the Greeks instead of the British 6-inch and went on to be mounted on the battle cruisers *Hood* and *Furious* and later the aircraft carrier *Hermes.* But among these super-star names was the *K17.* The other 'K' boats were to have had the 5.5-inch weapon, but the plans were amended on all but the *K17* to the 4-inch calibre. The manually operated and elevated 5.5-inch gun was designed in about 1913 and came into service in 1915. The weapon had a weight of 15,600 lbs (7.07 tons/7,076 kg) and a length of 284.7 inches (7.232 mtr) overall. The bore length was 275 inch (6.985 mtr) and had a rifling length of 235.9 inches (5.992 mtr), with 40 grooves. The twist was uniform RH 1 in 30 and the chamber volume 1,500 in 3 (24.58 dm3). The weapon had a maximum rate of fire of 12 rounds per minute.

The shells used by the weapons were:

1. Common: 82 lbs. (37.2 kg)
2. Shrapnel: 82 lbs. (37.2 kg)
3. HE: 82 lbs. (37.2 kg)
4. Shellite: 82 lbs. (37.2 kg)
5. HENT: 82 lbs. (37.2 kg)
6. HE Mark ID: 82 lbs. (37.2 kg)

The bursting charge was 5.25 lbs (2.4 kg) and in 1921 is listed as using a propellant charge of 22.25 lbs (10.1 kg) and in 1930 that increased to 22.54 lbs (10.22 kg), but by that date the *K17* had been broken up. The weapons muzzle velocity was CPC: 2,790 fps (850 mps and the working pressure was 18 tons/inch (2,531 kg/cm2). Unfortunately, the barrel life is not recorded. The propellant charge was of a single bag style.

The range for the 82 lbs (37.2 kg) CPC shell, with a 25 degrees elevation was 16,000 yards (14,630 mtr) and at 30 degrees that increased to 17,770 yards (16,250 mtr). The weapons muzzle velocity was 2,287 feet per second (697 mtr per sec) and the manually elevated weapon could elevate to 20 degrees and propel its 31lb shell over 10,210 yards (9,340 mtr) or 5.8 miles (9.33 km).

The *K12* had the best sea keeping qualities owing to the construction of her fore gun platform and to her carrying less fuel, making her more buoyant. The fore gun platform for the forward 4-inch gun was originally on the upper deck but it had been raised to a part of superstructure located forward of the bridge, (by 1925) like the K26 design. The anti-aircraft 3-inch or 12-pdr (76.2 cm) weapon is harder to identify but the 20 cwt QF HA Marks I, II, III and IV was in general use on British submarines at the time.

The large number of deck mounted weapons (and the necessary ammunition) greatly increased the vessels total displacement and to a degree effected their surface speed.

.

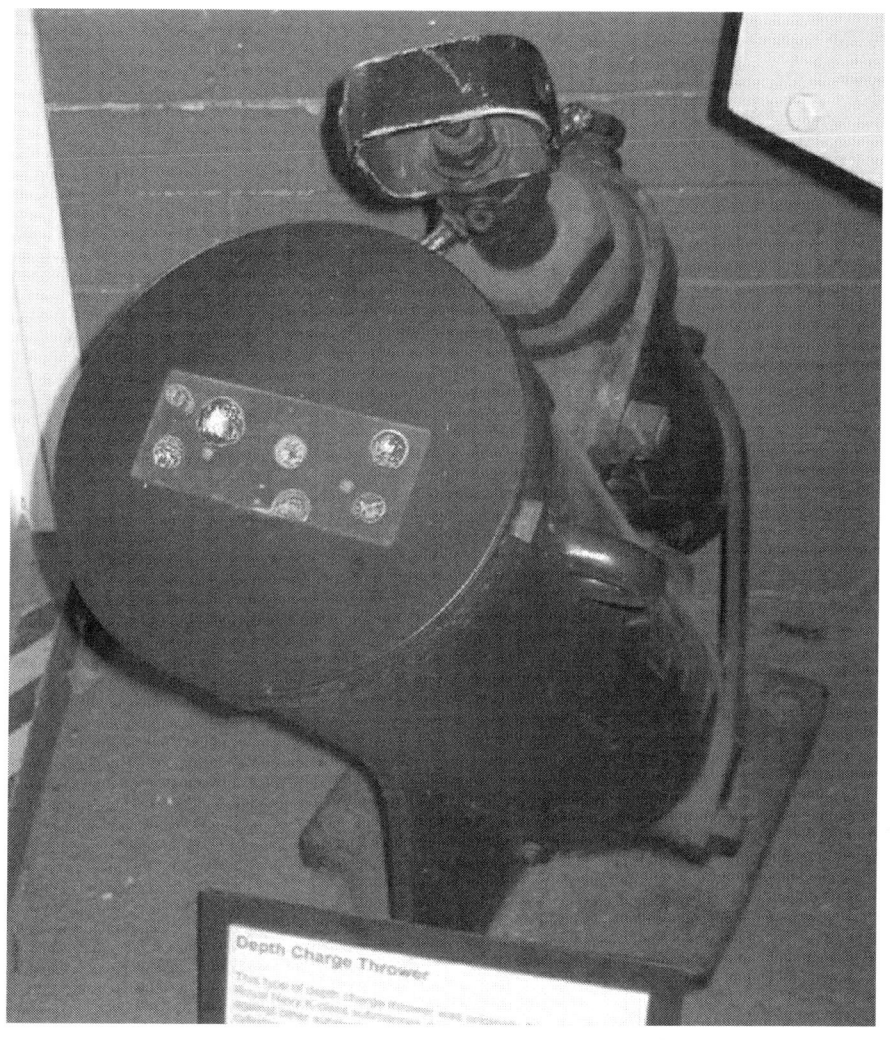

A 'K' BOATS DEPTH CHARGE (GOSPORT SUBMARINE MUSEUM).

Once it became clear to the Admirals that there was unlikely ever to be a Jutland II, the 'K' boats were moved away
from fleet operations and to a role of North Sea watching
patrols. In this function a few of the class were to be fitted
with depth charge throwers for an anti-submarine surface
capability. The *K3* was to receive her depth charge addition
during her March 1918 refit, with one on each beam and

"stowage for spare charges". The official range of the thrower was listed as 40 yards (27 mtr) when using the Thornycroft MkI and II depth charge. But there is no record of the 'K' boats ever using their depth charges in action and its unlikely they ever were. As a final note on these weapons they would be safe from detonation having been stored (assumedly) within the hull. But if they, were on deck when the boat dived, they would require arming and priming before any use was made of them in action.

PREVIOUS PAGE. THIS IMAGE OF THE K22 GIVES A VIEW OF HER DECK ARMAMENTS. LOCATED JUST TO THE REAR OF THE AFT FUNNEL LOCATION IS HER DEPTH CHARGE THROWER. THE ABSENCE OF HER FUNNELS INDICATES THE BOAT IS MOST LIKELY IN THE PROCESS OF EITHER DIVING OF SURFACING.

1: Coxswain Moth gives the number as 20 in his biography.

Range Finders

By 1921 the 1st flotilla's (Rosyth) 'K' boats had been equipped with a 3-foot range finder, but anything beyond 4,000 yards and the item was deemed to be inaccurate.

Masts, Periscopes & Aerials

The 'K' boats were equipped with two periscopes which extended to a height of 36 feet 9 ½ inches (10.98 mtrs) and were 17 feet 6 inches (5.33 mtrs) when retracted, (bar the exposed part of the extending portion). The normal length of a British periscope at this period was on average 30 feet which with their additional 6 feet, gave the 'K' boats an advantage with their depth keeping.

The 36-feet periscope in *K12* made her depth keeping in a heavy sea much easier than was the case in K2 and *K22* which were fitted with the normal 30-feet periscope.

The 'K' boats were equipped with two periscopes which extended to a height of 36 feet 9 ½ inches (10.98 mtr) and were 17 feet 6 inches (5.33 mtr) when retracted, (bar the exposed part of the extending portion). The normal length of a British periscope at this period was on average 30 feet which with their additional 6 feet, gave the 'K' boats an advantage with their depth keeping.

The 36ft periscope in *K12* made her depth keeping in a heavy sea much easier than was the case in *K2* and *K22* which were fitted with the normal 30feet periscope.

THE BOATS TELESCOPE FOREMAST:*

- Construction material: steel,
- Lower part: 14 ft 7 7/8 inches (7 inch diameter),
- Middle part: 14 ft 6 5/8 inches (5 3/8 diameter),
- Top part: 14 ft 2 inches (5 1/2 inches diameter),
- Housing of lower part: 2 foot 6 inches,
- Housing of middle part: 2 foot 6 inches,
- Housing of top part: 2 foot 6 inches,
- Total weight 0.4 tons.

TELESCOPIC MAIN MAST:*

- Construction material: steel,
- Lower part 14 feet 7 3/8 inches (7 inches diameter),
- Middle part: 14 feet 6 5/8 inches
  (5 1/2 inches diameter),
- Top part 15 feet 5 inches (3 1/2 inches diameter),
- Weight: 0.4 ton.

TELESOPIC MAIN MAST:*

- Construction material: steel,
- Housing of lower part: 2 feet 6 inches,
- Housing of middle part: 2 feet 6 inches,
- Housing of upper part: 2 feet 6 inches.

TELESCOPIC SIGNAL MAST:*

- Construction material: Norwegian spar,
- Lower part: 11 feet 3 inches
  (5 3/4 inches diameter),

- Middle part: 11 feet 5 1/4 inches
  (4 2/3 inches diameter),
- Upper part: 11 feet 9 1/4 inches
  (3 3/4 inches diameter),

(Weight 0.9 ton).

DERRICKS:*

- 14 feet 6 inches (5 ½ diameter) 0.137 tons weight,
- Construction material: steel.

JACK STAFF:* 14 feet 0 inches (2 ½ diameter) weight   0.13 tons.

ENSIGN STAFF:* 14 feet 0 inches (2½ diameter) weight).13 tons.

SPAR FOR BULLROPE:* 14 feet 2 inches (6 inches diameter) weight: 0.43 tons.

* figures based on *K1* in 1917.

Radios & Fessenden Gear.

By November 1918 all the 'K' class had been supplied with a 3 kilowatt Poulsen wireless set, which provided a range of 200 miles (321.86 Km) for submarine-to-submarine communication and 300 to 400 miles (421.80 to 643.73 Km) between shore stations and submarines. Reception with shore stations of 400 miles distant was not uncommon and high-power shore stations could be received over 500 to 600 miles (894.67 to 965.60 Km).

The boats were also fitted with a set of the American Fessenden Underwater Sound Telegraphy equipment to allow them to communicate with the surface ship they were working with. The plans called for the fleets destroyers to accompany the 'K' boats and to maintain contact with the rest of the fleet by W/T. The Fessenden would be used to communicate with the submarine once they had submerged. But the Fessenden gear was rarely to be made use of given its limited ability and a perceived danger that its use could plausibly give away the fleet's position to nearby any lurking U-boats.

By November 1918 all the 'K' class had been supplied with a 3 kilowatt Poulsen wireless set, which provided a range of 200 miles (321.86 Km) for submarine-to-submarine communication and 300 to 400 miles (421.80 to 643.73 Km) between shore stations and submarines. Reception with shore stations of 400 miles distant was not uncommon and high power shore stations could be received over 500 to 600 miles (894.67 to 965.60 Km).

The boats were also fitted with a set of the American Fessenden Underwater Sound Telegraphy equipment to allow them to communication with the surface ship they would working with. The plans called for the fleets destroyers to accompany the 'K' boats and to maintain contact with the rest of the fleet by W/T. The Fessenden would be used to communicate with their submarines once they had submerged.

But the Fessenden gear was rarely to be made use of given its limited ability and a perceived danger that its use could plausibly give away the fleet's position to nearby any lurking U-boats.

Boats

Located within a recess, (covered by steel doors) on the boats casing was a 12-foot dinghy. The dinghy was hoisted on a small stump derrick out and into the water. The craft had six big brass screw plugs which were taken out of the bottom of the boat, so that on the 'K' boats submergence the water could flow freely in and out of the boat and have no effect on the trim of the submarine.

CHAPTER TWO. A
GUIDED TOUR.

*"I Never Met Anybody Who Had The Least Affection For The 'K'
Class And They Were Looked On With Fear And Loathing. After
All, They Murdered Many Of Their Officers And Crews".*

(*Commander George F. Bradshaw, R.n. (Retd & Captain Of K15, 1959).*)

T he 'K' (Group 1) were divided into the following eleven compartments from the bow forward:

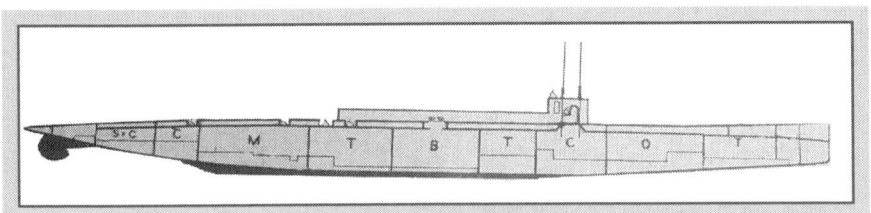

THE 'K' BOAT COMPARTMENTS

1)   Auxiliary Ballast Tank,

2)   Bow Torpedo Room (T),

3)   Officers' Quarters with Fore Hatch (O),

4)   Control Room with Conning Tower
     and Wheel house over and double Hatch (C),

5)   Amidships Torpedo Room with Torpedo
     Hatch (T),

6)   Boiler Room (B),

7)   Turbine Room with two Hatches (T),

8)   Motor Room with Hatch (M),

9)   Crew Space with Hatch (C),

10) Steering Compartment (S & C),

11) Ballast Tank.

The Group 1 and Group 2 boats were at a basic level the same. Its fortunate that in 1929 a crew member of the *K26* was to write and published a book about the boat on which he had served. The crewman went on after he left the service to become a writer and broadcaster under the name of Colin Clemack. Chapter 2 of his book is worth reproducing here in full, as it leaves us with a rare and maybe unique picture of life on the *K26*, (and by default a picture of all the 'K' boats):

"SOME SORT OF DESCRIPTION OF SUBMARINE K.26, IN 1929 THE ONLY STEAM SUB IN THE WORLD, ON THE SURFACE THE FASTEST IN THE WORLD, INCIDENTALLY, MY STEAM SWEETHEART.

I have described myself joining K.26 in 1929, at the age of twenty four, but what about the vessel? When out of the water sitting primly on chocks in a dry or floating dock she could be seen to be long and shapely. Standing right back, her lines were much like a garfish and if you have not seen a garfish lately you can look one up in the encyclopedia and imagine a straight superstructure amidships and a conning tower together with three separate nicely faired-in four inch guns, two short funnels and a bit of a cat's cradle

THE GARFISH & THE 'K' BOAT.

of wire aerials. Two fine Brass periscopes stood on top of the conning tower, or slid down into their controls. Between the periscopes and under periscope standards was a three-foot square wooden box its narrow side running fore and aft. This was the box which contained coils of cab tyre cable on which simple aerial the Morse signals from Rugby could be heard on long wave wireless. Even when submerged these very low frequency signals could be read by the telegraphists in the nine by eight silent cabinets in the Control Room.

Already K.26's wireless gear was achieving museum value. Broadcasting was well advanced. Moving pictures were getting sound through new valve amplifier techniques, aircraft carriers had short wave type transmitters. In K.26 the gear was old, tried, tested, it tried and tested the skill of the POTEL and his men,

Petty Officer Tel. Sabin, Leading Tel. Liddiatt and Telegraphist Lemaire were well versed in flying kite aerials, transmitting on the 1910 style Poulsen Arc Transmitter, listening on the quaint old bright emitter valve receiving gear. As the Leading Tel. said, "Your man killed by bow and arrow is just as dead as the one hit by a fifteen-inch shell." I saw his point. Economy was being preached. I saw no new gadgets in K.26's wireless office.

Well let's start from for'd, the bows, the pointed end. The bow was vertical and the 'free flood space' somewhat bulbous. Each side of the bow there were three torpedo tubes shaped into the pressure hull with streamlined shutters very sharp and clean she clove the water well. Round the tubes there were tanks and air vessels and the gear for loading and firing torpedoes, the tube space or 'fore ends' could be shut off by two high oval watertight doors, then came the spare torpedo stowage, racks, chains, hanging bogies with chain purchases that rattled Metallicaly if loose, another watertight bulkhead and then a passage lined with Officer's bunks, carefully curtained and with drawers beneath. In the same passage two electric cooking ranges, an ice-box, two air operated WCs and a lot of controls for pumping and flooding. Each side of the boat a Fessenden oscillator for making Morse to submerged submarines, generally its use was confined to occasions when submarines were missing. In this passage the Officer's steward and a seaman sometime cooked for the Wardroom, the cooking smells were wafted through a fan system which either distributed it around the boat when dived, or up through a discharge outlet when on the surface. Another bulkhead and the boat appeared to broaden out below.

The Wardroom was fitted with a round table, a side-board and some quaint Victorian-like armchairs. In a brave attempt to appear neat but not gaudy, the Wardroom corticene (1)was painted a nice shade of light green with the edges held down by polished brass strips. A strip of carpet ran fore-and-aft in the Wardroom from the for'd W/T door to the after W/T ditto. This was a good policy, when the boat was at sea with hatches closed down, or dived, all traffic for the Torpedo Room had to go through the Wardroom.

Shale oil in the Torpedo Room soaked into boots and shoes, plimsolls, some of it found its way into the Wardroom carpet which now and then got a hefty wash and was dried in the sun. Through the Wardroom after door and you were in the switchboard. A small brightly lit compartment through which the greater mass of electricity never passed, the intercourse between motors and batteries taking place without the intervention of the so-called switchboard. Still going aft the Control Room, an example of what might well be done without, except that you had to have it on the surface, steering wheels, hydroplane wheels, deep well to take the periscopes, panels of air controls, dials, pressure gauges, a tiny log that lied consistently and could not be made to tell the truth. It was an old type called Forbe's Log, out it was always called Forbe's Liar. It theoretically told you how fast you were traveling, how for you had gone, but it lied, how it lied. As voice pipes on long runs impress their own tune on words you have some standard messages that are unmistak-

able. Navigating from; the bridge the Officer of the Watch of K.26 would call down "Feed the dog" at this the helms-man or messenger on watch would read the two dials and report the result. It was up to the Officer of the Watch to interpret Forbe's liar. When dived, hydraulic power brought up the periscopes smoothly and silently and the training was by hand and two grips like cycle handlebars. The gyro compass tick a ticked in a space on the port side of the Control Room. At the after end of the Control Room the wireless office with a door like a butcher's refrigerator stood, it's interior lined with sheet lead and with bright copper wires running here and there on stand-off insulators of porcelain. Stuck on the outside of the door was an ominous notice about the Official Secrets Act applying to Wireless Offices. It was a bit of unconscious humour really, there was a need to keep quiet what was in the W/T Office. It was almost pre-Marconi but no doubt it was policy to let the world think that here lurked many secret and mysterious devices. A few 10-year old schoolboys of 1929 might have given poor old K.26 a lesson in DX hunting. The best gear however was the little detailed pieces like the operator's phones. These were made by a firm called S.G. Brown, were then the best in the world. Called Brown's 'A' they made a good job of the Morse signals of the time, even now are looked up to by specialists. One very special gadget hung in the Wireless Office it was called an Aerial Tuning Helix Mark something or other. Polished Copper, it looked like a piece of early movie prop. An occasional tearing blue spark crackled across it breaking the long monotony of longs and shorts that formed themselves into requests for oil fuel on arrival, or meat and potatoes before departure.

The Wireless Staff all three and later four were compatible. In harbour with a cushion middled across the rather sharp door sill of the W/T Office Petty Officer Sabin would sometimes play his violin the acoustics of the Control Room being slightly better than the lead lined silent cabinet. The bulkhead aft of the Control Room, this led to a passage down the side of the two Boiler Rooms. A small escape hatch not designed for a really fat man led out of the after Boiler Room into the passage. Out of the after passage door and you were in the Turbine Room and to get to the Boiler Rooms you walked across to port and then for'd to enter the airlock. This entering of Boiler Rooms is something that was clearly not for me, when lit up anyway. The pressure, the moving air flapping your overalls and seemingly designed to blow you through a small aperture into a blazing mass of oil, had no charms for me, when my duties took me there I worked hard and got out fast, my ears going in and out with the varying pressure. The Stokers on watch, normal in their cases seemed like devils in hell tending the boilers. I used to shudder at the thought of all that hot water, steam, flame. The Turbine Room hummed, the E.R.A.s controlled the steam the Stokers made; some curious looking clock gadgets ticked away, I felt glad they were non-electric, a carefully guarded small valve worked only, as far as I could see, by the Chief E.R.A himself, delivered hot distilled water from the Boiler or the Vaps. If we wanted hot water we had to work a hand pump, cold drinking water, up to a bucket which we balanced on an electric radiator until warm. I will speak of submarine hygiene later.

The next bulkhead was pierced with one watertight door leading into the Motor Room. The Turbine Room, due to escaping steam, oily atmosphere, condensation, heat, was a bit dank and depressing. Entering the Motor Room from the Turbine Room was like going from East Side New York to Broadway. The lighting was better the brass and copper shone, the paintwork was dazzling white, red voltmeters stood on the switch panels the copper bars, the bright brass fuse ends all spoke of a lived in space, yes, about 18 of us packed like herring in a barrel. No reminders of home, not a calendar or a pin up, or even an official notice, just utility in a shiny solid setting.

Under the brass rimmed corticened shaped wooden boards there was the underground. Beneath our feet a compressor, a large D.C. dynamo, both huge components, the compressor noisy with it, fortunately it was only used to top up the air bottles to about two thousand pounds a square inch at intervals. The more diving the more compressing. Unfortunately this compressor was temperamental. ERA Webb worked under our feet with his Stoker mate Joe Lough in a sweat of apology, he didn't like to intrude he said. The motive power for the generator and compressor was an eight cylinder diesel engine of 850 horse power, said to have been one of the main engines of submarine E.4 many years before and taken out and rebuilt when that vessel had sunk and been raised. I think this story authentic because, our Captain had been in E.4 himself and might have discounted it if untrue.

When this diesel and generator and compressor were started up the Motor Room vibrated and with the rounded hull the echoes were enormous. The idea of the diesel generator was to be able to charge the batteries when [the] submarine had no steam, we had to be moving in order to charge from the Main Motors geared to the turbines. But we could run the diesels to charge the battery, clutch up the motors to the screws, lower the funnels and move slowly about as diesel-electric, very useful too when seas came down the funnels and the fires went out. As the diesel was in the centre line there was a fair amount of room at the after end and two little steel cabinets stood on the port side, one for Chiefs' and P.O.s, one for 'Other Ratings'. Air driven W.C.s always referred to in crude submarine jokes that I will not repeat. They sent their charge out into the sea with a bottle of compressed air behind it; if you threw your head right back when you pressed the steel ball to operate it, you were safe - and dry! Not used in harbour their duties were taken over by a W/C in the upper casing on the top of the Conning Tower and a picturesque urinal device called a pig's ear on top of the conning tower. It was possible, so it was said, for the Officer of the Watch to make water into the pig's ear just below the coaming of the top of the Conning Tower, whilst standing at the salute when passing the Fleet Flagship, thus combining courtesy with bodily comfort.

Another bulkhead a centre waterline door in it and the Stokers Mess deck popularly called the Dope Den. Bunks both sides & long Mess table down the centre and as the diameter of the pressure hull was now decreasing everybody had to walk with a slight stoop. For convenience some Stokers sat up in bed to breakfast and others sat on the lockers. Beyond the Dope Den another bulkhead, the Coxn's stores including rum; and the steering mechanism electro-hydraulic one set and a tremendous hand wheel for use if all power failed. This steering gear occupied the thicker part of the piece called for its shape the duck's arse. Up top this piece was always awash on the surface whatever the trim. Painted black with boot topping it was always a bright green with short weed, slippery to the touch. Below, sticking out a little under fin-like guards the big twin screws, framing: them the rudder and the after hydroplanes. In the clear Mediterranean water the twin three bladed screws of phosphor bronze could be seen easily. Starting again from up on the duck's arse and going for'd a slim piece of free flood along the centre line ran to hip height. In this generously perforated casing were stowed fenders, ropes, und securing, wires and two hatches led down through it, one to the Stokers' mess and one further for'd to the Motor Room. Open in harbour except when very rough, sometimes by special permission at sea, at the pipe "hands to bathe". Stokers and seamen could come out of both hatches run along the rounded hull and dive into the sea. A few feet before the Motor Room hatch the upper casing, also 'free flood' began. It was some nine feet tall and had steel doors in it only on the starboard side. The top of this casing had a slightly flanged finish, the idea being that a wave would hit, run up and be deflected back, it sometimes worked, but big waves would go down the funnels from time to time. The after end of the upper casing had a recess to take a 12 foot dinghy and steel doors to cover the space, when the dinghy had been hoisted on a small stump derrick out of water it was lowered into its nest and the doors were shut. First, however there were six big brass screw plugs to be taken out of the bottom of the boat, so that on diving the water could flow freely in and out of the boat and have no effect on the trim of the submarine.

Next thing still going forward the after 4 inch quick firing gun which when in its normal position pointed for'd and remained level

A streamlined shield eased it through the water when submerged. Next the after funnel which protruded from a deep well in which it was pivoted, worked by oil pressure from vertical to horizontal. At the funnel base on top of the pressure hull a big domed door was also pivoted as the funnel tilted over this big circular plug moved into place sealing the boiler flue off from the sea. The for'd funnel came next with its attendant machinery. One to Starboard one to Port stood the steam sirens, the same type used in destroyers. A diesel submarine had an air whistle with a different note, in fog you could distinguish any submarine, except K.26, whose siren was the same as a steam man o' war.

The culinary coal as it was called was good stuff it lit easily and burned well. Cookie leisurely pumped more water into the back copper, not too much because it was tiring work, because anybody who came later to get hot water for tea or any other purpose, was bound *by custom of the boat to pump back as least as much cold water into the back copper as he took out. The system worked with a few hints from time to time to the nationality and background of the man asking for 'hotters': which was submarine slang for hot water. For cold water the term 'colders' was used, the cook would say, "I exchange you de hotters for de colders".*

Once the coal had burned up, almost everything was forthcoming from that tiny galley boiled, fried, baked, stewed and roasted. The Wardroom Cook, another who did his best in harbour beside the Boat Cook. The one with the apron called Nelson, was the Wardroom Chef. In a tiny recess next door to the galley reposed the butcher's block tied down to stop it floating to the top of the compartment when the boat dived. Standen, a Seaman Gunner, held the offices of "Jack Dusty" and Butcher. He officiated in the issue of rum and meat and spuds. It was once unfortunate that the issue of meat from the "Beef Screw" was later than the issue of rum from the after rum store. A badly directed swipe of the cleaver at a forequarter of meat hit a hydraulic pipe severing it and causing the foremost wireless mast to sink slowly down into its place of rest during the transmission of a signal. Consternation below when the transmitter was suspected. Eventually an oil-soaked bystander who was waiting for No. Two Mess's meat went down to the wireless office and shouted out "Sparks' your for'd mast has sunk'. As by this time the various parts of the arc transmitter were being spread around the table, the Leading Tel was duly grateful. A snug place the galley though painted with red oxide all the way round, the Q.M. used to keep the fire going at night, his rounds started and finished at the galley door, the log being tucked behind a convenient pipe, the sea thermometer hung up outside on the hand rail. Immediately abaft the galley was a full length door in the upper casing and beneath it, in the pressure hull, a large oval watertight door. Kept open on fine days in harbour it was only a few inches above the level of the water. The long part of the oval went athwart ships because this was the entry for the 'Beamery' torpedoes. At this time a 'Beamery' was fashionable in most submarines, a compartment right across the boat with torpedo tubes in. 'L' boats had two tubes, but 'K' 26 had four, the manoeuvre to get the torpedoes in were long and laborious. To get them out, provided you were afloat, was simple, you just fired them out in a positive buoyancy state without starting their engines, they surfaced and were lifted out of water by crane or towed by a boat to the torpedo depot. Later the four beam tubes were removed, as they were my pidgin I was glad. This hatch also led to the Chief and Petty Officers Mess, to the ERAs Mess, two very crowded places above the Beamery. In none of these spaces could you stand up straight you walked with a stoop or cracked your head. A bulkhead divided the Beamery from the for'd stoke hole. Another tall steel door in the upper casing opened to a space where a hatch went down into the Turbine Room, a big heavy watertight door that dropped into place with a sound as of a not-too-distant gun. Near it were strung up the petrol cans, full of either petrol or salt sea. Those full of sea had a piece of rag tied on the handle as a marker, but this code was not to be relied on. On the starboard side of this compartment there was a Heath-Robinson or perhaps an early Emmet W.C. with a long waste pipe running down through a pipe which took a rout through one of the external main ballast tanks to the open sea. The 'throne' as it was called, was an exact steel plate cone with an exactly circular wooden seat. There was no flap valve as would be expected in a device open to the sea one end. It was as crude as a Durer woodcut of a wheelbarrow, its action even cruder. On a day of flat calm it was faultless, you removed your belt undid your four buttons etc., perched on the throne. When finished a can on a piece of tarred rope was slung down the rounded side of the boat and poured carefully into the upturned cone. It did not do to wet the seat if another customer waited. But on a day of swell, it was different, you listened to the magnified gurglings' in this long pipe with its megaphone-like end, you saw little splashes appear. You chanced it standing up on the little platform if you heard a larger gurgle than usual. If you were lucky you got away with it by means of quick jumps to your feet. Occasionally you got caught, as constipation was an occupational disease in submarines your time on the throne, always called correctly "your reign" was too long for the waiting heir presumptive. The sea is often cold, but the compressed air w.c.s inboard were for use only at sea.

In the same compartment you bathed, taking in a bucket of "hotters", a flannel and soap and towel and hanging your clothes on a piece of spun yarn. A draughty bathroom, but like the steam room of a Turkish bath a place of stimulating conversation sometimes between two bathers one prospective bather and a man presiding on the throne. After dark the wide ocean was our urinal, but in daylight we crept in and used the inverted cone and on rough days stood care-

fully where our shoes would not get flooded. The decoration of this compartment too was red-lead. The floor to this magnificent free flood compartment was the pressure-hull rounded and thick. This w. c. was never known to clog, be the toilet paper ever so thick. Occasionally, economy was urged in the use of 'paper sanitary' as toilet paper was designated and it became scarce. It was a mistaken economy for sailors then adapted signal pads of nice printed paper to the toilet to use at about eight times the cost to the taxpayer. A better quality paper, but certainly more expensive. Of course, the Times of Malta, old newspaper sent out from England etc. helped out, or a very calm day, it was a good place to read your letter from home during working hours. A pity when they broke the boat up at Sliema they didn't think it worth shipping the throne back to England for exhibition in the Tower Museum alongside the rack and thumb screws.

In the smooth very end of the free flood the overtaking light at which any C.O. on a following L boat must have gazed with mixed feelings as he smelled our smoke and watched our wake in its glow. Ahead of the conning tower, the third gun, laid by the Senior Gun Layer. Identical with the two others fixed ammunition that is cartridge and shell joined together like a rifle cartridge. No electric firing circuits and, "What happens to the gun when you dive?" a question asked by a pretty girl visitor, answered by "Honey" Standen, "Why it gets wet". The breech is opened the water runs through all the mechanism, which is well-greased and well cleaned later. The conning tower, which would have looked ideal much later in the new Coventry Cathedra1. Tall, *stately, of brass painted grey, with brass rimmed portholes round it in a single line two tiers with a helmsman in the lower tier with telegraphs, compass, etc., a wooden rim or fairing round the top edge looking as if all it needed was an Archbishop of the Anglican Church resting on arm on it and blessing the crew with the other. Before it a highly polished bell with H.M.S/M K.26 engraved or cast in it, seeming to wait for book and candle and Priest. Around the base of the brass conning-tower a piece of solid brass deck kept shiny by pints of bluebell, a mysterious concoction of Petty Officer Sowden's* (Second Cox'n) called 'Scourers'. (*Petty Officer (SG) George Sowden O/N J20021 (Ch) rumour having it that a basic ingredient was a. rather plentiful sauce known as "Ally Sloper's." Stoker Faulks who was by way of analysing most things; being an amateur chemist, said the sediment was mostly bath brick and the fluid shale oil. This, the Second Cox'n denied, which was natural because all shale oil was the property of the fore end torpedomen under Petty Officer Joe Blake*, who would have propounded an awkward question (*Petty Officer (TGM) Frederick James (Joe) Blake O/N J46983 (Po). Just for'd of the conning tower was a vertical post for mounting the torpedo derrick to take torpedoes inboard and lower them down the fore torpedo hatch. On normal days a white drill cover fluttered like a Sultan's tent on a steel frame- over this the main hatch of entry, down which many a pretty pair of size threes have proceeded as Junior Officers showed their ladies round the boat. The quartermaster headed the procession through the boat discretely moving one compartment ahead of the visitors to see that no one was undressed or using language unsuited to Hansard or the Times. We knew the Captain's wife and the Engineers wife by sight, they knew the names and duties of the people they saw busy about the 'Wardroom Mess.*

Mrs. Garnons-Williams was reputed to have said, "Nelson and Avery, what a splendid pair of names, just like Fortnums and Mason, practically in the same trade." Nelson was the A.B. Wardroom Cook and Avery was the Officer's Steward's Assistant, another A.B. from Nottingham, with such a husky voice he might have smoked half the cigarette output of that famous city. If you had asked the crew where Nelson came from you would undoubtedly be told he was a Turk", "A Turk?" "Yes, a Turk, from ruddy Gosport". It seems that in the early 19th Century a Turkish ship foundered and the bodies floated ashore at Gosport, where the kind population buried them. So well and expensively, that relations between the 'Sublime Porte' and England were rendered most cordial. So, it became Turk-Town,, from that a man of Gasport is a Turk. Well the Officer's Steward was not a Turk, he was an Irishman, Mike Regan. With a napkin on his arm and his doeskin suit he could look the part of a Hilton wine-waiter. Still going for'd again up in the fresh air just before the bell on its little gallows there were in the pressure hull four little pieces of round brass that were the actual tops of the main vents.

To dive, these and others like them, opened and the air rushed out to be replaced by salt sea water. Normally shut, by the way no vent in a submarine is allowed to be called closed, only open or shut, because of the confusion in long voice pipes of the similar sounds of "open" and "close". Well the vents for'd were almost the same thing as the quarterdeck of a battleship. Here the defaulters were seen, the liberty men inspected, the big noises piped aboard, the bumboat men shooed away from. Here Able Seaman Jeffreys explained how the lady he had stopped with misdirected him in the morning, when he was one hour and seven minutes absent over leave. Here the Church service, here the goodbyes when anyone left for home or hospital. Boats came alongside a ridiculous little ladder with no more than three rungs. All this was encompassed by the word "Vents". "Fall in on the Vents", "The mail is now being distributed on the Vents". "Liberty men fall in". "Where?" "On the Vents – new boy". Four brass discs, the holy of holies,, steady now. On warm nights in Malta the Captain, oh great personage, would say to the Chief Q.M. "Didwell, have my bed made up on the Vents." A scurry round and at ten o'clock a camp bed made, covers turned back, meticulously placed fore and aft above the Vents. As Tims the funny Q.M. said one with his finger tip touching his lower lip, "God's in his heaven, all's well with the world." We were creeping out of a late Dghaisa and up the saddle tank inboard, the Captain's snores told us Tims was right. The saddle tanks ring a bit being full of air so we tiptoed aft and down the Motor Room hatch where our mess mates were snoring in a different key. Hammocks on high, hammocks on lockers, two bunks over the motors occupied, a hammock or two further aft secured on solid points on the solid centre line diesel that had been dead, drowned, deep under the ocean but had been miraculously raised and ran noisily to prove it. I wonder if, in 1931, that engine was again reprieved".

1: Corticene was a brown linoleum type decking used on small ships in areas where the crew required a good foot grip as timber would have been too heavy.

PART THREE. THE COMMISSIONS (1915 TO 1926)

HMS K3 WITH THE GRAND FLEET.

CHAPTER ONE.
BONUSES, TRIALS
AND A 'JINX'.

"Considering that these boats were of the a highly experimental type, they have turned out remarkably well" (janes fighting ships 1919).

EMERGENCY WAR PROGRAMME

GROUP 1

HULL NO	SHIPYARD	ORDERED	LAID DOWN	LAUNCHED	COMMISSIONED
K1	PORTSMOUTH (1)	08/15	13/11/15	14/11/16 (2)*	18/12/16*
K2	PORTSMOUTH (1)	08/15	13/11/15	14/10/16 (3)*	03/12/16*
K3	VICKERS (4)	06/15	21/06/15*	20/05/16*	04/08/16
K4	VICKERS (4)	06/15	28/06/15*	15/07/16*	02/02/17 (5)
K5	PORTSMOUTH (1)	08/15 (6)	15/11/15*	16/12/16*	06/05/17
K6	PLYMOUTH (7)	08/15	08/11/15*	31/05/16*	21/11/16 (8)
K7	PLYMOUTH (7)	08/15	08/11/15	31/05/16*	124/01/17*
K8	VICKERS (4)	08/15	22/09/15	10/10/16	06/03/17
K9	VICKERS (4)	08/15	28/06/15	08/11/16	09/05/17
K10	VICKERS (4)	08/15?	28/06/15	27/12/16	06/17
K11	ARMSTRONG'S (9)	08/15	01/10/15	16/08/16	01/02/17
K12	ARMSTRONG'S (9)	08/15	01/10/15	23/02/17	01/-8/17
K13/22	FAIRFIELD (11)	08/15	01/10/15	11/11/16	10/17
K14	FAIRFIELD (11)	08/15	01/11/15	08/02/17	22/05/17
K15	SCOTT'S (12)	08/15	01/06/16	31/10/17	03/04/18 (14)
K16	BEARDMORE (16)	08.15	01/06/16?	05/11/16	13/04/18
K17	VICKERS (4)	02/16		10/05/17	03/18

* = KEW FILES. 1 = PORTSMOUTH NAVAL YARD. 2 = UNDOCKED. 3 = FLOATED.

4 = BARROW-IN-FURNESS. 5 = LEFT BARROW, 6 = 08/15 HULL TENDER 10/15 MACHINERY ORDERED. 7 = DEVONPORT NAVAL BASE, PLYMOUTH. 8 = 12/02/17 INSPECTED*.

O n a summer's day in June 1915 in the north west corner of England, at the Vickers Shipyard in Barrow-in-Furness, his Majesty King George V presided over the keel laying of the Royal Navy's first 'K' boat, the *K3*. A week later, (this time without the Royal visitor), the keel of her sister, the *K4* was laid down in the same yard. Eleven months later that first keel was released into the Walney Channel, but the *K4* was to spend a longer amount of time under construction, not being un-docked until the 15th July 1915. In comparison the more conventional submarine *J6* was laid down on the 26th April 1915 and was not floated out until five months later on the 9th September 1915, which would imply the complexity and size of the 'K' boat design kept the hulls longer on the originality, slipway.

AN ADVERTISMENT IN JANES FIGHTING SHIPS. NOTE THE
THE K BOAT IN THE LOWER RIGHT CORNER.

Down on the south coast of England in the Portsmouth dockyard, the third and fourth keels (*K1* and *K2*) were laid down a few months later in November 1915. The two Vickers boats had both been ordered and laid down within the same month of May, but the Portsmouth boats had a three-month delay from being ordered in August, until work began on their keels.

On the 4th April as the *K3* slowly took shape, her first commanding officer, Commander Ernest W. Leir assumed command. Then on the 20th May with the traditional pomp and circumstance, the 'K' boat was un-docked into the waters of the Clyde. By the days end she was secured alongside in the fitting out basin in the Devonshire Dock and the final stages in her construction could be undertaken.

REPORTEDLY ONE OF THE FEW PHOTOS OF THE K13 BEFORE HER LOSS IN GARELOCH. THE SUBMARINE IS LAUNCHED. THE LINES OF THE ORIGINAL BOW SHAPE ARE PROMINENT

The K3 was soon ready to commence both her basin and then her sea trials. The Captain and his new crew, in company with a number of dockyard employees put the boat through her paces, but sea trials are never trouble free and with the added complexity of learning the ways of a steam powered submarine, the trials were a 'challenge'! But their very purpose was to test the craft, resolve those 'teething' problems and confirm she was finally ready to be commissioned. As the officers and men learnt how to operate their complex submarine, Leir compiled lists off "problems to be resolved" before he would sign for her on behalf of the Admiralty. It quickly became apparent that the deck mounted torpedo tubes, combined with the *K3's* low freeboard and her abnormal length made her an awkward craft to handle when surfaced. One of the early critics of the class was to question the wisdom of combining such a large hull with an unusual surface speed, (for a submarine). In effect producing a vessel with the speed of a cruiser, but the turning circle of a battlecruiser.

As the 'K' boats one by one undertook their trials, the Captains quickly found them to be awkward beasts to handle and the admiralty were in time to come to accept something needed to be done. During the first few years of service, the vessels were to be returned one by one to the shipyards and a bulbous 'swan' bow was added to each bow. While the boats were having their 'bow-lift's, their deck torpedo tubes and one of the guns was removed. The *K6* was to be the first of the 'K' class to have its bows raised by converting it into the prominent "free floating" bulbous swan shape. The new bow incorporated a 'quick blowing' ballast tank to improve the classes handling. An Admiralty report at the enquiry into the loss of the *K5* noted:

> *"The behaviour of the 'K' boats in all weathers experienced was good and they appear to make better weather of the long Atlantic seas than they do of the short seas encountered in the North Sea. The high buoyant [Swan] bow holds the boat up well in a head swell and there is comparatively little jar on the after hydroplanes".*

THIS IMAGE IS REPORTED TO BE THE KEEL OF A 'K' BOAT BEING LAID DOWN.

While officers and crews discovered the 'problems with the design, the shipyard labourers were equally struggling with the boats. As the 'K' boats underwent their individual trials, their crews would be joined by dockyard workers and management. The combined civilian and service crews had to suffer the poor working conditions that seemed standard with this new class of monster submarine. The boats suffered from humid interiors and were often, with the mixed crews, overcrowded. In addition to the humidity and crowded conditions there was the smell! All warships carry a scent of oil, diesel and 'odour-la-Naval'. But the 'K' boats brought extra with an unpleasant smell that filtered through the compartments. It was to become generally considered by the workmen that putting to sea in a 'K' boat was by far much worse than the more conventional diesel submarines. The interior of the boats contained countless sharp edges and oily surfaces as well as wet oily floors, making any effort by the workmen to maintain their clothing in a good condition, almost impossible. With the overcrowding, the odour and the sharp edges came the heat!

AN UNKOWN K BOAT ALONGSIDE THE KING GEORGE V IN SCAPA FLOW, (SOURCE IMPERIAL WAR MUSEUM

The working conditions were to become to be regarded as so bad that the Barrow Amalgamated Engineering Society asked for additional wages to be paid to its members. In particular, work was conducted within the boats numerous tanks was disliked. After 'negotiation' it was agreed to pay each workman an additional 10 shillings (2017= £29.50/$36.22) per day. The sum equated to a tradesman daily wage and was payable for each steaming trial conducted within the dock, with an extra allowance of 5 shillings (2017=£14.75) while the batteries were being recharged. The workers who were employed either within the boat's tanks or on top, received a further 5 shillings a day while the batteries were being charged.

Any 'main motor trials' with the propellers brought a bonus of 5 shillings for each trial on Port and Starboard, if conducted during the same day. The workman received 2 shillings 6d (2017=£7.37/$9.05) for any unsuccessful trials. For full speed 8-hour trials using the steam turbines brought payments of 42 shillings (£129.78/$159.34) if successful and a lesser 21 shillings (£64.89/$79.67) if they proved to be unsuccessful. Diving trials were awarded with a bonus of 21 shillings, if carried out on the same day. An allowance was also to be made for all pressure trials. For trials with high- and low-pressure compressors and pumps the bonus was 2 shillings 6d per trial. Work with the diesel engine was granted 16 shillings (£47.19) and for an unsuccessful trial lasting over 2 hours, 10 shillings (£29.50). For workmen employed on shifts other than their regular one, there was an additional 25 per cent added to wages for the first two hours. After the second hour the bonus increased to 50 per cent. In the event of an emergency there was a bonus, which is unfortunately not recorded. To allow for a level of comparison, in 1917 London bus drivers earned £3 per week, which equates to 60 shillings (£176.98).

On the 14th December 1916 the *K2* commissioned and was appointed to serve as tender to *HMS Fearless* in Scapa Flow.

In October 1916 the 'curse' or 'jinx' of the 'K' class made its most prominent appearance too date, on a test dive by the *K3* during her trials. But her trials had not been plain sailing up to that point and had seen her progress with a series of recurring problems. During her speed runs, the boiler and turbine rooms became so hot that the hatches had to be left open to try and gain some cooler air. In addition, a head sea cracked the conning tower windows and at one point she refused to answer commands to either her helm or diving planes and ploughed her bow into the seabed of Stokes Bay, in the Solent.

As the boat had slipped below the waves, her crew adjusted her trim, but she suddenly lost control and plummeted down to the seabed. As she headed towards the bottom, the crew and their visitors clung on, while others less fortunate slid along the decks plating. At 150 feet (45.72 mtrs) the *K3* ploughed her bow into what was fortunately a soft muddy bottom. As she lay with her bows buried, 150 feet above her stern stood proud of the sea. The channel at the point of this uncontrolled dive was only 240 feet (73.15 mtrs) deep and 55 feet of 'K' boat stood clear out above the waves, the three propellers whirling above in the air. She was to be stuck in this embarrassing predicament for 20 long minutes, but fortunately, no one was hurt. But to the navy's embarrassment on board that day was the Duke of York, (the future King George VI and father of Queen Elizabeth II) in company with the C-in-C of Portsmouth (Admiral the honourable Sir Stanley Colville), which made the debacle especially embarrassing for the 'Senior' service. Commodore Hall was heard to ask one of his Captains *"what on earth can we do with these 'K' boats if they won't dive"*.

Having extracted herself from an embarrassing situation, the *K3* went into dry dock for the necessary repairs and the removal of gravel from her forward torpedo tubes. December 1916 was also to see the *K3* establish unintentionally an unofficial record for a maximum diving depth (266 feet (81 mtrs)) following an uncontrolled descent to the bottom of the Pentland Firth. As the crew worked to return their errant craft to the surface, they must have cursed the lack of under-water escape gear the 'K' boats carried! The ship once more managed to surface without further mishap despite spending an unrecorded period 66 feet beyond 'crush depth.'

On the 9th December 'Bertie' the Duke of York was to write to his father from Admiralty House in Portsmouth:

" Late Tuesday Sir Charles [unreadable] was down here and the admiral took us on board the new submarine K3. I went aboard her in October when she was in dock. We went out into the Solent and dived. It was rather an unfortunate dive as we stuck her nose in the mud for a 1/4 of an hour. Her crew were quite new, and they had forgotten to flood one of the forward tanks when they flooded the remainder. So, when they did flood it the bows went into the mud. It was not serious, and they soon blew the water out again. It was most interesting and quite an experience".

On the 21st November 1916 the *K3* slipped away from Portsmouth's Royal Dockyard and she was eased across the harbour's waters by her electric motors, to be secured alongside Fort Blockhouse, the navy's submarine establishment in Gosport. Once in place her crew started to work on bringing onboard both the stores and ammunition that the vessel required. The following day, four torpedoes were moved from her bow to the beam tubes and the diesel engine was used to recharge her electric motors.

On the 23rd the crew worked at preparing the torpedoes while other crew members painted the ship and the engineering department resumed charging the boats electric motors with the diesel engine. The submarine departed the 'Fort' the following day under steam to conduct a dive off Spithead, before being secured to a buoy for the night. In the morning she returned to Fort Blockhouse and the crew were set to shifting the ballast and un-docked four dummy torpedoes from the bow tubes as a training exercise. The task of moving the ballast was resumed the next day, with help from a Fort Blockhouse working party.

On the 27th the crew were ordered to prepare the *K3* for sea. Off Spithead she fired two starboard beam torpedoes, as well as bow tubes 1 to 4. Having conducted a dive exercise, she returned to port and was secured to No 3 buoy.

The next morning saw five torpedoes transferred on board from Fort Blockhouse and the crew working at preparing nine of the weapons for use. On the 29th the *K3* was back out to sea once more under steam and off Spithead she fired tubes 1 to 4 as well as 4 torpedoes from the beam tubes and 5 from the deck mounted weapons. Having spent the night secured to a buoy, she returned to Blockhouse the next morning, where she loaded 5 new torpedoes.

On the first day of December her crew prepared her for sea and on her electric motors she made her way to Spithead once more, where she fired one weapon from each of her beam mounted tubes and having spent the night secured to a buoy, returned to Blockhouse, to charge her batteries the next day.

Then on the 3rd the log lists the crew as *"wiping over batteries"* and the 4th was one of cleaning the ship and loading torpedoes. The next day while secured alongside at Fort Blockhouse the crew loaded 5 torpedoes and prepared once more for sea, the *K3* making her way out too St Helens Bay. Diving exercises were conducted off Spithead before securing once more alongside Fort Blockhouse.

The 6th brought one torpedo on board and with no log entry for the 7th, the 8th found her having departed Portsmouth and on route for Scapa Flow, via Harwich in escort with the modified Acheron-class destroyer, *HMS Lurcher*. At 10:30 the vessels passed Folkestone Gate and by 15:30 *K3* was secured alongside the depot ship *HMS Pandora.* Her first full day in port found the *K3* preparing her torpedoes and guns. The 10th was to bring the crew much welcome shore leave, (once the boat had been cleaned). After two days in port the *K3* departed Harwich on her next leg north. On route the crew exercised at action stations off the Firth of the Forth, before steaming into Scapa on the 14th. During the latter part of her voyage north, the submarine while making 11 knots suffered in a heavily moderate sea and was rolling badly. In response and to keep her bow more buoyant the forward external tanks were blown. Leigh on entering the great harbour departed from the tradition of dipping his boats flag to Admiral Beatty, but instead dipped his two funnels. It was not appreciated by the admiral. Once in the Flow, the boat was moored in Gutter Sound and the crew were set to cleaning ship. The next three days were ones that saw her moored to a buoy. Her crew were employed at their diving station, as well as working on the torpedoes and around the boat as required. They also took on 850 gallons of fresh water for the crews use. In addition, the boat was cleaned and with an oiler secured alongside, she replenished her fuel tanks. On the third day the ship cleaning continued, and a party were employed working with the hydroplanes and steering gear. The afternoon was one of rest with 'Make and mend'.   On the 20th December the K3 moved out to the Flow under steam. The log notes that the boat *"Host[ed]"* a diving exercise and fired a 'Mk V 261' torpedo from one of her starboard [beam or deck?] tube. But the recovery party was unable to locate the missile to recover it and finally had to report it to be lost. The submarine was secured to a buoy for the night.

The 21st December was one of preparing the torpedoes and painting the boat. The next day having charged both the torpedoes and the ships electric motors, a diving exercise was conducted before going alongside the fleet's flagship, *HMS Iron Duke*. The C-in-C Admiral Jellicoe paid a visit to the 'unusual' addition to his fleet. Then with their visitor back onboard his flagship, the *K3* moved off to be secured to a buoy. Next, she was joined by an oiler on the 23rd and having refuel went alongside the flagship of Rear-Admiral Sir William E. Goodenough, *(HMS Orion)* who paid a visit to the craft. Then on her electric motors she made her way along-side the 5th Battle squadron flagship, *HMS Barham* and Rear Admiral Evan Thomas paid a visit.

Christmas day commenced with the crew cleaning the boat and then 'Sunday routine'. Having had a quiet 25th, the K3 made her way out to sea on the 26th under steam to conduct diving and wireless exercises, after which she was secured to a buoy. The 27th saw her steam into the Flow for additional diving exercises and firing from her bow torpedo tubes. The crew spent the 28th "employed about [the] batteries" and the 29th cleaning the guns and preparing the torpedoes for "running". Then with her boilers lit she made her way out to conduct more diving exercises and bow tube torpedo firing. In the process the log notes the loss of *"No 261-mark 5 torp"*.

The penultimate day of 1916 found the crew cleaning the

boat before mooring alongside *HMAS Australia* (flagship of Admiral Sir Arthur Cavenagh Leveson). She was alongside for four hours after which the K3 moved to buoy No 2. But the log makes no note of any flag ranked visitors? The 31st December found the crew *"wiping over batteries and cleaning ship"*.

The first day of 1917 brought a diving exercise before her return to Scapa Flow. The crew spent the 2nd refitting and cleaning two torpedoes and the men had a medical examination as well. But the day ended better with a Recreation party at 13:00.

The next day was cleaning ship, taking on stores and another diving exercise in the Flow. The 4th notes the taking on of one-mark VII torpedo and 'collision heads'. In addition, a court of inquiry was held onboard *HMS Orion* into the lost torpedoes. While that was underway the crew cleaned ship.

The next morning having prepared for sea, a diving exercise and the firing of four bow torpedoes was undertaken. Then it was alongside an oiler for refuelling. Over the following two days the boat was cleaned, and her torpedoes prepared. She was at sea on the 8th and once back at her buoy, the boat was cleaned and her torpedoes worked on, with liberty leave granted in the afternoon.

On the 9th January 1917, the K3 was patrolling the North Sea, (58°.17h.lat. 2°.0 E long @ noon). On this day *K3* was making 10 knots on the surface with a strong breeze to port. The log notes the seas at *"rough"*, *"heavy swell "* and *"force 6"*. All morning waves had been breaking over her, but suddenly at 06:37 a wave broke over the boats superstructure and washed down the two funnels. The deluge of seawater doused and put out the boiler's fires. The boat broached too, as a fresh wave of water poured down the funnels as she passed the Pentland Skerries. By the time the hatches were shut the boiler room was two thirds filled with icy cold North Sea waters. Commander Leir ordered tanks 8,9,10, Q and Z blown but despite the engineers' best efforts, the boilers were to remain unlit for the rest of the patrol. Fortunately the auxiliary engines Admiral Fisher had insisted on were able to limp the flooded 'K' boat westward and after a long slow voyage, (at half speed on her diesel engines) to her home, a journey which she commenced at 06;50. She limped into Scapa at 02:50 on the 10th January, securing alongside *HMS Fearless.* Once fastened, an Engineer work party from the *Fearless* came onboard to assist in the repairs needed. On the 16th she cast off from Fearless and made her way out into the *"Flow"* for a successful dive. Over the next three days the boat was cleaned and once the Fearless party returned to their own ship on the 12th, *K3* moved to a buoy.

The 15th was one of cleaning for both the guns and torpedo tubes, after which she made her way into the Flow to conduct a test diving exercise. The next day the *K3* was deemed fit and her crew prepared her for her return to sea. The boat headed out under steam for a diving exercise and then she returned to her buoy. The 17th was one of preparing for sea and then heading out under steam for a series of diving exercises and wireless experiments. Once in port she was secure to an oiler to refuel and then with her tanks full, she was secured to a buoy. Finally, before we move on, the 18th brought cleaning guns as well as the torpedo tubes. Warheads were off loaded on to a drifter and she took on both water and provisions. At 13:30 liberty men were landed... And so, the daily routine of a fleet-submarine working-up went on within the fleet's anchorage, training, cleaning, maintenance, training, cleaning...

The *K3's* working-up stretched further into January 1917 and one source noted (surprisingly) that her crew were in the majority *"very pleased"* with the boat, a comment that seems implausible and maybe from the lips of an officer saying what the admirals wanted to hear?

While the *K3* had steamed past the Firth of the Forth, on the 14th December the *K1* was *"un-docked"* from her place of construction and was to be commissioned as a tender to *HMS Fearless* on the 14th January 1917. Also, on the 14th December 1916 the K2 had commissioned and was also appointed to serve as tender to *HMS Fearless* in Scapa Flow.

The *K7* was one of the boats to undergo her trials in 1917 and on the 18th January while running between Polperro and Plymouth she achieved 10,000 shp over a four-hour run. During her run the boat was heavier than the designed displacement having had several of her tanks flooded. In addition, her underwater hull was clean of marine growth and the day was one of a moderate force 2 swell and force 3 wind. Her Ship's Book records speeds of between 22.25 and 23.35 knots having been achieved, with a mean speed of 22.69 knots. While the *K7* sped over the Cornish waters, her book records temperatures of between 68 and 80 F in the boiler-room, but the engine room peaked at 100! The *K2* ran her own trials off Spithead in January 1917 and achieved 10,000 shp following a spell in dock.

THE K4 AGROUND.

In 1917 the run of bad luck for the class set a new benchmark when in early January the *K4* was undergoing her own contractors' trials. While trying to navigate a difficult exit from Barrow in his new command, the *K4's* Captain, Commander David de B. Stocks ran his boat hard aground onto Walney island, due to a narrow channel and difficult tides. The boat lay beached on the sandy shore for all the world to see and was a brief but popular local attraction, before she was once more floated, making her way south. By the 18th January the freed *K4* was in a dock at Portsmouth Naval yard for 9 days of work to both her machinery and hull. Sixty years later the Resolution class submarine, *HMS Repulse*, would run aground in the same area of beach.

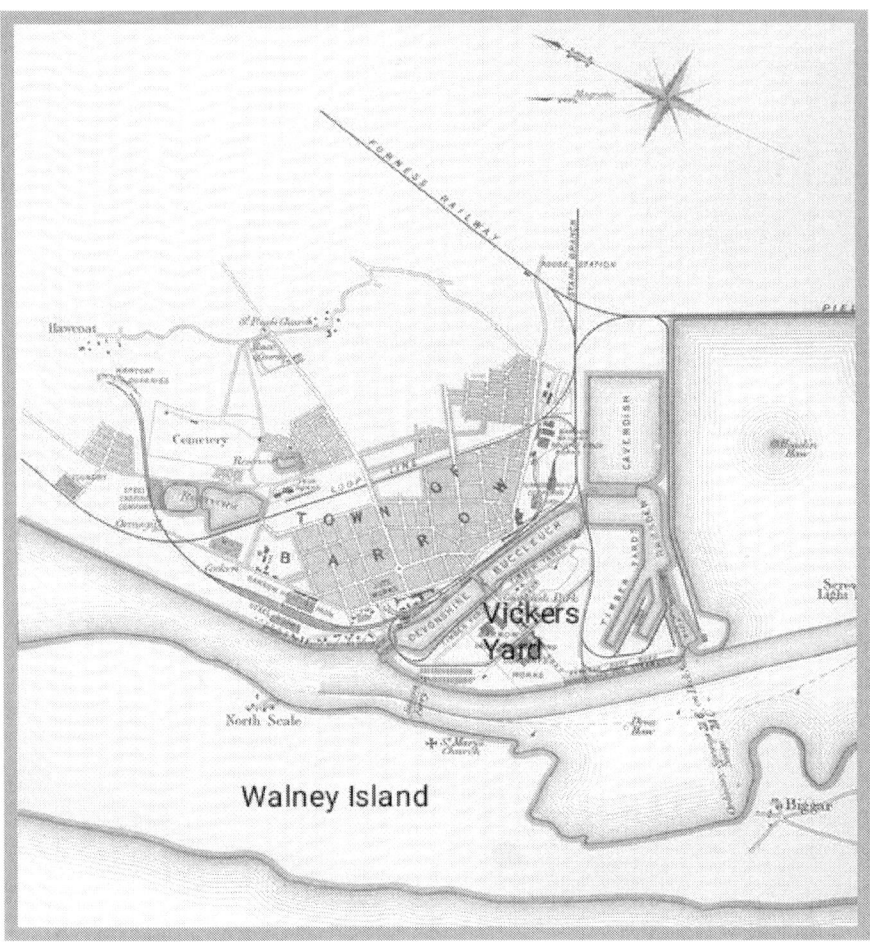

Stocks (despite the running of his new command aground and publicly embarrassing the Royal Navy) retained command of the repaired craft and was to be her sole Captain, until the day of her loss.

*THE K4 AGROUND, ALLOWING A CLEAR VIEW OF HER PROPELLOR
AND RUDDER CONFIGERATION.*

While the *K4* encountered Lancastrian beaches, off the Cornish east coast the southern built 'K' boats undertook their series of steam trials, in the waters between Plymouth and the fishing port of Polperro. On the 6th February 1917 the *K6* took her turn to run her trials and for three and three quarter hours she steamed at full power (10,000 shp). Her trim established the draft on the day at 16-foot 1 1/2 inch forward and 16 ft 11 inches to the stern. The Ship's Book which sits today in the National Archives Kew, notes her hull lines as clean (having only exited her dry dock on the 27th January), which would have allowed the sea waters to flow unencumbered along the hull and help her on her run. The day was one of a force 4 wind and the sea was force 3. Her run was without trouble and she achieved 23.211 knots.

K4 AGROUND BUT WITH THE TIDE COMING IN, (OR GOING OUT).

Having served seven months of her first commission, the *K6* was placed into dockyard hands an Invergordon between the 26th July and the 1st August 1917. Her boiler room intakes were adjusted and storage for a skiff dinghy was created. The aft hydroplanes had brake gear fitted to them and stowage for boxes in the control room were installed. A "portable gangway" was fitted over the torpedo hatch and her upper deck torpedo tubes removed. Her funnels were re-placed with new ones of a longer, (but unspecified length).

There were seven other boats in the vessels that comprised Group 1 which were projected to have been built. But with the admirals finally excepting that the 'K' class was to not too live up to their expectations, four of the seven took another non-steam powered route and three were to be scrapped having barely begun their construction.

The *K18* was to become the diesel powered 12-inch gunned *M1*, having been ordered during February 1916 from the Vickers yard in Barrow-in-Furness. Then on the 9th July 1917 she was launch and was to be completed on the 17th April 1918. She would then serve for just over a year before being paid off on the 27th July 1919 in Malta. On her voyage home she would call briefly at Algiers during October and on the 2nd December 1919 entered care and maintenance at Portsmouth. But the navy had not done with her yet.

The vessel that was to have been the *K19* was ordered from Vickers in the May of 1916. She too was to be completed as both diesel powered and armed with a 12-inch gun. In 1927 her lone gun would be exchanged for a hanger and launching system for an aeroplane. She was launched on the 19 October 1918 and entered service as the *M2* during November the following year.

The *K20* contract was awarded to Armstrong Whitworth in Newcastle during December 1916 and she was laid down in the same month. The boat was to be re-designated as the *M3* on the 6th December 1918 and was commissioned on the 16th March 1920. The Ships Book notes the commission date, but then adds, "Handed over 9.7.20". She commenced life with the single 12-inch gun but would later be adapted to serve as a mine layer.

HMS K4 UNDER STEAM. THE HUGE STEAM CLOUDS ROBBED THE SUBMARINE OF THE INVISIBILITY THE LOW PROFILE BROUGHT TO MOST SUBMARINES.

The *K21's* contract was granted to Armstrong Whitworth Newcastle in August 1916. Her keel was laid down the following December, being launch on the 28th July 1919. She had been re-designated as the *M4* on the 6th December 1918. But by the 23rd October 1919 all work had stop on the hull and the Admiralty authorized it to be cut up. Then on the 21st May the order was reversed, and she was offered for sale as she lay at the Walker naval yard in Newcastle. What was to have been the *M4* was sold as an incomplete hulk on 30 November 1921.

The orders for the three vessels *K23-K25* were awarded to the Armstrong's yard, but were to be cancelled before work progressed by any measure.

❖ ❖ ❖

1) *Reproduced with kind permission of the Royal Archives*

Windsor Castle and Her Majesty Queen Elizebeth II. All copy-writes are the property of the above and the content is not to be reproduced.

CHAPTER TWO: THE K13 & THE 'JINX'.

Triskaidekaphobia or Fear of the Number 13.

By the start of the third year of the war the *K13* had commenced her own set of trials off the Scottish west coast. Through the whole of January, the crew were employed with the ongoing trials. All had so far gone without a hitch, resulting in the officers and crew being pleased with their 'K' boat. As the *K13* approached the final few trials, the 'K' boat 'Jinx' quietly bid its time as it lurked in the shadows and in a few more days it would lay claim to its first fatalities.

Early on the morning of Monday 29th January 1917 Lieutenant-Commander Godfrey Herbert (the *K13's* Commanding officer, who had joined the submarine on the 11th October 1916) bade farewell to his wife and made his way from their rented accommodation, down to the Fairfield shipyard, in the Govan area of the Clyde, for a day of diving exercises with his new command. He found the *K13* laying moored alongside the quay, awaiting her captain and what was believed by all concerned would be the final day, of her trials.

Herbert had undertaken a full inspection of his new command the day prior and on this new morning, having run a cursory eye over the boat, he descended into the control room. On board the submarine for the days planned agenda was her crew of 53 naval personnel. These had been joined by 14 Fairfield employees (Directors & shipyard workers), 5 sub-contractors, 5 Admiralty officials and a river Clyde pilot, all of whom had come on board for the day's trials.

*THE K13 AT FULL STEAM ON THE WATERS OF GARELOCH
(SOURCE THE IMPERIAL WAR MUSEUM).*

With the crew, civilians and the boat ready Herbert ordered her eased away from the shipyard and guided her out into the busy river Clyde. But even before she had managed to clear the shipyards waters, the day started to go wrong. As the colossal submarine was gently moved away from the Guilders Basin, an unsecured mooring wire became fouled around one of her two propellers. Her departure was interrupted even before it had begun and for half an hour, the yard's diver worked to free her propeller of its entanglement.

Once the divers had released the propeller, the *K13* edged out into the Clyde and made her way downstream. But she had barely steamed a mile before one of her crewmen managed to accidentally turn off the steering gears starter motor. Before his error could be remedied, the giant submarine's bow swung round to port and 300 yards below the Whiteinch Ferry, *K13* pushed her bows into the Clyde's muddy banks. As she lay there, her bow in the grip of the thick gluttonous mud, the ebbing tide took hold of the beached submarine and pushed the stern around to face across the river. While the tide quietly toyed with the 'K' boat's stern, the Clydebank steamer Sonnava was sighted from the conning tower, making her way slowly upstream. Herbert quickly ordered a series of 'D's sounded in Morse, (-...) on the submarines siren, to warn the approaching steamer off. But those on the bridge of the Sonnava seemed to be oblivious to the 339 feet of submarine that lay across her intended path, as the steamer drew remorselessly ever closer. The horrified onlooking conning tower crew could only assume the steamers master was intent on steering his ship to pass between the moving 'K' boats stern and the dredger Shieldhall, which was moored alongside a wharf close by the submarine. But if that was the Sonnava's master's plan, his calculations were to prove to be fatally flawed and to the screeching sound of metal on metal, the *Sonnava* became wedged between both the submarine and the dredger.

The busy river Clyde was now blocked by a dam constructed of a submarine, a steamer and a dredger. But the steamer's master ordered his ships engines to be put in reverse and to a second cacophony of metal on metal, the *Sonnava* pulled herself clear. Herbert with his boat still remarkably watertight, aside from scratched paint and scrape marks, decided to let the Clyde's ebb tide continue its work with the *K13's* stern and with the additional aid of two tugs the submarine was finally pulled free of the mudbank's grip. Once they had reached (traveling stern first) 'The Cart', tributary Herbert calling on his boat's engines swung the submarine round to face downstream once more.

By 11:00 the *K13* had reached the Craigendoran Pier and having moored alongside, the Fairfield director Hugh McMillan and the company's naval architect Professor Percy Hill came on board. With the two additional civilians squeezed on board, the submarine eased her way once more into midstream and resumed her passage.

To date the crew of the submarine had run several exercises within the waters near the Fairfields shipyard and on the river Clyde. But Herbert had now progressed to conducting the trials in the waters of Gareloch.

The loch lays only thirteen miles northwest of Glasgow and its waters are seven miles in its length. This beautiful expanse of water nestles amongst the stunning foothills of the Scottish Highlands and in 1917 was a quiet location with only a few small rural villages. The lochs water lay in a quiet, secluded piece of Scotland and was by 1916 being used regularly by the navy for the diving trials of the Clyde built submarines. The boats could be put through their trials on the loch, safe in the knowledge that U-boats would not threaten them. The mile (1.5 km) wide loch flows in a southward direction, opening onto the Firth of Clyde and it was into these secluded seven square miles of water that Herbert brought the *K13* late that winters morning.

Prior to the 29th 'K13's crew had been exercised by Herbert a few times at their diving stations, but they had so far submerged the boat only three times. Today was scheduled to be their fourth submergence. While the boat had been worked in the waters nearer the yard, each day after the crew's dinner, the First Officer, (Lieutenant Singer) would exercise the crew at their diving stations, a process he had conducted to date at least twelve times. It is only to evident that as the submarine steamed into Gareloch's waters, the crews experience at diving in one of the navy's most complex boats was still very limited, but with each exercise they became more familiar with the *K13*. During her previous trials the *K13* had already covered the measured mile, (while surfaced), at 23.84 knots traveling at 405 revolutions per minute, which to her crew's delight, established her as the world's fastest submarine. During the *K13's* run a number of her ballast tanks had been flooded giving her a greater draught than had been designed. In April the *K9* was to run her own series of trials and in the course of them she achieved a rate of knots 0.34 less than the *K3's* record at a mean speed of 23.5 knots with 10,900 shp at 400 revs per minute. But the *K9's* mean draught was 18 feet 3 inches (5.56 mtrs) which was over 1 foot deeper (30.48 cm) than the normal draught, due to a number of leaky main tank vents. She was also minus the emergency oil fuel, which would have served to increase her surface displacement and her speed would most likely had drop by around half a knot.

A SUBMARINE CRUISER, K CLASS.

Central News

HMS K3 (CENTRAL NEWS)

As *K13* made her way into the calm waters of Gareloch, events had so far gone smoothly with her trials and the crew must have had a growing sense of confidence in their skills. The morning was a fine one, cold but with no wind as the submarine travelled through Gareloch's waters, her crew on deck watching the Scottish scenery pass by on either beam. As the *K13* was gently navigated further into the loch, Herbert ordered four tanks on each beam to be flooded. In company with the submarine was the twin funnelled *Comet* (1905), which was to act as the *K13's* tender for the day. The Comet was to be the grandstand view from which a director of Fairfield's, Alexander Cleghorn (1859-1922), would watch the submarine that his shipyard had built progress through another of her trials.

The *K13* was to spend what remained of her much delayed morning conducting a series of surface manoeuvres, (turning, stopping, starting, varying speeds, going astern...) and by midday all that remained was just one last dive.

At around noon, Herbert stood on the conning towers bridge watching boat and crew perform their roles in almost perfect unity. He now ordered the crew to prepare for the scheduled dive. The funnels were electrically folded down into their respective recesses and sealed watertight. Then in addition the four large openings that supplied air for the boiler fires were sealed with a series of large mushroom shaped valves. All the other hatches were closed and the submarine slowly commenced her dive to a depth of 80 feet (24.38 mtrs), where she was to remain for 15 to 20 minutes in order to test the water integrity of the hull.

On the K13's return to the surface, Engineer Lieutenant Lane commented to his Captain how he had observed the boat slowly increasing her depth while she was submerged, almost as if they were steadily gaining weight. Captain and Engineer discussed the fact that during her time submerged, water had leaked into the boiler room. They decided that as there was now around 200 gallons of water in the compartment that there must be a small leak! But with the combination of both the heat and steam that had built up within the boiler room, finding the leaks source was proving to be impossible. The heat had also made examining the water tightness of the funnel covers and boiler room ventilators difficult. As a result, Lane asked his Captain that once the boiler room had been properly vented, if he would agree to a second dive.

Lane in addition to the 'small leak' had several serious concerns about the operation of the mushroom valves. Having spoken to Herbert, Lane asked Frederick Searle, (the Admiralty Overseer), if he would look at the valves. Lane was worried about the 37-inch (940 mm) diameter openings to the valves as over the past few weeks, he'd found them to be prone to sticking and he showed Searle the open hatch with its rubber seal, which was jamming by three quarters of an inch. But after his inspection, Searle announced that he was happy and assured Lane that he had nothing to worry about. Strangely despite these 'minor matters' the Admiralty and Fairfield Officials were all pleased with the performance of the 'K' boat and they uniformly praised the submersible.

With the morning's agenda complete, Herbert brought the *K13* alongside the Comet for the crew's midday meal, (or "dinner"). Over his own meal on board the Comet, Herbert told the shipyard officials that he was happy with the boat, provided she was taken into dry-dock for the mornings damage to be fixed at the shipyards cost. Herbert was now happy to agree he would be accepting his new command on behalf of the Royal Navy. Coxswain Moth noted how *"Our Captain being quite satisfied with the boat now took her over"*

At this stage the *K13's* engine room crew had already lit the boilers in preparation for an afternoon of further surface manoeuvres, but Herbert now ordered them to be extinguished to allow for the second brief dive of the day that was to follow "dinner". Lane ordered that the vents be opened to cool the boiler room as much as was possible and he sent his Chief E.R.A. to confirm if these vents were now fully open.

There was an end of term air amongst the crew as they turned their minds from their meal. The trials were almost complete, just one final brief dive to check the troublesome vents. As submarine and tender lay alongside each other, those not required for the dive were transferred across, where they were to enjoy their own lunches.

As several of the shipyard's personnel crossed over to the Comet, Commander Francis Goodhart (1) came onboard. Goodhart was awaiting on the completion of his own 'K' boat, *('K14')* and had decided to take the opportunity to join the *K13* on her day of sea trials. He wanted to gain some first-hand experience of how a 'K' boat was handled. In addition to Goodhart, his engineer, Lieutenant Leslie Rideal accompanied the Commander.

Commander Francis Goodhart was posthumously awarded the Albert Medal for attempting to get help for the stricken submarine.

Those crowded into the cramped interior for the afternoons brief dive totalled 80 persons. The Royal Navy's element was comprised of 55 Naval Officers and ratings:

- Lieutenant Commander Godfrey Herbert, DSO, Captain of *K13,*

- Commander Francis H. H. Goodhart, DSO, Captain of the *K14,*
- Lieutenant Singer, First officer,
- Engineer Lieutenant Lane, engineer to K13,
- Lieutenant (E) L. C. Rideal, engineer to K14,
- Boson H. Pratt, gunner,
- Petty Officer Moss, coxswain.

There were 48 other ranks and 11 Admiralty and Sub-Contractor's men:

- F.C. Cocks, RCNC Admiralty Representative,
- F.W. Searle, Admiralty Overseer,
- Fred Hole, Assistant to Admiralty Overseer,
- Donald Renfrew, of Kelvin, Bottomley & Baird, (2)
- Sydney R. Black, of Kelvin, Bottomley & Baird,
- William Wallace, Director, Brown Bros, & Co, (3)
- E. Hepworth, Admiralty Boiler Overseer,
- W. U. Hancock, Admiralty Electrical Overseer,
- Edward Powney, Chadburn's Representative,
- Robert Lake, Brotherhood's representative,
- Joseph Duncan, Pilot.

In addition to the above, from the Fairfield shipyard's Engine Department were 14 officials, (on-board as observers while the ship was being worked by her own crew:

- John Steel, Foreman,
- William Lewis. Leading Hand,
- William Strachan, Leading Hand,

- William Kirk, Leading Hand,
- Donald Hood, Leading Hand.

From the Fairfield Shipyard other Departments was:

- William McLean, Manager of Submarine Department,
- E. J. Skinner, Manager of Electrical Department,
- Frank Neate, Skinners Assistant,
- William Struthers. Assistant Manager,
- Frank Bullen, Assistant Manager,
- John Green, Head Foreman mechanic,
- Percy Hillhouse, Naval Architect.

By early afternoon the weather had remained fine and seemed set fair for the remainder of the day. There was still no wind across the loch's waters and over lunch the lochs tide started to rise.

With her crew fed, the *K13* eased away from the Comet to lay slightly off the shoreline, a short distance from the Shandon Hydropathic hotel. As she rode gently in the calm waters her crew began the process of trimming the boat for its second dive and the Comet made her way back towards Shandon's Pier with the redundant personnel on board. As the submarine (with the bulk of her crew on deck enjoying the moment) and the tender drew slowly apart, Herbert gave the command *"Hands to diving stations"* and the boat became a hive of activity as everyone assumed their allotted stations. While his crew were busy with the inordinate complexity of diving a 'K' boat, Herbert cast an eye over his command. He missed little and ordered a stoker not yet at his diving station yet, to make haste. Without the rush that a war patrol can demand of a dive, the afternoons preparations were conducted at a slower and more careful pace. With the dive order given, Herbert walked aft along the superstructure, puffing on his cigar and repeated the order down the open engine room hatch. The Captain paused as he made his way back to the bridge and watched as the electric motors lowered the funnels for the second time that day into their respective deck wells. The holes left by the collapsed funnels were then sealed shut by their motors and the hatch below was sealed by hand. Once all was ready Herbert ordered a dive to 20 feet, confirmed and underlined by the diving klaxon as it sounded out across the loch.

Having watched the preparations from the superstructure abaft in the Bridge Shelter and satisfied the funnel doors were clipped down, he stumped out his cigar and descended at 15:15 down into the conning tower, before dropping further down into the control room. As he secured the hatch behind him, he noticed the 'shut' red light, (The light was engraved with the words "shut off")... A 'visitor' recalled after the day's tragic events that he too had noticed the red light in the engine room, but that it seemed to him to be flickering. When he questioned it, he was told that it was simply due to poor wiring and all was in fact ok. Lane ordered the engine-room hatch to be shut and secured, before checking verbally that the control valve was in the closed position.

The first officer Lieutenant Singer called out "engine room shut off" and Herbert ordered *"Half speed, ahead both"*, as well as *"Flood all externals"*, flooding all but four of the ballast tanks. Once the boat had sufficient speed a dive to 20 feet was ordered with the command *"take her down"* K13 commence a dive to 20 feet. As the boat passed eleven feet Coxswain Moth notes,

"...we got a terrible pressure on our ears. From experience we know that something very large had been left open and that water must be coming in very quickly".

As the massive submarine reached 18 feet Lane despatch the Chief Engine Room Artificer aft to the boiler room, to see if he could identify the source of the troublesome leak that had plagued them on the day's first dive. But the Artificer was not gone long before he quickly returned frantically reporting that the boiler room was *"flooding freely sir"*.

In the control room, unaware yet of the event's unfolding in the rear compartments, Herbert was watching the bows through one of the two periscopes. But the Captain was to quickly realize things were turning wrong, as his command having reach the 20-foot point, refused to come level and continued down towards the loch's bed. Herbert ordered the hydroplanes moved to "hard a 'rise" and for compressed air to be pumped into the ballast tanks to try and blow them clear of the inflowing seawaters. But to no effect. Herbert called out to the crew around him "Try to fetch her to the surface", but it was looking already a forlorn wish.

An urgent message arrived from Lane in the Engine Room stating that they needed to surface immediately as the Boiler Room was flooding. Herbert immediately gave the order *"Surface blow 2 & 3"*. As the crew blew the tanks a rush of air from aft filled the control room which only serve to confirm that they were taking on water aft. Herbert now had to accept that the decent would only stop when the submarine found the bottom of the lochs waters and ordered as the depth gauge showed 35 feet with a 4-degree inclination by the bow. Both the boats electric motors were shut down and every tank available was ordered to be blown, but still with no effect. In the engine room Lane quickly slammed and sealed the boiler room watertight door, as water poured along the passageways within the turbine room. But with the invading waters flooding onboard, the K13 was already too heavy and she continued in her uncontrolled dive. Lane having confirmed the water-tight doors were being closed, gave the order to drop the 10-ton forward keel and turned to the water-tight door in the after-control room. He discovered one of the doors 'indicators' was the wrong way, it could not be shut.

It was at that moment that the main motor fuses blew. With the troublesome door finally shut Lane went forward to confirm the ten-ton keel had been dropped. Letting one of the boats two keels go was always a desperate attempt to arrest a dive and orders were given to "blow all forward tanks" to try and arrest the boats sinking, but again with no success. Hepworth, (the Admiralty Boiler Overseer) who was in the boiler-room passage when the dive had been commenced had looked through the bullseye window in 'Admiral Fishers' side-passage and watched as the loch's water poured into the boiler room. He rushed into the engine-room and then back through the passage towards the control room to report the flooding. He was to be one of the last men to escape through the watertight door between the passage and the amidships torpedo room. The final person to get through the door that day was William Struthers from the Fairfield's party, who had only made it forward when the watertight door was held open for a few more precious seconds.

K13's uncontrolled dive came to its conclusion 50 feet (15.24 mtrs) down as the submarine settled on the bottom of the loch with a slight list to port and with her bows four degrees lower than her stern. As the boat settled into her resting place the naval crew and the civilians waited for the sound of the tanks being blown and to feel the boat lift as she slowly returned to the surface. But those hopes were to be short lived as water started to cascade into the control room from the voice pipes which were in the corner of the room, blowing in the process the adjacent port switchboard. As the switchboard sparked and flashed it started a fire burning the cables at the back of the board. The personnel nearest made frantic attempts to smoother the flames using cloths soaked in 'voice pipe' waters, but their efforts were frustrated by the electric shocks they received from the highly charged switchboard. Finally, a quick-thinking crew member pulled out a drawer from the chart table and having smashed it into 'firewood', used pieces of the drawer to poke the wet cloths onto the burning cables and the fire was extinguished. Another eyewitness states that wet sacks were used, but cloths or sacks, the oxygen consuming fire was extinguished. The control room was now full of smoke and fumes which rendered the crew to fits of coughing and stinging eyes.

Herbert and Hillhouse, (the Naval Architect) discussed the situation they were now in and Hillhouse could not give any real hope that by raising the bow of the boat, the hull would lift, even if every tank forward was empty. Both the Captains, (Herbert and Goodhart) were now of the opinion that there was nothing to be done until such time as a diver found the boat. But even if they received air and food, the Commanders felt that nothing short of blowing off the after part of the boat would bring the *K13* back to the surface. The beam Torpedo tube Room was taking in about one foot of cold Scottish water an hour, but it was easily kept down with the forward pumps.

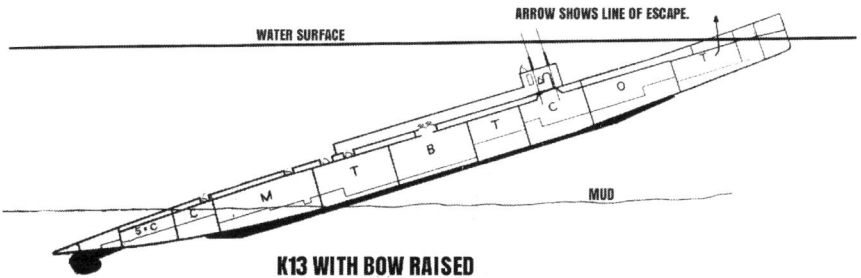

K13's POSITION ON THE SEA BED.

While the fires were being fought, other crewmen had stuffed rags into the voice pipes to cut off the flooding sea-water. With fires and the flooding voice pipes finally under control the crew in the control room made repeated tele-graph signals to their shipmates in the engine room, but all were to go unanswered and it was now only too apparent those men aft had been lost to the flooding.

In their frantic attempts during the dive to try and arrest the boats descent, half of the supply of compressed air had been used to try and blow the forward tanks. But now as the remaining reserve of compressed air was low, any ideas of further efforts were abandoned. The tanks would not be able to be blown until they had a new source of air, which at that moment seemed highly improbable. To compound matters, the proposal of dropping the aft 10-ton keel was no longer an option, as the controls for such an action were in the flooded part of the boat. Fortunately, the boats batteries were fully charged and uncontaminated by sea water. With the batteries intact the survivors were able to retain the use of the electric lighting, pumping and air compressor. But they had little idea as to when or even if they would escape the 'K' boat, so their limited supplies of power needed to be carefully husbanded. Lights and other electric items were run on reduced settings.

Coxswain Moth was to describe those hectic moments fighting the fire and water in his biography:

> *"The scene is very hard to describe and nobody can imagine what it really was like. My description is that it was like an inferno, with men fighting for their lives, battling with the water and trying to beat out the flames with pieces of sacking which had been torn up from the battery boards. At last success attended our efforts and the water was stopped and the fire put out, but you can guess what the air was like. We had the full pressure of air from the flooded compartments, which of course had come in before we could get the watertight doors closed and besides this the air was very foul with smoke and gas which had come from the switch-board".*

With the fires out and the waters stopped, Herbert took the moment to conduct a roll call. Forty-eight men answered their names, but another thirty-two were no longer alive to respond. The service personnel crowded into the forward portion of the ship were:

- Captains Herbert and Goodhart,
- Lieutenant Singer, Lane and Rideal,
- Bosun H Prattle,
- Petty officer Moss,
- 48 ratings.

Those civilians who were fortunate to be forward when the K13 plunged to the loch's bottom were:

- Searle,
- Cocks,
- Renfrew,
- Black,
- Wallace,
- Hepworth,
- Hancock,
- Duncan,
- Hood,
- Mac-Lean,
- Skinner,
- Struthers,
- Bullen,
- Green,
- Kerr,
- Hillhouse,
- Lake,
- Powney,
- Chatburn.

Three of the survivors had a lucky escape and were fortunate to be alive. Donald Hood of the Fairfield group, Chathburn, the telegraph engineer and another engineer (whose name was not recorded), had gone forward prior to the order to dive to loosen and oil the forward torpedo shutter. It had been found during the morning to be stiff and they went to resolve the problem. They were to be the only members of the Engine Room staff to escape the flooding. Unbeknown to the men in the un-flooded forward compartments, locked in the amidships torpedo room were two men who had been shut in during the *K13's* uncontrolled.

As the *K13* lay marooned on the loch's bed, on the surface Annie Macintyre, a maid at a local hotel had sighted two men a mile offshore in the water, but her report was to be ignored. Later it was concluded that the maid really had seen two people who had possibly escaped from the engine room. These were, by a process of elimination, established to be Engineer-Lieutenant Arthur Lane and Fairfield foreman John Steel. Lane's body was two months later to be recovered from the Clyde, but Steel's body was never to be found. It was concluded that the two men must have opened the engine room hatch, with the pressure being equal on each side and had managed to reach the surface. But they must have succumbed to the sudden reduction of pressure and surfaced unconscious, drowning in the loch's cold waters.

Fortunately for the survivors it had been near to high water when the *K13* had taken her plunge to the bottom of the loch, resulting with the boat laying closer to the shoreline, as she hadn't needed to move far from the shore to have sufficient depth in order to conduct her dive. The Clyde Pilot Duncan informed the Captain that he believed that the keel was lying on a surface of clean hard gravel. In addition, the day had remained calm and the loch's waters were both smooth and sheltered from the weather. The third plus was that the disaster had happened near to the greatest shipbuilding and engineering centre within the world at that time and not in a remote corner of the British Isles. All the resources of the Clyde could, (once the boat was located), be directed towards a successful rescue.

With the boat now stranded, thoughts naturally turned to the finite amount of oxygen available to the survivors and how long it could last. For the 48 men the unflooded portion of the hull that they now occupied was calculated to be of about 12,000 cubic feet, giving each person about 250 cubic feet of air. The air around us contains about 20 per cent of oxygen and should this become reduced by 4 per cent, death is the result. This meant that each survivor had an allowance of oxygen that was equal to 4 per cent, or 10 cubic feet of oxygen. A person at rest consumes about 3 cubic feet of oxygen per hour and this gave everyone enough for approximately 15 hours. But that figure was based on a regime of non-activity and if they had to perform any tasks, the rate of consumption would increase rapidly. Any hard work or exhaustion brings a consumption to a level 9 times greater, or 6 cubic feet per hour. That left the trapped men being forced to remain idle, which meant they were using oxygen at an average rate of about one cubic foot per man per hour. At this rate, unless the air could be renewed, in 8 hours their allowance of oxygen would be used up. They were in the end to last for around 42 hours, having supplemented the available air with their precious compressed air supply. At intervals McLean would release a small quantity of air into the torpedo room and at the same time was to force a portion of the used air back into other bottles by use of the air compressor. As the oxygen was consumed, it was replaced by the carbon dioxide the men exhaled. One per cent of carbon dioxide is something that can be detected as it has a scent and produces dyspnoea (which is the medical expression for 'panting'). At three per cent, the panting becomes painful and at 5 per cent any form of exertion becomes impossible. As the air in the submarine was slowly consumed exhaling became extremely painful. For some of the men the very process of breathing in became more painful and difficult than for their shipmates. Several men discovered that standing was the easiest posture, while the pilot, Captain Duncan, during almost the entire time the boat was on the bottom, paced the control room, as though still in command on the bridge of his own boat. But in the main the greater majority were reduced to doing nothing and they lay down around the areas not flooded, half asleep and breathing a harsh snoring or a gasping sound. There were a few bunks and each of these was to usually hold two or three occupants, while the officer's mess armchair was in great demand. A few crewmen discovered, that if they lay under the officer's dining-table they were less trodden upon, than in places more exposed to traffic. But as they lay there, with little to do it became 'clear' to some that their position was desperate, and they gave up hope of ever seeing the blue sky or sun again.

Hepworth was to comment to one crewman *"This looks like the end"*, to which the sailor replied, *"I am afraid it is".* Coxswain Moss, who had been through the Dardanelles in an 'E' class boat and on into the Sea of Marmora is recorded as having said "he wouldn't have minded losing his life in a fair fight with the enemy, but considered this a "rotten" way to die". But despite a growing fatalism there was no panic at any time, just serious faces and subdued conversation. Their chances of survival were discussed endlessly and at great length. The boat had commenced its second dive at 15:15 and as yet the Comet had no reason to be concerned and would not for another thirty minutes. The submarine *E50* was also in the loch that day and had watched as the 'K' boat had dived, but by now the *E50's* Lieutenant Commander Kenneth Michelle, was beginning to be concerned that the *K13* had yet to return to the surface. He had been uneasy at the amount of air that had bubbled up from the depths following the 'K' boats dive and now he took a ship's boat to the patch of water where *K13* was seen to have dived. The boats crew dropped a buoy to mark the spot and found the water to be contaminated by traces of oil and that a steady stream of bubble's was still breaking to the surface. A sample of sea water was taken and on being tested was found to be free from acid. Whatever had occurred to keep the 'K' boat beneath the waves, her crew had not been gassed. E50's officers still assumed and hoped that in time K13's crew would solve whatever the problem was, blow the boats tanks and return once more to the surface. K13's skipper was considered within the service as a 'prankster' or joker. Once when in command of *HMS C36* he had submerged the craft until only the periscopes remained above the surface. He then clung onto these as the 'C' boat moved beneath the waves, leaving him looking as if he was walking on water. *E50's* Captain was aware of how resourceful *K13's* Captain could be, as his stunt had demonstrated. If anyone could resolve the 'K' boats problems, it would be him. The boat dropped a buoy to mark the spot and Cleghorn telephoned Fairfield immediately to set in motion a rescue operation. He also sent a W/T to the Senior Naval Officers of the Clyde district asking for help. In response Captain Barttelot who was the Senior Naval officer of the Clyde was to arrive quickly on the spot to assume command of the rescue. In the meanwhile, a small ships boat was stationed over *K13's* last known position.

Fifty feet below the surface, having conducted a roll call and calculated the oxygen left to them, the Captain ordered an exploration of the areas not flooded. It was found that they were unable to gain access to the officers' quarters or the bow torpedo room as the watertight door clips had dropped down on the other side and there was no one alive in there to lift them. The trapped door meant they were deprived of the air beyond the door and of a potential escape route. Herbert also ordered Singer to send a distress signal to E50 on the boats Fassenden, an underwater communication device. But it was never to be received.

Other crew members explored the aft sections that they could access and began to cautiously open the watertight doors once more, to gain admittance to the air those compartments held. The watertight door leading into the amidships torpedo room was opened and the two men who had been shut in during the *K13's* dive were finally released. The torpedo-room was discovered happily to be all but free of sea water, but its aft bulkhead was constructed to withstand a pressure of 15 lbs per square inch and was now combating nearer 25 lbs. Not surprisingly given the greater pressure being exerted, it was leaking. There was also found to be a considerable quantity of water coming through the compartments voice pipe, the holes in the bulkhead for cables, telegraph shafting, etc.

Attention was now turned to the jammed door forward of the control room. There was no way to bypass the door and the clip could not be raised back up, thus leaving the door closed and the oxygen within the space beyond out of reach. The clip was fortunately not tight and with an effort the door could be pushed slightly away from its seating. But no matter how hard they pushed; it was insufficient to allow a hand to be squeezed through to reach the troublesome clip. For around two hours McLean, Struthers, Green and Bullen worked at the clip and finally after stripping all the rubber packing off to allow for a little more play on the hinge side, the clip was raised by means of a bent wire. As the door finally swung open a cheer rang out within the boat as one of the few victories that day, was won.

While the four men struggled to defeat the troublesome door, the loch's water was slowly gaining about 2 feet (60.96

cm) per hour in the amidships torpedo compartment. It became necessary at intervals to run the electric bilge pump for short periods to lower the water level once more. By 20:00 the trapped men had come to resign themselves to a night of waiting and maybe ultimately, their deaths. There were enough sandwiches on board for half a round per man, but no one was interested in the food. To add to the list of troubles facing the men, the seawater had contaminated the boats drinking water tanks.

TWO MODERN DAY HOPPER BARGES, BUT IN THE CENTURY SINCE THE K13 SANK THE DESIGN HAS CHANGED LITTLE.

In the waters above the trapped men, at 20:00 the first rescue craft finally arrived on the scene, in the form of the old gunboat *Gossamer* (4). In addition, the salvage vessels *Tay* (5) and *Thrush* (6), in company with two large un-powered hopper barges with cargos of wire were now on route to the scene. Nearly two more hours were to pass before the Admiralty in London learnt of the unfolding event's at 23:56:

"Submarine K13 on bottom off Shandon in Gareloch details not yet known am sending salvage vessels Tay and Thrush and two large hoppers with wires etc. Depth of water (?) 12 fathoms Captain Corbett is at

176

Shandon in charge of operations will report in morning".

*Leading Stoker Frederick James Howard, one of
the crewmen who persied with the K13.*

❖ ❖ ❖

*1: Goodhart was awarded the Cross of St. George by Tsar Nicholas
II for his role in sinking the armoured cruiser Prinz Adalbert
while in command of E 8 on 23 October 1915).*

*2: Kelvin, Bottomley & Baird were scientific instrument makers,
ship's compasses, sounding machines, general nautical instruments, electric measuring instruments...*

*3: Brown Bros and Co were manufacturers of steam, hydraulic
and electro-hydraulic steering gears, telemotors for steering and
helm signals...*

4: Chadburn's Turbine and Telegraph Tell-Tale was an electrical data system used to support a mechanical engine room telegraph with an electrical indication of roughly what the turbine was currently doing.

5: HMS Gossamer was a Sharpshooter-class torpedo gunboat of the British Royal Navy. She was built at the Sheerness Dockyard in 1891 and was converted to a minesweeper in 1909. Gossamer was sold for scrap in 1920.

HMS SPANKER, SHARPSHOOTER-CLASS TORPEDO GUNBOAT

6: HMS TAY, ex-gunboat, described as miscellaneous special service vessel. Launched 19th October 1876 Palmer. 363 tons, 110(pp)x34x5 ft. Avg 400ihp, 9kts. Served as tender at Devonport. Sold 22nd October 1920.

7: HMS Thrush was a Redbreast-class composite gunboat, her first station was the North America and West Indies Station based in Halifax where, in 1891, she was commanded by HRH Prince George, later to become King George V of the United Kingdom. In 1896 Thrush, along with Sparrow, played a part in the 40-minute Anglo-Zanzibar War. She was also on active service during the Second Boer War, which lasted between October 1899 and June 1902, where she was commanded by Lieutenant

Warren Hastings D'Oyly. In early 1902 she helped a British force in Nigeria re-open trade routes on the Lower Niger, closed by piracy of some locals. Lieutenant Hector Lloyd Watts-Jones was appointed in command on 5 July 1902.

HMS THRUSH, AS BUILT.

From 1906 Thrush worked for HM Coastguard before becoming a cable ship in 1915. She then became a salvage ship in 1916 before being wrecked off Glenarm in Northern Ireland on 11 April 1917.

CHAPTER THREE
THE RESCUE

*"This Memorial Has Been Created In Memory Of Those
Officers And Men Of The Commonwealth Who Gave Their
Lives In Submarines While Serving The Cause Of Freedom."
K13 Memorial Carlingford, New South Wales, Australia*

By midnight both the *E50* and the Gossamer lay stationary over the *K13's* suspected location. The *Gossamer's* Captain (Acting Commander Charles E. Aglionby) had earlier ordered the launch of two of his ship's boats and that a wire sweep be run between them. The cable was lowered into the loch's depths and dragged along the bottom to find the lost submarine by attempting to snag on to its hull. In less than two hours, at 02:00 the wire sweep found the missing 'K' boat. Now with her exact location known, a diver was ordered to be prepared to go down and try to establish if there were any survivors on board. Unfortunately, whilst the Gossamer did have a diving suit, she lacked the diver himself. A car finally turned up with the diver's assistant and he was quickly transferred over to the *Gossamer.* The assistant having donned the suit descended the ships side, into the water at 04:00. But the suit had not seen any use in several years and once in the water, it burst. The bedraggled diver struggled back onboard, wet through and the suit was discarded. The car raced back to Fairfield and a second (and newer) suit was urgently collected. Over the next few days that car was to drive the distance between Shandon and Fairfield no fewer than 14 times and altogether covered around 400 miles.

Source: Janes Fighting Ships 1924

THE DIVERS HEAVY ALL ENCOMPASSING STYLE OF EQUIUPMENT USED FOR THE RESCUE.

A trawler was the next addition to the 'rescue' squadron, having just completed the salvage of the mined steamer *Mavisbrook* on Loch Maddie. She was moored at Greenock when the news of the *K13* sinking broke and had only just completed towing the *Mavisbrook* into port. The trawler was low on the necessary gear, having neither a diver nor a suit. But regardless she departed to Gareloch at 06:00 the following (Tuesday) morning. Soon after dawn with his new suit now ready for him, the diver's assistant returned to the water. He descended into the loch's depths sometime after

08:00 and on reaching the *K13* he had been ordered to walk along the hull tapping with a hammer on the metal casing, seeking any trapped survivors. But as soon as his weighted boots landed on the hull, he drew a response from the trapped submariners. Moss recounted:

> *"As soon as possible divers were sent down and on Tuesday morning we in the boat knew help was at hand, for we could hear a diver walking about on the hull of the boat. You can guess we were very much relieved to know that we had been found and we were now wondering what they would do. We knew what a big job they would have especially as they didn't know under what circumstances we were, neither did they know how much of the boat was flooded. Our only chance was to get into some kind of communication with then and this we tried to do by making signals in the "Morse" code, which we did by tapping the hull of the boat. We got no answers and afterwards I found out that although the diver could easily hear the tapping he had no knowledge of the "Morse" code and could not receive our signals. Anyhow, those who were working on us knew that there were men alive inside the boat and this of course made them put every ounce of energy into their task".*

The trapped men finally heard the welcome sound of the diver's metal soled boots walking along the hull. Their cries to the diver were even heard on the surface and a lead line was lowered to the diver allowing him to tap on the hull. The unnamed diver unfortunately did not know Morse code, so the signals were made by raising and lowering the lead and the diver guiding it. The 'K' boats crew responded in Morse *"all well before engine room bulkhead"*. It was to prove to be the only successful Morse exchange as the men on the surface were to be unable to decipher any of the succeeding messages.

Through the 'bulls' eyes' or portholes in the sides of the conning tower the men could see the wire guard rail which ran around the topsides. They tried raising the masts to indicate the 'K' boats position, but they would learn later that they had not broken the surface, though the top of the foremast was bent over, having been struck by one of the salvage vessels hulls. As the wire sweep had grated its way along the outer hull, the trapped men cheered, but even with the succeeding sound of diver's boots, it was a false bravado. They were rapidly becoming resigned to the steel hull being their tomb. Moth again:

> "Everything was now as quiet as the grave and we simply looked at one another and then we began to look around to see if there was any chance or any possible means to escape from this "Death Trap". There certainly seemed to be very little cause for hope and in our own hearts each man knew, in all probability, that K13 would be our tomb"

After having spent near on 24 hours encased within the forward part of K13, the men were beginning by now to suffer from the effects of oxygen starvation. With every breath drawn by each of the 48 men, the reserve of breathable air was a fraction more reduced. As the air reserves shrank, the exhaled carbon dioxide took its place. The air was by now becoming foul and less breathable with each passing minute. The very act of breathing was becoming an effort as air starvation (or 'Dyspnea') began to impact upon the trapped men. They began to experience a shortness of breath and a feeling of being smothered with each succeeding laboured breath. Their chests slowly grew tighter and the struggle to inhale was becoming both rapid and shallow. Coordination had by now become a lost art and 'visual disorders' where causing problems with the crew's vision. As daybreak broke over the scene, at around 08:00, the trapped men had become convinced they could see a greenish light coming through the periscope. Some specks on the glass of the scope created an illusion of a light green sunlit sea, with a man rowing in a small boat. But the immobility and unchanging nature of the scene showed it to be non-existent. Some of the men experienced a growing sense of euphoria and blinding headaches were now a common infliction. It was by this stage they began to suffer confusion, as well as feel both a dizziness and an enveloping sense of restlessness. Individuals were suffering heart palpitations and the achievement of drawing breath was accompanied by the sound of wheezing. As the oxygen was consumed and the carbon dioxide level increased, *K13's* interior grew steadily colder and the growing lack of oxygen created a dampness that permeated throughout the hull. Any exertion or effort to perform a task brought on the sound of coughing and wheezing and the men simply took to laying or sitting around in the limited space available to them and waited for death to come and finally release them. Men lay around with each lost to his personal struggle to breath the shrinking supply of cold damp. But before they ran out of breathable air, the carbon dioxide they were exhaling would kill them. Hillhouse recalled afterwards

> "As the air in our submerged prison became more and more foul, so did our breathing become more and more difficult, we had to inhale and exhale with painful rapidity. For some the process was carried on only under great pain and difficulty. Many found standing the easiest posture. The great majority, however, were

rendered more or less inert and apathetic, lay down
anywhere and everywhere, half asleep, half awake,
breathing or snoring noisily. And so, the long night
passed away."

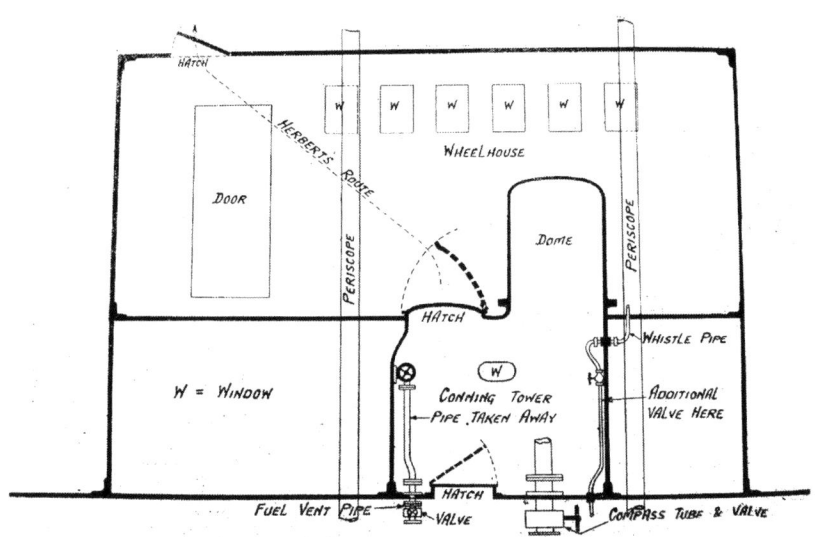

THE CONNING TOWER ESCAPE ROUTE PRESERVED IN THE NATIONAL ARCHIVES.

Shortly after noon, (12:30) Herbert asked Commander
Goodhart if he would consider undertaking an attempt to
reach the surface at low water. After some thought Goodhart
agreed a try should be made. They both knew time was running short and a way of escape needed to be found. Their
growing fear was that their rescuers would concentrate on
the raising of the boat and not to make the provision of
air their main priority. The two Captains decided that they
needed to ensure that the supplying of air became their
would-be rescuers first goal. It was obvious to the Captains
that Goodhart would be the better choice, allowing Herbert
to remain with his crew. The escape attempt was to be made
using the conning tower as an airlock.

With the decision made to try to reach the surface, the vent pipe within the conning tower was removed below the valve. This would allow through the opening of the valve, sea water to pour into the conning tower. The Projector Compass and its tube were removed to make more room within the confined space and its dome. The Captains also adapted the lower portion of the pipe within the control room to be used as a drainpipe in order to allow for the removal of the water from the conning tower, once Goodhart was heading for the surface. In addition to these refinements, a flexible hose was attached to the lower end of the pipe and it led into the amidships torpedo room to allow the water to be drawn off. The siren's pipe was also split at a joint, a valve removed from a second piece of piping and it was secured to the upper end of the pipe leading from the high-pressure air system. The new set up would permit pressurized air into the conning tower by opening the two-valve adaption. In addition, the incoming air could be shut off by use of either valve. Any holes as a result of the work, were plugged with small wooden plugs so that the tower was once again made watertight. The Captains did much of the work to prepare the conning tower themselves. Moth described the preparations in his biography:

"The magnetic compass was taken down and all the electric leads running through the conning tower were taken down also. When the holes through which these leads had been taken were plugged with small wooden plugs so that the tower was again made water tight. The next thing to do was to run a length of copper pipe from the "Whistle Pipe", which came off the HP system and fit valves to it. These were taken down from another part of the boat and the reason they were fitted

was so that they could control their own air.

It took me hours to complete the work but, at last, it was finished to their own satisfaction...".

One of Herbert's most vivid recollections of that day as the conning tower was adapted was that of a prawn who had somehow lodged himself against one of the bull's-eyes. Herbert wrote:

"I can see him still with his little black eyes pressed against the glass; he must have been attracted by the light. The plan was for both Commanders to enter the tower and close the lower hatch beneath them, which would also be clipped shut from the control room. The Captains would then un-clip the upper hatch and open the sea valve, allowing a strictly controlled amount of sea water to slowly flood into the conning tower. The incoming water would push and squeeze the air towards the ceiling, until its pressure became equal to the weight of the sea water pressing down onto the upper hatch. Then the hatch could be opened, while the two Commanders stood with their heads in the Projector Compass dome, in which would remain a last small pocket of air. At this point the water that had been drawn into the conning tower would be around three feet in depth. Then once the upper hatch was lifted, the air above this level and below the dome would escape and be replaced by more incoming sea water. Then once Goodhart had made his escape and was headed for the surface, Herbert was to signal his crew by tapping on the lower hatch. They would then drain the conning tower, before letting their Captain back into the control

room.

Goodhart was dressed, in just a shirt, trousers and sea boots, while Herbert was in his shirt, cap, trousers and sea boots. The sea boots were worn on Coxswain Moss's suggestion, knowing that Herbert was to return to the boat's interior and that it is difficult to keep your feet when standing in water, unless your weighted at the feet. Both men gave their thick 'watch' coats to crewmen and Goodhart his watch, handing it to the second coxswain, saying, *"I might ask you for that later on"*. Herbert also wrote a brief report for Goodhart to take with him, as well as a list of the survivors which he put into a small tin watertight cylinder about 8 inches by 2½ inches. Goodhart having tucked it under his belt said, *"well if I don't get up this will"*. Around midday, (at low water) both men climbed into the conning tower wearing only socks, trousers and a shirt. With the hatch shut and sealed the valve was opened and the cold Scottish waters poured in until it reached their waists height. Turning to Herbert, Goodhart said *"well I'm off"* and Herbert wished him *"good luck"*.

THE MESSAGE CYLINDER

Herbert then:

"...turned the air on, the force caused him to lose grip of the valve and he did a complete double somersault and found himself out of the airlock, but in an enclosed place. This must have been the wheelhouse for he groped about and it was some time before he got out. He felt the tremendous pressure on his body and he thought he would lose consciousness when he found a hole (which I believe was the side door) and got through it. Having been by pure good luck propelled by the escaping air aft and up through the hatch in the after-end of the wheelhouse roof. He partly swam and was partly swept along by the rising air, to the surface, breathing most of the time and brushing aside the "wireless" wires as he shot past them. He then found himself rapidly coming to the surface and, just as he was losing consciousness, he broke the surface and was immediately dragged by surprised but willing

hands into a boat".

Of Goodhart, the intended escaper, there was no sign. His body was to be recovered later when the submarine was salvaged and it was assumed the same rush of expanding air forced him into the dome, where he struck his head on the ceiling. He was found to have a broken neck and having been concussed, left unconscious. The brave but unfortunate Captain must have died quickly and with little suffering, drowning whilst insensible. Moss has given us a description of the escape in his account allowing us an insight from the survivor's perspective:

"After we had closed the lower lid we simply listened and waited very anxiously. At last we heard the noise of the clips being knocked off the upper hatch and then we heard a rush of water and knew the tower was being flooded. Minutes seemed hours to us, but at last the rush of water stopped and we know the tower must be full. There was a dead silence now and we looked at one another not daring to speak and. then we heard the noise of the upper lid being thrown right back and from this we knew everything had gone off according to plan.

"It was some minutes before we heard anymore. I suppose this was the time when Goodhart said his last farewell. At last we heard a tremendous rush of air and by looking at our high-pressure gauge we could see two thousand pounds of air disappear very rapidly. We knew in our own mind that this shouldn't have happened, but knowing that they had a valve in the conning tower, we didn't think it was right for us to

interfere with the air from below.

As soon as the rush of air had finished, it was all still again and we were beginning to wonder if success had crowned their efforts. We now waited to hear the noise of the upper lid closing and the signal to drain the conning tower, but none came. A dead silence reigned every-where and we simply looked at one another not daring to voice an opinion, although I am sure we all had aching hearts for we thought the whole enterprise had failed and that both of these brave men had lost their lives.

I think myself that at this time things absolutely looked their blackest, for we had lost what I considered the brains [of] the boat and I was wondering who we would have to take their places".

As the two men prepared for the escape attempt, above them on the surface the senior naval officer of the Clyde, Captain Brian Bartelott and the company executives of Fairfield's had formulated a plan. Their idea was to run a 6.5-inch cable between the Thrush and the trawler, creating a cradle for the K13 hull. Then with the hawser run under the boat, her bow was to be raised up to the surface. Moth explains once:

I expect a good many of my readers will be asking why the air wasn't pumped, into the boat to breathe? Well the reason is this, inside the boat we already had a tremendous amount of pressure, but there was no means of telling the amount, as we had no barometer to measure it. We ran our low-pressure compressor from time to time to take air out of the boat, but after a bit we considered it unwise, for the simple reason we didn't know whether we had taken the pressure down to normal or not. Of course, we found afterwards that there was still a tremendous pressure, but we thought it wise to leave things as they were, for the present at any rate.

Another reason we didn't use the LP compressor is, that it is run by the same motor which runs the Ballast pump and we needed the pump very badly. This motor can either be clutched into the compressor or the pump, but only one thing can be run at a time and as the pump was most needed, we kept it clutched in, the best part of the time.

Our biggest trouble was the watertight bulkhead between the boiler room and the beam tube room. This was leaking very badly and it will easily be seen why it did leak. This was only a collision bulkhead and was tested to a pressure of fifteen pounds and as we were below seventy feet, the pressure on the bulkhead would be thirty five pounds, so we must think ourselves very lucky it held as well as it did."

But the Fairfield executives, who still technically owned the K13, were opposed as they feared it would break the craft in half. Their alternative proposal was to construct a 27-inch (0.685mtr) diameter tube which was to be 60 feet long (18.28 mtrs). A discharge pipe was to be secured to its lower end and run up to the surface, parallel to the tube. The top of the tube was then to temporarily be closed by a bolted plate and the water in the tube blown up the discharge pipe. Once completed it was to be connected to the bow torpedo tube, caulking it watertight. Then having been pumped dry, the trapped crew could make their way to the surface through it.

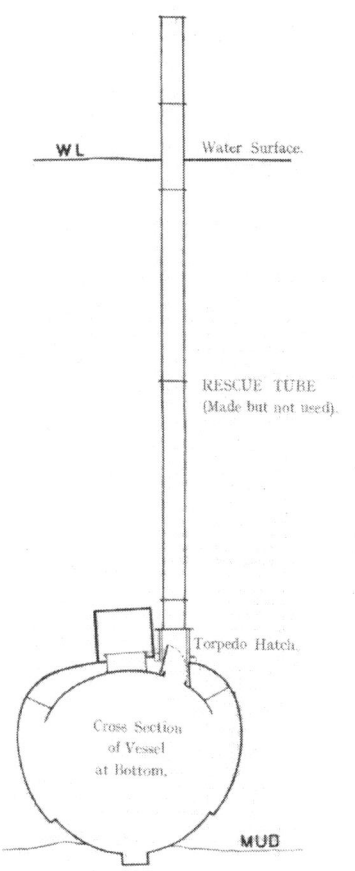

WL Water Surface.

RESCUE TUBE
(Made but not used).

Torpedo Hatch.

Cross Section
of Vessel
at Bottom.

MUD

E50's Captain, (Lieutenant-Commander Kenneth Michell), was opposed to the idea believing that such a tube would take far too long to build given the finite amount of time available to them and told supporters of the cable plan to proceed. Lieutenant Ivo Kay (RNR.RFA) Commander of the Thrush, oversaw the passing of a cable beneath the 'K' boat' bow to the trawler, which was achieved fortunately on their first attempt. By midday as the two Captains in the submarine prepared for Goodhart's escape, both the Thrush and the trawler were ready to take the strain onto their capstans.

OVER PAGE: THE PLANNED BUT REJECTED RESCUE TUBE.

However, as the order was given and the cable was slowly hauled in lifting the 'K' boats bow inches off the loch's bottom, the trawler's bulk was seen to be leaning into the

193

growing weight that lay beneath her. As the concern steadily grew over her increasing list, a huge bubble erupted in
the waters between the two vessels, causing the onlookers
to assume the worst, that disaster had struck and the wire
had penetrated into the hull. They feared that the cable had
snapped the hull in two and those trapped inside were now
all dead. But as the water slowly subsided a lone head could
be seen in the water, as Herbert burst to the surface. A diver
was quickly despatched across to the man in the water and
helped him on board the Thrush. Mitchell made his way
on to the salvage vessel, to discover what had happened
and who the lone survivor was. In addition, the man would
surely prove to be a much-needed source of what the actual
situation on the *K13* was. But despite Mitchell's questions,
Herbert's first concern was for Goodhart, however it was
rapidly becoming apparent that tragedy had struck and only
Herbert had made it to the surface. He could only hope now
that Goodhart had somehow made it back into the control
room. Herbert's second concern was that the provision of an
air supply to the 'K' boat was achieved as fast as was technically possible. It would then allow the trapped men to blow
the boats tanks and thus be able to help with the lift. Time
was of the essence as Herbert advised Mitchell

*"...the engine room bulkhead is leaking badly and the
bilge pump is running on makeshift leads which might
break at any moment".*

Fifteen minutes after having climbed out of the water, wearing a borrowed suit, Herbert was busy assisting and advising
the rescuers.

Two more divers had by now arrived on the scene and the
E50 was eased alongside the trawler to help with the plan

for lifting the *K13's* bow. She also had four lengths of 5-inch high pressured air hose onboard, which was soon to be put to good use. But until the three divers manage to find the 'K' boats 'External Connection Point', the hoses remained high and dry, coiled up on the *E50's* deck. During the late afternoon the HM Naval Salvage Adviser, Captain Frederick Young, arrived on the scene and he dispatched orders to the Fairfield's shipyard for the escape tube to be constructed. The disaster with the Royal Navy's latest submarine concept was in theory a closely guarded secret, but by this stage in the unfolding drama, crowds had gathered along the shoreline to watch the activity happening on the waters of their loch. It was evidently a submarine that was in difficulty, but it was most unlikely many of the onlookers even knew of the steam belching monsters. The next addition to the small but increasing armada was a tugboat which arrived from the Scots Shipbuilding and Engineering Company, the yard that was currently building the *K15*. The tug had on board a group comprised of the best men within the shipyard suited for the operation now unfolding on the Scottish loch: · Two Shipwrights,

- · Two Riggers (2)
- · Three labourers.

The seven men had brought with them additional tools, wire hawsers, timber, hoses…. The men and their equipment had been hastily loaded when the tug made a brief call at Fairfield, before departing on to Gareloch shortly after 06:00, with the parting words of the Head Foreman Shipwright Alan Aitken, *"do your best to save these fellows lives and I know you won't let them down."* As the tug made its way down the river, it made a second brief call, this time at Clydebank where they took in tow a quantity of heavy timber logs.

On the bottom of Gareloch the air on *K13* had by now easily exceeded Hillhouse's calculations and the clock had crawled to 24 hours, three times longer than they had expected to have breath for. But even though they could still breathe, the quantity and quality had diminished to such a degree that by now when a crewman struck a match it produced merely a slight wisp of smoke and no flame. The crew had finally given up what little hope they had left when their Captain had not returned from the conning tower, leading them to assume that both Captains had been tragically drowned while trying to save the crew. *K13's* First Officer, Lieutenant Singer was with the Captain's loss now ranked as senior and in theory took command. But he had resigned himself to an airless fate and simply sat on his bunk, morose and calling for a cup of tea, which was never going to arrive. Fred Searle the Admiralty Overseer, the man who all those hours ago, had inspected the four ventilators between the funnels and assured Lane that there was nothing to worry about, requested of the depressed Singer that he be permitted to assume leadership, a request that wasn't refused. The enquiry after the rescue drew attention to Singers failure to live up to his training and expectation. The air growing thinner and more unpalatable with each laboured breath and leading seaman Arthur Riley took to banging in Morse on the inner hull, *"give us air, give us air"*, again and again... Men lay everywhere, their throats parched and their tongues discoloured from the growing lack of oxygen. The submarines interior was gradually getting colder but that seemed not to affect them with the growing scarcity of breathable oxygen. The deprivation dulled the individual's senses and the biggest man on board tried to open a hatch in his need to escape and had to be felled by a spanner.

Finally, after hours of trying, at 18:00 the divers found and connected an air hose to the elusive external connection valve, or the 'Diver's Connection'. Moth describes the linking point as the "forward four-inch Gun connection", but whichever the name, the join was finally made. While his colleagues fastened the hose, another diver flashed signals by a torch down the periscope, trying to tell the trapped men to open the appropriate valve. But for a while the signals went unnoticed by the submariners. Finally, having persisted and after many repeated efforts, the diver's signals were understood and the *K13's* crew warily opened the valve. But to their horror instead of fresh crisp air filling the submarines fetid interior, they were met by an inflow of bubbling Scottish loch water. The crew grabbed two buckets and caught the invading water into them. They bailed bucket after bucket in the hope that each one would be the last and the desperately needed air would follow. But finally, they had to accept defeat and the valve was shut once more. Their fragile morale dropped even further at yet another failure. How many more trials need they suffer, before this slow tortuous entombment would end, for good or bad? On the surface the *E50's* compressor was working hard at pushing 2,500 pounds per square inch of air through to the submariners, but the air was going nowhere. The frustrated divers placed a hydrophone on the hull and heard Arthur Riley still tapping out his plea for air. They could only assume, (wrongly) that the crew had yet to open the valve. Mitchel had a metal oil drum put on *K3's* deck and a klaxon put in it to message the trapped men in Morse code. But he had to finally accept something must be at fault with the hose and ordered it to be unattached and the end brought up for checking. It was quickly found to be blocked by ice. Seven precious hours had been wasted, for which Mitchel blamed himself.

Freed of the blockage, the hose was once more reconnected

and the signalling through the periscope resumed instruct-
ing them to open the valve once more. After 35 hours sat
on the seabed, the valve was finally opened, and fresh wonderful air hissed in through the valve slowly expanding into
the dark, damp stale interior. The trapped men gathered
round as the invisible nectar slowly filled their small world
and each man savoured every wonderful lungful. As the air
permeated around the interior, finally the doubt and nega-
tivity were replaced by something better, a hope and a belief
they might yet just escape their underwater prison. After
35 hours trapped on the sea floor, reduced to laying on the
decks too sick to move, the survivors started to recover and
move about once more. Seale ordered that the air be directed into the empty air bottles, up to a pressure of 2,500
pounds.

Once the bottles were replenished, he ordered the ballast
tanks blown, but as much as the submarine groaned and
her crew wished it, she refused to lift free of the loch's bed
and stayed stuck fast at 4 degrees. Seale had all but two of
the tanks blown and it was looking to have been a futile
effort. But then suddenly they felt a movement within the
boat, as her bow heaved itself free of the loch's bed. As the
bow slowly came up to the surface, both the Thrush and
the trawler frantically hauled in the wire that ran beneath
the submarines hull. Finally, at 03:00, after nearly a day
and a half submerged, the 'K' boat's forward mast and periscope broke the surface. But even as the rescuers cheered,
the weight of the submarine and her internal trapped water
caused the trawler to heel even further over. However, success was too close to admit defeat to a 'mere' steep list. Then
finally the lochs waters were parted as the tip of the 'K' boats
bow broke the surface and the rescuers watched as that 'ex-
tremity' slowly grew into 8 foot of solid 'K' boat bow. The
waters around that small mountain of steel erupting from

the depths, churned and bubbled from the air expressed by *K13's* venting ballast tanks. Mitchel called a halt to the winches, but the divers were unable to work in the waters while the *K13's* ballast tanks vented a mixture of water and air. It was to take a further 15 minutes of signalling through the periscope before the *K13's* crew understood, and they ceased blowing the tanks. Herbert now ordered a brass plate covering the 7½ inch ventilation and ammunition 'hand-up' shaft over the officers' quarters to be removed and brought to the surface. The diver also connected an air lead to the foremost guns recuperating cylinder. This was to supply HP air to the tanks. Herbert's next step was to have a 4-inch diameter flexible hose welded over the shaft. An air supply pipe was passed down the flexible pipe, as was food in a liquid form. With the bow now free of the water it was possible to tow the steeply angled submarine closer in shore, her stern leaving a furrow in the seabed as it was dragged along.

The men inside the *K13* could hear the noises coming from beyond their metal walls, as if coming from another world, unseen but almost with in touch. But while still suffering from a degree of oxygen starvation, the trapped men were unable to understand Mitchell's request to open their end of the shaft. Food and an unlimited supply of air would be available to them, if only they could be persuaded to open the hatch. To complicate matters for the crew who must have been struggling to interpret what the noises and lifting of the bow signified, the hulls incline had brought the bilge pump clear of the water, making it no longer effective. Now slowly the waters within the hull resumed their advance through the interior, drawing nearer to the boat's batteries. The 'K' boat crew started to fear that the saltwater would finally reach the batteries and the combination produce the toxic chlorine gas that was the stuff of submariner's nightmares. In desperation the crew formed a bucket line that ran from the forward torpedo room to one of the bilges. Holding on with one hand to combat the boats steep deck slope and with one of the two buckets leaking, they bailed the water into a tank. After an hour and little real progress by the bucket chain Mclean and Bullen decided to try to lift a man-hole cover in the torpedo room floor. The two men stood deep in the ice-cold water and a job that should have taken five minutes took the shivering waterlogged men near two hours. But with a persistence born from desperation they finally prized the cover open and the water quickly drained away into the empty tank.

As the crew bailed and struggled with manhole covers, above them Captain Mitchell sat in the dark for two hours in a bosun's chair slung from the *K13's* bow, from where he signalled the men inside to open the small hatch. At dawn Herbert relieved Mitchell and soon after the exchange the *K13's* crew finally understood Herbert's signals and opened the hatch. As the men swung the entrance open a cloud formed of a black mist and with an unpalatable stench, (the submarines foul air) escaped from within the boat's inter-ior. The escaping smell was so strong that Herbert was un-able to tolerate it and had to move clear until it was vented. With the opening of the hatch the change in pressure tore at the *K13's* crews' eardrums, but once the worst had escaped Herbert called down the hatch, *"Can you hear me down there"*. McLean was nearest the hatch called back up *"yes we can hear you loud and clear"*. Herbert then enquired *"How is everyone?"*. McLean told him *"were all holding out, but we need air badly and water"* adding, *" have you seen Commander Herbert?"* Herbert was able to reassure them by calling down "this is Com-mander Herbert speaking" and on learning that their Cap-tain was ok, the men cheered as they gulped in more of the fresh cool air. The crew next asked about Captain Goodhart, but Herbert had to report that there had been no sighting of him.

One of the first items to be lowered down the hatch by Herbert was a stone bottle of brandy, but which with no trays available, Searle made use of a brass cover from an electrical switch to serve the brandy. Milk, coffee, soup and Bovril in stone bottles followed. Chocolates were dropped down as well but the sandwiches from earlier had remained untouched. Once the entire fiasco with K13 was over a rumour gained traction that the entombed crew whiled away their time by playing cards. But as one survivor said:

"I can assure you and I have no doubt you will readily believe that no one felt the least desire for any such occupation. There were cards on board, but they were never used. I still have two much-discoloured packs which were taken from the vessel in a very sodden condition, after she was raised. The story probably arose from the fact that after we had got fresh air, food and liquid and as we began to nurse a faint hope of ultimate rescue, our spirits revived wonderfully and in reply to a question from above as to whether we would like anything else to be passed down the tube some joker replied, "Nothing but a pack of cards." It was also rumoured and by some believed, that the Captain had been shot out of a torpedo-tube with such force that he had landed at Row!" (a small village just outside the lower end of Gareloch, towards the Clyde and is now known as Rhu).

With the change in the air pressure the water started to rise once more in the mid-ship torpedo room. To compound matters, a stone bottle of soda water became jammed in the pipe and the 'K' men had to shut the hatch while the tube was unfastened and cleared of its blockage. With the angle the boat now rested at, her stern had sunk under the pressure from the rising bow, 12 feet (3.65 mtrs) into the mud and the now rising internal waters were putting dangerous pressure on the internal bulkheads. Moth again:

> *"inside the boat were exhausted men, some working in spells and some working all the time. They were fighting the water which was pouring through the bulkhead and which threatened to reach our batteries, which if it had done would soon have suffocated us. To alleviate what was becoming a dangerous situation both the Thrush and the trawler hauled on the wire lifting the bow higher out of the water, until it stood ten feet clear of the loch's surface. With the forward tubes now clear, Mitchell told the men that in an hour he hoped they would finally be able to make their escape through the tubes. That news brought a resounding cheer and a surge by the men into the forward compartments. The small fleet on the surface had been increased further by the addition of two barges which were secured on either side of the now risen K13's bow. Once in place they had seawater pumped into their holds to lower their draft. Mitchell now told the men in K13 that once the torpedo tubes were clear of the water, he would hammer on the hull and they were to make their escape. The cheering crew gathered in the forward torpedo room expectant and excited.*

The *Thrush* resumed once more winching in more of the wire and the barges commenced pumping out their flooded stern sections. Seizing the moment Herbert made the decision that now was the time to start bringing his crew out through the torpedo tubes. But as the barges slowly lifted from water and the *Thrush* winched, *K13's m*assive bulk started to slip from out of her single wire cradle. Spotting the danger of losing all that had been so far achieved, Herbert quickly ordered the lifting operation as well as the crew's quick extraction to be sharply brought to a halt. To avoid the threatening catastrophe several fresh wires were passed from the barge's capstans, through the *K13's* hawsepipes (1) and then back to the *Thrush's* capstans. But having seen the *K13* slip once, Mitchell was now understandably nervous to resume the lifting. Inside the K13 the main fuse chose this time to finally blow, plunging the interior into pitch blackness. After an hour working in the stygian darkness by torch light, they managed to restore one light to a half intensity and were reduced to the lone bulb and the three remaining battery powered torches. The submarine had now reached an angle of 16° with the oil and water covered decking making any effort to stand unaided all but impossible. Bruises and scrapes became common place as crewmen lost their hold, sliding and banging onto the many sharp edges the K13's interior had.

It must have been with a sense of excitement and possibility that maybe they could survive this, that the trapped men found the surface was now visible through the periscope. The discovery led to the thought that the upper torpedo tubes must surely be clear of the water and that an escape was in fact possible. The crew quickly set to work to loosen a hatch, but as it came free, water poured in. The hatch was pulled shut and secured; the 'K' boat 'Jinx' was not quite ready to release them yet.

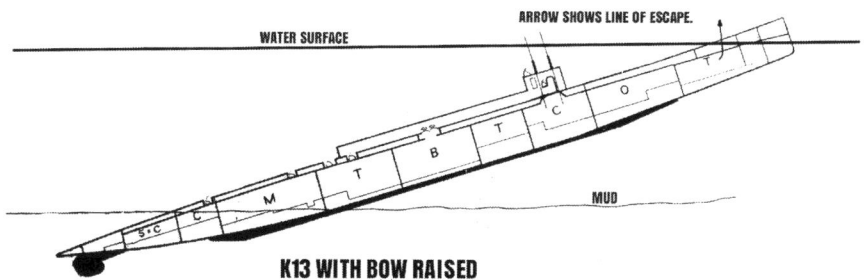

K13 WITH BOW RAISED

K13 WITH HER BOW HAVING BEEN RAISED TO THE LOCH'S SURFACE.

Both Mitchell and Herbert felt the next step for those above the water, was to cut a hole (between frames 17 & 18) through the bow with an oxy-acetylene torch. But Captain Young, the naval salvage expert was opposed to the plan, feeling that it was a bad idea and instead that they should look to carry on with the lifting of the *K13,* until her torpedo tubes were clear of water. An executive of Fairfield's added his voice, fearing that cutting with a flame would only serve to ignite any gas that must surely by now have built up inside the hull. But Captain Bartelott ended the debate and instructed that Mitchell go ahead and order the use of the oxy-acetylene torch. As the men had argued about the wisdom of using the tool, a lorry from Shandon had arrived on the scene carrying a cargo of rescue gear which had been manufactured through the night and the morning at the Fairfield's yard.

It was at 14:00 that the *Thrush's* chief engineer commenced the task of cutting through the outer hull. But shortly after the torches flame sliced into the casings metal, a fire broke out on the *Thrush* destroying in the process the equipment. New gear now had to be rushed from Shandon before the work could resume once more and a lorry was dispatched on the urgent errand. While the new equipment was on route to the scene, a crewman onboard the K13 reported that he could smell something odd. Maybe gas? With the crewman's claim, the interior of the 'K' boat became filled with crewmen sniffing the atmosphere. Some could smell the 'gas', while others found nothing.

Petty Officer Moth had for some time been the man stationed under the pipeline, from where he passed messages to and fro. He had only just been telling Herbert of his concern at the crews growing tension and unease. Moth choose the moments prior to the 'gas' report to go to the toilet and whilst he was 'indisposed' he heard someone shout through the pipe *"we're getting chlorine gas, Captain"*. The claim not unnaturally caused panic on the surface and it was calculated they now had barely 30 minutes to affect a rescue. But without the replacement torch it was figured that there remained no other option but to resume the hazardous lifting procedure. Moth was furious and asked Professor Hillhouse for one of the three torches, so he could check the batteries under the deck plating. They were found to be dry and, on his discovery, Moth shouted up the pipe *"Captain there is no gas down here. We are all right.* Please *ignore the earlier message. One or two of the lads are a bit jumpy, that's all"*. A much-relieved Herbert shouted back "thank god" and ordered the lifting to be stopped. The episode and panic were a symptom of how frayed the men's nerves were becoming after so long trapped within the 'K' boat. They needed to be free of the boat (and her jinx), as soon as was achievable .

By 15:00 the replacement equipment had arrived on the scene and the chief engineer of the *Thrush*, with the water of Gareloch lapping around his feet started cutting a hole two-foot square within the forecastle of *K13*. Herbert yelled down the tube that the job would take only 20 minutes to cut into the pressure hull and then they could start to escape the dark, damp, interior of the submarine. But as they cut away a piece of the hull, water was found to be filling the space between the outer and the pressure hull. With the news relayed down the pipe, the crew recommenced bailing with the two trusty buckets.

While some bailed the water out, others started to pull away both the wood and machinery equipment from the area where the hole was expected to appear. After so many hours inactivity, *K13* was transformed into a hive of action. For an hour the submariners bailed, but in the haste, no one thought to check if the four valves that accessed the flooded space were in fact closed. No matter how fast or how long they bailed, the level of the water remained unchanged. As time passed and as they bailed the crew within the *K13* were impatient and frustrated that the water level stubbornly refused to drop. It was Herbert who called down asking the crew if the valves were open or closed, while the Thrush's crew prepared a malleable material to block the valve which must surely be jammed open. The hole being cut through into the hull was a bare six inches above the lochs water level and with every minute the tide continued to rise, making time critically limited. Moth went forward in company with Mclean to check on the 4 valves. He found all the valves to A1 and B1 were jammed wide open, although they had the appearance of being closed. They were quickly shut. Once closed the bailing was resumed and the water level finally started to drop.

One of the barges had rigged a suction pipe running from the engine room and it was lowered through the now completed hole and into the water between the two hulls. Once in place it quickly sucked away the water and by 20:00 the gap between K13's outer and inner hulls was finally dry. An Engineer could now climb down between the hulls and the oxy-acetylene torch was passed to him. As he commenced the final cut, the crew in the dark interior could see the red glow of the cutting flame as it melted its way through to them. They watched almost mesmerized as the red line expanded marking their 'door-way' to the surface. Lieutenant Singer who with the reversal of their fortunes had recovered from his depression, gave the order that the civilians should be the first out when the time had come. At 21:00 the hole was cut, and the world of the living could be seen through the opening. The exodus could commence.

The escape hole was a mere three inches above the current water level, but fortune now seem to favour the 'K' boat, as the tide had reached its peak and was in the process of ebbing. Arc lights from the small rescue flotilla pushed the darkness of the night away from the scene that was unfolding on the Scottish loch. The first survivor to emerge through the hole was aided from above by Herbert and his appearance brought cheers that rang across the water, reaching out to the onlookers along the shoreline. Herbert helped each man ascend from the submarines interior and each new person brought a fresh round of cheering from his rescuers. As the men emerged from the dark depths into the bright floodlit world, they were led across a gangway of planks and onto the waiting Thrush. One of the Admiralty Overseers, in his white overalls, emerged carrying one of the three torches, a notebook in his breast pockets and his gloves in his hand. He looked as if he was merely emerging from a tank in his shipyard, having conducted another routine inspection. The inner exit hole through which the men crawled was a mere 18-inches square and the bigger members of the 'K' boats crew had to be pulled through the gap, but desperation is a great motivator and each man made it through. Moth recounted:

"What a beautiful night it was and what a treat it was to breathe the fresh air once more. There was not a breath of wind and the water was as calm as a mill pond. Everywhere there was a blaze of electric light and we could see the small rowing boots taking the men ashore.

I am sure there was an extra cheer for me as I came out of the hole, for I was very well known to the whole of the crews of E50 and E51, in fact quite a few of these men I had put through their course of submarine training. The Coxswain of E51 was one time my Second Coxswain when I was Coxswain of C24, so you can guess he was especially pleased to see me. He told me he thought I must have been one of the unlucky ones, when so many come out and yet I hadn't made my appearance.

I was now helped into a boat and was taken ashore and then we were all helped to walk to Shandon Hydro where we spent the night and best part of the next day. Everything that was possible for human hands to do, was done for us and after having a bath and a cup of beef tea, I went to bed and slept.

I think everyone slept the sleep of the just that night, I myself can remember nothing from the time my head touched the pillow until I was awakened by a pleasant faced maid. The sun was streaming in on me and I had to shake my scattered brains together before I could remember what had happened. She told me that there was hot water for my use, but they were waiting below for breakfast.

I hurriedly dressed and went below where I found the best part of the survivors having breakfast and they didn't look much the worse for their trying experience, except that our clothes which we had worn in the boat were all we had and you can guess it was in a pretty pickle.

The staff at the Hydro did their best for us and borrowed clothes and we didn't look much like "Navy Men" after they had finished with us. I had some very pleasant memories of kindnesses which I received from time to time from the staff at "Shandon Hydro", as well as from the good folk who live on the Gareloch side. I did the trials of two boats in the Gareloch at later dates, so you can guess I became a well-known figure there"

Singer, with the aid of Hillhouse and William Wallace a representative of an Edinburgh boiler firm carried out a final check to confirm that all the watertight doors, forward of the beam torpedo room were closed. The last man off the boat at 22:00 and after 57 hours trapped was the first officer, Lieutenant Singer. The K13 now lay with her bows above the water, deserted of the living, but crewed by her dead, thirty-two remained onboard at the places they had fallen. Thirty-two men who had lost their lives to the 'K' boat jinx. The next day Moth recounted:

.

"...after breakfast was over, I was employed, with the Captain and we were very busy letting the Admiralty and also our Depot know, who were lost and who were saved. I had quite a long yarn with the Captain and he told me, that we would all have to go south to Fort Blockhouse. It was decided that I should take the crew back to Glasgow that afternoon and get things squared up there so that we could go on leave on the Friday night.

We left Shandon by train and there was a great many of the staff of the Hydro to see us off. When we got to Helensburgh there was some very distressing scenes for the news had spread like wildfire and some of the relatives of the deceased men met us. I was very pleased to get in the train again and I must say I heaved a sigh of relief when I got to my lodgings at Govan.

The next morning, we were employed in getting the effects of the unfortunate men together, as well as our own and this was then despatch to the Submarine Depot at Gosport. That night we were sent on ten days leave, at the expiration of which we were to return to our depot.

THE BOW OF THE K13 IN HER WIRE CRADLE BETWEEN THE TWO BARGES. SOURCE IWM

> *Before going on leave, Herbert (our Captain), had the whole of the survivors of the crew mustered and he read a telegram of congratulations from the King, who had also sent a telegram of thanks and congratulations to the men who had worked so hard and had helped to save our lives."*

As the survivors had savoured the breakfast they thought they would never see and come to terms with the fact that they had escaped what should have been their deaths, families and loved ones of those poor soul's less fortunate received a knock on the door and a telegram.

> *"C. E ADMIRALTY S.W.*
>
> *1st February 1917.*
>
> *Madam,*
>
> *My Lords Commissioners of the Admiralty have*

this day received an intimation that your father, Mr.F.Hole, Assistant Admiralty Overseer, has, owing to an accident, lost his life while on board one of his Majesty's ships, I am commanded by Their Lordships to express to you their regret at receiving this intelligence and their sympathy in your bereavement.

I am, Madam,

Your obedient servant

(Signed) W. GRAHAM, GREENE.

Mrs, Neath.

174 Cross Loan Road.

GOVAN".

In these days before 24-hour news cover and social media, the relatives would most likely have heard nothing of the disaster (unless they lived in Govan or its surrounding area) and the telegram would have been the bearer of news from out of the blue. Maybe they knew their loved ones where 'working-up' a new submarine and assumed that for now they were safe, but the small envelope with its single sheet telegram tore that illusion to shreds and destroyed their world's.

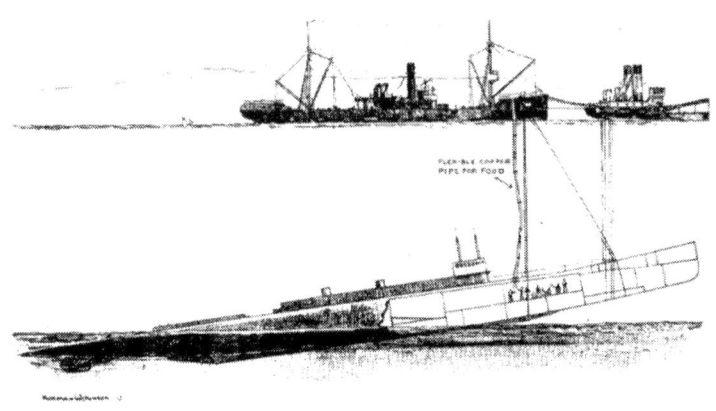

THE K13 IS BROUGHT TO THE SURFACE. THE LENGTH OF STERN THAT SANK INTO THE MUD & WOULD GO ON TO CAUSE SO MANY PROBLEMS LATER, IS ILLUSTRARED.(SOURCE:WARSHIP WEDNESDAY: OCT. 2, 2019, HMS UNLUCKY KILLER NO. 13/WWW.LASTSTANDONZOMBIEISLAND.COM)

At the court of enquiry, it looked as if the Admirals had decided before hand to hold a dead man accountable for the disaster, rather than allow any criticism of the 'K' class. The 'escape goat' was to be the boats Engineer Lieutenant Lane, even though the evidence showed he was the only man to have stated concerns over the operation of the boats mushroom valves. He was also the only officer to despatch a crewman to look for leaks in the boiler room and alert the Captain as to the flooding. If he had raised the alarm a few seconds earlier, the submarine could have surfaced before it was too heavy, and he would have been a hero. But instead in death he was to take the full blame for both the disaster and the heavy loss of life.

The court of enquiry found that four of the 37-inch diameter ventilators had been left open during the dive and that indicator lights in the control room had showed them as open. The engine room hatch was also found to be open, surely the route by which Lane and Steel had made their ill-fated escape? The Admiralty gave orders, following Goodhart's death, that all the upper hatches of the conning towers be fitted with a second hatch beneath it.

On the 19th February 1917 a letter from the court was despatch to Captain and Superintendent Barttelot, Clyde District:

Fairfields and Company

19th February 1917

ENGINEERING CO., LIMITED.

19th February 1917

Captain Brien Barttelot.R.

Captain Superintendent, Clyde District.

Sir,

We have the honour to report that in compliance with your memo of 15th February 1917 we have this day held a full and careful investigation into the cause of the accident to H.M submarine "K.13" and the subsequent foundering in the Gareloch.

It would appear from the evidence that

(a) the foundering was solely due to boiler intakes being open.

(b) the electrical indicator showed that the intakes were open.

(c) Engineer lieutenant Lane believed the intakes were closed.

(d) there is no statement to support this belief of lieutenant Lane.

It is possible that lieutenant Rideal was mistaken in supposing that lieutenant lane was referring to the intake indicators, but there seems no doubt that he believed the boiler room intakes to be closed and that he reported his department shut off for diving.

The evidence clearly shows that the intake indicators had been working correctly and there is no reason to suppose that they did not do so on the last occasion

We are therefore of the opinion that engineer Lieutenant Lane was solely responsible for the accident.

We consider that Lieutenant Commander Herbert was fully justified in believing that the submarine was all shut off for diving, but me would suggest that as a check on the electrical indicator it would seem desirable to make use of the voice pipe also.

In conclusion we suggest that the names of

Mr. Frederick William Searle. Admiralty Overseer

Mr. William McLean

Mr E. J. Skinner

and Mr F. Bullen Managers at Fairfield be submitted to Their Lordships for commendation on account of their able services which undoubtedly contributed materially towards the saving of the survivors.

We have the honour to be,

Sir,

Your obedient Servants.

Searle was to be prompted to the position of Established Assistant Constructor in recognition of his services during the incident.

On the 1st March 1919 The Times, much to the Admiralties concern published an account of the incident and the article was the first mention of the disaster in a newspaper.

THE TIMES, SATURDAY, MARCH 1, 1919.

STORY OF K 13 REVEALED.

CREW SAVED BY OFFICERS' GALLANTRY.

In November last year an account was published in *The Times* of the sinking of a British submarine in Gareloch, near the Clyde, and of the thrilling rescue of 42 out of the 73 people (including naval contractors and men from the yard where the vessel was built) who went down with her. It was then stated that the late Captain Goodhart, D.S.O., in an attempt to open the conning tower and float to the surface so that he could give the rescue party information as to the condition of the people below, struck his head against a support of the tower and was instantly killed, and that "his example was followed by another ship's commander on board who was fortunate enough to reach the surface and was caught and saved by the salvage men."

It can now be said that the submarine was the K 13, and that the officer who got clear through the conning tower was Commander Godfrey Herbert, D.S.O., in command of the ship. Commander Herbert and Captain Goodhart went into the tower together but the intention was that only the latter should attempt the task of reaching the surface. The plan formed was that with the aid of high-pressure air bottles Captain Goodhart should be projected through the tower and shot into the water. To achieve this he dressed in very light clothes. Unfortunately, there was no means of estimating the air pressure established, and when the lid of the tower was opened the officer was hurled upward at terrific speed.

Commander Herbert, who was more heavily attired, and had intended to remain in the submarine, was also forced up, but at a rate which enabled him to reach the water safely. After his rescue he gave information which led eventually to the release of the imprisoned men he had left behind. He gave the greatest possible assistance to the salvage workers engaged in the rescue operations, and worked indefatigably himself, his knowledge of the ship being largely instrumental in saving the lives of those below.

PREVIOUS PAGE: THE TIMES 1ST MARCH 1919.

◆ ◆ ◆

1: Hawser is a nautical term for a thick cable or rope used in mooring or towing a ship. A hawser passes through a hawsehole.

2: "Riggers in the shipbuilding environment are responsible for the lifting and moving of heavy and bulky objects, whether aboard ships or around the shipyard ". (www: ingalls.hunting-toningalls.com)

CHAPTER FOUR.
SALVAGE.

*"Without Any Doubt Whatsoever, A Fast Battle
Fleet Which Can Always Be Accompanied By
Submarines Under All Circumstances Would Possess
An Overwhelming Fighting Advantage". A*

Admiral Fisher

The morning of the 1st February 1917 brought an almost peaceful scene to the beautiful waters of Gareloch. The men rescued from the *K13* were enjoying breakfast at the Shandon Hydro. Lieutenant-Commander Kenneth Michell had departed in the E50, returning to her yard of construction on the Clyde, John Brown. The cause of the past few day's activities, the *K13* had not seemingly moved since the men had crawled from out of her dark damp interior. The portion of her bow that stood proud of the water was supported by a series of cables and on either beam she was moored to a barge. Captain Frederick William Young, the Naval Salvage Advisor in an effort to try to raise the bow further out of the water, had ordered additional cables to be drawn under the submarine's bow. The support of cable was there, he hoped, to hold her up until she could be fully raised. Young had also ordered more air to be pumped into her to increase her buoyancy and eventually to ease the task of lifting her. Things looked hopeful on that Thursday morning.

THE RESURFACED K13, PRIOR TO HER SECOND PLUNGE TO THE SEABED, SOURCE IWM

Yesterday before the final man had crawled through that small hole to the world of light and air, a tour was made of the compartments they had access to, and all the watertight doors were shut. But already with the boat silent and empty, the cold Scottish waters were seeping in from between the watertight bulkheads and slowly once more returning to invade the K13's compartments. The water having been held at bay by the heavy doors, sought and found other ways past. The pumps fought to hold back the slow but remorseless invasion, but it was a battle they could only ever really lose. Slowly the water seeped in and gradually the submarines weight increased, bringing a downward pressure on the straining cables.

As the weight increased both the *Thrush* (1) and the trawler were forced in response to slacken the cables that held the K13. The two hoppers each in turn supported the six 4½ inch cables that ran beneath the raised bow and a 7½ inch cable was planned to be added to the wire cradle. But despite his efforts the lochs waters continued to seep into the hull slowly and remorselessly. It was rapidly becoming too much and at around 18:00 the quiet of the loch was torn apart by a loud explosion as the weight of the *K13* tore the bollards from out of the supporting hoppers and the 'K' boat, free of her cable support, dropped once more, 12 fathoms (72 feet/21.94 mtrs) to the bottom of the loch, taking her dead with her.

With the *K13* once more on the bottom of the loch what had been a mission to re-float the stern portion of the boat was now vastly more complicated. The entire length of the monstrously huge submarine would need to be filled with pressurized air and pumped dry. Young was quickly aware that he would need extra resources and the salvage vessel *Ranger* (2) was already on route. The admiralty issued orders to the iron hulled dockyard tug and lift craft *Alligator* (3) to depart from France and make her way at speed to Gareloch. But she was to be delayed until (unspecified) damage to her could be made good. The salvage vessel *Hughli* (4) however arrived on scene that day with a barge in tow, a tug and a supply of lifting cables. Captain Young (the man in charge of the operations) dispatched several telegrams to the Admiralty requesting that lifting vessels be sent to Gareloch as soon as was possible. On the second day of February the divers entered the conning tower and recovered the body of Commander Francis Herbert Heaveningham Goodhart from the place of his tragic death. Sadly, although the Commanders body had been recovered, the remains of 32 of the crew remained in the submarines stern section, beyond reach, for now.

Two days later a telegram was dispatched to the Admiralty by Captain Young briefing the Sea Lords of the depth the K13's hull rested at on a high tide:

- *"No 1 fore end 56 feet".*
- *"No 2 Midship 61 feet".*
- *"No 3 Midship 72 feet"*
- *"No 4 aft 77 feet".*

The salvagers in an effort to retain the K13 at her current position and prevent her bow sinking further, added an 8 inch cable to the two Clyde hoppers that held either end of the wire cradle, which now once more kept the 'K' boats bow off the loch and its mud , which would become such a problem in the coming weeks.

On the 5th, having been repaired, the Alligator finally departed from Boulogne with a *"good supply"* of cables on board and made her way northwards along the English and Welsh west coasts. On the same day beneath the waters of Gareloch, two of the divers, working from a diving bell, managed to secure the first air hose to the K13's compartment number 18. With that first hose secure, the supply of pressurized air was turned on at 15:00, (at 50 lb per sq. inch). As the pressurized air was forced down the pipe, the pumps extracted the compartments water at "full bore". As the water came out and the air replaced it, the forward section of the *K13's* hull rested in a cradle constructed of 16 wires, but that number was increased with the addition of a further 6 new cables of "50 fathoms". As the slow battle to bring the submarine to the surface was waged, the salvagers waited for the arrival of the salvage vessel, *Alligator.* But two vessels in the meanwhile joined the growing squadron of salvage ships, the former screw gun boat and now salvage vessel *Hughli* arrived that day with the 'lift craft' *Dromedary* (5) in tow at 9:00. However due to poor planning or the rush to reach Gareloch, *Dromedary* had arrived on the scene with no lift cables on board. In addition, the *Hughli* was low on coal and was reduced to burning timber to maintain steam in her boilers. A trawler was ordered alongside and the crew's transferred 10 tons of coal to tide the *Hughli* over. In support of the operations Fairfield's was also in the process of sending extra barges, anchors, air piping and a wide selection of other tools. A Foreman Rigger named Hyland in company with 4 riggers had been despatched from Boulogne, but they were ordered in error to Liverpool. At their arrival on the Mersey, they were redirected to the Clyde's waters.

On the following morning the forward bow room was finally pumped dry and work on new series of connections to the hatch to number 18 compartment, (which held the officers' quarters), were underway. In addition, the divers discovered that number 9 compartment was found to be dry. As the flooded compartments content of water was replaced by pressurized air the bow slowly lifted higher, creeping back towards the surface. But as the bow rose, the weight of the water still trapped on board and combined with the sheer bulk weight of the *K13* herself pushed the stern further into the mud. It was hoped that if the mud could be removed then more cables could be passed underneath, where the drop keel had been, before it had been abandoned in *K13's* frantic attempt to reach the surface back in January.

The divers having successfully connected two 3/4-inch air connectors to the number 18 compartment started the process to feed air into the compartments on the 6th. As the air was forced in, the water was pushed out through a 3½ copper flexible pipe. In addition, a 2½ inch pipe was successfully connected to the ammunition "hand up". By this stage the growing armada had been increased with the addition of the arrival of the Alligator as well as a tug and a barge. With the Dromedary now on the scene one of the Clyde hoppers was released to return to the Clyde. The *Hughli* had in the meanwhile been dispatched to Greenock where she was busy replenishing her coal bunkers.

Divers were in the interim working at the air connectors that were linked to the control room. They had also managed to close some troublesome vents that fed into the boiler room. The covers that had been constructed for the vents were finally ready to be fitted. On the same day Herbert made a visit to the site, where Captain Young briefed him on the events to date and the plans to complete the refloating of the *K13*. Herbert left, happy with how things were proceeding with his boat.

The day after the Lieutenant-Commander's visit, (on the 8th) the second Clyde hoppers, (the 'no 7') was released back to the Clyde and on the 9th the divers partially closed vents to the boiler room by the use of screw jacks.

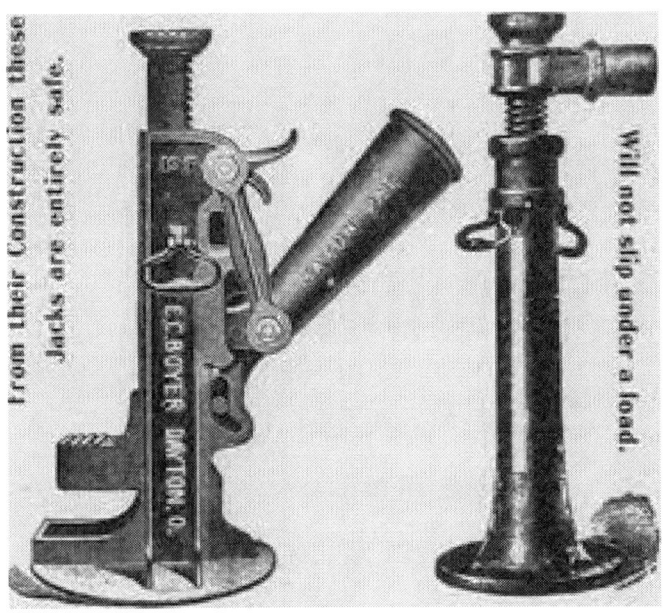

PREVIOUS PAGE. LOCOMOTIVE JACKS, WHICH WOULD NOT HAVE BEEN DISSIMILAR TO THOSE USED AT THE K13'S SALVAGE.

Two days later the divers discovered that the depth of the Lochs water amidships of the submarine was off to greater depth for them to work safely from the diving bell. Another setback was the discovery that the pneumatic drill they were using was, due to the high pressure, leaking lubricant. On shore the salvagers had approached the Clyde Navigation Trust who agreed to make a loan of a Grab Hopper to undertake the clearance of the mud that covered the stern portion of the *K13*. By this stage in the operation a pipe had been connected to the Control room and now air was being pumped in under pressure, as the water was forced out. Twenty-four hours later the divers managed to successfully close one of the boiler room vent and commenced the process of "Jacking down" the others.

The *Avenger* finally arrived in Gareloch at 13:00 and as with the *Alligator,* the new arrival was moored aside the Dromedary. Once the *Alligator* was secure, the salvage teams set to work preparing four 9-inch wires for use with lifting the bow. At the same time divers used the diving bell to try (and fail) in drilling through the torpedo hatch. It was decided after the failure to make use of the explosive Gelignite (in small quantities) to destroy a stubborn valve, which would then allow a pipe to access into the flooded hull. The salvagers had also managed to secure a 4-inch wire under the forward end, abaft of the hydroplanes. But as good as progress was with the hull connections, the divers faced a new problem with the lochs muddy bottom restricting their ability to open the external tanks. As divers and mud gave battle, the *Avenger* was despatch to Greenock.

On the 13th an air connection was finally made, through the boats Siren, to the torpedo room. The connection had required the lower part of the stubborn siren to be blown away with a small controlled Gelignite explosion . In addition, the day saw the external vents 7, 8 and 9 cleared. The divers were also successful in the removal of the manhole cover off tank number 8 for an air connection to be made.

Also on the 13th The Liverpool Salvage Association despatched for the attention of Captain Young:
- 3 lengths of hand hose, with couplings complete,

- 4 new diving dresses
- 9 pair drawers (for divers)
- 3 pair stockings (for divers)
- 4 pair cuffs (for divers)

While the siren had been frustrating the divers, others made efforts to raise one of the folded funnels. Finally, a charge was used to blow off the hinges as they had proven to be too heavy to disconnect conventionally. One hinge was shattered, but the charge on the remaining hinge misfired twice. A third attempt was abandoned as it was by this stage growing too dark to work. The Divers also found that their access to the engine room was restricted by one of the boats 4-inch guns and it would need to be disconnected and hoisted away to permit sufficient space for them to work in. But the day brought some success when the Manhole cover on external tanks 8-10 was removed and a new drill machine from Pneumatic Tool Company finally arrived on the scene.

The 15th was a productive day, with the obstructive 4-inch gun hoisted clear and the two funnels removed. But problems were never far off and now it was found the lochs mud made a hose connection to the engine hatch impossible. A request for the *Clyde Priestman* was made, her grabs would easily lift the mud clear. It was also planned to use a submersible pump to suck the mud away. The day also saw the insurance underwriters being refused access to the site by the Admiralty, which while it was unusual, the goal was to keep the *K13* was a 'secret'. They were told:

> *"If underwriters apply to Captain superintendent permission may be granted to a proper and trustworthy representative of underwriters of the "K"*

vessel on promises of secrecy to visit the wreck of
the wreck. His visit should be in the company of cap-
tain Young..."

By the 17th 20-feet length of steam hose had been lowered
down to the *K13* and connected to the engine room door by
the divers, who were working from their bell. Twenty-four
hours later the divers reported that all the compartments as
far as the motor room were now under their control. Slowly
they were winning the battle against the flood waters that
held the *K13* prisoner. Now only the crew space waters were
left to be dealt with.

A 12-inch steam pipe was run down to the submarine from
the Ranger, as well as an 80-foot length suction hose. The
hose was set to the task of pumping the mud off the aft deck
and once the deck was clear of mud, the salvager waited to
see if the exposed deck plates would silt up once more. The
divers were having trouble finding a path through the maze
of pipes in the motor room and the crew space, for their drill
to get through to allow the connection of an air pipe. To try
and see what they were dealing with the Chief diver Lambert
and lieutenant Kay travelled to the Fairfield's yard on the
Clyde to inspect the 'K' boats under construction there.

Over the next few days, the mud was slowly pumped clear
from a depth of three feet. A 4-inch "submersible" pump was
lowered down to the *K13's* stern to stir the mud up for the
12-inch hose to then extract.

The diver working on the crew quarter hatch found that the
space was too cramped to work within. But despite that,
there was a steadily growing confidence that if things con-

tinued as they were, the *K13* would be ready to be brought back to the surface towards the week's end or at the latest, early the following week.

By the 21st 25 feet of the aft portion of the hull was finally clear of the mud, to a depth of 8 to 10 feet. The divers discovered a considerable leak coming through one of the *K13's* bulkheads, but it was hoped that as more air was pumped into the compartments, so the bows would lift higher. But despite the optimism there remained a large amount of water to be removed from the stern portion of the hull. But that part of the boat was still firmly in the grip of the mud.

After several attempts, on the 23rd an air connection was finally made to the motor room and it was successfully tested. As the mud was pumped away the freshwater link became free and a hose joining was made to it, as well as the aft crew spaces.

It was found the next day that the divers were suffering from a form of compression sickness and the men were now ordered into a decompression chamber on their return to the surface. Through the passing days the pump worked remorselessly to remove the mud from the stern portion of the hull and it was hoped that by tomorrow the Thrush would join them, bringing a 12" pipe to join with the muddy battle.

By the 26th the divers work was finally all but done. Now the crews could turn their full concentration onto the mud that still refused to let the stern and its hydroplanes come free.

The 28th February was a day of air pipes blowing air in and pumps sucking mud to the surface barges. With each barge full the *K13* came closer to becoming free and buoyant enough to float once more. By 19:00 the number 9 fore torpedo room, number 10 officers' quarters, number 20 the control room and part of the beam torpedo room were all now free of water. The boiler, turbine and motor rooms were still having water extracted at "full bore". At 20:00 the air pressure was lowered to 35 lbs per square inch until 20:00 when it was raised once more. But a heavy leakage was noticed, forcing the pressure to be reduced once again. Once it was lowered the divers investigated the source of the leak and found some of the pipes to be chaffed. After they were brought to the surface, replaced and reconnected there no further issues. On the shore of the loch, off the K13's bows, in preparation for the next phase of the operation, anchors were laid out, with 30-ton purchases attach to wires. Two tugs were also placed on standby ready to lend a help in pulling the hull out of mud when it was clear.

By the 17th 20 foot length of steam hose had been lowered down to the K13 and connected to the engine room door by the divers, who were working from their bell. Twenty four hours later the drivers reported that all the compartments as far as motor room were now under their control. Slowly they were winning the battle against the flood waters that held the K13 prisoner. Now only the crew space waters was left to be dealt with.

On the a 12 inch steam pipe run down to the submarine from the from Ranger, as well as an 80 feet length suction hose. The hose was set to the task of pumping the mud off the aft deck. Once the deck was clear of mud, the salvager waited to see if the exposed deck plates would silt up once more. The divers were having trouble finding a path through the maze of pipes in motor room and crew space for their drill to get through and allow the connection of an air pipe. To try and see what they were dealing with the Chief diver Lambert and lieutenant Kay travelled to the Fairfields yard on the Clyde to inspect the 'K' boats under construction there.

Over the next few days the mud was slowly pumped clear from a depth of 3 feet. A 4" submersible pump was lowered down to the K13's stern in an effort to stir the mud up for the 12 inch hose to then extract.

The diver working on the crew quarter hatch found that the space was to cramped to work within, but despite that there was a steadily growing confidence was growing that if things continued as they were the K13 would be ready to be brought back to the surface towards the week's end or at the latest, early the following week.

By the 21st 25 feet of the aft portion of the hull was finally clear of the mud, to a depth of 8 to 10 feet. The divers discovered a considerable leak coming through one of the K13's bulkhead, but it was hoped that as more air was pumped in to the compartments, so the bows would lift higher. But despite the optimism there still remained a large amount of water to be removed from the stern portion of the hull. But that part of the hull was still firmly in the gripe of the mud.

After several attempts, on the 23rd an air connection was finally made to the motor room and it was successfully tested. As the mud was pumped away a connection the fresh water connection became free and a hose connection was made to it, as well as the aft crew spaces.

If it was found the next day that the divers were suffering from a form of compression sickness and the men were now ordered into re-compression chamber on their return to the surface. Through the passing days the pump worked remorselessly to remove the mud from the stern portion of the hull and it was hoped that by tomorrow that the Thrush would join then bringing a 12" pipe to join with the muddy battle.

By the 26th the divers work was finally but done. Now they crews could turn their full concentration onto the mud that still refused to let the stern and its hydroplanes free.

The 28th February was a day of air pipes blowing air in and pumps sucking mud to the surface barges. With each barge full the K13 came closer to bring free and buoyant enough to float once more. By 19:00 the number 9 fore torpedo room, number 10 officers quarters, number 20 the control room and part of beam torpedo room were all now free of water. The boiler, turbine and motor rooms were still having water extracted at "full bore". At 20:00 the air pressure was lowered to 35lbs per square inch until 20:00 when it was raised once more. But a heavy leakage was noticed, forcing the pressure to be reduced once more again. Once it was lowered the divers investigated the source of the leak and found some of the pipes to be chaffed. Once they were brought to the surface, replaced and reconnected the was raised once more with no further issues.. On the shore of the loch, off the K13's bows, in preparation for the next phase of the operation anchors were laid out, with 30 ton purchases attach to wires. Two tugs were also placed on standby ready to lend help in pulling the hull out of mud when it was clear.

It was discovered on the 4th March that as the water level steadily dropped the air pressure was increasing. Doors and decks now started leaking, particularly the funnel covers. The hatches were "shored" down and throughout the hull the only large body of water onboard was within the crew space. But still the hull was stuck fast in the mud. Heaving on anchors ashore was found to be of no use, not even with the tugs aid. While the stern remained gripped by the mud, the bow had lifted by inches bringing the forward hydro planes two feet clear of the water and extra anchors were laid out. The *Ranger* now joined the tugs and all three vessels and anchors strained at the hull. But the mud refused to let the boats stern come free, despite 60 foot of the bow now being clear of the lochs water at the days end. The external tanks were by now all but empty and most of the forward hull free of water. With the hulls reluctance to come free, a fear was growing that with the contained internal air pressure, the hatches would blow, and water would once more flood into the boat's interior.

The surfaced portion of the bow was attached by wire cables to the *Alligator* and *Dromedary* to prevent the stubborn *K13* from falling back. It was planned to shift more of the mud and use both the *Thrush* and *Ranger* over the stern end, but that plan was rejected as being considered unsafe for the hull and generally just not a good idea. The use of grab or bucket dredgers was unfeasible given the depth the stern rested at. It was decided instead to make use of a dredgers suction pump to lengthen the reach of the suction hose. But now the weather stepped in to delay that operation. The site was battling strong south west winds and heavy snow brought any work to all but a halt. On the 6th despite the weather lashing the workings the dumping unremitting and the bow continued to inch up, until both the very fore edge of the conning tower and the fore W/T mast was visible. But as much as the bow moved, the stern was still a prisoner of the lochs mud. The 7th March brought a stop to all work on site and overnight a gale battered the scene on the loch and the lighters pressurized air pipes and steam pipes were unconnected. But by morning the weather was moderating, and the air supply could be turned back on, finally clearing the aft crew space of water, allowing the mast to show. Divers descended at 16:30 to test the external tanks numbers '6' and '7' which by this stage should be free of water, unless it had seeped in once more. The goal now was to obtain the loan of two sand suction hoppers and to clear the upper surface of the ballast tanks. Divers, once the weather had moderated enough, drilled through the port and starboard external tanks, numbers 7 and 8. Three tanks were found to be disappointingly still full of pure Scottish loch waters. The fourth was only three quarters full. The divers tapped the tanks and the waters were sucked out through a fresh pipe connection, with the hope of gaining an extra 100 tons of buoyancy. The *Ranger* was moored over the stern and a 12-inch steam pipe was lowered down to the aft portion of the K13. The divers reported the mud to be of a 12-foot depth from the Sampson posts aft. It was hoped by Sunday that with the tanks empty, the *Thrush* and *Ranger* lifting and the anchors pulling, the stern would finally come free. The files also imply that the hull was raised and lowered through this phase to try and break the muds suction. On a requested visit by the underwriters, they was told there was nothing to see as the hull was now below the water level.

On the 8th March the Admiralty (Sir Douglas Brownrigg, formerly of Fairfield's ship builders, now Chief Censors at the Admiralty) issued an order (originating from Captain Young) prohibiting any civilians from boarding what they saw as a 'top secret' boat for any reason. Even Fairfield's employees were prohibited on board and the underwriters were not to be responsible for either the salvage or refit costs as the ship now belonged to the navy . By the 12th March the correspondence between the insurers (London Salvage Association) and the admiralty staff on site refer to the *K13* as *K22* as well *"no 522"*.

By the 11th the hull had risen to being "upright" and the after stern crew space manhole covers on the casing could be lifted. The divers could not enter through the newly opened hatch due to an unseen obstruction, but the stern remained stuck even as more mud was pumped away. The lifting craft *3* and *4*, (both busy at Dover raising *TB 24*) were offered to Captain Young, if the operations in Dover were abandoned. The *Hughli* would be available to offer towing after the 16th, but despite the urgency, there was a general shortage of tugs. The site was battling freezing conditions and one telegram reports the drills freezing up.

The Admiralty was advised on the 12th March that both the divers from the Thrush were now under the doctor's supervision. Lambert had been suffering from pressure, but he was on the path to recovery once more.

K13 WAS RAISED AND RETURNED TO FASLANE, RETURNING TO SERVICE
AFTER A SEVEN-MONTH REFIT I WM.

After 43 days on the muddy bottom, on the 15th March, despite every effort by Captain Young and his teams, at a time of
her own choosing, the stern came free of the muds vice like
grip and *K13* returned fully to the surface as unexpectedly as
she had gone down. At 14:32 the Admiralty Superintendent
Glasgow telegrammed the admiralty and the C-inC Rosyth,
two much sought for words, *"K13 floated"* . She surfaced to
20 feet 6 inches aft and 19 feet 6 inches forward. Searle the
Admiralty Overseer had examined the interior and found it
in the main to be free of water. He also reported that all the
hatches aft of the engine room were found to be open, Now
with the *K13* afloat, all the wires cradling the hull, the pipes
and the hoses could be disconnected while the anchors and
moorings could be recovered, but both the pumping and
draining continued. It was expected to surrender the *K13* to
Fairfields on Monday 18th March. The *Thrush* was ordered to
Greenock to offload her salvage equipment onto the lighter,
from where the *Ranger* would collect them. All the Admiralty salvage vessels were ordered to be over hauled and to
have their boilers cleaned, while the crew members that

could be released were to be granted leave.

PREVIOUS PAGE. *THE K13 MEMORIAL*
"SACRED TO THE MEMORY OF THOSE NAMED WHO LOST THEIR LIVES IN H.M.
SUBMARINE K13 IN THE GARELOCH, 29TH JANUARY 1917. ERECTED BY THE SHIP'S
COMPANY OF H.M. SUBMARINE DEPOT FORT BLOCKHOUSE, GOSPORT." {6}

The *Thrush h*owever remained moored alongside on her port anchor and all cables out. An anchor and wire were off her port quarter, one anchor astern and two anchors ashore.Two wires ran ashore and mooring ropes were secured to the trees. In addition she was supplying air to blow out the *K13's* external. She was in company with the Thrush and the Douglas, Ranger having departed the day prior. On the 17th the managing director of Fairfields visited the submarine but stipulated she required additional buoyance before she could be safely towed to the shipyard. The afternoon of the 15th saw the sad task of removing the dead from the 'K' boat commence and the last victim was brought ashore on the Friday morning. Twenty nine bodies were recovered, but after 45 days immersed in water, ten of the men were tragically unidentifiable. The men were laid to rest than same afternoon in Shandon, overlooking the scene of their death. Two bodies were missing, these most likely being the two men seen in the lochs waters by the hotel maid, Annie MacIntyre. The engine room was empty of bodies, but Lanes coat was found there and the hatches clips were undone.

CAPT SUPERINTENDANT W/T SIGNAL TO THE ADMIRATLY ADVISING
K13's DEAD HAVE BEEN RECOVERED.

On the 19th March the *K13* was lightened sufficiently to draw 16'3" forward and 17'3" aft. Two tugs were on route to take her upriver to the Clyde and the Fairfield's yard. But a change in the weather brought a postponement of the plan. Now only six wires were holding the vessel up.

On the 20th at high tide the two tugs eased her southward towards the loch's exit and she arrived on the 21st March at the Fairfield's yard where she was to be refitted. The *K13* and *K14* were to be the last submarines the yard was ever to build. Of the survivors many were never to serve in a submarine again and few if any of the civilians ever boarded one after their escape.

The *K13* having been repaired (at Fairfield's expense) was re-commissioned and renamed as *HMS K22* to sidestep the curse. But sailors are a superstitious breed and not so easily fooled. In a recognition of the entire saga and to avoid the risk of a repeat, the Admiralty were never again to allocate the number 13 to any submarine.

The Admiralty confirmed that all the costs incurred with the salvage operation were to be met by Fairfield's and their insurers. The Kew file provides us an insight into both the equipment and the costs the recovery had in part totalled:

"List of expenses incurred R.N factory Greenock in connection with salvage of submarine k13 in the Gareloch- February and March 1917

Use and wear and tear of diving launch. 1 hand pump, 1 power pump, air tubes, re-compression chamber and 3 diving dresses (one of which had to be replaced by a new one.

31 days at £2

£62.0s 0b

pay of chief gunner- 3 days £3.0s.0b

diving allowances paid to diver and assistant £56.13s.1b.

Subsistence allowances paid. 5s 0b.

Actual pay (including overtime) of 3 men £73.4s 7b

£195 2s 8b".

Payment to

- *Warnock bro (attendance of vessels etc) £360.0s0.b*
- *British marine salvage comp (dive gear etc) £35 3s 3b*
- *Mr David Budd (Labour etc) £2.8s 0b, (2018=£141.58)*
- *Cost of salvage work £195.2s.8b (2018=£11,511.34)*
- *Wages of depot artificers £130 2s 8b, (2018=£7,676.85),*
- *Other charges £65.0s.0.b (2018=£3,834.49),*
- *Total £195 2s 8b (2018=£11,511.34),*

The Kew files, among the pages arguing to who the different categories of payment should be directed or claimed from is a breakdown of ships and the dates they are employed.

- *Trawler Tay 29.1.17-24.3.17.*
- *Salvage vessel RFA Thrush 29.1.17-24.3.17.*
- *Clyde Conservancy barges 29.1.17-08.02.17 & 09.02.17*
- *S.S Ranger 30.01.17-21.03.17.*
- *L.C.1 (Alligator) 05.02.17-21.03.17.*
- *L.C.2 (Dromedary) 01.03.17-21.03.17.*
- *R.F.A Hughli 01.02.17-08.02.17. Towing L.C.1 at that time parent ship to HMS Ganges and former tug.*
- *Tug Avenger (hired and outfitted by Admiralty. Charged to Fairfields).*
- *Captain Young 29.1.17-22.3.17.*
- *Lieutenant-Commander Kay 29.1.17-20.3.17.*

1:THRUSH, cable ship, later salvage vessel, ex-Coastguard and Fishery Protection, C.76 (1914), X.56 (3.16). Launched 22.6.89 Scotts. 805 tons, 177(oa), 165(pp)x31x11ft. TE 1200ihp, 13kts. Armament: 4-4in (originally 6-4 in). Ex-1st class gunboat transferred to Coastguard 1906. Cable ship, based at Berehaven 1914-16, salvage vessel 1916. Wrecked 11.4.17 near Glenarm, Antrim.

2:RANGER. 1880 launched as the gunboat HMS Ranger 1892/3. She was sold to Liverpool Salvage Association and converted to a salvage vessel in 1904 converted to a salvage vessel named Linnet, Liverpool Salvage Association

3: ALLIGATOR lifting craft. Built 1897, 704grt. Large dumb barges with horned bows, normally working in pairs with wreck on cables between them. In service 15.2.16-10.11.20, renamed LC.1, 3.17.

4: HUGHLI, salvage vessel, W.82 (9.18). Built 1894 as tug, 513grt. In service from 23.2.15. Foundered 15.5.19 off Nieuport

5: DROMEDARY (2), lifting craft. Built 1897, 706grt. Large dumb barges with horned bows, normally working in pairs with wreck on cables between them. She was built by Russell & Company Port Glasgow, Yard No 422, in 1897 as a Steel Hopper Barge for Joseph Constant. Her displacement and dimensions were 706 tons and 167.8 ft x 35.5 ft x 13.2 ft. The ship had horned bows to take lifting cables. They operated in pairs, flooded down, attached their cables and then pumped out to lift the wreck. They were then towed to shallow waters. She was requisitioned on the 15th February 1917 by the Admiralty and converted into a Lifting Craft. In March 1917 she renamed LC.2 and returned to her pre-war owners on the 10th November 1920.

https://www.gracesguide.co.uk/Frederic_William_Young

6: K13's CASUALTY LIST: See appendix section.

CHAPTER FIVE: TRIALS AND TRIBULATIONS.

(JANUARY-JULY 1917)

"I Say Sir, My Ends Diving. Whats Your End Doing?"

The First Lieutenant Of A 'K' Boat Reporting From The Engine Room That The Submarine Had Decided Upon Itself To Flood Ballast Tanks, But Only Aft (C.1917)

By the close of 1917 it was apparent that the Royal Navy had a problem with the 'K' boats. In the short time since their conception they had proved to be nothing but problematic. Within the service they were becoming known as the "Kalamity'" class or the "Suicide Club" and with the submarine service being a volunteer one, manning the 'K' boats was becoming harder with each 'Incident'. Between January and May 1917 all thirteen of the 'K' boats were to undergo their sea trials and of the thirteen, the majority suffered problems. But by this stage too much money and reputation had been invested in the class and cancelling the project was not conceivable within the corridors and boardrooms of the Admiralty. Plus, pre-commissioning work was traditionally the time for 'issues' to be discovered and the solutions found. In addition, the appointed Captains were all men of proven experience and if anyone could tame the 'K' boats they would be the ones.

K13 lay in dock being repaired, her dead having been buried overlooking the scene of their deaths.(1) The work went on with the class which represented one thousand and three-men's postings, but money and reputation were seemingly more 'important' than life's.

"THE K13/22 IN DRY DOCK AT ROSYTH, WITH THE BOW HELD UP BY SCAFFOLDING. A FEW MEN STAND ON THE SCAFFOLDING WORKING ON THE BOW, IN THE RIGHT FOREGROUND. OTHER MEN STAND ON THE DECK OF THE VESSEL". THE BOAT LACKS HER SWAN BOW AT THIS STAGE IN HER CAREER AND THE IMAGE IS DATED HAVING BEEN PAINTED 1ST JANUARY 1918. THE ARTIST IS CHARLES PEARS AND THE SOURCE IWM ART 1359 FROM THE COLLECTIONS OF THE IMPERIAL WAR MUSEUMS.

The omens continued to look poor for the boats with the lead vessel of the class the *K1* developing so many faults on her own series of trials that they were to last from January until May 1917, a record of five months!

Towards the later end of January 1917, the *K2* was based

at Fort Blockhouse in Portsmouth for the start of her own acceptance trials. Her first run on the measured mile was paused for 15 minutes due to a pump failure and in a later run an accident with the hydroplanes injured two of her crew, necessitating a return to Portsmouth.

On her first dive the *K2* was to be rocked by an explosion and a resulting fire. It was found that the insulation on the electric motors had disintegrated. Before the fuse could blow, a flame flashed across the engine room igniting in the process the oily waste and planks left by the dockyard workmen. As smoke permeated through the 'K' boat Commander Laurence quickly ordered his craft to return to the surface. Once the boat was surfaced, the crew scrambled onto the submarine's casement bearing buckets. The sea water filled pails were passed down the engine room hatch and the fires were extinguished. Then the wounded *K2* limped back to port, entering the dockyard for the necessary repair work to her damaged engine room.

January was not to be kind to the *K2,* on another winters day the weather was colder than on average, the sea was choppy and on shore things were icing up. But once the K2 was clear of the sheltered harbour waters protection and out in the Solent, things got yet more difficult for her. The seas waves washed over the hull, freezing on the outer hull as the water poured into the casing beneath the funnels and through the mushroom shaped vents that accessed the engine room. Once the icy *K2* had made her way out into Stokes Bay, (between Gosport and Lee-on-Solent), the diving hooter was sounded and as the frost-bitten bridge crew dropped down into the conning tower, the boats ballast tanks were flooded. In the engine room an E.R.A threw the switch required to close the boiler room vents, but the indicator light stubbornly stayed off. The Engineer officer, (Alexander Mark-Wardlaw) quickly realized something was wrong and every crewman knew a 'K' boat was not a place to run risks. The *K2* dive was rapidly brought to a stop and Wardlaw found icy seawater had solidified the oil in the hydraulics system. On her return to port, the oil was sent ashore for testing and was found to freeze at 30°(-1C) Fahrenheit. On that first dive the temperature had been nearer 25° (-3C). As a result of K2's failed dive, the Admiralty ordered that the oil used throughout the class was to be changed.

On the 1st January 1917 the *K2* had made a six and a half hour run averaging 22.45 knots on a ship's hull that had been cleaned beneath the waterline on the 16th December 1916. The *K3* had however achieved 23.9 knots at Skelmolie in North Ayrshire, Scotland on a deeper draught. It was scheduled for the *K6* to make her measured run off Polperro in Cornwall the following week and she was to achieve 24 knots. On the 6th March off Stokes Bay in the Solent while under the watchful eye of Engineer Commander W.H. Wood R.N (retired) the *K1* ran a measured mile. She commenced the run with a draught of 15 foot 7 1/4 inches (4.74 mtrs) forward and 16 foot 3 1/4 inches (4.95 mtrs) aft. At the conclusion she was 16 foot 1 1/4 inches (4.95 mtrs) forward and 16 foot 4 1/4 inches (4.97 mtrs) aft. Her average speed with two boilers in use, had been 23.02 knots, (with a clean hull beneath the waterline, having last exited a dry dock on the 15th Feb 1917). The sea had been rough forcing the run to be made with the hatches closed. She had been underway for five and a half hours, of which 4 had been continuous. She was to commission on the 1st April 1917, 'All fool's day'.

A02585

*THE CONNING TOWERS OF K7 ,K6 AND THE K7. THE K6 APPEARS TO HAVE A
RATHER JAZZY PAINT JOB. ALL THREE CONNING TOWERS STILL HAVE THE ORIGINAL
CANVAS CONNING TOWER SCREEN.(SOURCE: AUSTRALIAN WAR MEMORIAL)*

On the 9th January 1917, having completed her trials and working up process, the *K3* was on a patrol out in the North Sea and the boat was struggling as the weather deteriorated through the course of the day. Yet once again the sea broke over the superstructure and washed down the funnels extinguishing her boilers and flooding the compartment. Despite the Admirals reassurance that in such circumstances the crews were to simply relight the boilers, the engine room crew were to be unsuccessful. Once more a 'K' boat limped home with her boilers out of action.

During July 1917 Commander Geoffrey Layton conducted the *K6* first 'static' dive in the 'safe' waters of the non-tidal basin, within the Devonport's dockyard. The craft had submerged with little issue, but then decided that like her sisters she would refuse to surface. As with the *K13* in Gareloch she too had on board both her naval crew and a few workers from the shipyard. It's not known if those on board the K6 where aware of the K13's near loss in the Clyde's waters, but the Royal Navy was a close knit community and it is more than likely at the very least they had heard rumours of the 'K' boats track record. As the boat sat at the bottom of the tidal basin, those on board must have feared they would not escape. Among the civilians was the Inspector of Engine Fitters in the shipyard, Selley. He managed to trace the fault to the compressed air system and over the next two hours worked at the fault. Once he had remedied the problem, *K6* returned to the surface as if nothing untoward had occurred. Selley now proposed that they conduct a second dive, but this time the civilian workers refused to board the 'jinxed' submarine. Selley was not one to be defeated and somehow assembled a scratch civilian crew. On her second dive of the day the K6 dived with no issues. The 'mutiny' and problematic first dive was to be 'hushed' up by the Admiralty. But two years later the 23rd April 1919 the publication, Naval and Military Review printed the following:

> *"... the lord Lieutenant of Devon presented l Selley*
> *the silver medal of the order of the British Empire*
> *for courage and devotion to duty on the occasion of*
> *the trial of a new submarine".*

Most of those who read the announcement had not a clue as to the story as to why he had been so awarded.

While *K6* was undertaking her trials off England's south coast, the *K14* was allocated the same Scottish loch the luckless *K13* had used. One night whilst riding at anchor in Gareloch , she sprang a leak. It was discovered when crewman Arthur Hime testing the specific gravity of the batteries stored in a compartment under the officers' quarters discovered they were full of water and creating toxic gas. With the plating over the ballast tank no one had noticed the chlorine gas gradually drifting through the submarine. With her crew most likely on deck and the boats hatches open to vent the interior, the *K14* was towed by a tug to the shipyard for repair work.

In the first few months of 1917, the *K11*, which had barely left the Armstrong Whitworth Yard on the Tyne, suffered seawater flooding down her funnels. She limped back to port and entered dockyard hands who fitted a new generator, as her original one had been wrecked by the saltwater. Even when the 'K' boats finally commenced their patrols, they experienced problems. Whilst out in the North Sea rough weather shattered the *K3's* bridge windows. The Admiralty ordered another 'fix' with thicker glass to be fitted throughout the class. This was not to solve the problem.

1 : The memorial erroneously awards commander Goodhart/Herbert? with a Victoria Cross)

CHAPTER SIX.
OPERATION 'B.B'.

I Think The Antipathy Toward 'K' Boats Was Universal Among Most Officers And Men. - Commander R. J. Brooke-Booth, D.s.c., R.n. (Retd, 1959).

In June 1917 Admiral Beatty, (the Grand Fleet's C-in-C) ordered that a number of his fleet's destroyers be detached in company with the submarines of the Grand Fleet to take part in Operation 'B.B', a large scale offensive he had conceived of. The goal of the operation was to launch attacks on the German U-boats as they made their way home from their Atlantic and Irish sea patrols. Seventeen submarines, in company with fifty three destroyers were allocated to form the core of the operation and were dispatched out to sea to patrol along the route the Germans used to transit between the Western Approaches, passing around the Orkney and Shetland Islands to reach the North Sea and Germany. By the operations conclusion on the 24th June, 61 sightings of U-boats had been made, of which 12 (19-20%) were attacked. In the limited actions not one of the U-boats was to be sunk or damaged.

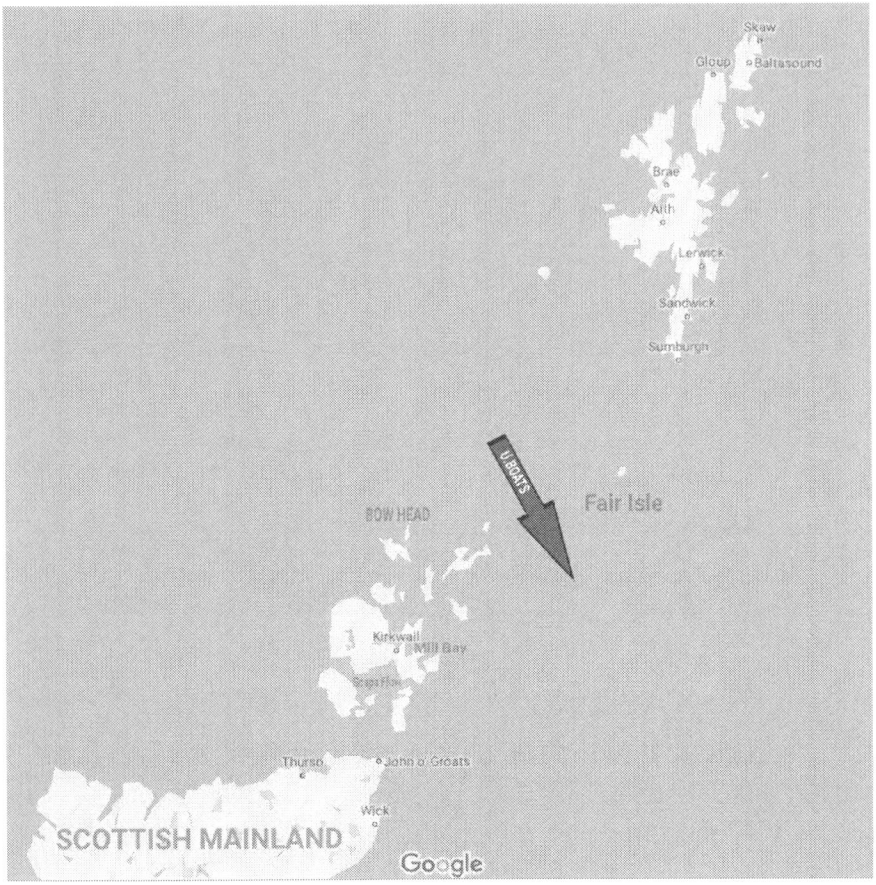

THE U-BOATS ROUTE HOME

The K7 under the captaincy of Commander Gilbert H Kellet was to have the honour of undertaking the classes only ever attack on the enemy. The K7 had departed from Scapa for her role in operation 'B.B' at 07:50 on the 15th June and was to spend the remainder of that first day patrolling off the Orkney's Mill Bay. The afternoon of the 16th was not to start well for the K7 when at 13:47 while running submerged she was mistaken for a U-boat by the two destroyers *HMS Observer* and *HMS Rocket*. Both destroyers swung on to a course to launch an attack on what they considered to be one of the Kaiser's U-boats. Kellet and his crew soon found depth charges were exploding all around them, but he managed to slip his boat clear and then having surfaced signalled that 'he was on their side'. Having managed to escape being destroyed 'friendly fire', *K7's* luck seemed to have changed for the better, when having submerged once more at 14:12, an hour later at 15:12 Kellett sighted a real German submarine, the *U95* (Kapitänleutnant Athalwin Prinz) running on the surface. To date Prinz had since departing port sunk two British merchants' ships:

- 3rd Jun 1917   *S.S Hollington*   4,221 tons,
- 12th Jun 1917   *S.S Polyxena*   5,737 tons.

Kellet having worked his submerged boat into a good firing position at 15:21 launched one of his 18-inch torpedoes from the *K7's* beam tubes(59deg 31' N., 1deg 0' W.). But with typical 'K' boat luck, it was to miss. Undeterred he followed up at 15:29 with a bow salvo of four, which all ran on the surface. Of the four torpedoes only one, (the third), struck the U-boat centrally under her conning tower but not unsurprisingly, it failed to explode. Reportedly, on her return to base U95 found the head of the torpedo lodged within her ballast tank.

Captain Kellet now brought the *K7* to the surface planning to make use of his boats greater surface speed to escape the by now alerted U-boat. But on sighting his mammoth adversary coming to the surface the U-boat's Captain turned and opened fire on the *K7* at 15:30 with his deck gun. The *K7* was to launch at 15:34 one more torpedo from her starboard tube, but it too was to miss. At this stage the German Captain took one look at the smoke belching giant as it ploughed through the sea like some primeval maritime monster and ordered his boat to crash dived. With *K7's* turn now to be exposed, (being unable to perform her own 'crash' dive) and vulnerable on the surface, Kellet steamed *K7* away from the area as fast as she could manage. By the 18th the 'K' boat was once more in Scapa, refuelling and replacing her expended torpedoes.

PREVIOUS PAGE. HMS K7 IN AN UNDATED IMAGE,

During Operation 'B. B' the *K2* (having joined the fleet from her Portsmouth trials), was on patrol within the same area of the North Sea as her sister, the *K7*. Laying to the north east of Scapa is the tiny island of Fair Isle with its two light-houses and during one of her 'B. B' patrols, the *K2* was in the waters off the small rocky outcrop. It was the Orkneys Fair Isle light keeper that was to wireless Scapa stating that he had seen a 'K' boat strike a mine and sink. It could only be the *K2!* The Admiralty dispatch telegrams to all the crews next of kin telling them of the loss. Two days after the light keeper's news, in the early morning, a Scapa lookout reported sighting a strange submarine approaching the Grand Fleet's anchorage. Alarms rang and patrol ships were ordered to close, identify, and engage if hostile. With the loss of the *K2* no friendly submarines were expected. But smoke belching submarines could only be one class and the intruder were soon recognized, it was the recently 'sunk' *K2*.

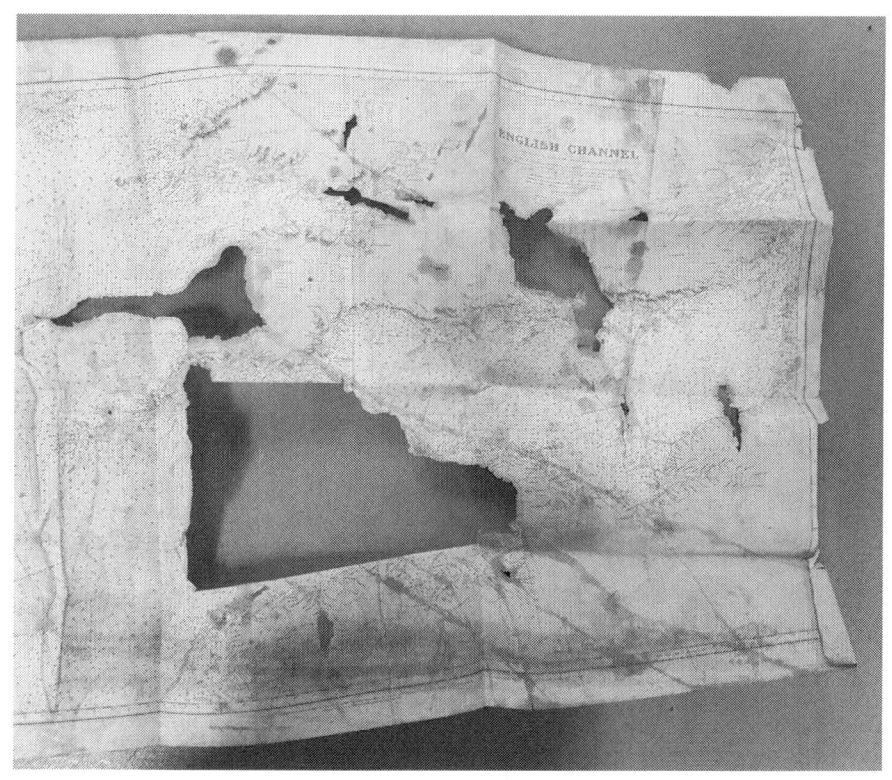

THE EXTREMELY FRAGILE AND ACID DAMAGED MAP K1'S CAPTAIN BENNING PRESENTED TO THE COURT OF ENQUIRY. BIZARRELY THE MAP IS OF THE ENGLISH C CHANNEL AND NOT THE ORKNEYS, WHICH LAY TO THE DISTANT NORTH OF THE BRITISH ISLES.(ADM 156).

The *K2's* Captain, Commander Noel Laurence had (having prepared his boat to commence a 'rapid' dive) ordered that a test fire be conducted with of one of her deck guns at a safe range, using the (out of range) lighthouse as her point of aim.

As soon as she fired, the *K2* had dived. By the time the shell hit the water, the submarine has slipped beneath the waves and the shells explosion made it looked to the watching light housekeeper as if she had struck a mine!

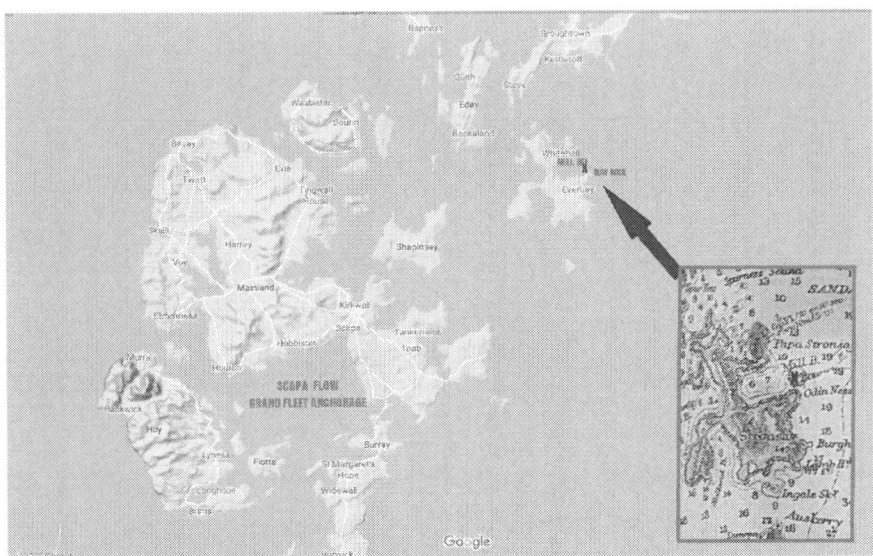

BOW ROCK, THE SITE OF THE K1's GROUNDING MARKED (BY THE AUTHOR) ON THE CHARTS PRESENTED AT THE COURT OF ENQUIRY. BOW ROCK WHILST SUBMERGED AT CERTAIN TIDES, IS CLEARLY MARKED ON THE MAP (SEE INSERT)

Operation 'B.B' was also to involve *K4* and her Captain David Stocks, who had in Mill Bay on the isle of Stronsay on the Orkney's found an anchorage where he could lay up and wait for any U-boats returning home through the Fair Island Channel. On K4's return to port Stocks told his colleague, the *K1's* Captain Stewart Benning of his new 'hidey-hole'. Benning, who was due to depart on his next patrol, decided to make use of the Bow Rocks information on the 26th June while on route between Scapa and Mill Bay on Stronsey. At 14:28 as *K1* eased her way into the bay, Benning took over navigation from Lieutenant Lowther (R.N.R) and personally took a few bearings, checking those taken by others who were on the bridge. But unfortunately for him, despite his navigation checks, he was to run his command aground at 14:32, on a day of excellent visibility while the boat was making 17 knots. Benning immediately ordered all engines stopped and the *"water bearers the oil starters were blown out"*, as well as the ballast tanks pumped out. In addition, the provisions room was emptied of its contents to lighten the boat sufficiently to enable her to float free. Benning also ordered the placement of a red flagged buoy at the end of the *"rock"* or *"reef"* to warn off other vessels and the waters around the grounded submarine to be sounded. While the boat lay stranded and vulnerable, several trawlers were detailed to patrol the bays entrance, to ensure she was not attacked by the U-boats that had been reported that day within the vicinity. Four attempts to tow the stranded submarine off at successive high tides (with a 3.5-inch wire) were made by:

- 14:00, Northesk (destroyer)
- *ANZAC* (destroyer)
- *02:15: Porta* (destroyer) attempted ended when cable parted))
- 03:00: *Hercules* and *Oceanic* (tug)

The *Hercules'* and *Oceanic* attempt were undertaken with the assistance of a destroyer rocking the stranded 'K' boat with her wash and the *K1's* main motors full astern. But at 04:32 the tide had dropped once more, and the attempt was brought to a halt. Unfortunately, in the process of freeing the stranded 'K' boat, at 16:10 the minesweeping trawler *Ida Adams* was also to go aground. But the 'K' had gone so heavily ashore that until her batteries, ammunition and stores could be hoisted out and removed, she was unable to be floated once more.

OVER PAGE: BOW ROCK, THE SITE OF THE K1's GROUNDING MARKED (BY THE AUTHOR)

ON THE CHARTS PRESENTED AT THE COURT OF ENQUIRY. BOW ROCK WHILST SUBMERGED AT CERTAIN TIDES, IS CLEARLY MARKED ON THE MAP (SEE INSERT)

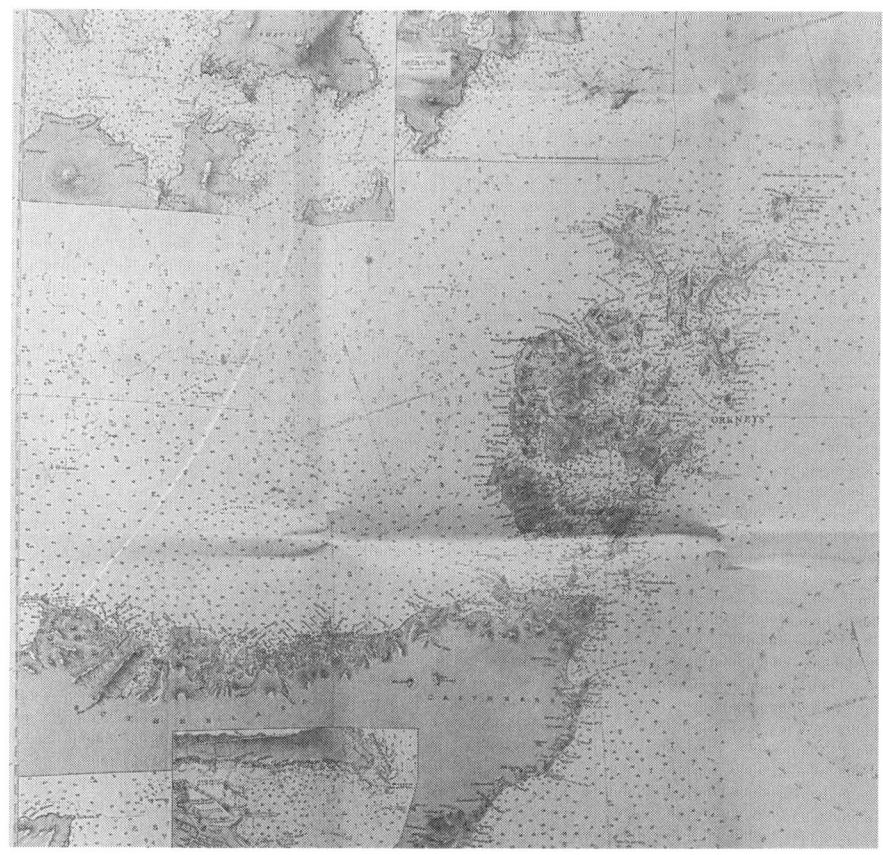

At 02:15 on the 28th the 'K' boats crew was set to lightening the submarine before the *Alliance* and the Oceanic took the submarine in tow, while the Porta made a *"heavy wash"*. This time the combined efforts worked and at 05:00, (after 38 hours and 3 minutes aground) the *K1* came free. She was towed from the bay at 11:30, to Scapa Flow, where a dry dock awaited her at 20:15.

The boat fortunately was not severely damaged. The navigator told the court of enquiry he examined the ship on her return to Scapa and found the fore part of her wooden keel was chipped, but overall there was little evidence as to the grounding, but navy rules demanded an enquiry. Charles Benning came up before a court martial on the 2nd August 1917 charged with hazarding his ship. Lieutenant Lowther was shown a chart by the court which was in a poor condition. He explained it was most likely damaged by acid:

> *"It was out about forty-eight hours before, being corrected and as we had been to sea for a good length of time and the batteries were always being charged up when we got in, an the chart table is right over the batteries, the density being taken while the charging is going on, also the chart table being small it is necessary to use the periscope standard as a table as well, I think that the acid pot which is sometimes standing up there or round that position must have spilt acid there on the chart table and it got into the drawer on to the chart with that result".* He added one other chart was similarly damaged, (chart numbers 1598 & 2180 were exhibited at the enquiry).

Common folk law claims that with a perfectly straight face Benning explained that a pet white rat (or a pair of rats, folk law is unclear on the number he kept in his jacket pocket) had eaten his chart of the anchorage. It was an excuse that only a 'K' boat Captain could have got away with! But the courts official file in Kew makes no mention of hungry mice. Ultimately the Board accepted the acid cause and issued him with only a reprimand. The ruling read that he had *"negligently or* default stranding and hazarding his majesty's submarine K.1." (1)

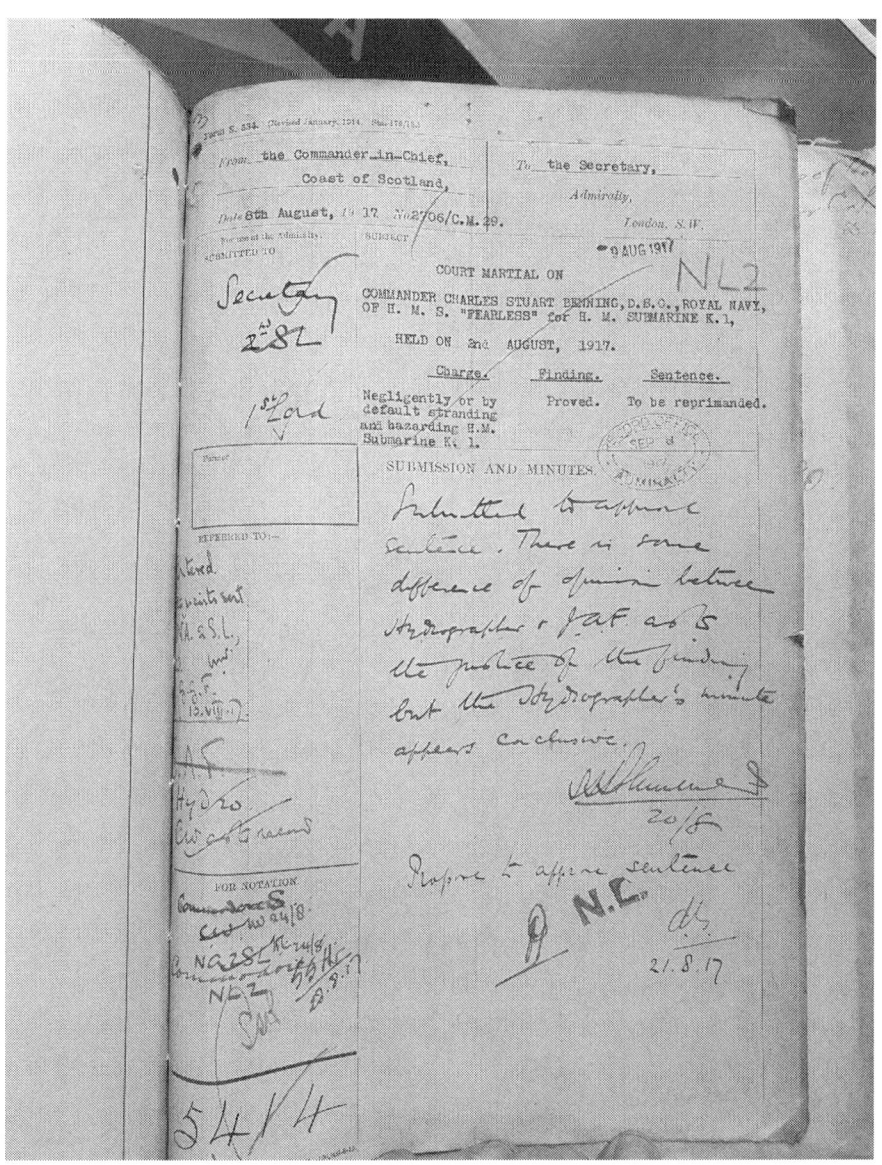

PREVIOUS PAGE: THE COURTS JUDGEMENT ON FROM THE KEW FILES.

On the 21st June 1917 King George V made another of *his visits to the Grand Fleet at Scapa, entering the anchorage on-*

board the destroyer HMS Castor. As the destroyer made its way into the crowded anchorage, she was battered by a force 8 gale and a thunderstorm. The King stayed with Admiral Beatty on the flagship, *HMS Queen Elizabeth,* where he was formally welcomed by all the fleets Admirals, his son Prince Albert (of *K13* fame and later King George VI), who was serving on board *HMS Malaya* and Midshipman "Dickie" Battenberg (later Earl Mountbatten). After a night onboard the *Queen Elizabeth,* the king woke on Friday 22nd to find the weather was still poor, making the plans for him to go to sea with the Fleet and watch a firing practice impossible and put on hold. Instead the King spent two hours touring the *Queen Elizabeth.* Then he went on board the capital ships *Revenge, King George V* and *Barham.* The following morning, he visited the submarine depot-ship *Lucia* (formerly the German *Spreewald*) and then lunched with Admiral Sturdee on *HMS Hercules.* Then he returned to the *Queen Elizabeth* to sail with her in company with *Barham, Malaya, Warspite* and *Valiant* for firing practice in the Pentland Firth. On the Sunday, after morning service, the King held an investiture and decorated over forty officers, including a Knight Grand Cross for Beatty and Insignia of Knight Commander of the Victorian Order for Rear Admiral de Brock. After lunch the King toure*d HMS K2,* (another report credits *K1* with the honour), but whichever 'K' boat it was, photographs were taken for the newspapers, but not before the funnels were retracted. The Admiralty feared the Germans would learn the source of the 'K' boats power and create their own version. He then toured the minesweeper *Godetia*, the hospital ship Plassy and finally his son's ship, *Malaya.* He departed Scapa on Monday, 25th June, steaming through the Fleet on the *Castor,* each ship cheering their monarch as he passed.

The 'K' boats would often conduct exercises with the battle fleet that they had been conceived to work alongside of. On an evening prior to such an event the First Lieutenant of the *K2* retired early to bed feeling unwell. The task of trimming the boat ready for the morning was left to another officer who was new to the 'K' class. The aim of trimming was to balance the submarine's tanks with water insuring that on diving she would have neutral buoyancy. On the smaller vessels it was common practice to make the craft slightly heavier for a swifter dive. The officer whose experience was with the smaller boat duly trimmed the 'K' boat accordingly.

The next morning the fleet and its submarine flotilla put to sea to conduct exercises. *K2's* Captain managed to work his boat into a position for a practice attack on the Grand Fleets 8th battle squadron. He then trimmed the boat and dived. But the *K2* went down fast and would not answer to her diving planes nor did blowing the tanks slow her ever downward plunge. At she shot past 100 feet her hull started to creak and groan under the growing water pressure and the seabed 360 feet below beckoned her on. Overhead, should she manage to reverse her dive, were the lethal bows of the capital ships, ready to cleave a 'K' boats hull in two. The First Lieutenant leapt to the master compressed air valve and emptied all the external trim tanks. The *K2's* dive was slowed and brought to a halt. Then she levelled out before she began a cautious return to the surface while the crew held their breath. Would there be a collision with a battleship bow? The *K2* happily made it safely to the surface.

HMS K2 IN AN UNKNOWN PORT, IN COMPANY WITH A LIGHT CRUISER.

The Kew files record that between the 5th May and 28th June 1917 the *K3* was in the care of Blyth Dry Dock in Newcastle. She was to undergo a boiler service and general maintenance during her time in dock. Her boilers and "associated machinery" had prior to the refit been rated as "good" and were "worn, renewed as necessary" and she had already undergone a similar dockyard visit in March 1916. She would repeat it a third time in February 1919.

The K5 (having been appointed as a "tender" to HMS Fearless on the 22nd May) conducted a steam trial off Spithead in the Solent on the 25th. In an unbearable 101-degree turbine room and 106-degree boiler room her engineer saw her achieve 23.653 knots.

*THE K5 UNDER STEAM PROPULSION. SHE SEEMS TO HAVE THE SAME WHITE
SUPERSTRUCTURE THAT K6 HAD IN AN EARLIER IMAGE?*

The *K7* entered a refit between the 24th July and 15th September at the Ferguson yard in Leith. She underwent alterations to her superstructure, adjustments to her blow down connections, etc...

It was the *K6's* turn between the 6th September and 12th November to go into dockyard hands, this time at the Swan hunter yard on the Tyne. The yard stiffened the deck under the broadside torpedoes and installed a 3-inch gun between the funnels. The 4 inch had adjustments made to her mounting. An "indicator" was installed between the boiler and the control room and the number 7 ballast tank was converted into an engineer's storeroom. A storage for ditty boxes was added in the aft mess and the hatch coaming in both the turbines and signal rooms was raised. Improvements to the casings watertight integrity were made and the guard rail on the aft upper deck extended.

The bow superstructure was extended as well, and a third W/T mast fitted. An Offal ejector was installed in the forward torpedo room and arm brackets added to the fore funnel. Mechanical indicators were mounted to the funnel doors, the funnel drain piped moved etc......

During September 1917 a few crew from the 'J' class boats received the unwelcome news that they were to be transferred to the newly refurbished *K22*, the former *K13*. Such was the superstition of the service personnel and the reputation of the craft that large numbers of the men reported 'sick' while some resorted to a selection of unspecified other methods.

But a crew was found and transferred to the K22. Her new Captain was Lieutenant-Commander Chris de Burg and Coxswain Oscar Moth, a survivor of *K13* was also serving onboard. He described how he came to join the former *K13*:

> *"On my return from leave to Fort Blockhouse, I was again put on the staff as an Instructor for new ratings joining the submarines, but I afterwards found out that this was only something for me to do, while K13 was being salved and afterwards overhauled. Of course, I didn't think for one minute that I should commission her again and when I was "told off" I was greatly surprised as well as were a good many more.*

Any how one evening; after tea I was sent for by the Drafting Officer, who I might remark was my Captain in H1 (Lt Wilfrid Pirie). He asked if I would go to K22 as a volunteer. At first my answer was "No" and I said I didn't think it was right to expect me to go back to a boat in which I had seen such awful sights. Anyhow after a bit I decided I would go; I think it was so that no-one could accuse me of having cold feet. Accordingly, I once more left the Depot and travelled to Govan where the boat was being refitted and soon I was installed as Coxswain of K22.

It was a surprise packet for the men at Fairfield's Yard to see me come up again for this boat and I soon had the civilians who were down in her with me, around to see me. They one and all told me I was a fool to tempt providence in her again and one of them told me he wouldn't go to her if he was dragged.

I simply laughed at them and told them I had just as well be at sea in this boat as any other and I also told then I considered she was a jolly fine boat. I also told them that they would soon hear about her, as I felt sure she would do something. I was quite right about this, but they heard of her in a far different way to that which I meant them to. Our crew came up in September and in October we were once more on the Gareloch doing trials. I shan't forget the day we first went inside the Gareloch for we anchored off Shandon in the exact spot where our accident had happened. Neither shall I forget the first dive I had in her as K22. I can assure you I had a jolly good look round myself this time, but it was next to impossible for the same accident to happen".

By October 1917 the resurrected *K22* had, following an extensive time in dockyard hands, commenced her trials. Her new Captain had joined the boat on the 18th July 1917 while she was in the dockyard and would remain with her until the 13th February 1918.

Moth recounts for us how the period during which *K22* underwent her trials was not all work

:

> *"One of the Sundays we laid off Shandon, we decorated the boat and threw her open for the people on the Gareloch side. We had a very big crowd aboard and they marvelled to think so large a boat could be so easily handled. There were two other boats on the Gareloch also exercising, they were K17 and N1 so before we left to join up with the Grand Fleet, the staff at the Hydro gave us a farewell dinner and dance. It was a really good show and I think everyone enjoyed themselves immensely. I am very sorry to say that a good many of the brave lads who were enjoying themselves, were "Down Under" within four months for K17 was lost with nearly all hands".*

With both her growing reputation and recent history, the *K22's* first dive in Gareloch drew crowds along the shoreline to watch. To try and come out from under the looming shadow of *K13*, de Burg asked Moth to show him the place where the *K13* had commenced her fateful dive. He then steered the boat to the indicated patch of water and once he had *K22* over the same piece of loch, he ordered "dive". For ten long minutes the crowd watched the empty patch of water. Would the 'resurrected' 'K' boat resurface, or would the 'Jinx' once more toy with her? While the crowds on shore held their breath, the crew no doubt offered silent prayers. Then de Burg brought the *K22* back to the surface and with no reluctance the submarine broke the lochs waters, with no issues. Two weeks later a four-hour acceptance trial was completed with no problems and in the middle of October the *K22* sailed from the Clyde to join the new flotilla of 'K' boats at the Firth of Forth. Her flotilla was number 13!

The '13th' flotilla had been formed in May of that year to support the efforts of the three other flotillas then screening the Grand Fleet (2). Two 'K' boats (*K9* and *K14*) had joined the new flotilla from the outset, under the command of the protected cruiser, *HMS Crescent,* which was not directly affiliated with the flotilla. The *K9* had previously been working up in the Sixth Submarine Flotilla, but the 13th was the *K14's* first posting.

Tragically on the 21st September 1917 *K2* lost one member of her crew, when 21-year-old Stoker First class Reginald Tinniswood on sea watch duty accidentally fell overboard and was drowned in the waters of Scapa flow

On the 18th November the Grand Fleet undertook a sweep out into the North Sea, steaming eastwards towards the coast of neutral Denmark, to lure the German battle Fleet out. The 12th submarine Flotilla, led by the scout-cruiser *HMS Blonde* and with four 'K' boats *(K1, K2, K3, K4* and *K7)*, traveling in her wake were conducting their portion of the sweep along the Danish Coast. The five 'K' boats and their light cruiser were in a line ahead that evening, with the *K4* 3.5 cables (700 yards/640 mtrs) in the wake of the *K3*. The cruiser was leading the 'K' boats of her flotilla in a line ahead at 16 knots. The sea was "very unpleasant" and the night was a dark one.

HMS K2 IN COMPANY WITH THE BATTLE FLEET. HMS REVENGE LAYS BEHIND HER.

Suddenly at 20:00 three dark shapes of cruisers running without lights appeared from out of the darkness. The *Blondies* lookouts on sighting what was most likely cruisers of the 4th LCS, passed a warning to the bridge as the in-truders passed across Blondies bow from starboard to port. Lieutenant L.C.Lush promptly ordered a turn to port and the navigation lights.

The *Blondies* bridge crew signalled the 'K' boats steaming in their wake "on navigation lights". The unexpected change of course had taken the 'K' boats, (which were traveling in her wake) by surprise. But as their flotilla leader turned, so to, in sequence, did her 'K' boats, switching on their lights as they altered course. *K1* was at this point two and a half cables astern of the *K3* and off the bow of the Blanche. The imminent collision between *K1* and *K4* would have been avoided but for the latter suffering mechanical problems.

The *K1* came to a rapid and unexpected halt when saltwater, (instead of fuel), had come through the sprayers and extinguished the boilers. *K1* had followed the *K3* in the turn and her Captain, (Denning) having arrived on his bridge, at the request of the officer of the watch (Lieutenant Robinson), assumed command. He ordered *"starboard 15, follow the Blanch"* to return his command to its allotted position, but the bridge crew sighted *K1's* stern light as it emerged from the nights darkness. Denning went to the bridge house to order his boats stern lights be increased to full, power and to check his side lights were on. While there he asked his quartermaster, (Able Seaman Henry Williamson) *"how's her head"* and was told *"350°"*. Denning ordered *"steady on that course"* as he was confident it would give the boats in his wake the best chance of avoiding the struggling *K1*.

Two minutes later the *K3*, (the boat astern of the *K1*) passed down the port side at between 6 to 12 feet. Denning next sighted the K4 as she emerged from the dark 3 points from right astern and the *K4's* Captain frantically ordered *"full astern both"* to minimise the impact. But the *K4* traveling in the wake of the *K3* was not to be so prompt. Her crew suddenly sighted the red light of the *K1* and although taking avoiding action, the *K4* struck the *K1* a glancing blow below the conning tower in the port beam tube compartment, (Stocks was to state at the enquiry, he was of the opinion that had he ordered hard a port his vessel would have sliced the *K1* in half). The *K4* (a few leaking rivets aside), remained watertight and was put full astern. But the K1's hulls was breached allowing the North Seas waters to pour into the control room. The watertight doors were quickly shut but within minutes, the water had invaded the battery compartments and chlorine gas was being released into the submarines enclosed atmosphere. In addition, the rising waters fused the lights, throwing the 'K' boats interior into darkness. Denning ordered the "blowers" on but instead of pushing the water in the tanks out into the sea, the damage to them resulted in the air instead being blown.

The stricken 'K' signalled *HMS Blonde*, (the signal man pointing his lamp through the conning tower windows), "am in danger of sinking" and shortly thereafter "am sinking". The cruiser having drawn closer, lowered two of her cutters under the command of Lieutenant Boys of the Fearless and Lieutenant Mason (RNVR) of the Blanche. The cruisers boat crews made five trips before all 56 of the stricken 'K' boats crew had been transferred to the *Blonde*. The two Captains debated about what to do with the submarine and if she could be saved. But they concluded:

"(a) The two largest compartments were bilged and she was considered to be settling slowly. This was confirmed by observations later.

(B) No man could remain on board without being gassed, unless he remained on deck.

(C) Men left on board to secure hawsers etc, were little likely to be saved if the vessel sank, as rising sea was making boat work most difficult.

(D) The bollards and cables for towing forward were already underwater.

(E) We had lain stopped for over an hour with

navigation lights burning and a searchlight on the wreck (at [the] request of "K.1" to facilitate rescue). The searchlights could have been seen for a great distance. Being in close proximity to enemy waters and the major duty of saving the crew having been performed, I considered the risk of remaining another hour or so to get her in tow would have been unjustifiable as well as fruitless.

(F) It was the opinion of all the submarine officers consulted that the chances of salving her were practically nil".

(Captain Earnie Erle Drax of Blanche in his report to Beatty).

Plus, with the proximity of the German navy's bases and the deteriorating weather it was finally decided to scuttle her. Using her 4-inch main calibre guns Blonde despatch the submarine at 22:00 in the approximate position 56.203 N. 5.44 E.

As the "K" boats made their way home a series of signals broke the news of the loss to the Admiralty in London:

BLANCHE to 3.0.5 B.3. and C-in-C (18/11/17. 20:31).

Am proceeding Rosyth with "K.3" damaged. "K1" sank, no casualties.

C-in-C. to "BLANCHE" (18/11/17)

If "K3" requires docking send her with destroyer to Tyne. Proceed with remainder of your force to Scapa.

"BLANCHE" to C-in-C. (18/11/17 21:00)

Vocabulary Code No.11 thrown overboard from "K.1"; other sunk inside her".

C in C to Admiralty. (19/11/17 10:56)

Regret to report Submarine "K.1" sank as result of collision with "K 3" in 56 17N 5 45E about 2000 18 Nov. No casualties. "K.3" is proceeding to Tyne for docking under escort of destroyer.

Admiralty to C-in-C. (19/11/17 18:45).

312. Your 677. Please confirm that submarine "K.3" was in collision with "K.1". Intercepted message appears in indicate "K 4".

C-in-C to Admiralty. (19/11/17 19:31).

677. Your 312. Original report stated "K.3". It is now evident or was K4.

C in C to S.N.O.Tyne. (19.11.17 19:11).

For Submarine "K4". No ratings from "K4" who are likely to be required as witnesses at Court of inquiry into collision with "K1" are to be sent on leave until Court of Enquiry has been held.

C in C to C in C Rosyth. (19/11/17 19:06)

56 survivors ex "K1" now on board "BLANCHE" have been directed to proceed Rosyth. Request they may be accommodated in "CRESCENT pending

Court of enquiry.

C-in-c. to Admiral Supt. Newcastle. (19/11/17).

Your 0651."K.3" should be docked immediately on arrival. Time of arrival uncertain

(12:18).

The court martial assembled on *HMS Revenge* on the 27th November 1917. *K1's* Commander, Charles Stuart Benning was blamed by some for not using his boats speed to swing clear, nor sounding the boats siren. He was however to be acquitted of any blame in the matter on the 16th January 1918. In addition, Engineer Lieutenant Cecil Heare was reprimanded for not testing number '7' starboard and '5' port for water, before transferring the fuel supply.

Things did not improve once the boats had returned to Scapa Flow. The morale of the 12th Flotilla suffered another blow when it was learnt that all 'K' boats were to put (in rotation) into a dry dock where the new "Swan" bulbous bows was to be fitted. The inference (and the facts) implied that the boats were not seaworthy in their present condition. Something the crews knew, but now the Admiralty acknowledged, which did little to calm the fears which the men felt each time the steam belching monsters left the sanctuary of harbour.

On a wet stormy North Sea day during 1917 four 'K' boats of the 12th Submarine flotilla under the escort of a cruiser (*HMS Fearless?*) were on route from the Pentland Firth to Scapa having conducted exercises as they had made their way northwards. The four boats were making 10 knots in a line ahead with the Commodore's light cruiser in the van, but the 'K' boats were struggling to make headway in a gale, that was rolling 20-foot waves over the 5 vessels. The officer of the watch on the *K2* watched as rollers overtook the ship and reared over her stern, at the very least threatening the boilers. Breaking every naval rule of procedure, without notifying or requesting permission from the flagship the officer increased K2 to 20 knots. The submarine surged past the light cruiser and scurried into the shelter of a harbour. In the meantime, her three sisters were forced to extinguish their boilers and dive to escape the seas battering waves. But once submerged they were unable to beat the 7.5 knot tide and had to seek shelter in a bay until the weather moderated. The forward planning *K2's* officer escaped any reprimand for breaking with naval etiquette.

The year was also to witness the *K11* damaged by a fire during another North Sea patrol. While on duty the lookouts had sighted a ship and made what was for a 'K' boat, an emergency dive. But as she submerged the stokers could not turn off the fuel pump and oil were sprayed into the compartment, catching fire. By the time *K11* lumbered to the surface the fire was out but during its short life it had melted the electrical cables in the boiler room, and she was left unable to reignite her boilers. The *K11* was forced to seek a tow home by a destroyer.

After seven months in commission, the K7 entered Portsmouth dockyard on the 29th October 1917 and was to emerge on the 11th February 1918 from dockyard hands. The refit had seen the installation of water pressure ammunition storage on deck for the 3-inch gun (10 rounds) and 4-inch gun (30 rounds), fittings and wires for a 10-inch search light, adjustments to the latrine door to make "more room". An "offal" ejector had been fitted in the forward pantry, indicators in the control room to show the status of the boiler rooms air intakes, rail ways in the beam torpedo room for torpedo transportation and funnel drainpipes. The telemotor was fitted with Artic oil. The 3-inch gun was relocated between the funnels and a 4-inch gun installed between foremost funnel and the bridge. In addition to these the mechanical aspects of the K2 underwent maintenance and adjustments.

On the 14th November 1917 Lieutenant-Commander Samuel Maryon Gorton Gravener took over temporary command of the K7 while she underwent her refit. He was to be surprised at the amount of off duty drinking that took place onboard and on his first 'post refit trials' dive in the Captains 'chair' was convinced the coxswain's knees were shaking as the boat dived.

With the fourth Christmas of the war passed, the *K9* left Rosyth escorted by the cruiser *Southampton,* bound for a refit at Chatham and the fitting of her new Swan bow. The *K9* or as her crew knew her "Ka-nine", carried a wooden plaque in her control room with the inscription "GARM" written onto it. "GARM" was both a Mythical Norse dog as well as King George V's dogs name and now the *K9's* nick name. But while off the Northumberland coast the submarine ran into heavy seas and while changing course a 'poop' sea launched a cascade of water down her funnels, extinguishing the boilers. To compound matters it was found she was unable to dive as the boiler room vents would not close, the seas having smashed the Coxswain's paint locker located within the funnel well. An examination revealed a lone tin of paint had jammed under the mushrooms shape vents and the weather was too rough for anyone to climb up and remove the offending object. In addition, the engine room reported the motor that pumped fuel into the auxiliary diesel had broken down. Despite the frantic rolling and pitching of the hull, twice over the few next hours the boiler was lit but twice the sea put it out. *HMS Southampton* stood close by keeping a protective eye on her smaller charge and at one stage made the attempt to tow her. But in the process the 'K' boat lost 12 men overboard. Finally, the Captain of the *K9* (V. Layard) decided to abandon ship but that too proved to treacherous. The submarine finally rode out the gale and then *Southampton* towed her into Tyne for repairs, before resuming her voyage onto Chatham.

Layard had for a 'K' boat Captain, an unusual 'troubled' pre-'K' boat career. In April 1913 while in command of the submarine C34, Layard collided her with the battlecruiser Invincible and blame was fully attributed to him, *"thereby arousing Their Lordships' displeasure"*. Then to compound matters her repeated his 'accident' when he collided C33 with the pre-dreadnought, Prince of Wales in June 1913. This time he warranted only a caution, but he seems to have suffered no long-term harm to his career with these two 'incidents'. He went on to a *"long and arduous services in command of* [illegible], submarines in the third period of the war" and was to earn a D.S.O between the 1st January to 30 June 1918, his time of command on the *K9*.

On the 13th January 1918 the *K5* steamed into the Rosyth dockyard and would remain in their hands until the 27th February 1918.

She underwent a refit in that period of just over a month and would consequently escape the Battle of May Island. The work undertaken involved:

- A Voice pipe installed from the bridge to the 3-inch gun,
- A 10-gallon petrol tank installed within the super-structure.
- Additional lockers,
- The 4-inch gun fitted onto the superstructure,
- The 3-inch gun moved over the boiler intakes.

But the planned high (or Swan) bow was postponed due to insufficient workmen being available. She would be dry docked on the 17th June 1918 for her hull to be scraped and repainted beneath the waterline.

1: During my research I was forwarded the following quote from a blog site: "Mum told a story about a naval vessel aground at Rothiesholm .The sailors came ashore, Granny made porridge for them. Someone had to go to Whitehall to telegraph (I guess) for assistance. Can anyone corroborate this story, Mum would not have made this up. She was young enough for one of the sailors to carry her around on his shoulder,so around WW1."

Although unconfirmed its plausible this tale relates to the period the "K" boat was fast aground?

2: 10th, 11th & 12th Flotillas.

CHAPTER SEVEN.
THE 'BATTLE OF
MAY ISLAND'.

"Early In The Morning The Inconstant Hoists A Signal ,
See The Little K-Boats All In A Row.
Man In The Control-Room Pulls A Lot Of Levers
Swoosh-Swish-Down We Go".

A 'K' Boat 'Ditty'.

As bad as 1917 had been for the 'K' boats, 1918 was to be no better for them. In December 1917 Vice-Admiral Beatty had ordered that the 12th (1) and 13th (2) flotillas, (comprised of the 'K' class submarines) be transferred from Scapa to Rosyth for a better strategic location. His aim was to ensure that the boats comprising the two flotillas were in an improved position from which to undertake their North Sea patrols. As the two flotillas and their escorting ships steamed past May Island and under the Forth Railway bridge into their new home port, they could have no inkling the 'Jinx' was traveling with them and had yet to play its trump card.

The 'K' boats duties during their period at Rosyth were not what would be considered 'usual' for a submarine and seemed to be more attuned to the role of a surface craft. Moss describes how they were:

> "... *employed with the fleet and although we did a good deal of running it was far different work to what I had been used to, for in this case we did all surface work, early in December we shifted our base south to Rosyth. Our "stunts" now consisted of work with the mine layers and mine sweepers. We used to go to sea with them and. after they had done their work over the "other side", we were used to cover their retreat. We saw nothing during these escapades, but we were always on the "Top Line" in case we were wanted to dive and attack anything. There was not a great deal of work to do and I would have far sooner been in a boat to do submarine patrols, but still we were kept with the fleet and had to put up with it. Christmas came with the usual jollifications and by this time we had settled down and I prided myself on having one of the best and I am sure the happiest boat, in the Flotilla."*

The 'Battle of May Island' has become over the succeeding century, the name history has given to a series of collisions that occurred during the Grand Fleet's operation 'E.C.1'. The 'battle' was to unfold on the night of Thursday 31st January 1918 in the waters around the Isle of May. The small rocky outcrop is located 5 miles (8km) to the north of the Firth of Forth and faces broadside out into the North Sea. The 'battle' involved ships of the Rosyth fleet, as it made its way out of port on route for a series of joint fleet exercises with the Scapa contingent of the Grand Fleet out in the North Sea.

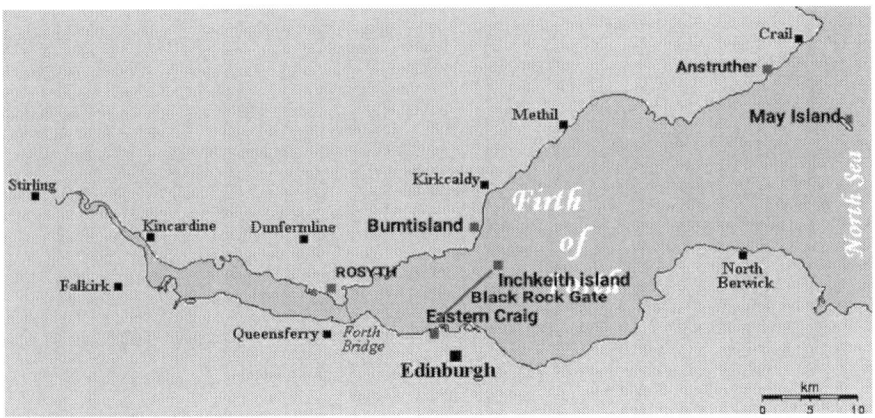

THE FIELD OF 'BATTLE'

On the misty night of 31st January/1st February 1918, (Thursday/Friday) there were to be five collisions between eight vessels. Two submarines were to be lost as a result and three others as well as a light cruiser were to suffer differing degrees of damage. But the human price was the 104 men who lost their lifes and almost On the misty night of 31st January/1st February 1918, (Thursday/Friday) there were to be five collisions between eight vessels. Two submarines were to be lost as a result and three others as well as a light cruiser were to suffer differing degrees of damage. But the human price that night was to be 104 men who lost their life's, all this taking place almost one year to the night the *K13* sank in the waters of Gareloch.

Only shortly before the scheduled date for the exercise the *K6* had return from the Tyne with her new 'Swan' bow and with her funnels having been extended to stop the sea from flooding down them. In addition, since her collision with the *K1*, her bow had been strengthened with 4 inches of solid steel. At a 'gathering' of the flotilla's officers onboard the *K4*, the Captains of the host boat and *K6* jokingly laughed about the depressing number of collisions to date within the class. Commander Geoffrey Layton, of the *K6* told his colleague Commander David de B. Stocks, of the strengthened bow and in humour warned him he would best steer clear. Words neither officer took seriously, but over their shoulders, the 'Jinx' was busy making notes.

As that fourth New Year of the war passed Beatty issued his orders for operation E.C.1, an exercise for both his cruiser and submarine squadrons, as well to provide an opportunity to practice the entire fleets manoeuvres. Beatty's plan was for the operation to comprise of the Vice-Admiral himself with his flag in the *Queen Elizabeth*, accompanied by 26 battleships from seven divisions, (1st, 2nd, 3rd, 4th, 5th, 6th and 8th). They were to be screened by 9 cruisers, 4 Light Cruisers and numerous destroyers. Rosyth was to provide the second element in the shape of three ships of the 5th battle squadron, (the squadrons fourth ship, the *Malaya*, was in dockyard hands) and the light battlecruiser *Courageous.* These were to be supported by the four ships of the 2nd BC squadron, (*Australia, New Zealand, Inflexible* and *Indomitable*) plus *Blanche* and fourteen ships of the 1st, 2nd, 3rd and 4th Light Cruiser Squadrons. The two 'K' boat flotillas were to be next, led by their own two escorts. (3)

The two forces, (Rosyth and Scapa), were scheduled to meet in the North Sea on the 1st February and then having united, to undertake a series of training exercises, with the additional hope of enticing the German fleet from its harbours. The two fleet's orders had been issued by Beatty on the 28th January 1918 and they required that Sir Evan-Thomas led his ships from Rosyth on the evening of the 31st. For such a large number of warships to sail, whilst it was dark, showing only solitary stern lights (with black-out shields that restricted the lights to one compass point either side of the boats' centre line) and in addition to maintaining radio silence, was never an easy task. Then to complicate matters further, a U-boat was reported by a patrolling Seaplane (N1665) as 5 miles south east of May Island. The German intrusion was confirmed by a signal from the requisitioned passenger ferry Nairana as 5 miles east south east of Fifeness. The submarine had responded by diving, but the threat was present, and the C-in-C was informed by telephone. As a result of this threat Evan-Thomas amended his fleets orders to include an increase of speed to 22 knots as the fleet passed the island, with confirmation that radio silence be strictly maintained. Departure was also to now be delayed by 20 minutes. Once clear of the U-boat and the island, the fleets speed was to be reduced to 21 knots, then after an hour a reduction to 16 knots was to be ordered. The fortifications on May Islands were ordered to run dark from 20:30.

The crew of K22 had enjoyed a good Christmas and New Year. Moth related how

"We went to sea with the mine layers and sweepers on the 29th of December and we returned on New Year's Eve. We secured to K5 in the pens at Rosyth at about 11.40pm so we were in for the usual sixteen bells at midnight. My crew were very lively and we sang the old year out and the New Year in and our greatest wish was that this year would see the trouble [war] all over. January passed along with nothing of unusual interest until the night of the 31st. I must here say that I had watched the anniversary of K13s fatal dive and I was very pleased we were in harbour for the 20th and 30th. On the evening of the 31st we had orders for sea and as we were leaving the "pens" we could see that the

whole of the fleet were preparing for sea. Both the 'K'
Boat flotillas with their leaders HMS Ithuriel and HMS
Fearless were ordered to anchored off the Burntisland
Roads and awaited the hours of darkness".

The 'K' boats were then to fall in behind the battle cruisers as they made their way out to sea. The Ithuriel was to position herself 6 cables in the wake of the Courageous. The fleets projected Northern Channel route had been swept in preparation for its departure the Thursday morning.

The *Ithuriel* and her charges raised anchor at 13:50 and made their way to Burntisland on the northern shore of the Firth of Forth, letting go their anchors there at 14:50. The two 'K' boat flotillas remained at anchor through the cold winters afternoon, only lifting them from the sea bed at 17:25. Then in a line ahead and at 12 knots Ithuriel and her charges assumed their place on the fleets line ahead. Ten minutes later the speed was dropped by 2 knots, but at 17:48 it returned to 12 knots.

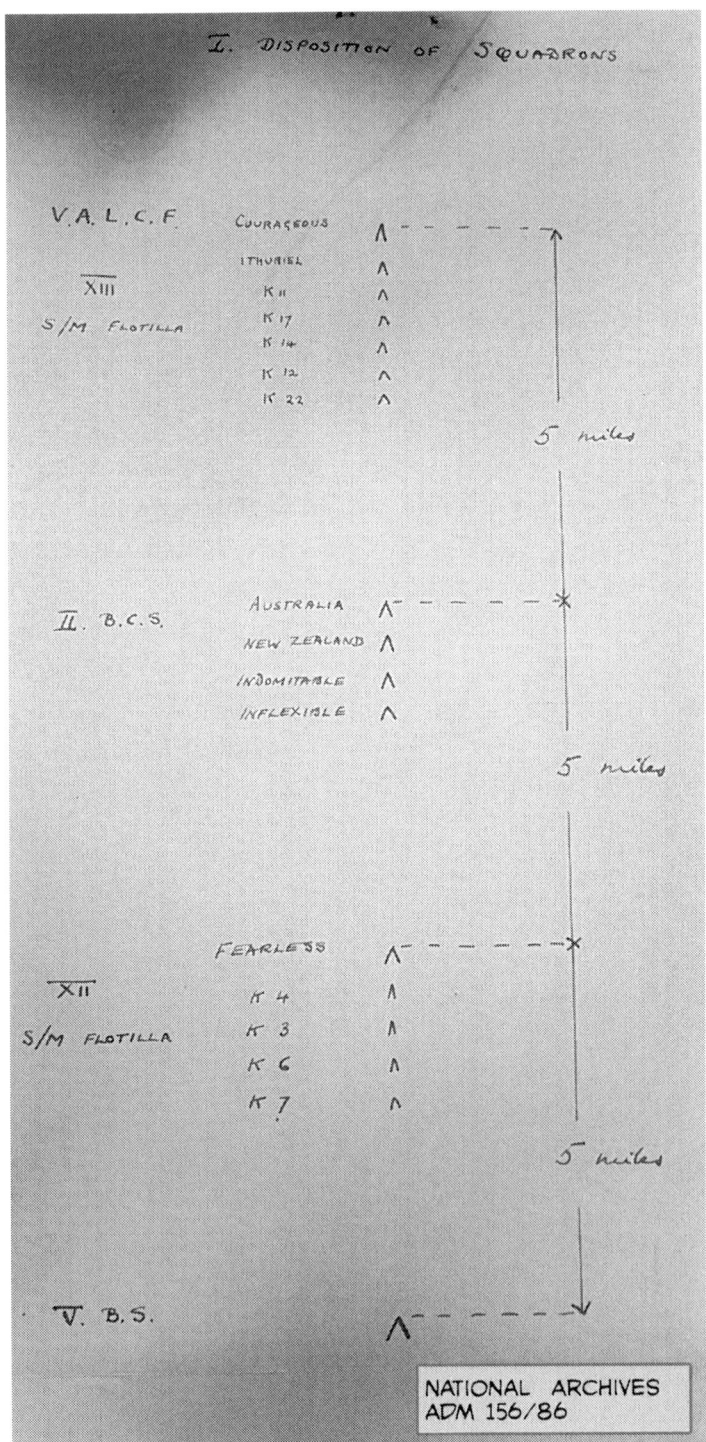

I. DISPOSITION OF SQUADRONS

V.A.L.C.F. COURAGEOUS

XIII

S/M FLOTILLA

ITHURIEL
K 11
K 17
K 14
K 12
K 22

5 miles

II. B.C.S.

AUSTRALIA
NEW ZEALAND
INDOMITABLE
INFLEXIBLE

5 miles

FEARLESS

XII

S/M FLOTILLA

K 4
K 3
K 6
K 7

5 miles

V. B.S.

THE PREVIOUS PAGE:
THE FORMATION OF THE ROSYTH FORCE. FROM THE COURT OF ENQUIRY FILES.

The evening of the 31st was a clear one, but typically for the Firth of the Forth, a cold night with the moon having not yet risen. As the evening drew on, the assembled vessels of the Rosyth force weighed their anchors. The ships under the command of Vice Admiral Sir Hugh Evan-Thomas, (flying his flag from *HMS Courageous*) formed into a single line of nearly 30 miles (48 km) in length. Leading at the head of the line was the flagship Courageous, followed in her wake by the Marksman class destroyer the *HMS Ithuriel* under the Captaincy of Commander Ernest.W.Leir. The *Ithuriel* led the 13th flotilla, whose 5 vessels followed, like oversized ducklings, behind the destroyer:

- *K11*, (Commander Thomas Frederick Parker Calvert),

- *K17*, (Lieutenant-Commander Henry.J. Hearn),

- *K14*, (Commander Thomas Cecil Benfield Harbottle),

- *K12*, (Lieutenant-Commander Graham Bower),

- *K22* (ex-*K13*), (Lieutenant-Commander Charles   de Burgh)).

But at 339 feet the 'ducklings' were 14 feet longer than their mother and 911 tons greater in weight! Five miles astern of the *K22* came the four capital ships of the 2nd Battlecruiser (4) Squadron, *Australia, New Zealand, Indomitable* and the Inflexible. The Battlecruisers on raising anchor lacked their allocated destroyer screen, which was to join them further downstream. The remaining four 'K' boats of the 12th flotilla was led by *HMS Fearless* (Captain J.C.Little) and were next in the line. They followed the *Fearless in* order of:

- *K4*, (Commander David de B. Stocks),

- *K3*, (Lieutenant-Commander Herbert William Shove),

- *K6*, (Commander Geoffrey Layton),

- *K7*, (Lieutenant-Commander Samuel Maryon Gorton Gravener).

Bringing up the rear of the line were the three battleships from the 5th Battle squadron, which were to be accompanied by several screening destroyers. The vessels orders were to sail in line-astern, 400 yards (370 mtrs) separating each ship from its neighbour's stern. Each stern was to show a half shielded low powered navigation light for the vessel sailing in its wake.

The evening was a clear one with a relatively calm sea, as the lead ship, (*HMS Courageous*) passed through the Black Rock Gate, a 6-mile defence boom controlled by trawlers. The 'gate' ran between the Eastern Craig, just east of Long Craig and Inchkeith island in the middle of the Firth.

At around 18:30 hours, the darkened *Courageous* steamed passed May Island which lay one and a half miles off her starboard bow and duly, as per orders, increased her speed to 22 knots, just as a low-lying bank of mist settled over the sea. As Ithuriel passed a light vessel at 18:33 she increased her distance to the *Courageous* by dropping back to 1,200 yards (1,097 mtrs) astern at 16 knots, allowing the battlecruiser's destroyer escort to adopt their allotted stations. As the 'K' boats made their way out to sea, with three cables (600 yds/548.68 mtrs) between them, they were making, as per orders, (in company with the rest of the fleet), 16 knots. As the 13th Submarine Flotilla in turn passed the island, 20 miles off their bows lay eight armed trawlers, (who were not part of E.C.1) from the port of Anstruther, who were busily sweeping for mines. No one had thought to forewarn either the trawlers Commander, (Temporary Lieutenant Robinson Rigby) or the navy's base on May Island that the fleet was heading out to sea that evening. In return the armada was equally unaware of the trawlers operating in the estuary that night. At 18:41 Evan-Thomas's lead ships ran into the low-lying mist and the lookouts on *Ithuriel* quickly lost sight of the *Courageous'* stern light as the capital ship was swallowed up by the enveloping mist. In an effort to regain the lost contact, Lier ordered an increase in both the Ithuriel and his 'K' boats speed to 19 knots at 18:54, but somewhere ahead, *Courageous* stubbornly remained lost to them, enveloped by the mist. As the flotilla chased the elusive battlecruiser, the two units had a disparity in their speed of 3 knots, with the *Courageous* pulling further ahead with every spin of her 4 screws. To complicate matters further for Ithuriel, the mist had dropped the nights visibility to around one and a half miles (2.4 Km).

As the *Ithuriel* and her charges further increased their speed to 19 knots, (still one knot slower than the Courageous), the eight mine sweeping trawlers green and white lights emerged from the mist and were sighted by the lookouts, as they approached the flotilla's line. Seeing the danger appear from out of the mist, Lier ordered the flotilla to alter its course sharply to port in order to safely clear the unexpected intruders and also signalled for a decrease in speed. But at that moment the 'K' boat 'Jinx' played its first card of the night. As Harbottle in K14 watched the navigation lights of the K17 and K11, (making visibility at this stage circa 1,333 yards (1,219 mtrs)), she appeared to decrease her speed and haul out of line to port. K14's Captain was puzzled by this unexpected manoeuvre as the flotilla was now at the point where an increase in the flotilla's speed was due to be implemented. Then for reasons unknown to a perplexed, (but wary Harbottle), the K17 mimicked K11's apparent change of course. Harbottle immediately dropped his boats own speed to 13 knots but stayed true to his own course.

At that moment two lights loomed from out of the mist half a mile ahead of the K14 and Harbottle realized the slower moving vessels, (most likely the trawlers) would be passing across his bows. "Starboard 15" was his immediate response, but the gap was closing faster and "hard a starboard" was next to be ordered as beneath Harbottle's feet in the wheel house, helmsman Able-Seaman Harold Curtis frantically swung the boats wheel to port.

But as Curtis spun the wheel and the bridge crew watched the diminishing gap, the helm of the K14 decided at that moment to jam, (28 degrees starboard). Curtis was left with only 3 inches (7.62 cm) of movement in the ships wheel on either turn. As K14 swung out of her place in the line, Harbottle was thankful to see the boat traveling in his wake,

(K12) turn on her navigation lights, confirming that she would pass astern of his circling boat with no danger of a collision. He then ordered, despite the reported U-boat, his own boat's lights to be switched on and *"slow both engines"*. For six minutes *K14's* helmsman struggled to free the wheel and regain directional control of their errant charge. With *K12's* location known, Harbottle knew *K22* would be traveling in her wake, but he was more concerned at the battlecruisers following four miles to the flotillas stern. Harbottle now ordered *"full speed port, slow starboard"* to try and clear the shoreline and to correct the swing to port. Then with typical 'K' class fickleness, as swiftly as it had jammed, the helm came free and control was back, as K14 veered out of the line. To correct her course *K14's* Captain ordered *"hard-a-port"* to enable the errant 'K' boat to return to her designated and vacated place within the flotilla's line.

As the *K14* swung out of her allotted place, the last boat in the flotillas line, *K22* lost sight of the navigation light of the boat ahead of her, the *K12*. But the *K22's* officer of the watch, Lieutenant Dickinson stayed on the set course, *"north 65 degrees east"*. For three minutes *K22's* conning tower crew strained into the misty night to try to see the elusive blue navigation light. That lone light would mark the rear of *K12's* conning tower and give them the reassurance that their boat was still within its allotted place. But as they tried to see into the mist, out of it drifted a single red navigation light, passing across their bow from starboard to port at 200 yards, (182 mtrs). The officer of the watch (Dickinson) desperately ordered *"hard-a-starboard"* but at 19 knots the distance and time available were not to be sufficient. It was too late to do much more than to watch and pray as the two 'K' boats drew ever closer.

The night's quiet was to be shattered by the sound of the 'battles' first impact. Both boat and the horrified crew were thrown about as 'K' boat tore into 'K' boat. *K22* had struck something, yet the bridge crew were unable to confirm who it was that they had run into. As his boat slowly ceased rocking, Dickinson ordered all engines stopped and the watertight doors to be shut. He also had more lights rigged to the rear of the conning tower, only to aware that yet further ships were steaming up astern of his stricken boat. Moth recounted that.

"...as near as I can remember it would be about 7pm and as it was the last day of the month, I was very busy with my Paymaster's accounts. I thought being that we were at sea on the last day of the month that I should be able to finish the accounts and have them all ready to send to our parent ship on our return to harbour. I was sitting in my mess and only one other Petty Officer was there with me, when I suddenly thought this was the anniversary of the night I came out of K13. I looked up from my work and remarked this fact to this Petty Officer and his answer was, "I hope we shan't have to come out of her the same way". I said "No. I hope we shan't and then I went on to outline what had happened on that night. All of a sudden, we got a terrible crash and it was like running bang into a stone wall and I knew in a minute that we were in collision with something and whatever that something was we had run into her and not her into us'.

I threw my books across the table and yelled "Close Watertight Door" and I rushed into the control room. I was going farther forward but I met a Leading Seaman who was rushing aft. "What's the damage I said?"

and he told me that we were holed very badly, but that he had closed the forward bulkhead door. He said water was rushing in very quickly and he was only just in time. I went forward and found the bulkhead was standing alright, so I got the crew underway to shore the bulkhead with beams of wood. Our Navigator who was in charge of the bridge, had sent below for our Captain, but he didn't want sending for, for he was up there like a shot. He found out that we had rammed another submarine, but we didn't know for some time which it was. We soon found out that we were very badly damaged forward, but there was no danger of sinking. The boat we had rammed was damaged a great deal more than we were and she lay on the surface in a very dangerous predicament with her stern sticking out of the water and her nose well down into it".

The former *K13* now lay hove too, all but a year to the date and 121 miles from where she had lain on the bottom of Gareloch. But this time she lay stranded on the surface, in an estuary filled with many thousands of tons of naval warships steaming towards her in a dark moonless mist covered sea. The cold Scottish waters flooded in unhindered through the holes ripped into the pressure hull, but this time it was the forward torpedo room that was the one to flood. The invading waters surged on into the next compartment as the crew worked frantically to brace the bulkhead and watertight door in the second compartment, making use of wooden beams. Sailors are a superstitious breed as *K22's* crew feared the 'K' boat curse had called once more to complete its fate for the former *K13*. Dickinson assumed that they had somehow run into the illusive K12, but they had in fact ploughed into Harbottle's K14. The two boats lay with *K14* at 313 degrees and the *K22 at* 60 degrees. Moth recounts those frantic moments:

"... *we had already shored up the bulkhead between the forward torpedo room which was flooded and the wardroom and we found this to be holding alright. We were a good bit down by the bows, so we blew the water out of the forward ballast tanks and also the fuel from the forward group of fuel tanks and this brought us right up out of the water and we could see that there was no danger at all of us sinking. I now thought I would go on deck to look at the damage and when I got up there I found our bows had been pushed back and squashed in just like a concertina. We could do nothing now but sit and see what was to happen to K14. She still had a very big angle on, but we could do nothing, unless they decided to abandon her, in which case we could have taken her crew on board us".*

The force of the impact to the *K14* had nearly severed her bow, breaching the double hull to the forward mess deck and disabling her W/T. *K22's* bow had torn into the port side crew space immediately behind the forward torpedo room and the impact had in turn destroyed her forward wireless mast. As the water swept into the forward mess deck, the night claimed its first victims, two torpedo men, Able Seaman Walter J, Bowell, Leading Seaman Alexander Scott, who were to drown in the first few minutes, in what would grow to be a full opera of tragedy over the coming hours. The First Officer (Gavin), moving in advance of his Captains orders, dashed down the boat to find the wooden door to the wardroom had been ripped off by the impact and was now jamming the watertight door open. With the strength gifted by desperation he pulled the obstruction free and slammed the watertight door shut, saving both the crew and their boat. Gavin then reported to the Captain that the forward two compartments were flooded, but that the watertight door in the control room was currently holding. From *K14's* conning tower Harbottle signal by lamp to *K22* asking de Burgh to report the collision and to seek help. At 19:15, despite the orders for W/T silence, *K22* signalled by wireless to Ithuriel:

> *"Priority, have been in collision with submarine K12.*
> *Both ships are flooded forward".*

De Burgh replied to Harbottles enquiry by lamp that *K22* was *"OK"* and would be able to make harbour unassisted. But Harbottle was not so fortunate and signalled de Burgh to *"remain on station"* and to stand by as *K14* was unable to move, being down by her bows and liable to sink at any moment. De Burgh maneuvered his boat about to face away from the oncoming fleet to avoid any further collisions. With the rear of her conning tower now facing the approaching ships, he hoped that in the mist his navigation lights would be sufficient to be visible to the oncoming fleet. *K22* was not so fortunate and lay stopped and taking on water, while the *K14* signalled on her Aldis lamp to the sea around her, hoping any ships nearby, (but hidden by the dark), would come to their aid. de Burgh also equipped a crewman with a Very pistol and a healthy supply of cartridges to warn off any ships, as he knew the darkness too the stern of his boat held 85,660 tons of fast moving and oncoming battlecruisers. The remaining three submarines of the flotilla were yet unaware of the events unfolding in their wake. As the night's agenda unravelled, the *K12*, (the boat Dickinson thought that he had struck) had also to swerve to avoid the two stationary submarines assuming one of them to be the *K14.* Having swerved out of line, the *K12* return to her place in the wake of the *K17.*

By 19:30 the four ships of the 2nd Battlecruiser Squadron, with their destroyer escort now in place, were bearing down at 22 knots on the two stationary 'K' boats. As the 12-inched gunned juggernauts drew ever closer, the submarine bridge crews on both the bridges frantically flashed into the night by signal lamp and broadcast on their W/T requests for help. The battlecruiser *Australia* had only just increased her speed to the 22 knots, when those on her bridge sighted a series of red very light's arching skywards off their port bow. From the darkness came the light of an Addis lamp signalling *"HAVE-BEEN-IN-COLLISION-REQUEST-ASSISTANCE".* The chance of the oncoming three mountains of finest British steel missing the patches of water that held the helpless 'K' boats was now long gone. The destroyer escorts hurtled passed the 'K' boats to starboard and the battlecruiser thundered past the two submarines on their port side. So close was the *Australia* that her crewmen were able to look down into the submarine's funnels and see the fires glowing below. As the capital ship swept past, her wake seized the smaller vessel and tossed it about, the cliff of thundering steel missing her by less than three feet (91 cm). *HMAS Australia* tore past and vanished once more into the night, the froth of her wake being the only sign she had passed by. As his flagship was swallowed into the darkness, Rear-Admiral Leveson signalled the destroyer *Gabriel* to go to the aid of the two stricken vessels.

Both the *K14* and *K22's* bridge crews had held their breath and looked up as the colossal cliff like bulk of the battle-cruiser and her destroyers swept past on either beam. A destroyer thundered past the *K22* with a bare 10 feet (3.04 mtrs) separating between them, while the signalmen tried urgently to signal the maritime express train, as it roared past. The men in the conning tower waited for the sound of metal on metal, for the boats to be flung about as if in the hands of a child playing in his bathtub. But nothing happened, the 'K' boats emerged unscathed and unharmed by their bigger cousins. The submarine's desperate pleas for assistance were to go unanswered, but the signalman's night was to grow worse for just 100 yards off a second battle cruiser's bow loomed out of the dark, her bow framed by two waves of water and was this time headed direct for the submarine's engine-

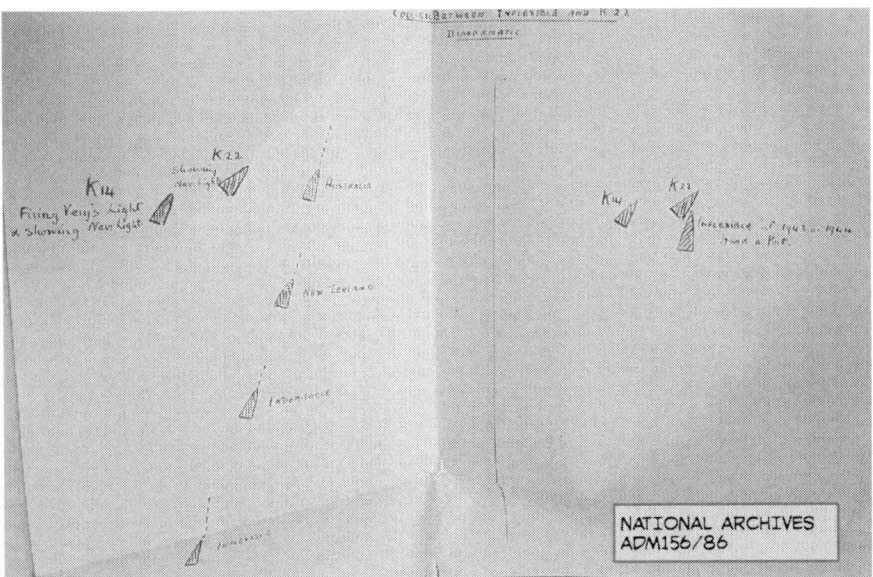

DIAGRAM FROM THE COURT OF ENQUIRY DETAILING THE COLLISION OF THE INFLEXIBLE.

The final battle cruiser of the procession was the 20,700 ton *Inflexible,* which had sometime prior lost sight of the ship in front of her, the Indomitable. At 19:30 her navigator Lieutenant-Commander Bernard Knightley Boase sighted a 'very light' and sent the officer of the watch, the Honourable John Bruce to report to Captain James Rose Price Hawksley. When Hawksley reached the bridge and while his eyes adjusted to the darkness, he could see nothing in the form of any hazard through his binoculars. Then after a minute or two white lights and the bow light of a small craft became visible to the Captain. He told Bruce to take their bearing, but Hawksley remained confident they would miss the source of the lights, whatever it was. Then directly ahead a third lone white light was sighted. Hawksley believing that at last he had found the elusive Indomitable's stern light, breathed a sigh of relief. But his reprieve was to be only too tragically short lived as a green navigation light leapt out of the darkness

400 yards (365 mtrs) distant. Orders were shouted for *"hard port"* and *"full astern"* as what was assumed to be a destroyer lay before the battlecruisers oncoming bow. But *Inflexible* ploughed onwards at an all too slowly diminishing 22 knots. Both crews held their breath as the distance grew less with every turn of the *Inflexible's* screws. Too slowly the battle-cruiser started to turn, but it was to be too little and too late. The 20,700 tons of battlecruiser ploughed in too and then rode over the diminutive 1,980 tons of *K22*, ripping and twisting 30 feet of her bows out to port forming a right angle. As the Inflexible slowly swung away her stern caught the 'K' boat at 165 degrees and ripped off both the submarine's external ballast and fuel tanks. De Burgh reported afterwards that at the time of impact *Inflexible* had been going astern, but regardless she did not stop.

The *K22's* bulk was forcefully submerged by the sheer mass of the colossal hull that had so suddenly mounted her, until only her conning tower and superstructure remained above the waves. Then having steamrollered the shocked submarine, the wake of the colossal battlecruiser flung the battered submarine about and swept over her as if she were a twig in its wash. The signalman on duty in the conning tower, having regained his feet frantically signalled the vanishing *Inflexible* for help. But the battlecruiser sailed on into the dark seemingly unaware of his pleas and the carnage that she had left lying in her wake.

Inside K22 the watertight doors leading through to the damage bows were holding, despite the pressure building up on the far side, but the loss of her tanks had given the wounded submarine a list to port. Captain de Burgh ordered 150 tons of water ballast be pumped out to restore the hulls lost even keel and that still more lights on deck be switched on. With every passing minute the conning tower crew fired a Very light aloft in a frenzied plea for help.

At 19:40 the Ithuriel lay 6 miles off the stricken *K22* and her Captain (Leir) had received the decoded *K22's* message about the first collision between the two submarines. The message read as if *K22* had been struck by a merchant ship named the *'Nova Scotia'*, the wrong code having been used to decipher the message. In addition, Ithuriel's log notes a signal lamp from another 'K' boat saying *K22* had not been seen for a while. Twenty minutes later Leir received a second coded message stating that both *K22* and *K12* had been in a collision. On the Courageous the 21:15 garbled message was taken in at 21:40; *"K22 to Ithuriel. K12 both....flooded ......"* If the night had been one of peace time, the fleet would simply have heaved too, illuminated their searchlights and launched the ships boats to bring assistance to the 'K' boats. But wartime brings the peril of the enemy submarine and even though this was an exercise, turning back to help them was not an option for the fleet. But the *Ithuriel* in her role as the flotillas flag ship had to render assistance and passed by signal light to the 'K' boat astern of her, orders to turn 16 points southward in succession, (a process that took half a mile of sea room) using 5 degree of helm at 20:10. The signal was then repeated submarine by submarine down the line of trailing 'K' boats. The *Ithuriel* regardless of the reported German submarine lurking off May Island switched on all her navigation lights to aid her 'ducklings' at 20:09. The manoeuvre was begun at 20:10 and seven minutes later, at 20:17 the last submarine, the *K12* had completed her change of course.

At 20:40 as his flotilla reversed its course to bring aid to the two damaged 'K' boats, Commander Leir ordered Lieutenant Taylor to despatch an encoded message by W/T to the flag officers on both the *Courageous* and *Barham.* Leir signal warned them of what was unfolding in the waters off May island,

> *"Submarines K-12 and K-22 have been in collision and are holed forward. I am proceeding to their assistance with 13th Submarine Flotilla. Position 18 miles east magnetic from May Island".*

But for reasons unknown, the message was to be delayed before it was finally sent.

At 20:18 the *Ithuriel's* lookouts sighted an oncoming darkened shape, as the *Australia* made her way remorselessly eastwards out into the North Sea, 45 minutes after her near brush with the 13th flotilla. The battlecruiser squadron was on a more southerly course, but the *Ithuriel's* turn had put both her trailing 'K' boats and herself on a course to cross the oncoming battlecruisers bow, in the parody of a 'T'. As his lookouts reported their sighting of the capital ships, Leir ordered a change of course to try to pass south of the *Australia* by 600 yard off the starboard beam. But time was no more abundant than earlier, and the 'K' boats were notoriously slow in completing any form of manoeuvre. They had the dexterity of a battlecruiser and the length of a small cruiser. The *K12*, (the last in the line) spotted the bulk of the *Australia* coming out of the mist, her bow pointed straight towards her. The *K12's* Captain, (John Graham Bower) frantically ordered his helmsman to swing the oversized graceless submarine "hard a starboard" as the *Australia's* lookouts in turn sighted the Ithuriel's group commencing its ponderous turn. But the 'K' boats slowness in turning on their lights had delayed the battlecruiser sighting the submarines lying in their path. It was by now too late for the *Australia* to make a full turn away and Leveson remarked to his flag Captain "if we turn our stern will swing round and bang the last submarine on the nose". *Australia* held to her course and was to be gifted by yet another paint scraping near miss with barely 2 to 3 feet separating the two hulls. As the battlecruiser hurtled past, her wake once more seized a 'K' boat and threw both submarine and her crew about.

The *Ithuriel* in turn managed to dodge the *Australia* and the battlecruisers escorting destroyers were fortunate to make a timely sighting of the oncoming submarine's navigation lights. The *Ithuriel* was quickly swung back to starboard and a destroyer ran close along her port side. Then as Leir ordered his command southwest yet another destroyer appeared from out of the darkness. One by one the 'K' boats managed to safely swing clear and in the space of just four minutes Leir had put his ship through five changes of course. But in all the twisting and turning the *K11* had fallen behind the Ithuriel, while the *K17* had in turn lost ground and now lay half a mile astern of the *K11*.

The capital ships that comprised the Rosyth force that night had on their approach to May Island maintained a rigid line ahead formation, but the numerous changes of course had unintentionally altered the fleets line formation to one of an irregular echelon. Before the 12th flotilla had reached May Island their flagship, (the Active class scout cruiser), *HMS Fearless's* W/T room had picked up at 19:45 the *K22's* coded distress call, the same one the Ithuriel had decoded. The darkness that surrounded the 12th flotilla was pierced by the flashing of a signal lamp as Captain Little ordered the *K3, K4, K6* and *K7* to keep a sharp look out and to increase their stern lights to full power. The battered, bruised and shaken

K22 radioed in code to the cruiser leading her flotilla to report that she should be able to reach port, but that the *K14* was not so fortunate and she lay crippled and sinking.

At 19:45 the *Fearless* passed May Island and a few minutes later Little ordered the scheduled change of course. After another thirty minutes the cruisers Captain relaxed believing he was now safely beyond the scene of the incident. At 20:25 Leveson ordered a signal to the three battleships, (*Barham, Warspite* & *Valiant*), following behind the 'K' boats, "priority have just passed Ithuriel and three submarines inward bound". The signal went out 15 minutes after the Ithuriel and her 'K' boats had begun their turn, but it was to be too late for the *Fearless.* As the signal was sent, officers on her bridge sighted white lights from two vessels moving in a line ahead and passing across the *Fearless* and the 'K' boats bow from port to starboard. The next sighting from the *Fearless's* bridge was a single light following in the wake of the preceding two vessels. Little ordered by lamp and radio that his 'flotilla' illuminate all their navigation lights, but he was to make no order for a change in their course and the flotilla held true to its current compass bearing. Little had assumed the other vessel would obey the law of the sea and 'port her helm' to pass down *Fearless's* port beam. But as the ships drew closer there was to be no change of course and as the distance grew dangerously ever shorter, ships sirens sounded three short blasts and another three 'S' in Morse (... ... ...) signalling that the *Fearless* was going astern. But by this stage the time and distance remaining were too little and too insufficient, as the cruisers forward momentum negated any immediate attempt to go astern.

HMS Fearless's bow, powered by the 3,390 tons of cruiser behind it, rammed into the *K17* on her starboard side, forward of the conning tower. As the cruiser sliced into the smaller craft, with her remaining forward momentum she buried her bow deeper into her victim and the *K17* twisting free of the cruiser passed down her port side. From the deck of Fearless it seemed as if *K17* had been dealt a mortal blow and had sunk instantly.

As the *K17's* bridges crew had come to realise the collision was to be unavoidable, with ten seconds to spare, the watertight doors had been ordered shut. As the Fearless rammed the submarine at 20:32, the K17 rolled and bucked under the impact throwing the crew around the 'K' boats interior and the internal lights were lost, plunging the crew into darkness. To make matters worse, water had contaminated the batteries and now a toxic gas was being released into the boat. Little ordered that all the cruisers watertight doors be shut and sounded 'D' on the ship's siren (-..), telling the boats astern to keep clear. It was now 20:32, an hour and a half after the nights first collision.

Lieutenant Gerald Edward Armitage Jackson was in the *K17's* wardroom when the order came through, 20 seconds after the impact to close all watertight doors. He made his way into the control room as the interior lights went out and the crew were plunged into darkness. Jackson with some help struggled to close the foremost door to the control room but the incoming waters pressure made it all most impossible and threatened to take the legs from under them.

But despite the horror of the impact and appearances, *K17* had not plummeted to the seabed and she slowly drifted astern, being swallowed up by the evening's darkness. As she fell astern of the flotilla leader, sea water flooded in through the wound in her side at the fore end of the wardroom. Despite the lethal situation the crew remained calm and went about their duties, waist deep in water as they struggled to shut the watertight doors, a fight they were only ever to lose. But Lieutenant-Commander Henry J. Hearn had to finally accept that his boat was beyond saving and gave the order all Captains fear, *"abandon ship"*. His crew scrambled up onto the submarines decking, emerging from both the control and engine room hatches as the sea water had by this stage claimed everywhere forward of the control room and the bows were awash. With the fore end of the submarine becoming more submerged by the minute, the Captain ordered his crew to move aft along the deck. The crew shuffled towards the stern as the bow sank beneath their feet and the stern lifted free of the water. With the stern rapidly becoming the only part of the hull still above the surface, the crew clung to the boat's guns, funnels and superstructure as the sea swallowed more and more of the drowning warship. The *Fearless* had by this time put her engines into reverse and sounded a blast of three on her horn once or twice and then a series of "D's" (-..) to warn the boats in her wake. The *Fearless* had come to an abrupt halt a skill the approaching 'K' boats would lack as they drew closer. As the Firth of Forth's waters reached further along the casing, men were washed off into the freezing cold Scottish waters from where they watched the *Fearless's* searchlights as she scoured the sea, finally finding the stricken 'K' boat. Then additional searchlights from the flotillas other boats swept over the submarine as her stern rose higher and eight minutes after the collision *K17* lifted her stern high into the night sky, her free stern light marking the summit of the mountain of steel, as she sank into 27 fathoms of water off May island, the *Fearless's* search light still illuminating her as she slipped 164 feet (50 mtrs) down to her watery tomb.

Four hundred yards astern of the *Fearless*, Commander Stokes in the *K4* could hear the flotilla leader's siren as it screamed out into the darkness. The Commander ordered his boat full astern and then to stop engine's. To mark their location and having also to ignore the U-boat threat, Stokes now ordered his boats navigation and stern light to be illuminated at full power, as he was close to the Fearless. The *K4* swung out too starboard unaware of the events unfolding in the waters surrounding her.

The next boat astern, the *K3*, had also turned on her own navigation lights having sighted the other boats illuminations. Unsure of the events erupting around them, the *K3's* officer of the watch called his Captain, Commander Herbert William Shove, away from his dinner and onto the conning tower bridge. The *K3* was slowly but gradually closing in on the lights at half speed and as the distance diminished Shove too was puzzled as to the source of the illuminations that had broken away from the flotilla's line. Suddenly out of that night's treacherous darkness loomed the *K4*, but the shortness of the distance left only seconds before the two submarines would make contact. Stocks frantically gave the order to swing the *K3* to port managing somehow to narrowly miss the *K4*, then having righted his stern the two boats missed each other once more while *K3* was going astern. A quarter mile astern the K3 finally came to a halt and Shove tried to peer through the darkness to see what the cause of the commotion was.

Off to the *K3's* starboard beam the *Fearless*, despite the reported U-boat, was making use of her searchlight and in the beams of light Commander Shove on the *K3* sighted a sinking submarine with its crew on the stern desperately waving their arms. But with two boats closer he decided to leave the rescue to the two unknown boats. The Ithuriel with *K11* in company slowly approached the scene of the first sinking unaware of the drama's second chapter unfolding behind them. Both had sighted the *Fearless'* lights and *K11* had maneuvered to give them a wide berth, while only one of the 'K' boats still trailed the *Ithuriel.*

In the searchlight illuminated evening the Captains tried to untangle and make sense of the drama being played out around them. The *K22* and *K14* had collided astern and the Fearless had sunk the *K17*. In addition, *K12* had just been missed by the Australia which was now on a collision course with the *K6*.

The watch on board the *K6* had managed to sight the navigation lights in sufficient time to allow her to make a turn safely to starboard. With the manoeuvre complete K6 once more resumed her original course, having lost sight of the *K3*, whom she had been trailing by 600 yards (548.64 mtrs) during the turn. But in the nights growing confusion *K6's* watch sighted a lone white light ahead and assumed a position astern of it, taking it to be a 'K' boat. As *K6* trailed the 'unidentified' vessel at 19 knots her watch could hear a siren in the distance that was emitting the Morse for 'D'. Unsure of what was unfolding around him, the officer of the watch despatched a messenger below to request Layton to come to the conning tower bridge. The watch now sighted the outline silhouettes of submarines off to their starboard as well as a light off the port bow. It was at this stage they realized they were most unlikely to be following the *K3's* stern light, but in fact another low in the water ship that was in the process of crossing their bows. At this stage Commander

Geoffrey Layton finally stepped onto the bridge and having seen the light, urgently ordered "slow both", followed by a frantic, *"stop both"*. Whichever 'K' boat it was, it now lay ahead of the *K6's* bow and broadside on to her. Layton realizing that disaster loomed before his boats remorseless but slowing bow, ordered a series of actions,

"full speed astern... hard a port... sound full stern on siren... navigation lights on... searchlight on astern".

But all was too late, and Layton could only hope to reduce the impact to that of a glancing blow. He watched in horror as the *K6's* bow sliced deep into the helpless *K4* at a right angle, almost severing her in two. The two 'K' boats lay at right angles to each other, in a horrific mimicry of the letter 'T', but the *K6's* engines continued to go astern. The K4 was mortally wounded and was starting a fatal dive to the seabed, threatening to drag the entangled *K6* with her. Layton ordered the closure of all the watertight doors and for *Fearless* to be signalled telling her what had happened, asking urgently for help. For 30 long seconds it seemed as if the *K6* too was destined for the seabed as the waters filling the *K4* threatened to drag them both down. But her net buoyancy and her hard-working propellers finally, to the sound of metal on metal, pulled the 'K' boat free. But *K6's* withdraw exposed the deep wound in her sister ship, allowing the invading waters to flood in faster and in greater volume. With his boat backing off from the *K4*, Layton ordered the engines to be stopped. He also sent Lieutenant Sandford forward to examine the forward compartments and the searchlight illuminated as a warning to the last in the line, the *K7*. By now all that remained of the *K4* above water was her conning tower. A post 1945 visit to the wreck revealed that the bow section of the *K4* was around 65 feet (20 mtrs) in length. It is speculated that it parted from the main hull immediately after *K6* and *K7* had rammed her, staying afloat for a while and drifting in the tide until it too sank.

At this stage in the unfolding drama, the *K7* lay half a mile astern of the *K6* and her Captain, Lieutenant-Commander Samuel Maryon Gorton Gravener was only to aware, through bitter personal experience, of the 'K' boats fault known as 'losing suction', which brought the boats to an unexpected stop. Through his time in command of the *K7* (14 November 1917 to October 1919) he would always add 100 yards to any distances and told other 'K' boat Captains he was just a poor judge of space. Thirty seconds after hearing the 'D' siren he brought *K7* down to 12 knots and ordered the navigation lights to be illuminated. Ahead and off to starboard he recognized the *Fearless* and off to port he spotted the *K6*. To give the *Fearless* some space he ordered his boat to be turned to port which unintentionally aimed his commands bows at the *K6*. But Gravener on realizing the vessel before him was hove too ordered the *K7's* engines to be stopped. Then he ordered hard a starboard and astern on both engines. As the *K7* passed down *K6's* starboard side she managed to just miss her. The *K6* switched on her searchlight and the beam revealed to Gravener yet another 'K' boat in the process of crossing her bows. But the vessel seemed devoid of any crew on her conning tower or superstructure and was bizarrely low in the water. As Gravener exclaimed *"hell its sinking"* the submarine vanished beneath the waves, going so fast that the oncoming *K7's* keel merely brushed the unknown 'K' boats bows. Once *K7* had finally come to a halt Gravener and his crew could hear the cries of the men in the icy cold water as they struggled astern.

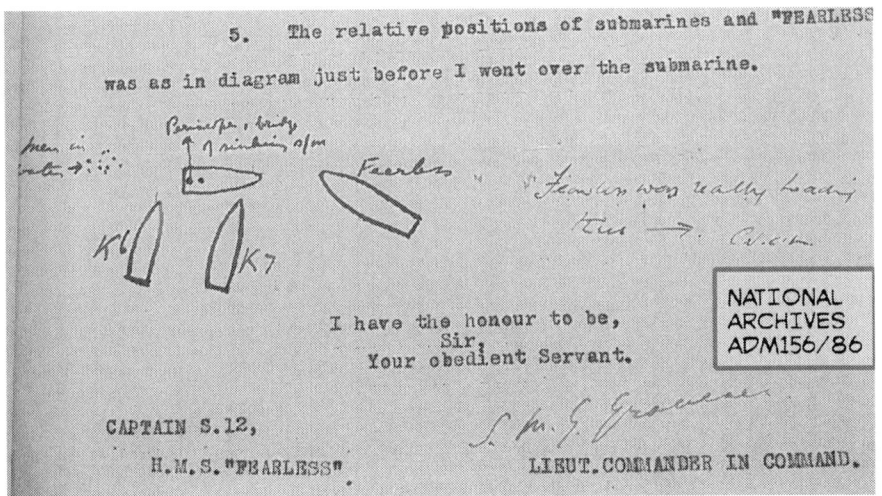

FROM THE COURT OF ENQUIRY FILES

The *Fearless* having switched on her own searchlights, passed the beams over the struggling men in the water. Little ordered via a signal lamp for the *K7* to recover the men and as she slowly went astern Gravener called his own crew onto the deck casing to rescue the men in the water.

As the Fearless swept her searchlights over the water and the K7's men prepared to rescue the survivors in the sea, four miles astern of the last 'K' boat was the 90,000+ tons of the 5th Battle squadron's three battleships. *Barham* had at 19:54 received the *Australia's* signal warning just that *a "vessel* [was] in distress in [the] *path of* [the] *fleet* [and was] *due north of May island* [and a] *destroyer* [was] *standing by".* The message relating to the *K14* and *K22* was transmitted 40 minutes after the collision, 20 minutes after the Australia had thundered through the scene of the accident and 13 minutes after the *Inflexible* had struck the *K22.* As the 'K' boat disaster played out in the seas around her, the Ithuriel wireless room had remained (and was still) silent.

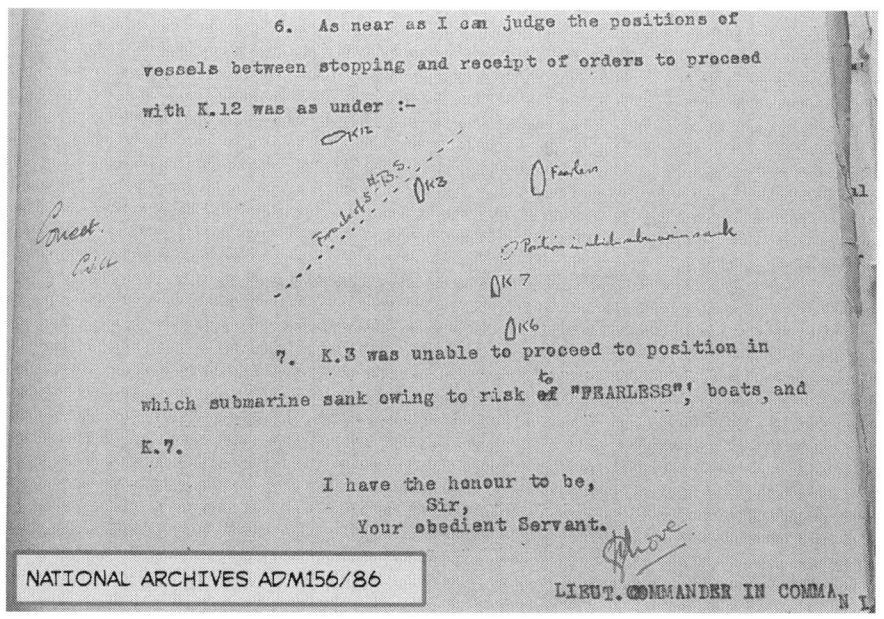

LT-CDR SHOVE (K3) DIAGRAM OF FEARLESS's COLLISION

The Inflexible's collision marked the anniversary of the

K13's sinking during her trials, something Moth was only to aware of;

"...I was still on the upper deck, when I heard a cry from someone who was aft. Everyone on the bridge turned and we could easily see the hull of a very big ship loom-ing out of the darkness. She was making straight for our Conning Tower at a great speed, but I think she must have seen us about the same time as we saw her, for we could see she was altering course. I am sure everyone must have held their breath for although she was altering her course, we could all see that it would be impossible for her to avoid us. We put our telegraphs to full speed astern, but all to no use, for she crashed into us at a terrific rate, the blow simply heeled us ever to a very bad angle and tore away our bow and pushed it around to port, for we had been struck on the starboard side. I think myself the ship must have been carrying extreme helm, for as she passed her stern swung in on top of us. Her port propeller or her rudder tore our ex-ternal tanks all along the starboard side and she also shoved us down in the water until the water was only a few inches from our conning tower and the boiler room intakes, which were of course wide open. I really thought it was all up this time for I thought it would be impossible for the boat to float after being so severely damaged.

But no! Up she came again and she put me in the mind of a living thing; who did not intend to give up so easily. As the stern of the ship swung by us, it was possible for us to make out part of her name and we found her to be HMS Inflexible. We immediately signalled her, told her we were in a sinking condition and asked her to stand

> *by us, but she didn't even answer us. I don't suppose she*
> *dared to risk turning back for she would most probably*
> *have had more trouble with the other ships who were*
> *now leaving the Firth of Forth. As we could see that we*
> *were going to get no help from anyone else, we set to*
> *work to do our utmost to keep the boat afloat. We blew*
> *all the fuel from the tanks leaving sufficient only to get*
> *us back. This brought us up in the water and we could*
> *see now, that we weren't going to sink".*

At 20.09 the tail end of the Rosyth fleet, the three battleships of the 5th battle squadron with their accompanying
destroyers steamed past May Island. As the battle squadron
passed the small land mass, the destroyer *Venetia* had a boat
in the water as she stood by to help the *K14* while a search
light played on the submarine and her own ships boat. The
battle squadron was able to see the scene unfolding on the
water before them and as a result passed the scene in safety
and with no additional life's lost. Once beyond May Island
the ships of the 5th Squadron, as per its orders, changed their
course. Fifteen minutes later the collision between the *K4*
and *K17* took place. The three battleships closed in on the
K3 laying off the *Fearless's* port beam with both the *K6* and
K7 lying astern of the cruiser. The *K12* was baffled by the
events and had stopped off the *K3's* port bow. All 5 ships had
lights on and many of *K17's* crew of 56 men were struggling
in the water awaiting rescue.

At 20:38 Fearless signalled the *Barham* that she had sunk
K17 and finally at 21.40 the *Ithuriel* broke her own W/T silence. She announced that she had turned back to aid the
K14 and the *K22*. Of the four 'K' boats she had led out to sea,
only the lone *K11* now trailed her. Neither of the W/T messages were to allow the speeding battleships sufficient time
to avoid what lay before them. At 21 knots the 33,790-ton

Barham led her flotilla through the disaster scene, all three of the colossal fast-moving battleships somehow missed the comparatively diminutive *K3* by mere inches. As the castles of steel thundered by, their wakes tossed the submarine about as if she was a cork. Her men clung on as the hull was thrown from side to side and the bridge crew looked up as the huge ship briefly towered over them. By a miracle, or by something the 'K' boats were unfamiliar with, good luck, the battleship and the submarine's hulls did not come into contact. The 5th battle squadrons escorting destroyers in turn steamed directly at the *Fearless*, while the *K7* made her way slowly astern with her crew working on deck desperately trying to help their colleagues in the sea. The destroyers thundered over the patch of water that the *K17* had so recently sunk in and on through the men struggling in the water. The destroyer's bows cleaved a path through the 56 men in the sea and those who had survived the speeding cliff size ships were dealt a horrific death by the spinning propellers. The men struggling and screaming in the cold waters of the Firth of the Forth were sucked down and into the mincing machine the destroyer's propellers had now become. The wake of the battleships in turn threw the rescue boat, (the *K7*) about, tossing several of her deck crew into the sea. Then as fast as they had burst from the night's darkness, the 5th Battle squadron and its escorts were swallowed up once more by the darkness and were gone, blood red water and minced carcasses marking the wake of their passage. Of the 56 men from *K17* who had been in the water moments ago, only 9 now survived to be rescued. The *K7's* men were to be the more fortunate and all were to be pulled uninjured from the sea.

As men struggled in the freezing cold water awaiting their rescue, the identity of a second submarine sunk puzzled Layton as he looked out from the bridge of the *K6*. He signalled the Fearless that he had struck the *K3*, given that she was next in the line to his craft. But his theory was to be disproved when the 'sunken' *K3* identified herself off the port beam of the flotilla leader. When Layton heard that the Fearless herself had hit something it was assumed to be the K7 as she was sinking. But the *Fearless'* officers rapidly concluded it was the *K4* they had sunk.

By this point the *K6's* fore compartments were flooded to a depth of six inches and the crew frantically in searching for the source discovered that the starboard torpedo tube was the leak. When the seawater was no longer flooding in, the water already onboard could now be returned by the pumps out into the Firth of the Forth. With the leak stopped and water being pumped out, a much-relieved Layton could now signal by lamp to the *Fearless* that his command was no longer in any danger of sinking.

At 20:58 the Cou*rageous* received the *Ithuriel's* 20:40:

"Priority. Submarine K12 and K22 have been in collision and are holed forward. I am proceeding to their assistance with 13th submarine flotilla. Position 18 miles magnetic from May Island. 2040".

Half an hour after the nights final collision Little ordered both the K3 and K2 to make their way back to the safety of Rosyth. He also had his ships boats scour the water for survivors, but after an hour no one was found to be alive, only the remains of the dead were to be seen.

The *Fearless* had lost a large slice of her bow and suffered flooding to a number of her lower compartments. Twenty feet of the top half of her bows over hung the water, looking as if a giant sea creature had risen from the depths and had bitten a chunk of her bow from the water line to two thirds of the way up to the deck line. On her starboard side a huge plate stuck out as if she had in addition grown a solitary fin and the flooding had reached to the number 17 bulkhead. But when the ship moved forward the waters pressure pushed the 'fin' against her helm and made the steering of a steady course difficult. At 21:49 Little flashed Gravener in the *K7*:

> *"I am going to return to harbour, stern first slow speed. Keep near me".*

For half an hour both the *K6* and *K7* stood close by as the Fearless made a mere 3.5 knots up the estuary. But it was soon to become evident that the exposed watertight doors would in fact hold, so Little despatch the K6 and K7 ahead to the Burntisland Roads which lies on the northern shore of the Firth of the Forth.

At the same time (21:10) Ithuriel and the *K11* went to the aid of the K14 and *K22*. The would-be rescuers arrived north of May Island at 21:15, but by that time the *K22* was already Rosyth bound, like the *Fearless,* stern first. The *K14* was low in the water, down by her bows and was about to follow in their wake, towed by the destroyer *Venetia*. The *Ithuriel* joined the procession at 22:00 going at 4 knots as far as Inchkeith where a number of harbour tugs took over the job of the towing.

OVER PAGE: CHART FROM THE ENQUIRY SHOWING THE TRACK OF THE TORPEDO BOATS DURING THE 'BATTLE'. THE CHART IS ON THIN 'WAX' PAPER, WHICH ALLOWS THE FOLLOWING PAGE IN THE FILE TO BE VISIBLE AS WELL.

Attached was a small card reading:

"6 pm   ELIENESS   Bearing   N.36 E Course E&N (Mag) Speed 10 kn.

6.05 pm   Do.   North 1   E&N   Do.

6.35 pm   Do.   N.89 W.4-4/6 Altered course to W&S (Mag)

7.10 pm   Do.   North 1'   Do   E&N (Mag)

7.40 pm   Do.   N.89.W 4-4/6 Do   W&S (Mag)

7.58   Do.   N.70.W.2'   Do   E&N (Mag) Speed 18kn

8.30 pm   Do.   May Island Bearing South 3 miles (estimated) High Light Visible.

Tracings from chart 114.A

TB's 25,28 &32 steaming in line ahead showed all navigation lights from 5.30 until 6.11 p.m, after which instructions were received to proceed to position 3 North of May Island all lights were shown (spelt shewn) and kept during throughout the search.

STAMPED BY REAR-ADMIRAL 2ND BATTLE SQUADRON 8 FEB 1918"

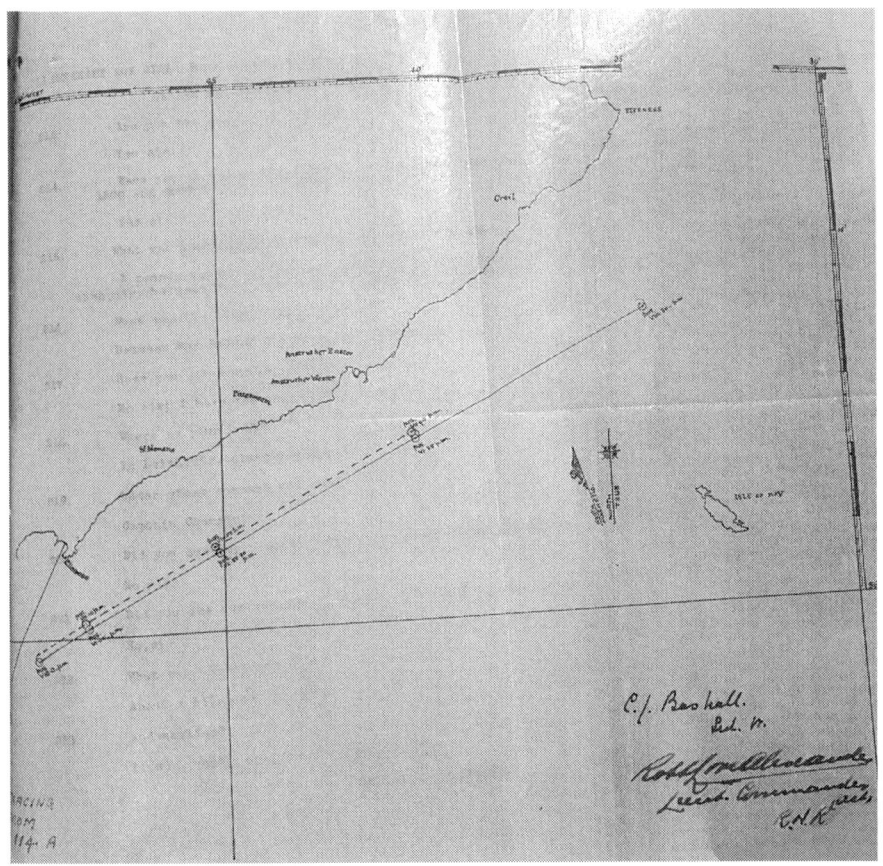

BELOW: *HMS FEARLESS IN DOCK WITH HER DESTROYED BOW FROM THE 'BATTLE'.' YOU CAN SCALE THE SKZE OF THE DAMGE BY THE FIGURE LOOKING UP. THE BULKHEARDS THAT SERVED TO KEEP THE SHIP DRY ARE VISIBLE BEYOND THE TORN BOW.*

As the evening's events had unfolded off May Island three torpedo boats (*T25*, *T28* and *T32)* were also at sea and by 18:00 they were running 'East by North and West by South' and were located two miles off Elisness. The crafts Commanders, (unlike the eight trawlers) were aware the fleet was in the process of heading out to sea and at 19:55 received a W/T message from the Extended Defence Officer of Inchkeith. He advised them that the *K14* had been in a collision

3 miles north of May Island and they were to 'render all and any assistance'. The three boats set a course at 18 knots for the reported location of the *K14* . The Commander of *TB25* ordered the other two boats to form a line abreast to starboard and port of his craft, half a mile out to sweep for the damaged submarine. As they approached the area the smell of oil greeted the crews and at 20:58 *TB32* reported by W/T, *"two submarines north of May Island"*. By this stage *Venetina* had the K14, which was illuminated by *TB26* and *TB32's* searchlights. The Extended Defence Officer signalled *TB25* at 21:17 to stand by *K12* and *K22,* ready to offer assistance should it be needed. Unable to see the two boats, TB25 called her two companions away and made 15 knots towards Fidra Gap, hoping to overtake the two 'K' boats. The searching TB's only found *K22* and *TB25* having signalled *TB26* and *TB32, "I shall take K22 into harbour. Return and search for K12".* They then parted company. TB32 eventually escorted *K12* and one other 'K' boat into port.

During the early hours of the morning the Admiral commanding Rosyth broke the news of the incident to the Admirals in London:

Sent 03:15

Received: 03:53

"555. Following from Captain (S) 12th submarine Flotilla begins. H.M.S. FEARLESS in collision with submarine K.17 lat. 58.15 N. long. 2.9W.Submarine

K.17 sunk.Submarine K.6 also in collision with another submarine probably submarine K.4 which has also sunk. Am ordering all submarines to return to base. H.M.S. FEARLESS and submarine K.6 damaged forward. H.M.S FEARLESS seriously requires docking.ends. Submarine K.14 has been in collision has two compartments flooded. Draught of water forward 22 feet.Submarine K.22 also in collision steaming three knots bows damaged unable to anchor".

PREVIOUS PAGE: THE FEARLESS' BOW SHOWING THE IMPACT DAMAGE FROM K17.

The new day revealed that a piece of the *K17's* plate had been forced into Fearless' bow. With the sun risen a fresh search for survivors was undertaken, but the estuary only offered up bodies. The two crippled submarines and the *Fearless* finally reached the sanctuary of Rosyth well after dawn on the 1st February and was secured at 12:28 to a buoy. At 13:40 with the aid of a tug she made her way into Rosyth's basin and was warped against the basin wall by 14:30.

During the early hours of the 1st February at 03:15 the Admiral of Rosyth, Rear-Admiral Henry H. Bruce, signaled the Admiralty:

> *"Following from Captain (S) 12th submarine Flotilla begins H.M.S FEARLESS in collision with submarine K.17 1st. 55.15N. long 2.9.W. Submarine K.17 sunk. Submarine K.6 also in collision with another submarine probably submarine K.4 which has also sunk. Am ordering all submarines to return to base. H.M.S FEARLESS and submarine K.6 damaged forward. FEARLESS seriously requires docking. ends. Submarine K.14 has been in collision with two compartment flooded; Draught of water forward 22 feet. Submarine K.22 also in collision steaming three knots bows damaged unable to anchor".*

Admiralty in London noted the signal received at 03:52

The morning after the 'Battle' was a hard time for the flotillas survivors and was to be the end of Moth's association with the cursed 'K' boats. He notes in his biography!

> *"What a gloom this cast over our flotilla. It is bad enough to know that a boat has been sunk by the enemy, but to know our own ships had done this was terrible. I lost a great many friends in those boats and as I have already said, the boys who were dancing with us a few months before at Shandon had now made the supreme sacrifice. Of course, this had to be kept quiet as it was War Time but in*

the 'K' Boat flotillas I have often heard this incident spoken of as "The Battle of May Island". I think it is a very good name for it, anyhow I expect if the Germans had heard of it, they would have had a good chuckle. We now waited for the Admiralty to decide what was to happen to us and when the news came, it was to say that K22 and K14 were to be paid off and put out of commission until they were thoroughly overhauled and the damage made good. My Captain was now appointed to K16, which boat was completing at Beardmores Shipbuilding Yard, Dalmuir. The reason he was appointed here was because the Captain who had been standing by her, was unfortunate enough to be out in K4 and so lost his life. I don't think my Captain was very pleased when he got his appointment, for he told me he had hoped to get an L Boat, as there were a good many of this class of boat building.

He sent for me and asked me if I would serve with him again, but when I found out he was going to a K, I thanked him very much, but said I considered I had had quite enough of Ks. I don't think any of my readers will accuse me of having cold feet, but my experiences in "K13/K22" had certainly made me think and I didn't intend to tempt providence for a third time in a K. I was also asked to stand by K22 and this meant a quiet time for nine months, but knowing if I stood by her, I should be expected to commission her, I refused. Accordingly, I paid off K22 on February 20th and proceeded on leave and again joined Fort Blockhouse on the 6th of March. Here I was again asked to go to K16 in fact my rating of torpedo coxswain was pointed out to me. The Drafting Officer said I was only allowed in the complement of 'K' Boats, but he said he could ask the

Commodore of the submarine service, if he could send me to an L Boat. I told him that I would revert to the General Service if I was again told off for a 'K' so at last consent was given for me to go to an L Boat commissioning".

With the demands of war, the Grand Fleet went on to conduct the planned exercises out in the North Sea, but on his return to port on the 2nd, Beatty ordered that a full enquiry be held into the events of May Island. The hastily-convened Court of Inquiry first sat five days later on the 5th February and was to last for five days. The Court's final report was released 14 days later, (on the 19th February) and it placed the blame for the 'battle' onto the shoulders of Commander Ernest William Leir and four other officers who were onboard the 'K' boats that night. The court recommended that Leir should be court martial, but it was found in the case of negligence against Leir for the loss of the K17, the ruling that it was "not proved".

In the matter of the collision by HMS Inflexible with the K22, the court placed the blame onto Lieutenant-Commander de Burgh, because his crippled submarine was in the way of the Rosyth fleet! The court knew K22 was both holed and standing by K14 to render assistance, but someone needed to be blamed. This despite the fact that the K22 was both well lit and flashing signals but the courts simply ignored this. Beatty was not to agree with the court and refused to except the ruling.

Both the investigation and subsistent court martial were kept quiet and much of the information was not to be released for seventy-six years, until 1994, by which time all of the participants had passed away and the delay saved any embarrass-

ment to the Navy.

Captain Little noted after the event that " I know it will be felt the flotilla made a mess of a difficult situation". The First Sea Lord, Sir Eric Campbell Geddes wrote that;

"I cannot but think as a layman of this chapter of accidents looks as if there was something wrong with the standard of the efficiency of the officers. Of course, naval officers will better appreciate the difficulties than I, but broadly speaking the catastrophe was caused by the cumulative mistake of those majority concerned".

The one factor the Admiralty never thought to place any blame on was the 'K' boats themselves. It had to be human error and not the fault of their flawed concept!

Those few hours of May Island brought the death of 104 lives, 55 from the *K4*, 47 from the *K17* and two from the *K14*.

Lieutenant Jackson, (who was the only officer to survive the loss of the *K17*), left the flotilla after only 8 days service in it. He was to be posted to two other submarine depot ships, the *Bonaventure* and *Alecto,* but there is no record that he ever served again on any other submarine.

Of the officers in command that night their careers took different paths of success or stagnation?

<u>***K22's***</u> Lieutenant-Commander Charles de Burgh was to go on to command the *K14.*

On the 9th September 1918 Commander Thomas Frederick Parker Calvert transferred from the *K11* to the post of Captain of *H.M.S Pegasus,* the seaplane carrier. He was to command the battlecruiser *Renown* between 1932 and 1933, completing his service in 1938, having served since 1936 as the Rear-Admiral Commanding the Second Cruiser Squadron.

K14's Commander Thomas Cecil Benfield Harbottle was to transfer to an 'L' class boat and was Captain of the depot ship *H.M.S Alecto,* between 1919 and 1921.

K12's Lieutenant Commander John Graham Bower left the K12 in November 1918 and was to be unemployed until becoming Captain of the depot ship *H.M.S Pandora* between February and November 1922. The remainder of his career would be a series of depot ships and training posts.

K3's Lieutenant-Commander Herbert William Shove ended his tenure as Captain to the *K3* in September 1919, being his last command with the navy.

K6's Commander Geoffrey Layton was to become Assistant to Admiral Sydney-Hall, handing command of the *K6* to Lieutenant-Commander Crowther. He had sailed for the first time on a 'K' boat that night of May Island and Layton handed command to Crowther with the words" *a bloody good introduction to 'K' boats".* Layton would progress through a series of commands until he was posted to cruisers and *HMS Renown* in the 1930s. He rose to be Rear-Admiral Commanding the Battle Cruiser Squadron between July 1938 and January 1939. The war would see him command cruiser squadrons before progressing onto flag commands in the Far East.

K7's Lieutenant-Commander Samuel Maryon Gorton Gravener stepped down from *K7* in October 1919 and his last command was the depot ship *Diligence* between May 1920 and August 1921.

HMS *Ithuriel's* Commander Ernest William Leir, (a former Captain to the *K3)* was appointed in command of both the scout cruiser *Fearless* on 7th March 1919 and the Twelfth Submarine Flotilla. Leir was promoted to the rank of Captain on 30th June 1919. On the 25th July, he was appointed the command of *HMB Dolphin* and an unrecorded submarine flotilla.

This position ended on 27th July 1921. He was promoted to the rank of Rear-Admiral on 8th October and placed on the Retired List on 9th October 1931. Leir was to be active with the Liverpool and Leigh Convoy Pools from September 1939 and in 1942 he was mentioned in dispatches for three years of outstanding devotion to duty as a commodore of ocean convoys. He returned to the Retired List on 11th September 1945, to receive class 'A' benefits in the rank of Commodore, Second Class.

Captain Little remained on board the *Fearless* until 1919 and retained his position as flotilla Commander. He was to progress through a series of shore and sea commands, reaching the post of senior officer in the Persian Gulf during the late 1920s. He retired in 1931 having served as Commodore-in-Charge, Portland between April 1929 and April 1931.

In 2011, surveyors were to undertake a full and detailed survey of the seabed for the Neart Na Gaoithe offshore wind farm and published sonar images of the wrecks of the two submarines, *K4* and *K17* that had been sunk during the 'battle'. The location of the two sunken submarines lay 328 feet (100 mtr) apart and about 164 feet (50 mtr) down and their location had long been known.

SECRET

S. 584a. (Established—January, 1914, Sta. 1305/14.)
(Revised January, 1916, Sta. 6071/15.)

No. 453/H.F.1100.

Date 19 February, 1918.

SUBJECT.

LOSS OF "K"-CLASS SUBMARINES.

FORMER.

ENCLOSURES.

(1). "ORION". 9th February, 1918, et seq.
(Finding and Minutes of Court of Enquiry).
(2). Rear-Admiral, Second Battle
Squadron, No.056/2 13th February, 1918.
(Two Track Charts - Under separate cover).

e Secretary

of the Admiralty.

"QUEEN ELIZABETH".

REPORT OR SUBMISSION.

Forwarded, concurring in the Finding of the Court
of Inquiry.

2. The following action is being taken as regards the
several collisions :-

Collision between K-14 and K-22 :-
Commander T. C. B. Harbottle, Commanding Officer
of K-14, is being informed that some responsibility for this
collision rests with him, in that he would have been better
advised to stop and sound 'D' on his syren when the helm
jammed.

Collision between "Inflexible" and K-22:
No action.

Collision between "Fearless" and K-17:
The Vice-Admiral Commanding, Battle Cruiser Force is
being directed to forward an application for the trial by
Court Martial of Commander E. W. Leir, D.S.O., to the Commander-
in-Chief, Coast of Scotland.

Collision between K-6 and K-4:
Lieutenant R. D. Sandford, Officer-of-the-Watch of
K-6, is being informed that blame is attributable to him for
not at once appreciating the necessity of getting clear and
for not taking action to do so on hearing D's sounded on the
syren ahead of him.

Lieutenant..

PREVIOUS PAGE: THE COURT OF ENQUIRYS SUMMARY.

THE WRECKS AS THE LAY TODAY.

❖ ❖ ❖

1 : 12th Flotilla, Flagship, Captain (S) Fearless

Submarines, K 2, K 3, K 4, K 5, K 6, K 7 & K 8.

2 : 13th Flotilla, flagship, captain (s) Ithuriel.

Submarines C 7, K 9, K 11, K 12, K 14, K 17 & K 22. (Oct 1917)

3 : Within the pages of the Court of Enquiry is a list of the witnesses the court called. The three pages allow us to see the ships that were in the vicinity during the battle.

Fearless   Captain C.J Little

Ithuriel	*Commander E.W.Leir*
K14	*Commander Harbottle*
K22	*Lieutenant-Commander de Burgh*
Australia	*Rear Admiral A.C.Leveson*
Australia	*Flag Lieutenant-Commander Warre*
Inflexible	*Captain J.R.P. Hawksley*
Australia	*Commander (N) W.E.Cornabe*
Inflexible	*Lieutenant-Commander (N) Boase*
Inflexible	*Lieutenant the Honorable J. Bruce*
TB 25	Lieutenant-Commander Love Alexander (RNR)
TB 28	*Lieutenant R. Gill*
TB32	*Lieutenant R.T. Park (RNR)*
K14	*Acting Engineer Lieutenant T. Gardner*
K14	*Able Seaman H Curtis*
K14	*Signalman W.H Fielder*
K12	*Lieutenant-Commander Bower*
Ithuriel	*Lieutenant Casey (RNR)*
K11	*Commander T.F.P Carfert*
K17	*Lieutenant G.E.A Jackson*
Rhouma	*Lieutenant A Darrock (RNR)*
Rhouma	*Mr. L.W.G Alford WT Tell (RNR)*
(Hired Grimsby Trawler)	
K17	*Stoker P.O J Stewart*
K17	*Leading seamen F. Brown*
K17	*Leading seaman A Westbrook*
K17	*Leading Seaman G Kimbell*
K17	*Stoker 1st class K Vass*

K17	*Stoker 1st class H Fulcher*
K17	*Stoker 1st class A Dowding*
Shemara	*Lieutenant A Badman (RNR)*
Shemara	*Lieutenant J McCullen (RNR)*
(Hired Yacht)	
K3	*Lieutenant-Commander H.W. Shove*
K3	*Acting Lieutenant L.F. Fowey*
K3	*Able seaman N Haley*
K6	*Commander G Layton*
K6	*Lieutenant R.D. Sandford*
K6	*Signalman F.G. Stockley*
K6	*Leading Seaman W. Pouste*
K7	*Lieutenant-Commander S.M. Gravener*
K7	*Leading seaman A.L. Martin*
Barham	*Captain A.W. Craig*
Fearless	*Lieutenant-Commander H.B. Maltby*
Fearless	*Staff-Surgeon A.F. Fleming*
Fearless	*Mr. E.W. Penny WT Tel RN*
Cave	*Temporary Acting Lieutenant R.B. Cuthbert (RNR)*
(Hired Hull Trawler)	
Good Hope	*Skipper Robert McKay (RNR)*
(Hired trawler or drifter)	
Culblean	*Temporary Lieutenant R. Rigby (RNR)*
(Hired Aberdeen Trawler)	

Ships in vicinity but witnesses not called.

Strathella* (Hired Trawler)

North King* (Not listed in RN Shipping list)

*Patrolling with the Culblean

.

4: Rather bizarrely (in relation to this narrative) the 2nd BCS was between November 1914 and January 1915 known as the "Cruiser Squadron K"

CHAPTER EIGHT. THE
FINAL YEAR OF WAR.

"To Sum Up In Brief The Use Of 'K' Boats, It May Be Said That:- As Surface Ships, They Can Get To The Scene Of Action And Choose Their Attacking Position, After Which They Have, Except For A Small Difference Of Speed, The Same Chance Of Making A Successful Attack As Any Other Submarine In The Same Position".

(N.s. Nash)

All in all, February 1918 was not a good month for the 'K' boats. *K4* and *K17* lay at the bottom of the Firth of the Forth and *K6, K7, K14, K22* and the Fearless were in the hands of the dockyard undergoing repairs.

The Admiralty strove to restrict the full story of the event's off May Island and until the 1990's the relevant files would be sealed shut. But sailors talk and news of the 'battle made its way through the messes and wardrooms of the submarine service. It had been hard to crew the boats before that night off May Island. But now it became all but impossible. By April the navy was forced to decommission *K14* and *K22* and reallocate their crews to other postings within the service. But by the 22nd August the *K22* was once more in service, as had been the *K14* on the 19th of August.

Between the 13th January and the 27th February 1918 the K5 was in dockyard hands at Rosyth. A voice pipe was run from the bridge to the 3-inch gun, a 10-gallon petrol tank installed within the superstructure, additional lockers fitted and a 4-inch gun installed on the superstructure, while the 3-inch gun was moved over the boiler intakes. It had been intended to fit the new 'Swan' bow but a lack of workmen in the yard saw that postponed.

Between the 9th of May and 27th July 1918, the *K3* had been in the hands of Armstrong's Wallsend's Newcastle yard, where her funnels were extended, and the superstructure adapted around the extension. Her aft 4-inch mount and deck torpedo tubes were removed, a search light was installed on the rear of the bridge, new additional bunks were fitted in the already cramped aft torpedo flats and the officers wardrobe bunks were adjusted. The torpedo flats also received "wooden flats", linoleum flooring and 7-foot tables. In addition, the port storeroom in the steering flats was converted to a bathroom. But the seamen's baths were to be removed in 1919. The broadside torpedo room received additional lockers, the upper deck a 'latrine' and the stern an additional shaded light. There was also a multitude of tweaks and changes throughout the hull.

K7's turn for her refit came on the 6th April and she was to remain in Browns Clydeside yard until the 28th August. The boat was to have work on her hydrophones, as well as a battery box charge and discharged switch fitted. A small fan was installed to ventilate the officer's quarters. She had her bow modified as her classmates also had. The 'A1' tank was fitted with additional telemotor vents and the 'B1' tank was fitted with extra flaps, as well as telemotor vent valves. A board was installed over the bow in lieu of the grating and lockers were supplied for storage of "gear". The 3-inch gun was relocated between the funnels and a 4-inch MK VI gun fitted between the conning tower and the foremost funnel. Storage on the starboard upper side for the spare torpedo was altered to allow for a longer warhead. Tanks 'Q', 'X' and 'Y' were converted to become oil storage. The guard rails were extended the full length of the aft casing and a splash plate was fitted between the 4-inch gun platform and the conning tower. Number '8' auxiliary tank was converted to become an engineer store and indicators were fitted from boiler room intakes to show in the control room. Mechanical indicator gear for the upper funnel doors was fitted. Plus, storage for small arms ammunition boxes and Very cartridges was installed. Storage for 'ready-use' was also built at both the 3-inch high angle and 4-inch quick fire guns. The storage held 20 rounds of 4" and 8 rounds of 3 inch, etc...

May of 1918 was to bring the Edgar class cruiser (and former guard ship to Scapa flow) *H.M.S Royal Arthur* (1891) for attachment as a depot ship to the 12th flotilla. The flotilla Flagship remained the Fearless, with the *K 2, K 3, K 5, K 6, K 7, K 8* and the *K 15* forming the submarine element. The flotilla would remain in this form until it was disbanded in March 1919.

HMS K15 (IMPERIAL WAR MUSEUM)

On the 13th February K22's commander Lieutenant-Commander Charles de Burgh, was transferred to the newer *K16* and in March he would see her commissioned. The newest of the 'K' boats joined the Flotilla Leader Ithuriel, the depot ship and another Edgar class former cruiser *Crescent* (1892), *K 9, K10, K11, K12, K14* and the *K22* which together comprised the 13th Submarine Flotilla. The K16 replaced the C7 which had been the lone non-'K' submarine within the group. During her trials and working up period, the *K16* undertook her measured mile run in the area around Skelmorlie in North Ayrshire, Scotland. The first run went with no problems, but as the submarine was turning to commence her second run, the turning gear jammed. The officers on her conning tower struggled to regain directional control of the boat beneath their feet, while yet another 'K' boat was not under its crews' control. The 'Jinx' set the

K16 on a course directly towards the beach and the humili-
ation it would bring down on de Burgh. But on the bridge
the boats navigator, by being none to gentle with her, forced
the errant craft into going astern and a 'fresh' chapter in the
'K' class 'Kalamity' was avoided. An examination after the
event was to establish that her hydraulic system had failed.

With the system repaired, the *K16* now set off for Gareloch
to undertake her diving trials, just as (and where) the unfortunate *K13* had. The Captain trimmed down the boat off the
Shandon Hydropathic Hotel and then with the boat running
on its electric motors, he ordered the forward hydroplanes
set for diving and the aft hydroplanes to rise. But as was becoming habitual with the 'K' boats, with no warning the bow
took a dive directly towards the lochs bed, just as *K13* had in
the same waters. As the boat descended the by now frantic
crew managed to blow 'B' tank first, then 'C' tank and finally
in desperation, every tank the boat possessed. But this was
to have no effect and at 112 feet her bow furrowed into the
muddy loch bed. With her bow resting on the bottom, her
propellers were over 100 feet above the waves, spinning in
the open sky, her air borne screws making any attempts to
go into reverse, futile. But once the crew managed to blow
the tanks and empty them of water, the *K16* lifted her bow
from the bottom of the loch and she rose to the surface. On
her return to port, it was established that the aft hydroplane
had been the cause of the fault and they had not been re-
sponding to the wheel commands. Once the dockyard had
corrected the fault, the navy accepted *K16* on the 13th April
1918, having commissioned the *K15* a few days earlier on
the 3rd of April.

The *K6* entered the Ferguson shipyard in Leith on the 29th
July 1918 and remained in their care until the 9th August.

During her time there, a Thornycroft Depth Charge was fitted and the electrical leads to the number 2 battery were amended. New and heavier plates were fitted to the external tanks at the waterline level. A voice pipe was run from the control room to the W/T cabinet. A depth gauge was installed in the turbine room, a metal bridge screen fitted, and the superstructure reshaped slightly. A voice pipe was run from the bridge to the gun positions, the aft casing extended to the galley area ...   On the 31st July 1918, two stokers from the *K5*, George Booker and Michael Jordan, were to be lost by drowning. The boats captain, (Hutchings) was held to blamed to:

> *"a certain extent" for not having had them "put on and blow up life belts in view that the rails were unshipped."*

On the 16th October 1918 the *K5* went into dock at the Earles shipyard in Hull. She would remain in their hands until almost a year had passed, the work being completed on the 20th September 1919. Among the long list of jobs undertaken was the fitting of a new and higher bow and the installation of a depth charge thrower, (the ships book refers to the installed DC thrower in the singular, but on other 'K' boats it's a plural reference?). The motor rooms ventilation was improved, vertical watertight bulkheads were added between frames 77 and 80, a number of hull plates were replaced by new plating which was twice as thick, alterations to the galley and the sink in the motor room, changes to the aft crew space, stiffening the bow shutters, a guide rail fitted for the periscope, updating of the communications in the aft crew space, stand pipes and a 'cock' fitted to tanks '6', '7', '8', '9', '12', '13', '14' and five oil tanks. The list of work undertaken covers two or three pages in the ship's book and there is, a second list of jobs that were not undertaken at the time, for reasons not specified.

The last year of the war was to see the 'K' boats relegated from fleet operations to patrolling in the waters of the North Sea. These patrols, (entitled 'K.K' patrols) were given the objective of establishing a patrol line, from which a W/T warning of any enemy warships could be made. The forewarning would then allow the fleet sufficient time to make its way out to sea and to ambush the unsuspecting Germans. Each patrol was of a week's duration, with the daylight hours spent running with only the conning tower awash, before surfacing fully at night to recharge the batteries and despatch a report to base by W/T. With no real prospect of action, the 'K' boat crews found the patrols were repetitious and boring, coming over the slowly passing days, weeks and months to loath them.

On her first 'KK' patrol the *K15* found herself struggling through a north-east gale as it battered the North Sea. The boat was steaming nearly beam on through the rough seas, which were rolling her around and leaving the crew struggling within the cramped interior to remain on their feet. Once more the seas were breaking over a 'K' boat (despite the *K15's* heightened funnels) and flooding down the twin funnels as the sea water filled both the casing and the air intake valves. The water on her decks was inevitably sucked down into the boiler room and flooded the compartment. The water cascaded into the adjoining engine room, flooding that in turn. With the weight of the water now on board the boat the crew found their submarine now had negative buoyancy. In addition, the waters in the boiler room extinguished the boilers fires. The Captain (Commander Hubert Vaughan-Jones), realizing his boat was now carrying several tons of sea water within her machinery compartments and that was in fact destroying her buoyance, ordered *"stand by for diving"*. This order brought the closure of the boats watertight doors and the water was now contained within the boiler and engine rooms. At this point the sources clash, some crediting the downward plunge of the *K15* to the Captain ordering a dive. But other sources claim the flood waters, combined with the fact that the swan bow was not providing sufficient buoyancy, dragging the *K15* down. But whichever was correct, the "stand by for diving" order had saved the craft. But now she dropped beneath the storm lashed waves and in the space of 4 minutes the *K15* was bound on an uncontrolled dive for the seabed, stern first. At 80 feet the stern struck the seabed and the unrestrained dive was over. Vaughan-Jones could see through the raised periscope day light, which reassured him they were not too deep. The electric bilge pump should have been capable of pumping the water out, but once it was started the water levels remained stubbornly unchanged. With the water level not decreasing a stoker volunteered to dive into the 7 feet of icy cold oily water that filled the compartment. Through the murky water he found the strainers to be blocked with cotton waste. The unfortunate stoker had to repeat his dive several times to finally clear the obstruction. Eight hours after having dived stern first, *K15* meekly returned to the surface.

In the design process the "holes" (or ports) in the funnel superstructure had been designed to open both ways, a questionable feature in a submersible craft. On her return to base on day seven of her patrol the *K15's* crew learnt that the fault was in fact already known about. The fault had been recognized and already remedied in all the boats within the class, bar the *K15*. The *K15's* stern 'dive' was the first recorded for the class and but for the cold, wet stoker, it was an incident that could have cost the lives of her entire crew.

From amongst the world's 'seven seas' and its oceans the North Sea was probably the most suited for the 'K' boats. On average its depth is less than that of the length of a 'K' boat. But there is naturally a location that defies the hull length to water depth ratio. The "Pothole" sits in the bed of the North Sea and is deeper by far. Given their accident rate a 'K' boat was always going to one day, find it. That day came on the 2nd May 1918 and the 'jinxed' boat was the *K3* under the command of Lieutenant-Commander Shove.

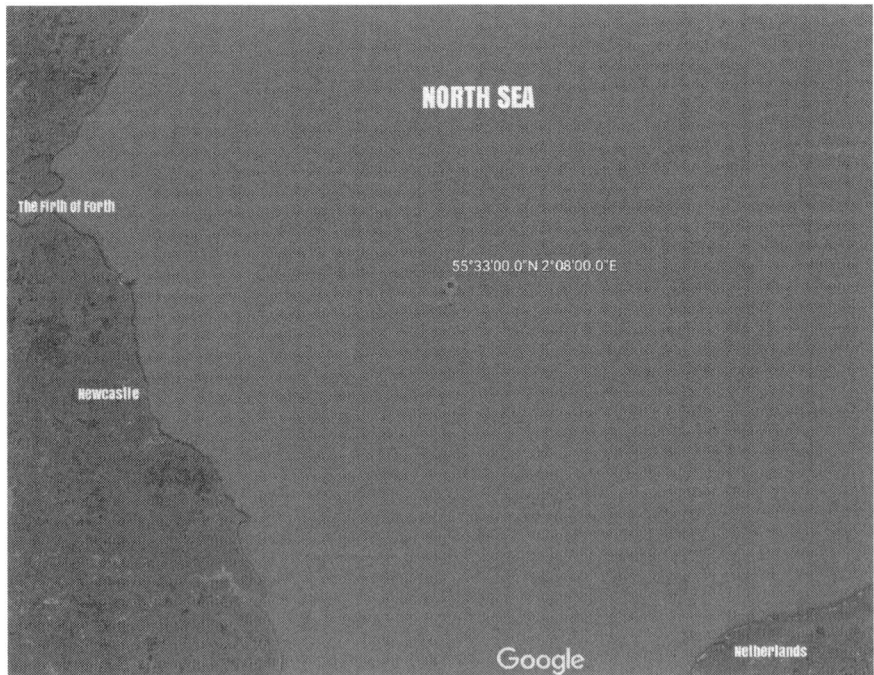

Latitude 55° 33'N. Longitude 2° 8'E

On that Wednesday morning the *K3* was making her way under steam in the waters of the North Sea (Latitude 55°

33'N. Longitude 2° 8'E) and as the new dawn broke the weather was fine and clear with a wind blowing force 2 to 3 in from the North East. The sea was calm at force 2 and with a slight easterly swell. The 'K3' was steaming at 12 knots on of bearing 180°, her passage marked by a long trailing cloak of smoke bellowing from her twin funnels. At 03:55 Lieutenant -Commander Herbert William Shove gave the order to *"Stand by"* to dive. Shove was to write:

> *"Upon this, in accordance with the routine observed in the vessel, the forward hydroplanes were run out, telemotor pumps started, preparations made for shutting off the engine room and the following tanks flooded:*
>
> *"B" internal,*
>
> *All fore flood spaces.*
>
> *"Q", "X", "Z" internals (these were already flooded but were opened to ensure their being completely full on diving), Nos. 8, 9 and 10 externals P. and S".*

Four minutes after having given the order, Shove ordered *"Dive"* and the diving horn sounded out across the Pentland Firth. Shove continues:

> *"... the remaining external tanks except Nos, 1, 2, 3, P. and S. and Nos. 6 P. and S. were flooded, the engine room and conning tower shut off and clutches charged from turbines to motor ,Nos. 1, 2, 3 external were kept*

closed by my special order until the E.R was reported shut off this being a precautionary measure, usually adopted by me in diving "K.3" when a trim has not been obtained for some time, when time admits to prevent the possibility of submersion before the E.R. is properly shut off, to ensure that the vessel has an inclination by the stern in the initial stages of diving.

As soon as E.R. was shut off the hydroplanes were put hard to "Dive" forward and hard to "Rise" aft, Nos 1, 2, 3 externals flooded and the motors started at "Half speed ahead together" (about 4 ½ to 5 knots) to dive the vessel. The helm was put 15° to starboard to turn to the new patrol course 0°."

The submarine slowly submerged beneath the waves and as she was trimmed by her crew, the 'jinx' stepped from out of the boats dark recesses and took the *K3* into an uncontrolled dive. As the bow dropped towards the seabed, its course was in line with the "Pothole" and its 266 feet depth. The seabed that awaited the *K13* as she dropped lower foot by foot, was at least sixty-seven feet beyond the hulls theoretical diving depth.

Two minutes after she had commenced her dive, the submarine's bow reached a depth of 55 feet with an angle on her of between 4° and 6°. Shove was only to aware of the 'K' classes record and urgently ordered the forward hydroplanes set to "rise" and the bilge pump on 'A' internal tank worked frantically as it became only too clear the runaway boat was heavy forward and that was only quickening her dive. But neither the bilge or hydroplanes nor the bilge pump had any effect and the depth gauge continued to drop. Shove now ordered that they blow external tank numbers '1', '2' and '3' and then in addition numbers '4' and '7'.

Shove resumes:

> *"... the air was admitted to the tanks very promptly and pressure kept to 15 lbs above sea (by differential gauge)".*

As the desperate and frantic crew sought to regain control of their sinking boat, the interior was filled with the cacophony of creaking metal, orders being shouted and the leaking of rivets that bound the boats hull plates together. As the depth grew, so did the crushing water pressure on the 339 feet of submarine hull and with each additional foot the danger grew remorselessly. The sounds of creaking metal and jets of water were joined by stays, angles and stanchions as they weakened and surrendered their shapes to the pressure. As the depth grew so too must have been those frantic men's fear the 'jinx' had them, but seemingly unstoppable, the *K3* descended towards the seabed. The crew could only accept they were to die when the boat came to rest, entombed to a slow death, unless the plating finally gave way.

Downward the 2,566 tons of submarine dropped as the dive grew steeper and as the bow grew heavier. The men clung onto anything within reach as the boat was now at 20° and continuing to descend rapidly. The desperate efforts to halt the death ride by the blowing of the tanks and the hydroplanes appeared to have no effect. The depth gauge continued to mark the boats decent into the depth as she stubbornly refused to answer any attempts to reverse the course. The boat dropped past 150, 160, 170, 180, 190 and finally 200 feet, her theoretical but before to date , unconfirmed diving depth. Then as fickle as a 'K' boat can be , as the 200 feet mark was passed, the 'jinx' released the submarine and *K3* straighten out. The crew held their breath and all eyes were on the depth gauges needle. Then slowly her hull's angle adjusted itself and reversed from minus figures to between plus 4° and 5°.

Shoves report noted how:

"... an attempt was then made to dive at 30 feet [?] the vessel being steadied on Co. 0° but in spite of all the water in "A" internal and a quantity from No. 3 auxiliary being pumped out, she seemed unmanageable, taking inclinations of 4° or 5° very rapidly under the influence of the forward hydroplanes, but appearing to be unaffected by the after ones. It was therefore suspected that the latter were defective but an examination of the gear disclosed nothing wrong internally".

But the errant submarine was a 'K' boat and the curse was a fickle mistress. As stubbornly as she had decided to dive into the 'Pothole', she then decided it was time to return to the surface at 04:40, demure, meek and with little resistance.

The log records the only dive for that day as :

"03:55 standby,

03:57 dived,

04:40 surfaced".

An understate if accurate entry!

After 43 minutes of hell and having surface, Shove decided it would be unwise to remain on patrol given the doubts over the watertightness and the unknown damage exerted by the water pressure on the hull.

Once the *K3* was safely back in the care of Rosyth dockyard, an examination on the after hydroplanes showed no defect. A search was also made for water in the forward compartments. It was found that the forward trimming tank, which would normally hold 250 gallons of water, held 890 gallons and was all but full. The remainder of the boat's tanks were found to contain the correct amount of water for the set trim.

In a Report of a Deep Dive by submarine *K3* which was written by Shove, he makes the following comments:

"The extreme rapidity with which the vessel went down after her first initial dive and the great difficulty experienced in checking: her is attributed to the collapse of No.6. external P. which should have been full of oil fuel but was known to have a slight leak into No.5 and thro' a top seam. No allowance had been made for this leak as it was impossible to measure the amount of fuel short in the tank and the effect should have been to make the vessel light so long as the tank was not vented.

As a matter of fact, it would appear that the oil had leaked away down very nearly to the normal waterline of the vessel, as is shown by the shape of the collapsed tank. This would be about 5 tons.

It has long been recognized that the arrangement of the external oil fuel tanks in the K. Class is unsatisfactory being in the nature of a makeshift and the approved alteration to make these tanks self-compensating will avoid the danger at present inherent in them. As this alteration is already being carried out in all K. class coming in-hand and is approved for I have no suggestion to make on this head.

The blowing of the main ballast does not seem so quick in its effect as might be desired. Conclusions on this head are, of course, affected by the considerations set out in paragraphs 14 and 15 above, but at the same time I beg to submit that a system of emergency blows direct from the High Pressure Service to the individual tanks cold be arranged without difficulty and would enable a large quantity of air to be turned into the tanks very rapidly. The objection to such a method on the score of danger to the tanks does not, it is submitted apply in the "K" class whose tanks are always open to the sea.

As regards the estimation of the depth reached and the inclination of the vessel on this occasion, these are of necessity only approximate as the depth was beyond the limits of the depth gauges and the inclination too great to be measured by the levels. The only definite statement as to the depth is the observation of the E.R.A. stationed in the turbine room who reports that the pressure shown on the gauges of the circulating water outlets was about 140 lbs. This must be inaccurate as the greatest depth shewn on the charts in the vicinity of the occurrence is 48 fathoms (288 ft - 130 lbs). But the graduations of the gauges are to 120 lbs and it is thought that the needles went at least beyond this. Allowing only the 120 lbs the depth would be 266 feet and this is considered to be approximately that reached. The inclination must have exceeded 15° as the wardroom table, which fell over, was found on subsequent trial to do so at this angle. At the same time, it was not my impression that the angle was extreme so that 20° has been accented as a probable limit. It is not established that the vessel struck bottom. Nothing was felt in the control room. Those aft report a slight bump but this may have been the collapse of No 6 external".

The crew, counting their blessings, were ordered to take their crumbled dented and leaking craft to Armstrong's Naval Yard Newcastle-upon-Tyne for repairs. She arrived on the 8th and was still in dockyard hands at the months end. The official report as with all the 'K' boat incidents fudged and simply said "the cause of the accident not clear". But the crews knew that the curse or 'Jinx' had once more taken a 'K' boats crew and having toyed with them decided to let them live, this time. June of 1918 was to bring a new metal bridge screen for the K3's conning tower and a "navy phone" from the engineers bank to the turbine room. The latter room also gained secondary lighting and in addition a considerable number of tweaks throughout the hull of a mechanical theme were undertaken.

Three months later, September 1918 brought a period of major work on the *K3* with the installation of her new bow at the Vickers yard. In addition, the upper deck boiler room casings were extended outboard and a "flape" fitted. The crewmen's lockers were lined and made watertight, the casing over the engine room hatch expanded, the galley extended by its aft bulkhead being moved one hull frame and a locker with flaps fitted to the wireless mast ram recess. "Grease cups [were] fitted to the bulkhead" glands of the steering revolution shaft. A new 4-inch gun was installed while the 3-inch was moved to nearer the boiler room intakes and water pressure resistant ammunition lockers were fitted with the deck guns. Two Thornycroft depth charges were added, one facing out to port and the other to starboard. With her new bow and revised weaponry, she returned to service, but the report omits a date for that event.

On the 3rd October 1918 as the *K11* was entering Rosyth Dockyard a wave washed over the deck casing throwing Able Seaman Ernest Robson Smith into the harbour's waters. Tragically while so close to the shore, the unfortunate sailor was drowned. Sometimes the 'Jinx' was happy with just one crewman, but there would come a time when it would demand and take a full compliment.

As the war came to its conclusion, on the 16th November 1918 *HMS K2* entered a refit that was to last until 18th June 1919 at the Brown's shipyard on the Clydebank.

CHAPTER NINE. THE POST WAR YEARS

"My Dad's Name Is F. F. Hills And He Was A Stoker First Class. He Joined K10 At Barrow-In-Furness In 1917.. .. He Hopes They Never Build Any More Like Them For Poor Men To Live In As They Made More Men Sick Than Any Other Boat"

Mrs A. I. Hammond, Of Barrow, (1959).

	GROUP 1 COMMISSIONED	FATE	PERIOD OF SERVICE (YEARS/MONTHS)
K1	18/12/16	17/11/17 (COLLISION)	0/11
K4	02/01/17	31/01/18 (COLLISION)	1/0
K17	20/09/17	31/01/18 (COLLISION)	0/4
K5	05/05/16	20/01/21 (SUNK)	4/7
K7	17/01/17	09/09/21 (SOLD)	6/5
K3	04/08/16	26/10/21 (SOLD)	5/2
K10	06/17	11/21 (SOLD)	4/5
K11	01/02/17	08/03/21 (SOLD)	4/10
K8	06/03/17	11/10/23 (SOLD)	6/5
K15	31/03/17	08/24 (SOLD)	7/4
K16	14/04/17	22/08/24 (SOLD)	7/5
K6	21/11/16	13/07/26 (SOLD)	9/8
K2	03/12/16	07/26 (SOLD)	10/4
K9	09/06/17	23/07/26 (SOLD)	9/2
K12	01/08/16	07/21 (SOLD)	9/11
K13/22	10/17	12/21(SOLD)	9/2
K14	22/05/17	16/02/26 (SOLD)	8/9

THE PERIOD OF COMMISSION FOR THE GROUP 1 BOATS, IN ORDER OF THEIR DEMISE.

Whil the guns fell silent on the 11th November 1918, there were fourteen of the Group 1 'K' boats remaining in commission. The class had been in service for barely two years, yet in that period three boats had been lost. The 'K' boats now numbered *K2, K3, K5 to K12, K14 to K16* and the former *K13*, the *K22*. The boats had ended their war still in the official role of supporting the Grand Fleet and patrolling the North Sea, while conducting the tiresome and dull 'KK' patrols. The fourteen remaining boats were divided between the 12th and 13th submarine flotillas. In January 1919 the two flotillas were comprised of the following boats:

12th FLOTILLA

Fearless (Flagship, (Captain (S))

Royal Arthur (Depot Ship)

Submarines: *K2, K3, K5, K6, K7, K8, K15*

13th FLOTILLA

Ithuriel (flotilla leader)

Crescent (depot ships)

Submarines: *K9, K10, K11, K12, K14, K16, K22.*

But three months later, in April 1919 the *K2, K10* and *K14* were reduced to reserve. Given the classes track record crewing the boats was becoming problematic, it is feasible the Admiralty were finding it harder to obtain personnel prepared to serve on the steam powered submarines.

THE K3 PASSING THE SURRENDERED GERMAN FLEET IN SCAPA FLOW.

By this period the *K10* had also decommissioned (on the 14th February 1919) and she was to be sold for scrap by November 1921. A month prior to the hauling down of the *K10's* White Ensign, (on the 12th February) two members of her crew were to be lost overboard. One was a married man, Able Seaman Sydney Charles Baker. The Kent born 23-year-old had joined the navy as a Boy 2nd Class on 7th January 1913, transferring to the *K10* on 1st January 1919, only a few weeks before his death. The second crewman was Able Seaman Herbert Henry Normington aged 20 and born in Plymouth. He too joined the navy as a Boy 2nd Class, (but on the 1st November 1915) and joined the *K10* on the 1st January 1919.

The two men were both working on the port side amidships employed with the fenders, as the *K10* entered Rosyth, manoeuvring around a dredger. They were equally leaning on the guard rail when it suddenly snapped, throwing both men into the water. The *K10* hove too immediately and boats where launched to recover the them. But the tide was ebbing fast and as the boats arrived on the scene, it snatched them away. The would-be rescuers could see the struggling men but were unable to reach them in time before they sank beneath the waves. It was to be a few days before the bodies were found. A Court of Enquiry held afterwards ruled that both deaths were accidental. The sailors were to be buried far from their homes in the Dunfermline Cemetery in Fife. As to the *K10,* having been sold, she was to founder whilst on tow to C.A.Beard at Upnor, on the 10th January 1922.

HMS K22 IN APRIL 1923. THE SMALL DERRICK AMIDSHIPS WAS FOR HANDLING THE SUBMARINES SMALL BOAT. (SOURCE:LASTSTANDONZOMBIEISLAND.COM)

In March 1919 during a post-war reorganization, the 13th submarine flotilla was re-designated as the Second Submarine Flotilla. This excluded the *Crescent,* which was transferred to the Firth of Forth, being replaced by the Edgar class cruiser *St. George* (1892). At the time of the changes, the flotilla comprised of:

Ithuriel (flotilla leader)

Crescent (depot ship)

Submarines: *K9, K10, K11, K12, K14, K16, K22.*

The same month was to see the 12th flotilla retitled the 1st submarine flotilla, but the boats within the force remained unchanged:

Fearless (Flagship, Captain (S))

Royal Arthur (depot ship)

Submarines *K2, K3, K5, K6, K7, K8, K15.*

While 'K' boats were decommissioning, the Jinx still had work to do with the remaining boats and May 1919 was to be a busy year for it with five 'incidents'. Twice in one month during the previous year, (18.05.18 + ?.08.18) the *K15* was to dive out of control while in the North Sea and both times she struck the seabed. But both times she survived to reach the surface.

The 16th May 1919 saw the K7 enter Rosyth dockyard for work on both her propellers and her underwater fittings.

The *K8* whilst undergoing a refit at the Chatham naval base was to catch fire and the *K14* suffered a boiler explosion which forced open the troublesome mushroom vents while she was diving. The boiler room was flooded and only the swift action of her crew got her back to the surface. Then having just completed her post fire refit, she suffered a second explosion and a resulting fire from her batteries.

On the 14th August 1919 the *K3* was given notice she too

would soon be offered for sale and on the 11th September in Chatham her white ensign was lowered for the final time. She was sold on 26th October 1921 to the Barking Ship Breaking Company for scrapping in London. But she was to lay at Chatham forlorn, neglected and humiliated, throughout November while awaiting the final tow to the breakers yard. Five months after her Rosyth refit, the *K7,* (the third 'K' boat to be decommissioned) hauled down her ensign during October 1919. A report had been issued prior confirming her magazines to be empty on 18th September 1919 in Devonport. She was to be sold for scrap on the 9th September 1921 to a Sunderland based company.

The year 1919 also saw a portion of the Grand Fleet undertake a Victory cruise around the country. Amongst the fleet of battlecruisers, cruisers and destroyers were some of the remaining 'K' boats. The fleet toured the British coastline visiting ports and towns, drawing the curious and excited public with every port of call. The crowds gathered to watch as the submarines approached their harbours, ports and bays, columns of smoke blowing out from just behind the conning tower. There is on You Tube a brief footage of Pathe news film which shows a lone 'K' boat steaming at full speed through a flat sea (1). The darken smoke emissions from the two funnels resemble a railway steam engine charging at full throttle, the bow waves throwing up a huge wave of sea water on either side of the bow as she powers along. But as spectacular as they looked at full throttle, such smoke emissions robbed the steam submarines of one of their chief assets, near invisibility on the surface. (To be fair, in practice the diesel powered 'D' and 'E' class submarines also tended to produce excessive quantities of exhaust). Once a 'K' boat was steaming along at full speed, she could not be mistaken for any other class of submarine, 'D' or 'E'!

The public, to who until the wars end, the 'K' boat was a 'secret', must have watched open mouthed as these giant steam bellowing monsters of the sea swept into ports around the United Kingdom. It surely must have seemed as if machines from a novel of H.G.Wells or Jules Verne had stepped out from between its book covers!

One year after the Armistice, in November 1919 the status of the surviving 'K' boats stood as follows:

- *K2* - 1st Submarine Flotilla, Rosyth, Atlantic Fleet (in reserve as of 31st December).
- *K5* - 1st Submarine Flotilla, Rosyth, Atlantic Fleet.
- *K6* - First Submarine Flotilla, Rosyth, Atlantic Fleet (in reserve).
- *K8* - 1st Submarine Flotilla, Rosyth, Atlantic Fleet.
- *K9* -1st Submarine Flotilla, Rosyth, Atlantic Fleet
- *K12* - 1st Submarine Flotilla, Rosyth, Atlantic Fleet.
- *K14* -1st Submarine Flotilla, Rosyth, Atlantic Fleet (in reserve).
- *K15* - 1st Submarine Flotilla, Rosyth, Atlantic Fleet.
- *K16* - 1st Submarine Flotilla, Rosyth, Atlantic Fleet (in reserve).
- *K22* - 1st Submarine Flotilla, Rosyth, Atlantic Fleet.

During December 1919 whilst on passage from Portsmouth to Rosyth the *K5* encountered a short but rough sea (1). Once she reached the calmer waters of a harbour, no damage by the seas battering was evident. But it was found on the flotilla's arrival in Gibraltar the next year that the 'December-seas' had bent the leading edges of the hydroplanes back and she was put into dock to have the damage repaired. The *K12* was also found while the flotilla was in Gibraltar to have developed a "bad" leak between the settling and the reserve fuel tanks. This had allowed large quantities of oil to leak into the boilers, a problem K5 had also experienced in 1919. When the flotilla sailed on into the Mediterranean, the *K12* was to remain in dock in Gibraltar.

During 1920 the Reserve Submarine Group "B" was based at Rosyth and was home to the *K14* and *K16*. The 'K' boats were under the collective command of Lieutenant Harry P. K. Oram and on the 20th November 1920, he was relieved by Lieutenant William Ibbett. The *K16* would never be recommissioned, finally being sold, after over 4 years in reserve, for scrap on 22nd August 1924.

Between the 6th December 1920 and the 6th May 1921, the *K6* was in the hands of Chatham dockyard undergoing a refit. The 4-inch gun was changed and covers supplied. An air duct from the boiler to the motor room was installed and the guns ready use lockers upgraded. Overhead storage for grenades, a fan to the ammo hand up in the wardroom and the bow shutters were strengthened. The engine room hatch underwent changes and Modified blowing and flooding arrangements installed in the external tanks. The yard fitted a *"4-inch SI mtg in lieu of existing 3-inch mgt"* and the dinghy storage was strengthened. Both propellers were refurbished, and the battery cells were repaired, renewed and replaced as required.

This long list of work,(a list not reproduced in full here) cost:

- Labour £27,436 (2017=£797,227),
- Materials net £9,932 (2017=£288,601),
- Contractors work £952, (2017=£27,662).

Three boats formed the Reserve Submarine Group "A" based at Rosyth and the submarines were under the collective authority of Commander John F. Hutchings. On the 8th March 1921 the *K2* was to be recommissioned manned by the former crew of K11 at Rosyth, which had in turn been decommissioned on the 8th. After 8 months quietly rusting at anchor, the *K11* was sold for scrap on the 4th November 1921 to P & W McLellan at Bo'ness.

The *K8* finally decommissioned on the 10 June 1921 and was sold for scrap on the 11th October 1923. Then a month later the *K9* was also to be decommission, on the 2nd July 1921 and after 5 years rusting at anchor, she was sold for scrap on the 23rd July 1926. Now there were eleven 'K' boats, *K2, K5, K6, K8, K9, K12-16, K22*.

As the 'K' boats slowly one by one decommissioned, the 'J' class submarines which had been also completed in 1916, remained in service and would do so until the last was decommissioned in 1929, having been transferred to the Australian navy in March 1916. It's evident the 'K' boats commissions were cut short, but the 'J' classes 14 years of commission, compared to the less than a decade for the 'K's merely serves to highlight it.

One of the eleven surviving boats, the *K6* was to be in the dockyard hands of Rosyth between the 4th and 21st November. She was placed into dry dock and below the waterline was scraped, cleaned and repainted. In addition, the rubber joints to the deck hatches were renewed, new lockers were installed in the stoker's mess, as was three-ply lino flooring. The 13 feet 5-inch dinghy was repaired, wood plating added in the control room, the bridge and the wheelhouse. A handrail and stanctions were added to the upper deck, a W/T mast installed, the periscope bearings replaced, covers, beams and grating added to the battery compartments, the bow caps worked on, valves added to the ventilation valves, etc... Her boat and torpedo derricks were found to be repairable and the order to replace then was cancelled, saving money. In addition, the cost of materials prices dropped and work on the thrust blocks and on the shaft, bearings was a smaller job than first thought. The boilers, funnels, main generators and motors were also found to be smaller jobs. The lower bill was also a result of labour being found in other dockyard departments.

The final bill was:

LABOUR

- Estimated £18,582 (2017=£1,096,193),
- Actual £17,741 (2017=£1,046,580),
- Difference £849 under (2017=£50,084).

MATERIAL NET

- Estimated £1,335 (2017=£78,754).
- Actual £1563 (2017=£92,204)
- Difference £228 Over (2017=£13,450)

CONTRACT

- Estimated £29,497 (2017=£1,740,092).
- Actual £29,150 (2017=£1,719,622).

- Difference £356. (2017=£21,001).
- Material £218 (2017=£12,860).
- Labour £18,592 (2017=£1,096,782)

HMS K12 IN 1924

1: *Short sea: a sea in which the waves are short, broken, and irregular, so as to produce a tumbling or jerking motion.*

CHAPTER TEN. THE LOSS OF THE K5 & K15.

*"Of All The Branches Of Men In The Forces There
Is None Which Shows More Devotion And Faces
Grimmer Perils Than The Submariners."*

Winston Churchill

On Friday 14th May 1920, the K5 had been exercising off Fidra island in the Firth of the Forth. Her captain, Lieutenant-Commander John A. Gaimes, ordered a preliminary trim to be undertaken and his Engineer-Lieutenant reported that in the aft machinery compartments all was prepared. All but the external tanks '4' and '7' where flooded, those tanks being retained as empty and the boat held on the hydroplanes until the order to dive was given from the control room. That order to submerge called for a 28-foot depth, but normally the boat *"hangs"* between 18 to 20 foot for a brief period. But on this dive the submarine passed the 18-foot mark and continued her downward course. Gaimes immediately ordered the number '4' and '7' tanks to be blown and the electric motors put at half speed, as well as all the vents closed to stop the tanks filling any further. But as if in response, the bow took a steeper angle towards the seabed and Gaimes now frantically ordered the external tanks '1', '2' and '3' to be blown, the motors stopped and tanks '4' and '7' to be shut off. The boat dropped passed the 30-foot mark and the decent only halted when her bow gently struck the seabed at 105 feet with an angle of 15 to 20 degrees on her.

Having taken her to over 100 feet, the 'Jinx' was finished with her for that day and with barely a complaint the boat returned to the surface. It was found afterwards that a large amount of sea water had flooded the 'D' main ballast tank by entering through a Kingston valve. The valve had not been fully closed and the boat had as a result dived uncontrolled to the seabed.

At the enquiry Grimes (who had assumed command 44 days prior on the 1st April) was to be blamed by the board for 'merely' repeating the operating procedure of his predecessor, Commander John F. Hutchings and failing to establish what they comprised of. But despite the reprimand Grimes was to retain his command, which was to lead to his death within the next twelve months.

But the 'incidents' paint a biased image of the classes record. Having suffered accidents and disasters during their war time service, the post war 1st flotilla's time serving within the Atlantic Fleet was to see the 'K' boats complete hundreds of hours at sea with no recorded incidents. However, the 'Jinx' may have been quiet, but it was not done yet. Every time a Captain ordered a *"dive"*, his crew must wondered if now the curse would step out from the shadows and claim them or if they would dive and surface with no incidents.

During the summer of 1920 the Atlantic fleet was to visit Arosa Bay in Spain, as well as Gibraltar, Majorca and Algiers in North Africa. At the tour's successful conclusion in Algiers the *K5* led the 1st flotilla, (in company with the fleet), out to sea at 18 knots and a course was set for their passage home through the Bay of Biscay. But as the fleet passed north through the Bay it ran into heavy seas. On the last night of the voyage the flotilla was making its way up the English Channel when two 'K' boats developed the old fuel problem of 'losing suction' and both came too an unplanned halt. Fortunately, this time with no collisions resulting. The next day the ships of the fleet were scattered to their various home ports for the crews to enjoy their Easter leave. During the summer of that year, the K5 was in Largo bay, part of the Firth of Forth's northern coastline, when she went out of control while diving and her bow struck the muddy bottom. Once more a 'K' boat hull lay at 45 degrees, but 120 feet above the bow, *K5's* stern stood proud of the water for all to see. With the propellers spinning in the air, reverse had no effect, but Gaimes ordered the forward props ballast tank blown and after 10 minutes the boat returned to the surface.

After a brief period at Scapa Flow, during July 1920 the 1st flotilla was ordered to Tor Bay on England's south coast, where they were to re-join with the Atlantic Fleet. The southward steaming 'K' boats paused overnight on the 7th July in the sheltered waters of the Welsh port of Milford Haven. But during the night they were ordered to sea with 'no waste of time'. As the *K5* made her way down the harbour and out towards the sea she collided with an obsolete destroyer under tow by a tug. Destroyer and tug had both hard moored for the night, but the tugs master failed to pull his charge alongside and instead moored the tug and destroyer in a line astern.

The *K5's* swan bow was crumpled with the force of the impact, but the damage was on inspection found to be superficial and the boat had retained her watertight integrity. Gaimes in company with the flotilla continued their route to Tor Bay, arriving 24 hours before the fleet was due to arrive in port. With a day to spare before the fleet arrived in the bay, Gaimes used those hours to have his crew construct a dummy bow. The new bow was composed of canvas and wire, to conceal the damage until he could be sure his report was on Admiral Sir Charles Madden, (the fleets C-in-C's) desk. For 3 days, with the Admiral's barge moored close by, but the false bow fooled all who looked on. Then the flotilla was given orders to make its way out to sea for divisional practice and the bow was finally unmasked in all its dented form. But by that stage the submarine captains report was safely on the C-in-C's desk. *K5* was to finish the year 1920 under refit at Chatham.

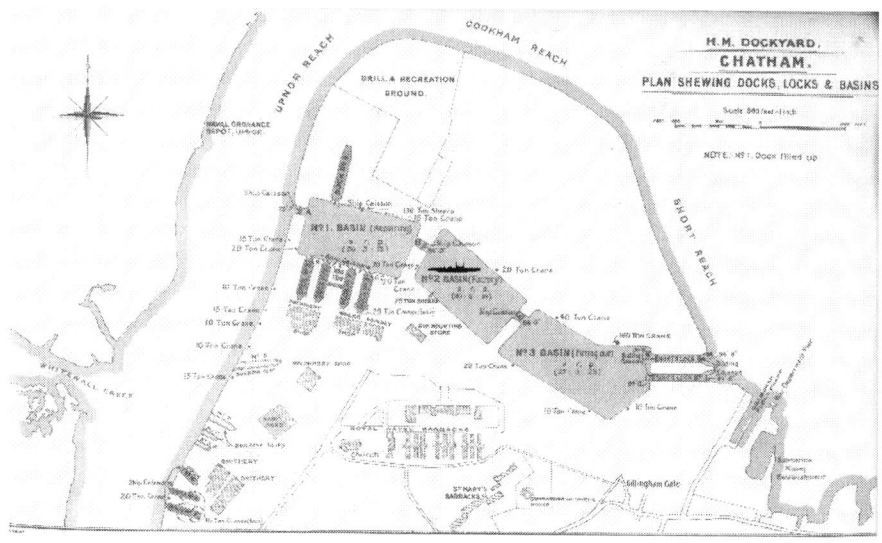

CHATHAM DOCKYARD & THE SITE OF THE K5 INCIDENT.

On the 29th November 1921 the *K5* lay alongside the 'wall' in Number 2 basin at Chatham dockyard, where she was in the process of undergoing a refit. On that day at 11:00 she was due to conduct a test of her foremost air compressor. But while the compressor was being run a crewman or dockyard worker, (the latter being according to the enquiry, the most likely) opened the 'blow to No 9 auxiliary ballast tank and the valve between the HP and LP line in the after 'manifold'. It was a chief ERA who was to discover the error, which was then under 80 lb's of pressure per square inch within the tank. The 8-ton compensating tank located between hull frames 194 & 199 lacked any Kingston valves to shut it off in the event of an emergency. Shutting it off quickly was not an option (1).

As the ERA tried to close the valve, a series of rivets blew along the top of the tank, around a dozen in number. Others showed signs of strain and the plate seams underwater opened, releasing a stream of bubbles to the water's surface.

Dockyard divers were sent down and were ordered to go aft to examine the damage underwater. But the harbours water was to prove to be too dark at the stern to see anything, leaving the diver to examine the damage by touch and as far as he could tell, the hull was undamaged! To compound matters it was decided against docking the boat, as that would only delay the refits completion.

After the damage had been done, the shipyard offered that if the matter were kept quiet, they would fix the damage and foot the cost. That way the refit would be completed on time! The seams were duly chalked from the inside and the missing (and strained?) rivets replaced. Problems were experienced in lining up the after hydroplane and the steering motors due to a distortion in the deck above the tank. After her loss, a witness (Whitfield) would describe K5's deck as buckled and visible as such to the eye. Once the refit was complete the tank was tested but not seemingly to the stipulated 50 lbs per square inch. No one seemed at the enquiry to give a definitive answer either way. In addition, the *K5* conducted a dive to 70 feet within the basin and experienced no issues. But the accident was to raise questions later in 1921 as to the *K5's* seagoing condition at the time of her sinking. The enquiry into her loss stated that a number of dives between the refit and her final dive were made, but was unable to give either dates or numbers, given the log and the crew had been lost to the ocean's depths by that stage.

After Christmas leave, (having spent a month in Chatham's dock), *HMS K5* with her new bow and a nearly **all new crew**, (but still under the command of John Gaimes), sailed from its port of repair, (Chatham) for Portsmouth. On the boat's arrival at Portsmouth, Captain Lewis, the divisional Commander, having learned she had yet to conduct a post refit dive at sea due to poor weather, ordered her out to Spithead where she conducted a trouble-free dive.

From there she was ordered to join with the *K9* and *K14*. Then on the 15th January 1921 the *K5* departed port in company with the Inconstant and *K9*, on route for Tor Bay. The small flotilla paused briefly at Portland (15th to 17th) to take on board Lieutenant-Commander Reginald Drake and to refuel. With Drake safely on board the boats made their way back out to sea, where once north of St Albans point, *K5's* Captain decided to order a test dive to trim the boat. The first tanks to be flooded behaved perfectly, but the red 'engine 'room shut' light was suddenly noticed by the control room personnel not to be illuminated. The Captain ordered all the vents closed and the dive to be immediately cancelled. Once safely back on the surface an inspection to discover the fault was undertaken. An officer found a heaving line had been stowed carelessly and had jammed under one of the mushroom vents, this being the cause of the problem.

Having made it with no further incidents to Tor Bay, *K5* and *K9* anchored near the *K15* and *K22*. The next morning the fleet was due to weigh anchor and make its way out into the English Channel and then set a course for Spain, conducting 'battle' exercises on route. But during the night a gale was to blow in from the English Channel and for 3 days the fleet lay hove too in Torr Bay battered by the weather as it rode at its anchors. By the 20th January the storm had finally eased off and the fleet sailed out in two divisions, one labelled as Red and the other as Blue. *HMS Inconstant* was to lead her 'K' boats out from Tor Bay with the K5 and *K9* on her starboard quarter and *K22, K15* and *K8* on her port. Through the day and the following night, the fleet sailed on a southwest course towards the pre-arranged battle zone. The night was to be a moonless one and the flotilla was to show only stern lights, which made keeping station difficult, but the nights passage happily passed without incident. But as the sun came up, the *K9's* officer of the watch realized he had lost sight of the next boat in the line, the *K5*. He was about to order an increase in speed to catch up, when a signal man spotted a lamp from K5 flashing "O.O.W (officer of watch) *to ditto, sorry lost suction"*. Another disaster was averted.

During the mid-morning of the 20th January 1921 the 'battle' was ready to commence. At 11:15 *HMS Inconstant* sighted the 'enemies' cruiser screen and signalled the 'K' boats to spread out and prepare for the attack. *K5,* (the

K9's divisional leader) ordered her to fall in with her wake and follow her. At 11:20 the oncoming 'enemy' sighted and opened fire on the Inconstant, who in response made a 180° turn as if she were beating a hasty retreat. The attackers had by this stage in return sighted the 'K' boats who were still riding the surface. The attacking forces were ordered by their Commander to switch targets and concentrate their fire onto the submarines. The plan was that once the boats had dived, the cruiser force was to remain within the vicinity. His goal being to ensure the Fleet-submarines did not surface and then steam off to reposition themselves ready for a fresh assault on his forces. The rules for the exercises stated that if a submarine was attacked while surfaced and she was within 6,000 yards, the boat was not permitted to take any further part in the exercise for the period of an hour. At 11:20 the K5 signalled the K9 "K.S.3.3.0" (33 being the "enemies' course) and both the 'K' boats crews prepared their vessels to dive. As the Inconstant lured the 'enemy' ever on towards the submarines, the 'K' boats lowered their wireless masts and uncovered the periscope wells. At 11:10 the destroyer HMS Spencer signalled by W/T (via the *Valentine*): *"For exercise - urgent - one light cruiser and submarines 130 degrees, 12 miles, course 060 degrees, position 260 V 50" (1106)"*. Then at 11:30 the signal, *"Detail one division to attack Western Submarines"* was dispatched. The 'K' boats had been sighted.

The K5 signalled the required course to her sister ship by flag and ordered the dive to commence. She was the first boat to submerge at 11:30, at a *"normal angle and without difficulty"* in *"92 fathoms"* of water. She was last to be seen when at 11:44 she reportedly resurfaced briefly. While dived the K9's Captain had watched the K5 (through the periscope) as the boat commenced her (second?) dive, with no visible problems. The K5 must have dived a second time at 11:44, turning to starboard to avoid the 3rd destroyer flotilla, as the destroyers senior officer reported only sighting 4 submarines on the surface. At 11:47 the battle squadron (*Tiger* (Flag of Rear-Admiral Sir Roger B. Keyes), *Renown, Repulse, Hood*)). engaged the two 'K' boats that were still on the surface. But the 'jinx' had a few hands on this day. HMS *K9* had duly turned 160 degrees on receiving the *K5's* 11:20 order "spreading course" and as the bridge crew descended into the control room, the *K9* commenced her dive. But she was immediately to experienced trouble as her angle of dive was uneven with her bow dipping and the boats trim no longer being level. The Captain ordered the aft hydroplanes to be raised to lift the bow and level the dive angle, but that drew no response. No matter how much her Captain tried, 10 foot of conning tower stood proud of the water. The captain (Lieutenant-Commander Alfred Hine), checked the telemotor panel but all 16 vents of the external ballast tanks were showing as correctly open. The ballast tanks were full, but a spirit level's bubble declared she was light in the bow. Hine ordered 'B' tank, an internal tank with an 18-ton capacity to be flooded. The conning tower dropped a few more feet but still 8 feet remained stubbornly above the water. If she were not to submerge soon the oncoming 'Enemy' cruisers would sight her. The First Officer finally looked through the forward periscope and saw the *"two manhole covers"* were shut tight. Orders to blow the vents were given but even though the operating lever for the vents was in the open position, two safety valves on each side of the lever had been overlooked. The bows buoyancy tanks were full of air! As a Seaman went to open the valves an officer physically stopped him. 'B' tank needed to be empty first. With 'B' tank empty the dive proceeded perfectly. But she was still to give trouble when she dived later in the exercises. *K9's* warning light had failed to illuminate during a preliminary trimming dive. On an inspection her horrified officers found a coil of rope had been carelessly stowed under one of the ventilators, where it prevented it from closing. Fortunately for the crew the almost unknown reluctance of a 'K' boat to take to the depths, saved them from a bad experience, or given the class of their boat, worse...

The *K9's* crew now sighted three 'enemy' destroyers closing in on their position and at 12:02 the boat surfaced with the destroyers now a mile off. The K9, having suffered troublesome dives, turned 16 points and steamed off to remove herself from the action. Having extracted herself from the exercise, her trim was adjusted and at 12:22 a fresh dive was undertaken to check she had been trimmed correctly. All the external tanks, bar numbers '4' & '7' were flooded and by 12:33 she had dived on a level angle to a depth of 28 feet. Seventeen minutes after having submerged the *K9* returned to the surface at 12:50. Her bridge crew noted that while the 'enemy' were still visible, they were a distance off. Prior to returning to the surface a check had been made through the periscope, but with the seas swell, plus a lack of height on the periscope, the 'enemy' had remained out if sight. *K9* quickly dived and was to remain submerged until 13:47 by which time she was well clear of both the fleets. On surfacing there were no other 'K's' to be seem by the *K9's* lookouts.

MAPS OF THE EXERCISE.

THE FOLLOWING MAPS OR DIAGRAMS ARE FROM THE COURT OF ENQUIRY FILES HELD AT THE KEW NATIONAL ARCHIVES.   THE CHARTS ARE LISTED HERE CHRONOLOGICALLY AND NOT IN THE OFFICIAL NUMBER SEQUENCE.

1.   DIAGRAM NO 2: 11:10 POSITION OF SPENSER & 2ND FLOTILLA.

2.   DIAGRAM NO 1: 11:17 TRACK OF SPENSER AT 11:10 TO 12:03.

3. DIAGRAM NO 3: 11:25 POSISTIONS OF SPENCER & INCONSTANT.

4.   DIAGRAM NO 4: POSITIONS AT 11:44.

5.   DIAGRAM NO 5: FLEET POSITIONS AT 12:00

6.   DIAGRAM NO 6 (?): FLEET POSITIONS AT 12:10

7. "ENGAGEMENT WITH INCONSTANT AND SUBMARINES 20.01.21"

ORIGINAL SCANS OF THE MAPS ARE AVAILABLE BY CONTACTING THE AUTHOR, SEE FRONT OF BOOK.

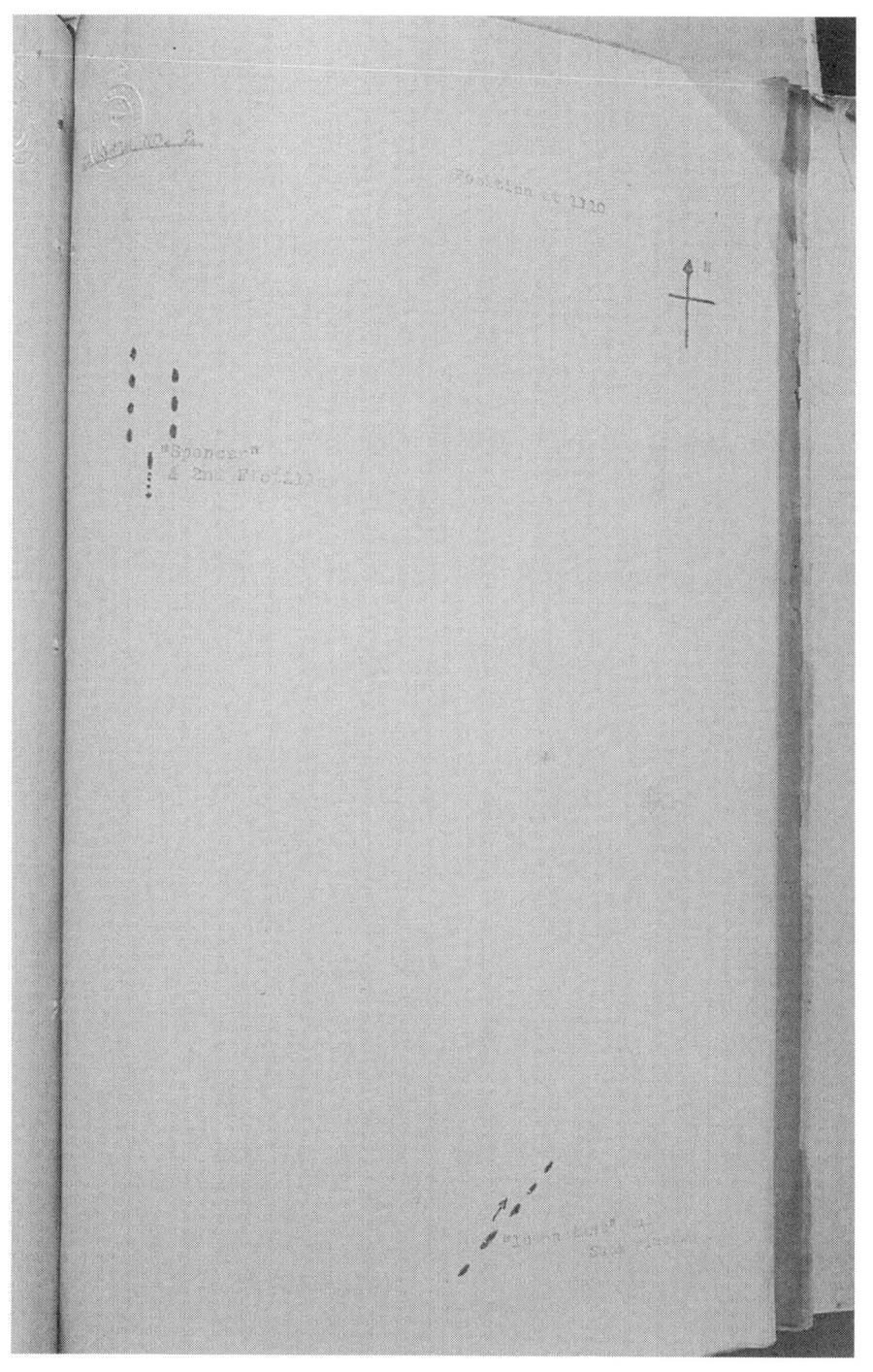

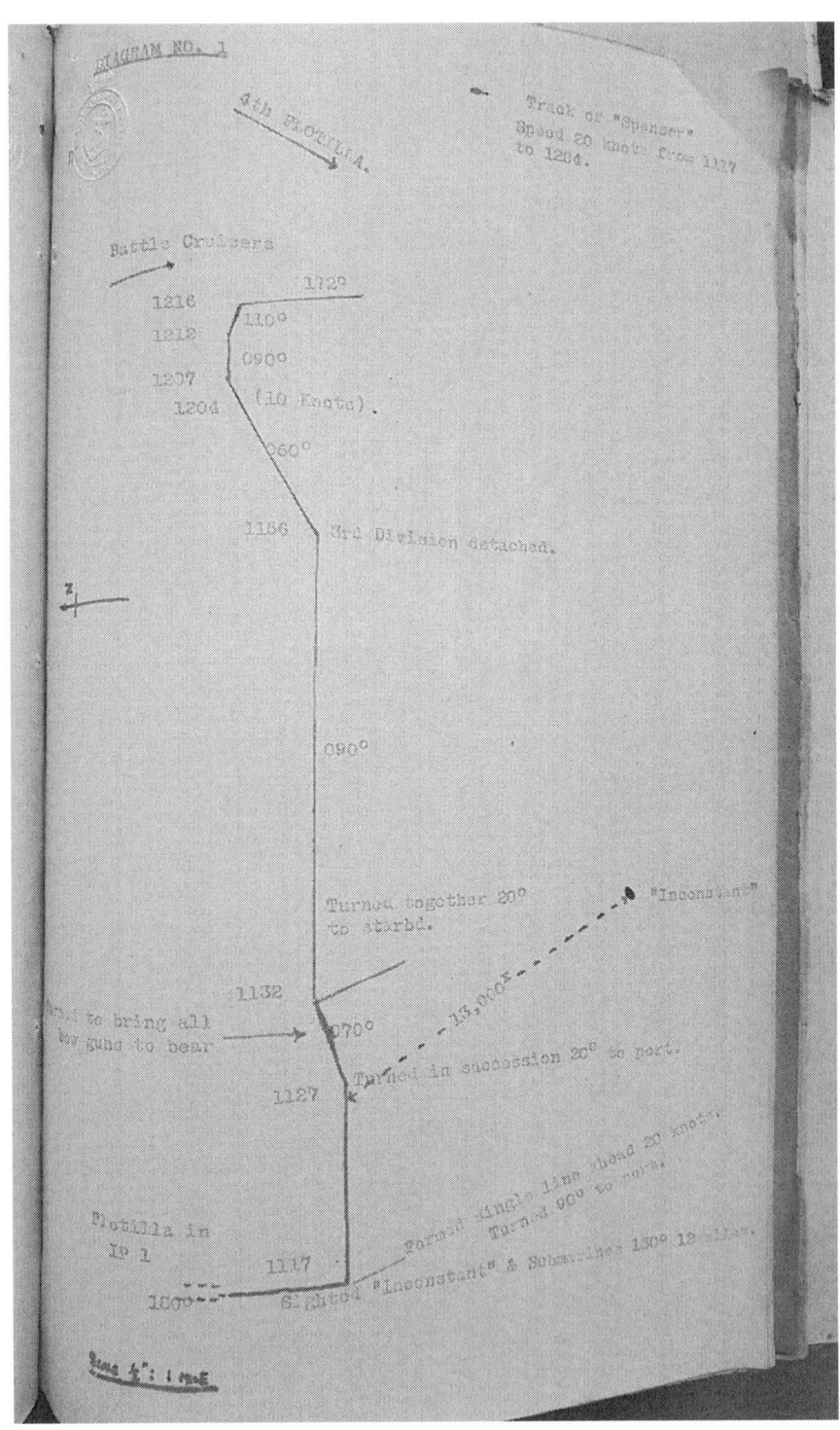

DIAGRAM NO. 1

4th FLOTILLA.

Track of "Spencer"
Speed 20 knots from 1117
to 1204.

Battle Cruisers

172°

1216
1212   110°
1207   090°
1204   (10 Knots).

060°

1156   3rd Division detached.

090°

Turned together 20°   "Inconstant"
to starbd.

1132
13,000x

...t to bring all   070°
...y guns to bear

Turned in succession 20° to port.

1127

Plotilla in
IP 1

Formed single line ahead 20 knots.
Turned 90° to port.

1117
1100
Sighted "Inconstant" & Subma...hes 130° 12 miles.

Scale ½": 1 mile

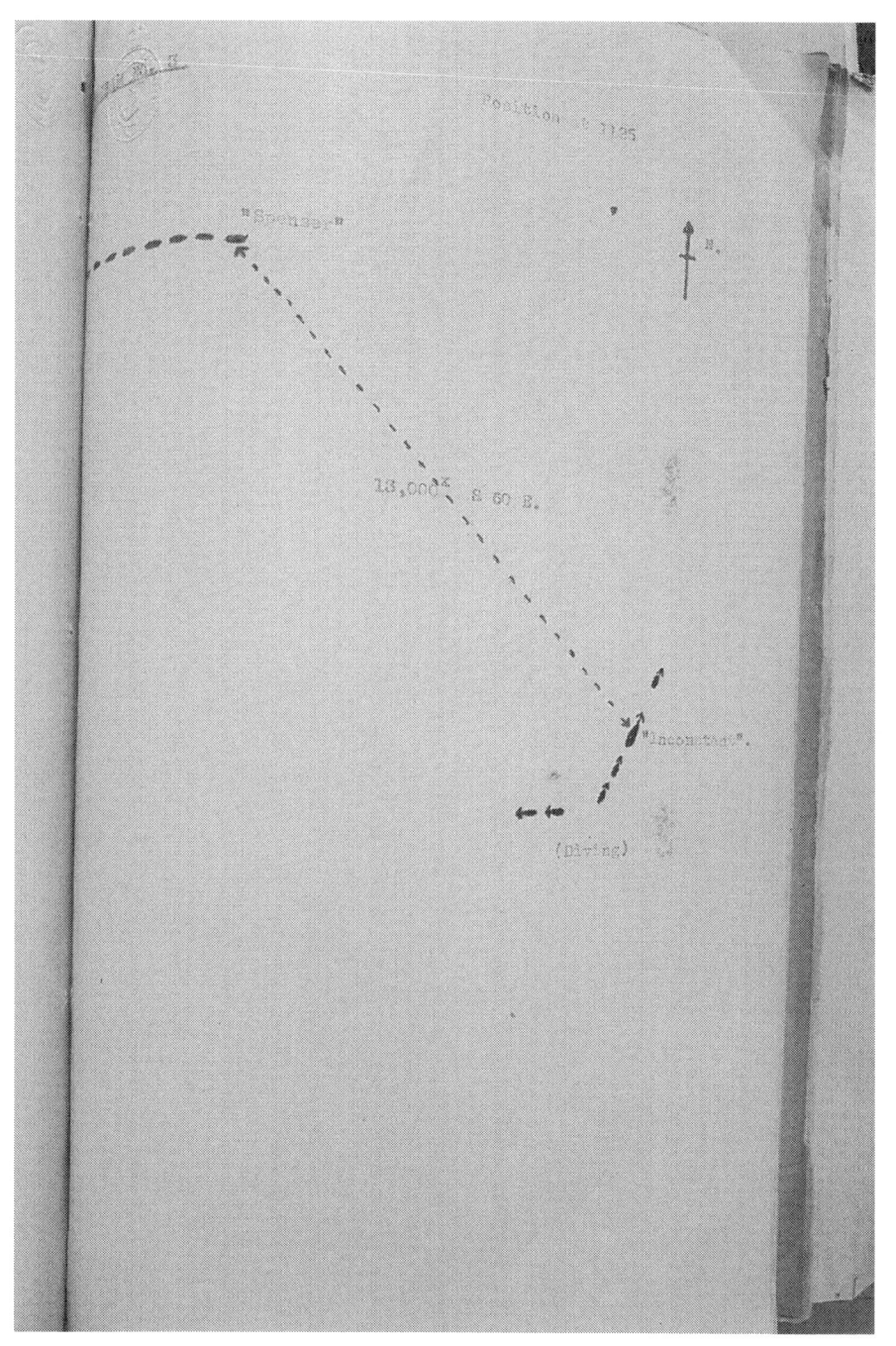

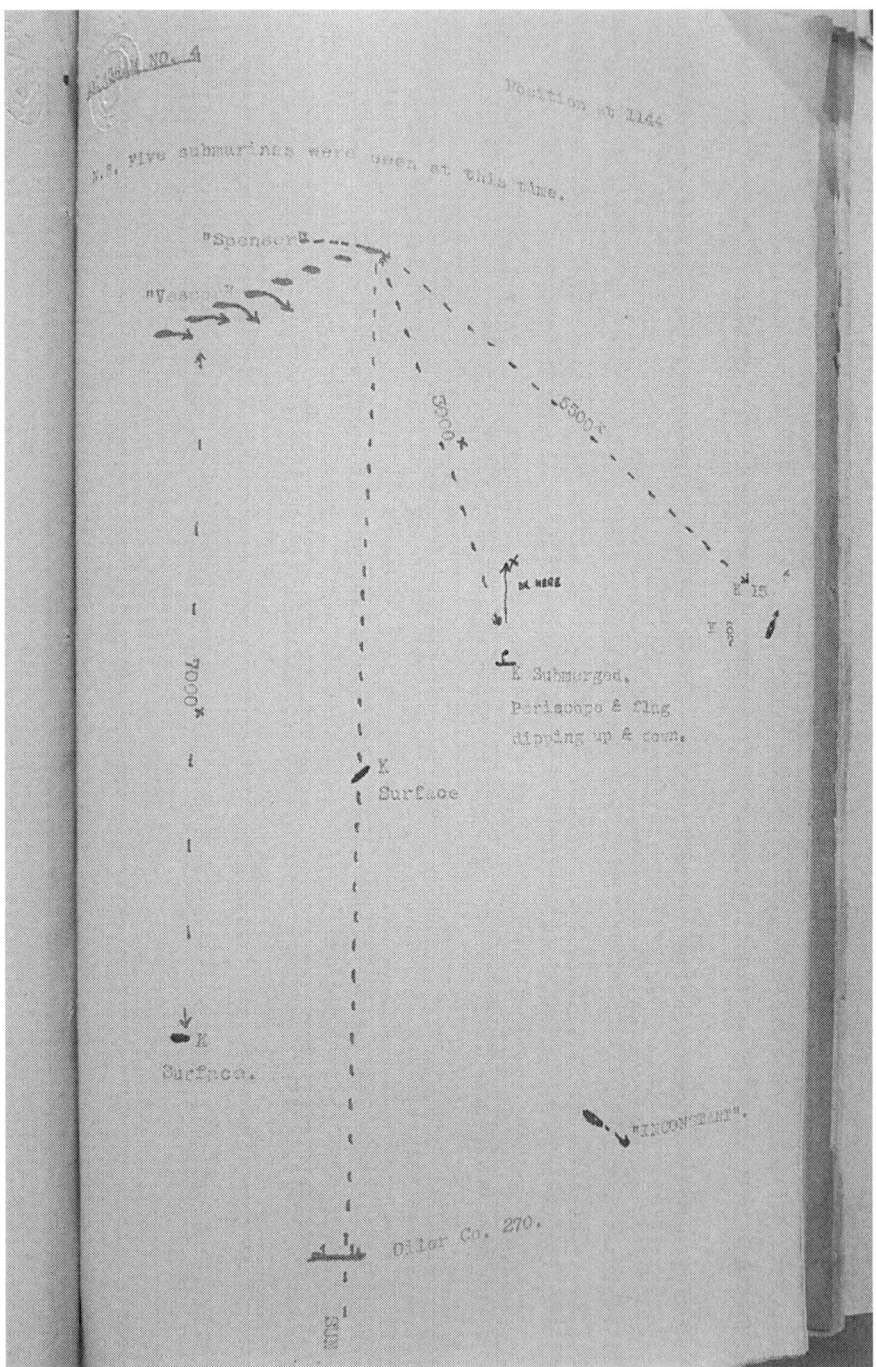

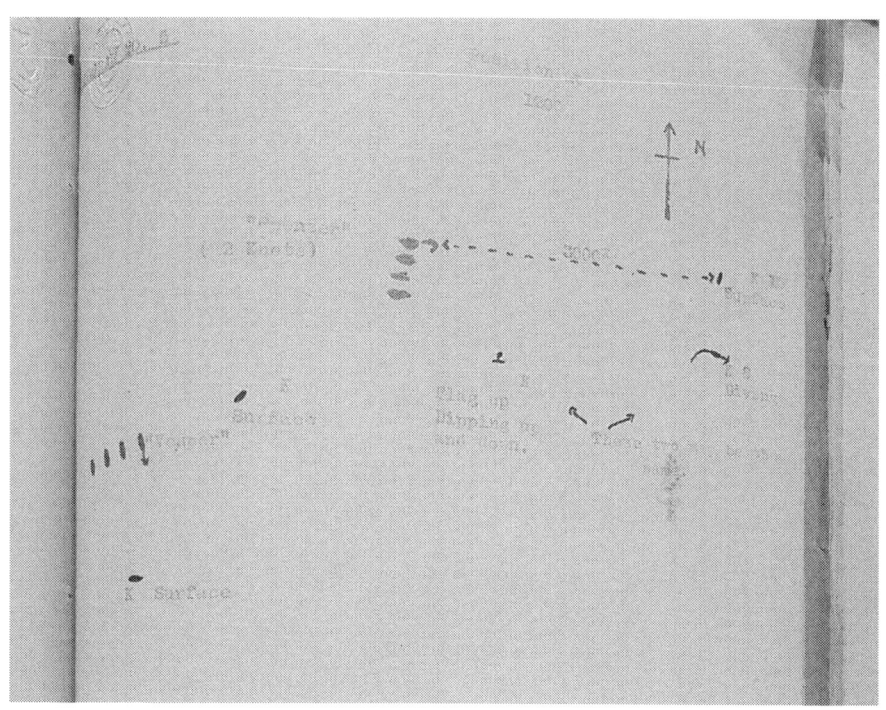

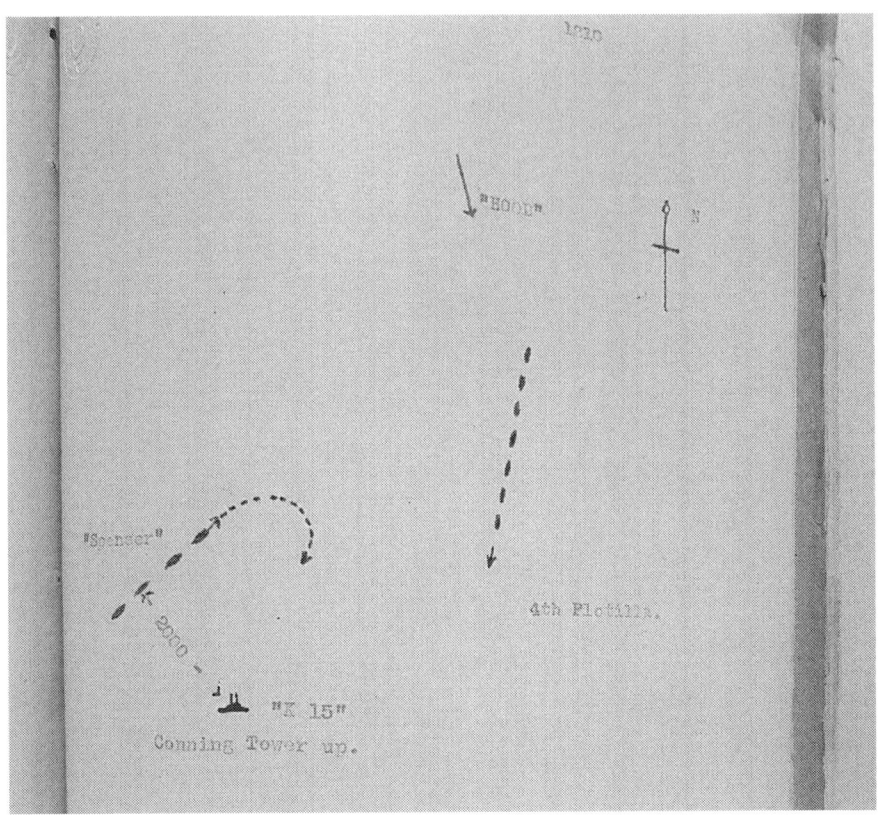

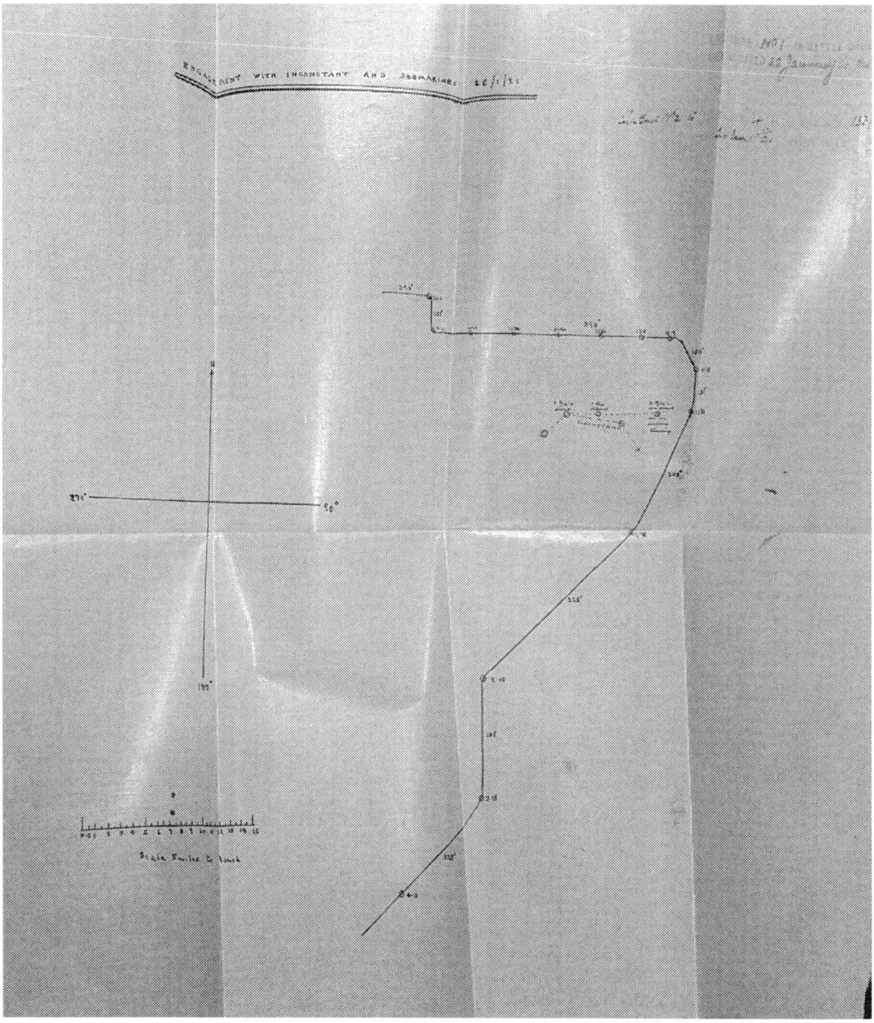

CHAPTER TEN
CONTINUED...

"the result of an unholy union between a destroyer and a submarine" (Anon)

At the same time the *K22* had struggled to regain the surface, when her dive took a nasty bow down angle. She had at 11:27 been ordered by Inconstant, to begin her attack and commenced her own dive. But as she submerged at 7 degrees (flooding tanks '1' to '4' at full pressure) she experienced trouble with her trim. Her Captain (Allen Poland) given the 'K' boats track record decided not to risk the dive and ordered full astern on both engines and all the boats tanks blown. The submarine surfaced at 11:47 and Poland abandoned his planned attacks and effectively dropped out of the exercise. He then went aft and opening the boiler room tried the test cock, discovering that the number '6' external oil tank had leaked six tons into the sea. This had made the boat light towards the stern and hard to dive on a level trim. At 13:20 after a successful dive *K22* closed with the *K15* at 11 knots.

K15's own dive was less problematic. The boat was the divisional leader and at 11:56 ordered the division to dive on *"333K.S spread"*. At 12:12 her Captain, (Robert Wartkins) having found himself a distance from the 'enemy' resurfaced the boat.

After an hour running submerged the 'K' boats role within the 'battle' was over and the submarines returned one by one to the surface, (*K8* surfacing at 12:29). Once surfaced they were found to be scattered over the expanse of water. As each boat came to the appeared it raised its W/T aerial to report its position to the *Inconstant*. Soon the light cruiser's Captain (S) Robert. R. Turner was asking each submarine in turn if they had seen the *K5*. Each boat replied in turn, *"no"*. No shipping had passed through her dive area, so a collision was quickly ruled out. The third division of the second destroyer flotilla had passed near her dive area and reported no oil being sighted. By midday concern was growing into alarm and the flotilla spent the afternoon looking for the missing boat and asking the ships of the fleet if they have seen her. At 14:09 a by now worried Turner had failed to get an answer to K5's call signal.

But by dusk no sign had been found and the flotilla returned to the location were the *K5* had been seen to dive. At 17:42 *Inconstant* found a square mile of sea water (1.5 miles off *K5's* diving location (2.41 Km)) that had the smell and calmness of an oily layer. Four destroyers were detailed to search through the night and by the morning the oil had spread over 8 miles of the sea. Two pieces of timber were sighted and the K9 recovered the floating debris. The pieces bore red sides with numbers in white along the upper edge. They were recognized as beams, (the largest being 9 foot 11.5 inches) for a battery cover, the movable floorboards from control room rested on these beams and the numbers were cell references. The ends of the beams were undamaged, implying they hadn't broken free, but that the boat had disintegrated around them as they were an internal element of the boat which with the oil, sadly made what was feared all the more likely. *K5* had been lost. That evening the C-in-C of the Atlantic fleet Sir Charles Madden signalled the Admiralty:

"Regret to report loss of submarine K5 with entire crew while diving to attack battle cruisers during tactical exercises in about latitude 49 N longitude 9 west at about 11.30 today. Thursday 29th January. Cause not known, patches of oil and wreckage have been located. It is hoped to ascertain definitely the nature of the wreckage at daylight. H.M.S Inconstant and destroyers last. are on in the spot. Am proceeding Arosa Bay in Queen Elizabeth with second and fourth destroyer flotillas. H.M.S Inconstant and first submarine flotilla to hold enquiry. Remainder of Atlantic fleet will proceed on spring cruise as already arranged".

The National Archive files provide us with a list of the signals that were dispatched that day, providing an insight into the exercise and its transformation into a search of the missing submarine:

11:10: A.C.Q & D.2 from "SPENCER" (via "VALENTINE) W/T. "For exercise - urgent - one light cruiser and submarines 130 degrees, 12 miles, course 060 degrees, position 260 V 50" (1106)".

11:18: "single line, speed 20 knots".

11:30: A.C.Q & D.2: "Detail one division to attack Western Submarines"

11:32 "Turn together 20 degrees to starboard".

11:35 D.2. TO 3RD DIVISION:"Attack Enemy Submarines".

11:35 A.C.Q. & D.2.

FROM "SPENSER" (VIA VALENTINE) W/T:"For exercise - urgent - 2 submarines have dived".

11:43 D.2. to "VESPER":"You should not exceed 20 knots".

11:55 A.C.Q. to D.2: "Attack Enemy submarines ahead of you".

11:56 D.2. TO 3RD:"Attack Enemy Submarines to South-west".

11:58 DIVISION D.2. TO 1ST DIVISION: "Form on a compass Iine".

1158 D.2 TO 1ST DIVISION: "Form on compass line of bearing south from "SPENCER".

12:03 D. 2. TO 2ND FLOTILLA:"Speed 10 knots".

1205 D.2. to 2nd FLOTILLA: "Form single line ahead"

12:09 & D.2. from "SPENSER" (via "VALENTINE") W/T:"One light cruiser bearing 170 degrees,14 miles, steering 270".

One light cruiser bearing 090 degrees, 14 miles, steering 270."

One light cruiser bearing 100 degrees, 14 miles, steering 270. (1201).

12:10 D.2. to "VESPER" (W/T): "Rejoin with all despatch ". (1208).

12:24 D.2 TO 2ND FLOTILLA: " form submarine screen No 6".

12:24 D.2 TO 2ND "Speed 10 knots".

13:15 A.C Q TO GENERAL: "Course 225, speed 16 knots, form single line abreast to starboard".

13:17 D.2 TO 2ND FLOTILLA: "Form Submarine screen No.9".

14:00 D.2. TO A.C.Q: "Submitted. 3 submarines were destroyed by 1st Division at ranges from 4,000 to 1,000 yards. One destroyed by 3rd Division at 3,000 yards. They were under concentrated fire for a considerable time". (Note-originally added "One escaped by diving".)

17:01 A.C.Q TO D.2: " Your 1400. What numbers of 3 submarines attacked by 1st division? Did they all remain on surface after action? (1650.)".

17:10 D.2. TO A.C.Q:" Two numbers were seen K.8 and K.15. They constantly dived and again broke surface except K.15 which was not seem to dive".

17:45 A.C.W TO D2: "Two submarines dived at 1121. At 1130 one division was ordered to cross in their vicinity. Which division did you detail? Did these submarines subsequently come to the surface? K.8 and K.9, the two (sic) testing submarines have been accounted for".

17:45 D.2 TO A.C.Q: "3rd Division was detailed. Both these submarines came up but a long way separated". (1752.)

17:58. A. C.Q TO D.2: "What about the third?"(1754.)

18:20.D.2 TO A.C.Q: "The third submarine which "SPENSER" 1st Division were engaging kept on showing between 3 and thousand yards away and closing. I think she wad left with conning tower awash, but in turning to avoid the 4th Flotilla we lost sight of her".

2026. A. C.Q. TO D.2. AND D. 4. (W/T): "Submarine K.5 has apparently been sunk. Report if any destroyer can possibly have struck her".

D.2 TO 2ND FLOTILLA: "Report immediately if any destroyer of 2nd Flotilla could have touched submarine to-day."

23:05. D.2. TO A. C.Q: "No boats of 2nd Flotilla touched a submarine".

SIGNALS PASSED ON FRIDAY, 21st JANUARY 1921

09:23:D.2. TO "VESPER": "When you first opened fire yesterday

I. How many submarines did you see on the surface?

II. When 3rd Division was ordered to attack, 2 submarines were separated to the Westward and dived. Did both come to the surface again?.

III. What was the closet any destroyer of your division approach a submarine?

09:45 "VESPER" TO D.2:"Your 0923

I. 4

II. Only one was seen.

III 3,000 yards (0940).

The accident was later recorded as having occurred at latitude 48° 51 ½'N longitude 9° 5'W, about 100 miles south west off the Scilly Isles. The next morning brought the recovery of a ditty box lid belonging to one of the *K5's* Petty Officers, Arthur Mould and it was most likely to have been stored in the control room. Nothing else was ever to be found. Six officers and fifty-one men had been on board. That second night the Inconstant and the 'K' boats headed for Spain's Arosa bay.

The enquiry as was becoming standard for a 'K' boat

achieved little but concluded the wreckage showed the submarine had broken up. She might have exploded, broken in half or gone out of control and dived too deep. But whatever the cause the limited wreckage all came from the control room. The weakest point of the hull was where the conning tower dome joined with the pressure hull and it most likely broke open here. The submarine had been commanded by an experienced officer, Lieutenant Commander John A Gaimes, but he had a new crew. The other officers on board were Lieutenant F Cuddeford, Engineer-Lieutenant E Bowles, Acting Engineer-Lieutenant G Baker, Lieutenant B Clarke and Acting Lieutenant R Middlemist. The full complement included 51 ratings on board.

A DITTY BOX OWNED BY SERGEANT FURLONG OF THE ROYAL MARINES. IT WAS AN ITEM SIMILAR TO THIS THAT WAS RECOVERED BY THE SEARCHERS. (SOURCE: NATIONAL MUSEUN OF THE ROYAL NAVY).

After her loss, Lieutenant George Whitfield (who had been present on the day in November the *K5* had had her valve problems), was ordered by Commander Kellett to write to the Admiralty telling them of the incident. He questioned if as a result, the *K5* was safe to go to sea, as he believed on diving the damage would inflict her with a heavy trim throughout the hull, dropping her quickly to 100 feet. He suggested with the tank having been chalked internally, on diving it may have given way. It would have filled quickly dragging the stern down too fast. The weakened deck would have given way and as the stern dropped the motors would lack the power to bring the bow to the surface. He also claimed to have overheard during the refit that although the repaired tank should have been tested up to 50 lbs per square inch, it had not been. The court of Enquiry was held on board *HMS Resolution* between the 24th to 26th January 1921.

The General Public had little idea of the 'K' boat curse and with the wars end, censorship was no longer in force. There was shock and surprise as they were unaware of the class's history. On the 24th January 1921 the retired Rear Admiral S. S. Hall RN, (who during the war had served as the third Inspecting Captain of Submarines) published his insight into the loss of the *K5* in The Times:

"The 'K' Class submarines were designed solely for action with the Grand Fleet in the North Sea. They are the largest and fastest submarines in existence, certainly by far the most complicated and they need an exceptionally well trained crew.

It is not know what rapidity of dive was being demanded by the operation orders, but it seems certain that the first Lieutenant (K5) on whom would fall the chief duty of supervision below was recently appointed and also many of the crew were newly joined. However, this may be, it may be taken as certain that the loss of the vessel was due to some delay to checking the downward momentum gained by the vessel being over-trimmed in diving, either by admitting compressed air too slowly to too many tanks at one time, to tanks only partially full, or to a sea connexion being closed prematurely....

K class submarines were designed solely for action with the Grand Fleet in the North Sea. They are the largest and fastest submarines in existence, certainly by far the most complicated and they need an exceptionally well-trained crew.

It is not known what rapidity of diving was being demanded by the operation orders, but it seems certain that the first Lieutenant, on whom would fall the chief duty of supervision below, was recently appointed and that many of the crew were also newly-joined....

The accident is deplorable in the loss of so many gallant officers and men and it is not clear why the 'K' class should be taken for cruises in the Atlantic in the winter. The vessels may with accuracy be described as 'freak' submarines, built entirely for the peculiar conditions of the last war. The high surface speed necessitates great length and the further complication of steam demands very large openings for funnels and air intakes to the boiler-rooms. These have always been a source of great anxiety in bad weather or in rapid diving..

Presumably these vessels are kept in commission in order to perfect the conduct of such submarines in a fleet battle, but it appears to be a very questionable policy, since the 'K' class will be obsolete long before such a battle can take place. They were designed solely for the North Sea and have not the qualifications nor the sea endurance to accompany a battle fleet under war conditions except in home waters.

The keenness of all submarine officers is well known. It is to be hoped that this has not been over strained from a lack of understanding of the delicacy of this very special type of submarine, with the result of the vessels' being employed on work for which they were never intended and for which they would be highly dangerous if the personnel were not thoroughly trained... .

It has always been recognized that owing to their size and complications the 'K' class cannot dive as rapidly as smaller submarines. For work with the fleet this was no disadvantage, since they could always expect to get good warning; but a highly trained crew, thoroughly familiar with every detail of the vessel, is required. With such conditions the 'K' boats could dive from twenty knots on the surface in about four minutes, but with anything but a perfectly trained crew, any attempt to do this would be highly dangerous in deep water. With water entering the tanks at two hundred tons a minute, the vessel might easily be trimmed to such an extent that the slightest hitch in getting the compressed air to act would take the vessel too deep for recovery. It will easily be understood that as the vessel now weighs over two and a half thousand tons and has way on her the downward momentum may be considerable. If there is much sea or swell it may be imperative to give her some negative buoyancy to get her away from the surface and though the compressed air will blow one or two tanks rapidly there is often considerable delay in checking the vessel's downward motion. This is especially the case if the tank or tanks to which the air is admitted are not quite full and the vessel is already getting deep. The air has first of all to raise the pressure in the whole of the empty portion of the tank. During this time the water is still entering and rising in pressure and only when the air pressure exceeds this and commences to drive the water out will buoyancy begin to be gained. Even then it will be an appreciable time before the vessel is checked and then begins to rise....

It will be readily understood that diving a vessel of this size and intricacy is a delicate operation, demanding the complete knowledge of his duty from every member of her crew and a perfect system of drill and control from the central compartment before rapid diving can be safely undertaken".In addition, he drew attention to the need for a thoroughly trained crew to operate them safely.

The Admiralty were to make no comment beyond stating how sorry they were for the loss. But a high-pressure air system was ordered to be fitted to the external ballast tanks throughout the surviving class. On the 25th January the *K2* was given a reprieve and removed from the for-sale list to replace the lost *K5*. The *K2* returned to service on the 9th March 1921, manned by the former crew of the *K11.*

The ill-fated Submarine "K 5."
Sunk with all hands, 57 officers and men, at the Western entrance of the Channel whilst exercising with the Atlantic Fleet, 20th January, 1921.

Previous Page. The Above caption: " ill-fated submarine "K5" sunk with all hands, 57 officers and men, at the western entrance of the English Channel whilst exercising with the

Atlantic Fleet, 20th January 1921. (copywrite Abrahams)"

On return from her exercises in the Mediterranean in 1922, the Battlecruiser *Hood* in company with the rest of the fleet dropped several wreaths and held a memorial service where the *K5* had been lost.

The fleet called at Parma Bay on Palma de Mallorca, Spain during early February, but by June the 'K' boat flotilla had returned to England. The 'Jinx' had not yet had its fill of the 'K' boats and now it turned its attention once more to England's south coast. Late on the 25th June 1921 the *K15* lay moored alongside the light cruiser *HMS Canterbury* in the tidal basin of Portsmouth naval base, where she was undergoing maintenance. Most of the crew were absent on leave, including the Captain, (Commander George Fagan Bradshaw), while those on board not on watch were in the majority asleep in their berths. Suddenly a watch keeper on the conning tower noted that the submarine was slowly sinking into the basin's waters, the stern already being awash. He frantically dropped down the conning tower's ladder and roused the off-duty watch. The half-awake crewmen scrambled aboard the Canterbury and the ropes binding cruiser to submarine were quickly unfastened. The submarine then slowly set-tled down onto the basins bed amid streams of bubbles as the boat flooded throughout its length, her hatches having been left open in the frantic haste to escape. By low tide only the funnels and top of the conning tower were visible above water, marking the 'wreck's location near the mouth of the tidal basin and for such a busy naval port, a navigation haz-ard. Divers were despatch soon after the *K15* had sunk and their examination found the vents on the external ballast tanks to have been leaking.

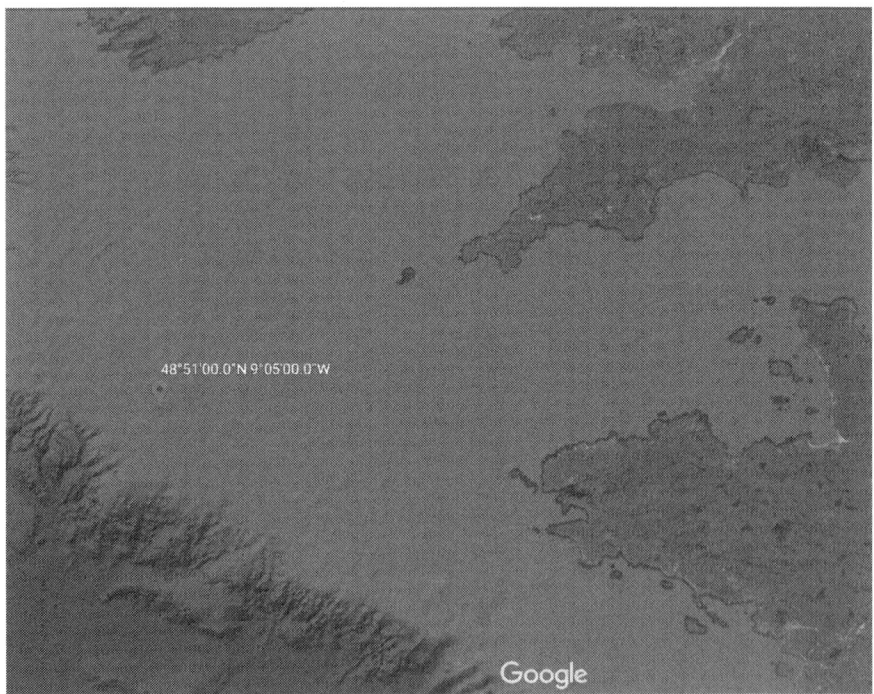

THE LOCATION OF THE K5's LOSS APPROXIMATELY.

The navy was faced with an urgent salvage operation as the craft could not remain where she now lay. Salvage was not going to be easy as the crew had abandoned the boat with little time to spare and all her watertight doors remained open and in addition the intake valves had also been left open. As a result, *K15* was now flooded from bow to stern. Also the day prior the dockyard workers who had been working on her refit, had drilled a hole one inch wide leading through the pressure hull and into the conning tower. The divers tried to plug it externally but that proved to be not possible. The Admiralty had in the meanwhile ordered *K15's* original Captain, (Vaughan Jones) onto the scene to help and advice with the recovery of his former command. One funnel was lengthened and the other sealed off after which the divers could then enter the interior through the funnel and successfully closed off the boiler room. Now compartment by compartment the hull could be pumped out. The men worked sixteen-hour day with one rest day over a thirteen-day period. By that stage the hull had regained sufficient buoyancy to be towed by a tug onto the mud flats south of Whale island where she was laid on a mud bank at Fountain Lake. The former *HMS K15* lay abandoned for a month on the exposed mud until in July 1921 she was made watertight and then towed the following month to Upnor on the river Medway for scrapping.

The accident was found afterwards to have been caused by the hydraulic oil expanding in the hot weather and contracting as the days temperatures dropped, causing a loss of hydraulic pressure and that resulted in the vents opening. As the air pressure dropped so the sea rose. In addition her Captain, the decorated and experienced sub Commander George Fagan Bradshaw, was advised that he would not be placed in command of a submarine again, due to the 'sloppy standards of attention and supervision' that had come to light on board the submarine by the Court Martial. Bradshaw had been in command of a succession of submarines, his first

Captaincy of a submarine being *HMS C7* on the 20th February 1914. On the 10th March 1917 he had while in command of *HMS G13*, torpedoed and sank UC43. He was awarded the Distinguished Service Order for this feat, on the 12th May 1917. Unfortunately, on the 22 November 1918 while in command of the *G11*, he ran her aground in fog. A Court Martial investigating the loss was not to attribute any blame on him. Following the loss of the *K15* he was unwilling to retire; Bradshaw underwent training in the Anti-Gas School later in the year before going onto half pay. On the 1st June 1922 at his own request Bradshaw was placed on the Retired List. He was promoted to the rank of Commander on the Retired List on 6th December 1927.

The year of 1921 had commenced with seven 'K' boats forming the 1st submarine flotilla serving within the Atlantic Fleet, while five others undertook a series of high-speed trials and torpedo testing. That year the Admiralty was to note in the Technical History and Index that,

> *"The K-class stands by itself. No other nation is building similar boats and our inception of them shows that our lead in design is very great."*

No other nation, (nor their crews) wanted them!

The *K22* was to be the first of the surviving Group 1 boats to be fitted (in 1922) with a new improved high-pressure system, for blowing the external ballast tanks. After her modification and while off Campbeltown on the West coast Scotland, (50 miles from Gareloch), she was ordered to conduct a dive in front selected officers from the Atlantic fleet who were watching the dive from the decks of the cruiser *Norfolk*.

But with typical 'K' boat 'flair' she managed to dive with at least one funnel raised, allowing water to cascade down and into the engine room. Fortunately, the tanks were blown and the red-faced Captain, Lieutenant-Commander Ronald W. Blacklock brought his command back to the surface.

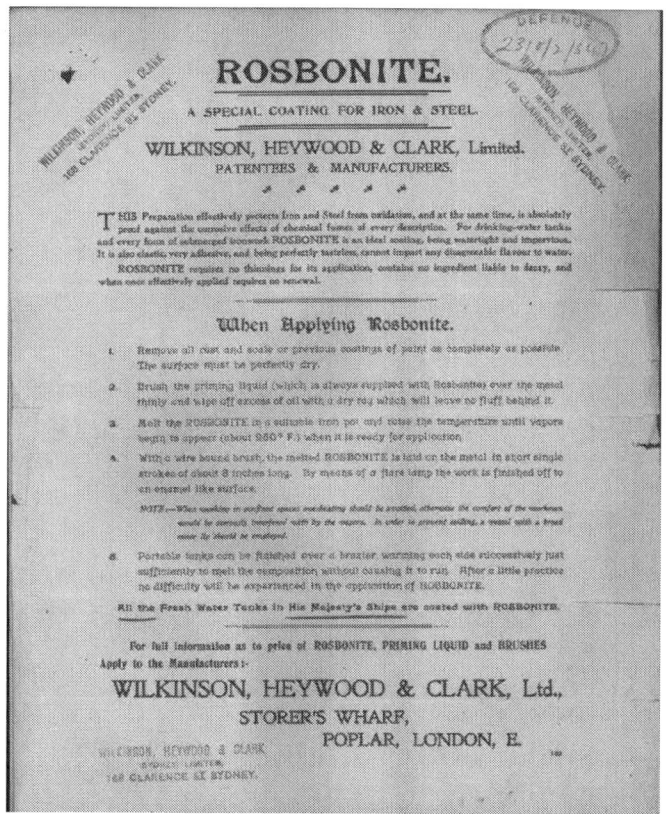

In 1922 the *K1* was to undergo a refit at the Chatham dockyard. Several of the tanks casing and the diesel engines were renewed. Her battery tank rivets had been found to be defective and needed replacing. The Battery tanks were scraped, cleaned and re-coated with 'Rosbonite'. Her water tanks were cleaned, oiled and coated with Rosbonite. The two boilers tubes were cleaned and re-coated with Bitumastic Enamel. All her tanks were cleaned and re-coated with Oxide. Her watertight doors, hatches, manhole covers, and fittings were tested and repaired as necessary. She emerged from the dockyard in February 1923. The records also note that by July 1923 the *K2* had received a set of new boilers and engines. This after only seven years' service and at least one of those years in reserve! But maintenance aside 1923 was to be an incident free year for the surviving Group 1 boats.

However, on the 11th January 1924 K2 and *K12* were both sailing from Portland Harbour when the former was to collide with the *K12*. She tore a hole in the forward casing of the *K12* and buckled her bows for about 6 feet (1.8 mtrs). *K12's* Captain, Lieutenant-Commander Christopher P. Satow was judged responsible for the collision. He was in command of the boat from the 15th November 1923 until 27th July 1924.

Next in K2's year was the death on Tuesday, 20th May 1924 of Christopher Stoneman, a Leading Stoker for reasons not recorded. Then as the year drew towards its end, on the 7th November, *K2* collided with the submarine *H29* as they participated in exercises off the Needles. The *K2* suffered slight damage to her bow and the *H29's* Captain was judged to be responsible for the incident.

The *K14* having been placed into reserve prior, was re-commissioned on 20th August 1924 under the command of Lieutenant-Commander James Lawrence Boyd. But just over a year later the 13th November 1925, she was reduced to the

Care and Maintenance at Chatham.

The *K6,* having had a new high-pressure system installed at Chatham in 1924, was ordered north for Invergordon. But as she made her way northward along the English East coast, she ran into a North Sea gale. The *K6* struggled with making forward passage as her bow rammed itself into and then through the mountainous waves. As the bow headed down into a trough and into the next wave, something felt wrong to the Captain, (Lieutenant-Commander Oswald E. Halifax). An examination of the forward compartments revealed that the rivets in the pressure hull were leaking. The boats speed was lowered to 8 knots and she limped into Invergordon. Once the weather had moderated *K6* returned south to Chatham for the necessary repairs. It was suggested that the weakness originated from her collision with the *K4* six years prior. But we have encountered failing rivets in a 'K' boat before...

On the 17th October 1924 the *K2* was reduced to reserve status and just under a month later, the 13th November 1925 brought HMS *K6's* reduction to a Care & Maintenance Party at Chatham. The next and final stage in the K6's demise was on the 13th July the following year when she was sold to John Cashmore Ltd for scrapping at Newport. The *K22* was during 1925 part of the First Submarine Flotilla, operating with the Atlantic Fleet. But on the 7th December, she paid off into Dockyard Control at Chatham, joining the *K12,* who had entered C&M at Chatham on the 13th November 1925. *K12* would be scrapped in July 1926.

On the 3rd September 1925 a planned refit for the *K2* was put on hold until it could be decided if she was to remain in service. A month later the 4th October it was decided she too was to be scrapped and on the 13th November 1925 the *K2* was reduced to C&M. She was finally paid off on the 7/9th(?) December 1925 being handed over to Chatham dockyard control and her batteries were removed. On the 23rd July 1926 she was sold to John Cashmore for breaking. Group 1 was reduced to two boats, the *K14* and the *K22*. By December they too would be sold.

Now there were no Group 1 boats left, just the lone Group 2 hull, the *K26* and her stepsisters, the 'M' class.

After all the 'incidents', accidents and losses, remarkably *HMS K8, K9* and the *K10* were to be unaffected by the "Jinx' and they completed their services with no blemishes in their Royal Navy career.

As the 'K' boats were gradually offered for sale and their disposal, Admiral Sir William "Blinker" Reginald Hall proposed that a number of the steam powered submarines should be made available for conversion to the role of coastal merchant ships. But it was concluded that they would need to be sold at a price lower than the market value and the amount of work for the conversion was deemed to be neither feasible nor cost effective. The idea was dropped.

In 1926 the Group 1 boats last few boats, the *K2, K12, K14* and the *K22* in company with the K26, had taken part in the fleets Spring manoeuvres. The weather during the fleet exercises was bad and they were eventually to be cancelled. A comparison was made after the event between the two groups of 'K' boats. There needs to be some allowance for the fact that the Group 1 boats were all completed in 1917 and were of wartime construction, whilst the *K26* was completed at a gentler pace in 1923.

There were several negative points raised regarding the 'K' Class. But given that the surviving boats were of an average 8.1 years in service, they were not sufficiently seaworthy to maintain a station within the Fleet while it was at sea. Their poor seaworthiness had escaped criticism during the war when the vessels were new, and the bow had been raised to combat the failing. In fact, as has been noted prior, in September 1918 two 'K' Class submarines overtook the Grand Fleet which was hove too in a heavy gale out in the North Sea. This showed on some level their seaworthiness, but it did not prove that they could keep up with the Fleet in calmer weather at a reasonably (or fleet) speed of 21 knots. But in part this criticism was the effect of the extra weight in the form of the oil reserve and the influence it had on their buoyancy. The emergency oil fuel brought the reserve of buoyancy down to 25%, which was still a reasonable figure even by post-war standards.

The hull structure was deemed to be too weak and caused excessive working within the boats frame in a rough sea. The fuel stowage in the external tanks was poor regarding the tank's location. In addition, the tanks were an add on to the original design and had not been purpose-built. The bow tube door gear was of a poor design and was unable to withstand heavy seas on the bow. But given a surface speed of 24 knots it was not really a surprise.

The boats suffered according to the author of the report:

1. "Poor habitability" or living conditions.

2. The electric generating plant was proven to be unreliable if it was run for extended periods.

3. The notorious slow rate of dive quoted as about 5

minutes.

4. Poor manoeuvrability underwater when compared to the navy's other submarines.

5. Group 1 had the older 18-inch torpedo tubes.

6. A comparatively low endurance.

7. A design failing in shipping water into the boiler room through the vents and funnels.

The boats usually operated with a particularly small amount of buoyancy. The *K26* clearly benefited from the experience with the original 'K' Class. The design work for the *K26* probably started at the beginning of 1918 and at that stage many of the 'problems' would have been known about by the designers.

1: "The first effective submarines, those of World War I era, had hulls that were broadly circular in cross-section, with a deck plate mounted midway. Their heavy battery tanks were mounted beneath this deck, for stability. The ballast tanks were mounted inside the pressure hull. For compactness the ballast tanks were wrapped around the batteries, low down and sharing the flat surfaces of the battery tank.

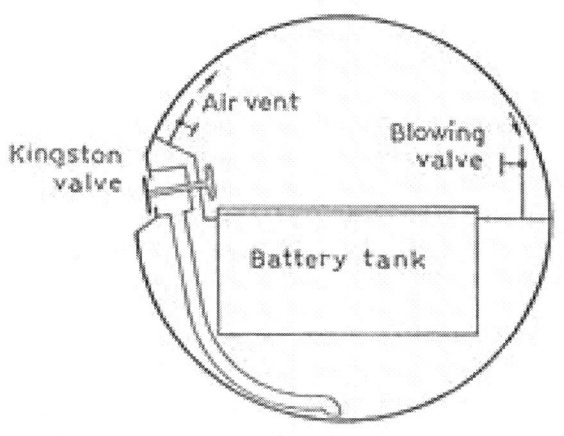

Early submarine cross-section, before saddle tanks

The Kingston valves linking the ballast tanks to the sea could be left open, a practice known as "riding the valves", and the water level in the tanks controlled solely by the vent and blowing air valves. The drawback was that the ballast tanks, open to sea pressure, had a flat surface to the crew compartment and were thus restricted in strength to the bursting strength of this flat plate. In particular this led to accidents where the boat bottomed safely after an accident, but the excess pressure of "blowing out" was sufficient to cause the internal tank wall to fail.[1]

A secondary drawback of these internal ballast tanks could be poor sea-keeping when surfaced. With the tanks full of water the submarine was stable, but when emptied, this large buoyant volume low down led to excessive rolling. This was a particular problem because early submarines spent almost all of their time surfaced and had little freeboard to begin with" (Mikhail Ryazanov).

PART FOUR. GROUP 2 (HMS K26)

HMS K26

CHAPTER ONE. BIGGER AND 'IMPROVED'.

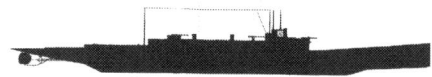

"It Is An
Extraordinary Fact That Even After The War Was Over And The
Lesson Supposedly Learnt, One More Of These Boats Was Built". H.
M. Submarines, By Lieutenant-Commander P. K. Kemp, R.N.

DIMENSIONS

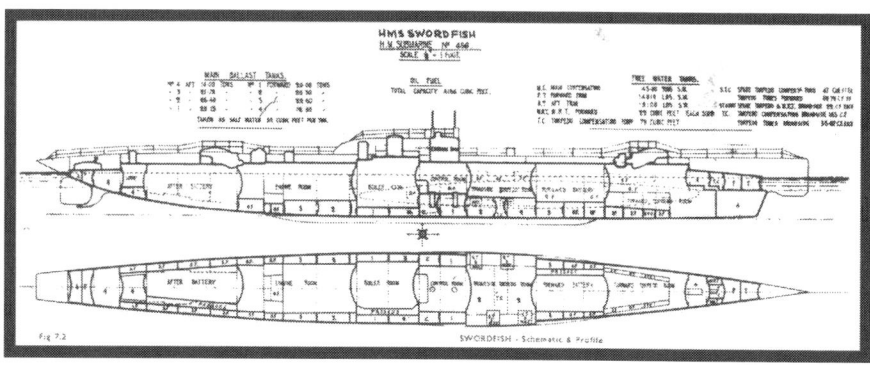

T he Group 1 boats were, (as we have discovered), uncommonly big for a submarine. But as large as the first group of the 'K' boats were, their successors, Group 2, were bigger from bow to stern by 12 feet (3.65 mtrs). This extra length of hull was caused by the *K26* being equipped with the newer 21-inch torpedoes, as opposed to their predecessors 18 inch.

The *K26's* hull length from bow to stern was 351 feet (106.98 mtrs) and her waterline length was 347 feet (105.76 mtrs). But allowing for the fact that the waterline under cut the underside of the stern by 4 feet (1.21 mtrs), the above figure is one to be wary of. The actual measurement was most probably circa 339 feet (103.32 mtrs) and 326 feet (99.36 mtrs) along the waterline.

The *K26's* mean draught was 16 foot 10 inches (5.13 mtrs) which gave a freeboard (the distance from the waterline to the deck), of 4 foot 2 inches (1.27 mtrs). But the measurement from waterline to bridge deck was 12 foot 2 inches (3.70 mtrs). Beneath the waterline the ballast keel was 15 inches (38.1 cm) in its depth.

The *K26's* inner or pressure hull width and depth was listed as 21 feet 9 inches (6.62 mtrs) and 19-foot 1 inch (5.81 mtrs) respectively. The external hull was 28-foot 0 inch (8.53 mtrs) in its beam and 19 foot 9 inches (72.23 mtrs) in its depth.

From the conning tower forward the main deck had an incline that reached along and up to the raised bow. This slope lifted the forecastle to a height of 13 feet (3.9 mtrs) above the Load Waterline Length. On the Group 1 boats (prior to their new bows being fitted) the same measurement was 9 feet (2.74 mtrs), but as we have seen, the fore part of the boat as fitted was prone to being wet over their bows. The redesign of *K26* with her additional 4 feet (1.21 mtrs) was an attempt to make both the conning tower, the bows and fore deck as drier places as was feasible. The raised forward section of the bow was sub-divided into three buoyancy tanks, which were there to help lift the bow higher above the waves.

Displacement.

	SURFACED	WITH EMERGENCY FUEL	SUBMERGED
Group 1	1980 tons	2093 tons	2566 tons
Group 2	2140 tons	2140 tons	2530 ton

After her completion the Department of Naval Construction issued a set of figures for the *K26's* displacement. They listed her as 2,530 tons whilst submerged, (later in her career a higher figure of 2,770 tons was given) and 2,140 tons when surfaced. From these two figures it is possible to calculate that the quantity of main ballast water used was 390 tons. The officers' quarters and control room were both 18 inches shorter than in the Group 1 boats and within this smaller area a switchboard compartment was now included. The boiler room retained its dimensions from the earlier boats, with the width being dictated once again by the scale of the two boilers. Although the boiler room and the beam torpedo tube space remained fundamentally the same, the turbine room and the engine room were both reduced in length by 18 inches. This despite the same machinery having been installed. The changes in the hull's dimensions included an increase in the aft crew spaces by a 'roomy' 36 inches (91 cm). What had been the aft main ballast tank in the earlier boats was amended into the steering compartment in the K26 and 18 inches was as a result saved at the stern end of the hull.

The other area the two groups differed in structurally was

in the external hull and the superstructure. The profile (or shape) of the exterior hull had remained the same with the top surface of the external tanks running to a middle line bulkhead as they had in Group 1. But on the *K26* they stopped at the longitudinal bulkheads on the port and starboard sides of the middle line. This was feasibly due to the external tanks stretching to the middle line, where they would have approximately an 8-inch depth at the top.

The capacity of the *K26's* fuel tanks was increased from 197 tons to 300 tons of oil and the hull carried an additional 12 feet of steel plating and framework, all of which served to increase the *K26's* tonnage. The superstructure was in addition modified and raised by 3 feet in the final design to try and resolve the earlier 'K' boats funnel 'issues'. The superstructure was extended forward of the bridge to allow for one of the 4-inch guns to be remounted to a higher and drier position. The enclosed bridge was raised by the same height and a sea (or open bridge) was built above the closed bridge.

In addition, while on the slipway and under construction her swan bow was modified, and the hydroplanes were moved to operate in the wake of the propellers. All these factors and alterations added weight to the boats hull.

Buoyance & Fuel Tanks.

The bulk of the fuel oil carried by the *K26* was stored with in a series of external tanks and a larger percentage of the boats main ballast water was carried within the hull's internal tanks. These design changes to the tank's storage methods was a redistribution of the hulls liquid tonnage in attempt to improve on the earlier boats slow diving times.

The 'K' Class had 56½ tons of controlled free flooding space built within the superstructures frame but this figure was not to be included within the crafts submerged displacement totals, it was instead included in the reserve buoyancy sum. The three buoyancy tanks in the bow were also not included in the submerged displacement and was most likely considered to be controlled free flooding spaces.

The controlled free flooding tanks were fitted with a series of high pressure blows which worked in combination with the boats main ballast tanks. The storage capacity of the main ballast tanks was included within the total of ballast water used in the boat's submergence procedure. Their total was also incorporated within the submerged displacement. The figures in the records for her submerged displacement quote the tonnage as 2,530, the reserve buoyancy being 29.4%. Judging from the above displacement totals there must have been little alteration in the design of the hull's scantlings(1) from those in the first group, despite the designed diving depth being increased by 50 feet. The overall width of the boats external tanks was increased by an additional 17 inches (43.18 cm), but the total from the top of the pressure hull to the exterior plating was decreased by 8 inches (20.32 cm).

The alterations made to the Group 2 design allowed for an increase in the number of watertight bulkheads, raising the total to ten in the *K26* and in general the watertight sub-division was considered by the navy as excellent.

In total the *K26* had ten main external ballast tanks as well as fifteen internal tanks. Of the 390 tons total of main ballast water carried within the boats tanks around 220 tons was stored externally and 170 tons internally. The internal tanks would most likely have had Kingston valves fitted, (given the *K5's* experience) but the externals were flooded through holes within the bottom of the tanks a design that had been adopted for the earlier boats. In the later years of the *K26's* commission the Rear Admiral (Submarines) put forward the idea that "scoops" be fitted to these tanks to improve flooding time. But there is no record or likelihood that this was ever carried out on the *K26*, although such scoops had been fitted to the former Group 2 boats, the "M" Class.

Machinery.

GROUP 1

STEAM TURBINES
2 × Brown-Curtis or Parsons, 21,100 shp (15,700 kW) 2 ×
Oil-fired Yarrow.

BOILERS
2 × Oil-fired Yarrow.

ELECTRIC MOTORS
4 × 5,760 hp (4,300 kW).

DIESEL
1 × Vickers, 800 hp (600 k)..

GROUP 2

STEAM TURBINES
2 × Brown-Curtis or Parsons geared, 10,500 shp (7,830 kW)
each

BOILERS

2 × Oil-fired Yarrow.

ELECTRIC MOTORS
4 × 1,440 hp (1,070 kW) each .

DIESEL
1 × Vickers, 800 hp (600 k)..

The two groups boilers, motors and turbines were identical in specifications, but several other issues connected to *K26* would impact on her speed through the water. The Group 2 design included, (as has been mentioned) the addition of 300 tons of emergency oil, to increase the new boats operational range. The *K26* was in fact to have a steaming range of 260 miles above that of the Group 1 boats.

ENDURANCE RANGES

GROUP 1
SURFACED: 12,500 nm at 10 Kt.
        800 NM at maximum speed.

Submerged: 8 nm at 8 Kt.
        40 NM at 4 kts

GROUP 2
SURFACED: 1,200 NM at full speed.
        12,600 nm at 10 K.

SUBMERGED: 8 nm at 8 at 8 kts,
        30 Nm at 4 kts.

The problems the Group 1 boats had experienced with the amount of time taken to dive was finally overcome on the *K26*, by an improvement in the ballast tank design. Her record diving time was a much improved 3 minutes, 12 seconds to a depth of 80 feet. In addition, the maximum diving depth was increased by an additional 50 feet to 250 feet (76 mtrs). But there was no apparent reason for the 50 feet increase over that of the earlier 'K' Class. Another advance was made in the K26's battery storage by the introduction of battery compartments, which were to become standard in the designs of the 1920s.

Both groups had two shafts and two 3-bladed propellers, but the *K26's* propellers were 2 inches shorter at 7 ft 6 in diameter. However, with the additional 12 foot of hull in her length, her designed surface speed of 23.5 knots was 0.5 knots slower than the original design. But during her service years, the reduction in her speed was to be frequently blamed on the repositioning of the stern hydroplanes, as they now sat in the wake of the propellers and increased the hulls draught. The Group 2's 'designed' speed of 24 knots was based on a displacement of 1,980 tons while carrying the normal load of 197 tons of oil fuel. But with the additional 300 tons of emergency fuel oil the displacement was increased to 2,093 tons and the full speed decreased to 23.5 knots. Plus, the boat had to contend with the additional 12-foot increase in length. The *K26* simply weighed more and that slowed her down!

On their completion the boats of Group 2 were to have had a surface range 1,200 miles (1931.21 Km) at full speed and 14,500 miles at 10 knots (23,335 Km). The designed submerged speed was for a maximum of 9 knots at 1,440 bhp. Although that figure could most likely be achieved, the electric motors would have to be run in a critical condition of up to 2,040 bhp for 20 minutes. It was concluded, as it had been with the first group, that the submerged speed and endurance for the completed *K26* was a disappointment.(2) Towards the end of her service career, (in 1930) the operational figures for the *K26* were:

- Surface speed 22.5 knots
- Surface range 930 miles (1,496.68 Km) at 22 knots
- 12,670 miles at 10 knots (20,390.38Km)

- Submerged speed 8 knots.
- Submerged range 8 miles at 8 knots (12.87 Km)
- 30 miles at 4 knots (48.28 Km).
- 45 miles at 1.5 knots (72.42 Km).

These figures refer to the *K26* on a calm sea with a hull bottom that was reasonably clean from marine growth. The state of *K26's* hull beneath her waterline (as with every ship) had a considerable effect on the speed she could make through the water. After only two months out of dock, it is possible for the maximum speed of a ship's hull to be reduced by as much as one knot. Given the short amount of time the *K26* had spent in the water pre-trials, it is possible she achieved the speed of 23.5 knots while her hull was new and unencumbered with marine growth.

	Surface	Dived
Group 1	24 kt	8 kt
Group 2	23.5 kt	9 kt
'J' CLASS	19 kts	9.5 kts

(The Navy's 'E' class could achieve 9.5 knots submerged.)

On the design board the speed and ranges the Group 2 boats could cover, once submerged at a slow speed was predicted to be 4 knots over 50 miles (80.46 Km).

The new group of 'K' boats also had within their design a new and an 'improved' system for the folding of the troublesome funnels as well as the air intakes that fed oil to furnaces and blow tanks. The 'improvements' were to be successful with the funnels and almost cured the unwelcome tradition of water entering down the funnels putting the boiler fires out in bad weather.

Armaments

The Group 2's design torpedo armament saw an increase both in the number of tubes and of their calibre. They were to carry six of the 21-inch (533 mm) torpedo tubes (that had been unavailable in time for the earlier group) in the bow instead of the four 18-inch (457 mm) of the Group 1. The upgrade in the torpedo armament resulted in the hull being 12 feet (3.65 mtrs) longer.

The torpedo room and the torpedo tube space were now separated by the addition of a watertight bulkhead which was to become standard in the navy's succeeding designs. But despite the extra 12 feet of space within the hull it must have still been cramped, as the new calibre tubes were several feet longer in their length. The hatch by which the weapons were brought onboard was re-sighted to be above the officers' quarters aft of the torpedo room. The *K26* carried 14 spare 21-inch torpedoes, of which six were reloads for the eight tubes. These were the Royal Navy's next generation weapon of choice for its submarines and the *K26* had six of the tubes installed within her bow, two more than Group 1. The 3,206 lbs (1,454 kg) weapon was introduced in 1916 and over a range of 8,000 yards (7,300 mtrs) had a speed of 35 knots. At 10,000 yards (9,150 mtrs) that decreased to 29 knots and at 13,500 yards (12,350 mtrs) to 25 knots. Aside from the 21-inch, the design retained the four 18-inch beam tubes of Group 1 amidships with eight of the 18-inch torpedoes carried. But six years after entering service in 1929, the beam tubes were to be removed.

The boats carried three 4 inch/40 (10.2 cm) QF Marks IV deck guns which were all installed on the superstructure. To make the gunnery position drier, the *K26's* forward gun was not to be mounted on the forward deck plating, but instead sat in a raised area before the conning tower. In addition, a streamlined shield was fitted to the guns to help ease its passage through the water once submerged.

CHAPTER TWO. THE COMMISSION

*"K26 Is A Bloody Fine Boat, Her Casings
Painted White, She Works Her Crew All
Through The Day And Half The .....Night"*

Earliest Date: 1987 (Tawney)

HMS K26

1922-1923   5th Flotilla,Gosport
1923-1927   1st Flotilla,Portland.
1927-1931   1st Flotilla, Malta

As the Group 1 boats were slowly decommissioned and sent to the breakers yard, work was finally resumed on the one remaining keel of the second group, the *K26*. The bulk of the Group 2 boats were cancelled on the 26th November 1918 and although construction of the lone *K26* continued, it was at a much-reduced pace.

THE K26, NOTE THE ALTERATION IN THE GUNS POSITIONING. THE FIGURES BY THE FORE FUNNEL GIVE A NICE INDICATION AS TO THE FUNNELS LOW HEIGHT.

She was 'launched' during August 1919 at the Vickers Barrow-in-Furness yard. Once she was afloat, her construction was put on hold. Then in 1920, she was brought down to Chatham's dockyard under tow. But now work was underway once more and the project included a few extensive modifications gained from the 'experiences' of the previous 'K' boats. During *K26's* time on the Malta Station John Colley who served onboard her, published his recollections in the Conway magazine, entitled Queen of the Undersea:

> *"I was lucky enough to serve in one of these steam monsters, K.26, she was a beauty, based on Malta and painted a very light grey.*

Our pet name for K.26 was "The Queen of the Underseas" but other sailors in the flotilla, all diesel-engined boats, called our vessel the "Steam Pig".

Having a large crew we were able to find plenty of volunteers for football, cricket, running and water-polo, often holding our own against teams from battleships. Being such a large vessel, 2,000 tons, we had a Commander in command, an Engineer Lieutenant , two executive Lieutenants, two Subs.

Right for'd there were six torpedo tubes in the charge of a Petty Officer Torpedo Gunner's Mate, immediately abaft them were six spare torpedoes for reloading. Then came a space filled with built-in bunks for the officers, after that, the Wardroom.

This was about as large as the living room in a small cottage, it contained a round dining table, three armchairs and four other chairs. Crammed into odd corners were a sideboard, a pistol-rack, a few cupboards, with an electric fan overhead to stir up the air.

In order to let the Officer's Steward lay the table, three officers would go out into the passage. Out of the after wardroom door you found a little place called the switchboard, in the middle of its deck a round hatch through which you got down on top of the battery, a group of 336 cells weighing half a ton each.

When being charged these cells produced a lot of hydrogen gas, explosive when mixed with air; and it had to be blown overboard by special fans. The valves on these fans were my special care, on diving they had to be shut or else!

Next aft, the control room crammed with pipes, instruments, electric motors, other machinery. In the centre line the brass periscopes hung waiting to be raised by oil pressure. Here also were the steering wheel and the two large wheels for the hydroplanes.

At the after end of the control room and through a sound-proof door was the W/T office. When the door was left open at sea the dit. dit. dah. dit of messages could be heard, but in harbour the P.O. Telegraphist used to sit there in the evenings and play a violin which he bought in Sicily.

The next compartment aft was called the "Beamery," the widest part of the vessel besides having two decks. Down below there were four torpedo tubes, two facing to port and two to starboard; on the deck above two messes, the P.O.s and Chiefs, the E.R.A.s. They were all very crowded, when all bunks were occupied it looked like a film set of an opium den.

Through another watertight door, a narrow passage led past the boiler room on the starboard side. Half-way along this passage was a little escape hatch so that men in the boiler room could crawl out, once when the sea came down the funnels they had to use this quickly.

Out of the after end of this passage you were in the tur-bine room, where an air-lock led into the boiler room in which stood the two oil-fired boilers. The boiler room was very noisy until the submarine dived. Then the stokers on watch saw the fuel supply stop dead, heard the funnels rumble over into their wells. The last of the oil fuel flashed back and flared up on the boiler fronts. They had wet sacks ready to beat out the flames, it always worked.

Above the after end of the turbine room there was a hatch that led into the upper casing. Once there was trouble with the hatch on diving; a petrol can from up above jammed in it. A solid stream of water plunged down the hatch but a burly stoker sprang up the ladder and wrenched the can free. The hatch shut with a clang - the stoker fell with the can into the bilges. He was called "Crash-dive Barton" after that.

Through another door, there was the motor room, the shining switchgear on top and the four huge main motors down below, with a large central dynamo on a shaft turned by an eight-cylinder diesel engine further aft. This was for charging the battery in harbour.

In the motor room between the switchgear lived the seamen, signalmen, telegraphists. Sitting at table we had to keep our elbows tucked in, for all the switch- gear was alive. Charging at sea, the temperature would go up to 120 degrees, only the torpedoman looking after the charge would remain there.

Through yet another watertight door going aft was the stoker's mess. Here you could not stand upright, bunks and lockers lined the central mess table, most people off watch laid in their bunks at meal-times to keep out of the way. It was a "glory-hole" no wind- jammer that every sailed the seas had a fo'c'le packed as tight as this. In this place right in the under- water tail of the submarine the stokers could make as much noise as they liked.

When they were not singing they were playing the gramophone. The favourite record was "Swing low Sweet Chariot," sometimes at diving stations when the submarine was very quiet a stoker would stuff a singlet down the gramophone to muffle it, make it grind out "Swing Low". Abaft the stoker's mess there was only a little provision store and the steering gear.

All the way through the boat - by the way, submarines are always "boats" to those in them, human beings were packed into the spaces between the machinery.

Submarine Dived.

In one part was a coal-fired galley. When submerged the fireplace, oven, coal-bunker, hot-water tank, all got washed through. There was a rumour, I never believed it; that once some fish were trapped in the galley and had only to be cooked and eaten.

However, it was in this galley that the sailor trusted to be butcher was allowed to cut up the meat. He had a sharp cleaver, but a poor aim. He missed a leg of beef and hit the oil-pressure pipes going to the rams of the telescopic masts. Telemotor oil poured all over the poor butcher and five day's meat, the oil caught fire.

The fire was soon out - we had corned beef, a change of butcher soon after.

On top of this casing were three four-inch guns for use in surface action; when the submarine dived the breeches were left open and salt-water just ran through them. On surfacing the water drained out and they could [be] loaded and fired immediately.

In a special well in the casing was a small wooden skiff, got out by means of a stump derrick. Down below in the pressure hull we had an outboard motor for this skiff. When the boat dived, six large plugs were left out of the skiff, so that the sea ran in and out of her easily.

Whilst in Venice an Italian thief stole the skiff from where she lay at the boom at night. The next day it was found abandoned, it must have been quite a shock for the thief to find those six large plugs in the bottom of the boat, making it the most conspicuous boat in Italy.

In this wonderful submarine we visited France, Italy, Jugo-Slavia, Greece, Crete where people were all very much interested in our funnels. The Chief E.R.A. had a standing joke with these funnels. In harbour he would run them down into their wells after dark.

Next day there would be much discussion on the jetties. The Chief would stand on the upper casing and smile at the crowd.

Someone with a knowledge of English would ask, "Does not your vessel have two funnels?" Chief would scratch his head. 'Funnels?", he would repeat innocently. "Chimneys," the foreigner would say. Then old Chief would laugh out loud, "Chimneys, funnels, why this is a blinking submarine."

The same night he would run the foremost funnel up and leave the other one down. This caused more argu-

ment ashore next day.

She was a wonderful craft, fast and safe; when worn-out she was broken up in Malta. Perhaps some of her metal has been melted down and is living again in plating for other ships and submarines, I hope so.

Now that the American atomic-steam submarine is nearing completion I wonder - yes - I wonder if they'd like an old torpedoman with several years' experience of steam submarines?"

On the 3rd November 1922 while under construction, the *K26,* was to claim the life of a member of her construction crew, when an explosion shook the hull. The detonation was established to be a result of valve tests being conducted with the turbines and the workmen were enveloped in scolding steam. The turbine room was suddenly filled with smoke and the boats interior plunged into darkness. Witnesses said afterwards that the steam came from the boilers and had rapidly reached 200 lbs of pressure. It rebounded against the waste pipe and was forced through the furnace and out into the boiler room. Pipe work was being adapted and the valve was working ok, but the oil sprayers were burning at the time. Charles Bailey died a few hours after an explosion and Archibald Stannard suffered severe burns and shock.

The Admiralty saw the *K26* as the lead ship of a new improved type of submarine and having between 1922 and 1923 been based with the 5th Flotilla, in Gosport, she was

Commissioned at Chatham on 28th June 1923 with great expectations amongst the Royal Navy's Sea Lords. She would surely prove the steam powered submersible a solid and well-conceived concept?

The new boat started her first commission under the command Commander G.P. Thomson O.B.E (naval intelligence) with the 1st Submarine Flotilla of the Atlantic Fleet. She was to remain within the flotilla for four years until 1927. The 1st Flotilla was then transferred to Portland and her final deployment would be between 1927 and 1931 with the 1st Flotilla in Malta.

In 1925 the Admiralty decided to despatch the *K26* under the command of Thomson O.B.E further around the globe than any 'K' boat prior. She was to sail from Portsmouth under the full glare of publicity to Malta, she sailed out into the Solent on the 2nd January commencing what was to be the longest Royal Navy Submarine voyage since the armistice in 1918.

Having steamed through the Bay of Biscay, the *K26* made a port call to Gibraltar before heading eastward into the Mediterranean and what the crew thought was their final goal, Malta. But on her arrival at the island, her voyage was extended to Singapore. The goal was to test the feasibility of operating steam submarines in the tropics and to test some unspecified equipment. Before she lit her boilers or turned a propeller the *K26* underwent a series of modifications to make her habitable in the tropics. It is worth recalling here the incredible heat generated within the boat from her boilers and wondering how the crew really coped as the equator drew ever closer.

Her passage to Singapore was to take her through the Red Sea and via the ports of Aden, Trincomalee in Colombo and then onto Singapore.

Her only incident of note that occurred was on the outward voyage while she was transiting the Red Sea, when she encountered the British pilgrim ship *Frangestan,* out bound from Bombay to Genoa and Barcelona. On board the *Frangestan* had 1,200 pilgrims bound for Jeddah and a Cotton cargo valued at over £250,000, (2017=£10,264,725).

The *K26* having received the distress call, found the *Frangestan* burning furiously 200 miles south of Port Sudan for over two thirds of her length. The cargo had started smouldering early in the day. The *Frangestan* masts had toppled into the blaze before the sun was up and by the time the *K26* chanced on the scene she was well alight. The submarines crew looked out at a hull that was becoming a charred shell at that point.

THE LAST OF THE FRANGESTAN BOATS ALONGSIDE THE K26. THE ILLUSTRATED LONDON NEWS 1924.

THE FRANGESTAN SINKS HAVING BEEN SUNK BY THE K26's GUNS. THE ILLUSTRATED LONDON NEWS 1924.

The passengers and Pilgrims had been transferred to the British merchant ship *Clan MacIver*, having responded to the *Frangestan's* W/T plea for assistance. The captain attempted to reach port refusing to abandon his burning wreck until he had no choice. The *K26* stood by the scene until the next day when Thomson received orders to sink her as she had become a danger to navigation. The gun crews took the opportunity for some excellent target practice and after 50 shells the *Frengestan* sank into 237 fathoms. The water around the ships was clear and the crews had the added excitement of several sharks in the neighbourhood.

As the submarine crossed the Indian ocean, she experienced a South East monsoon and a tropical thunderstorm during her time in Singapore.

She departed Singapore, after a two month stay, on the 10th June, arriving after a trouble-free voyage in Portsmouth between 17:30 and 18:00 on the 12th August. She was moored alongside the cruiser Conquest in the dockyard's tidal basin. The voyage had seen a 22,000 'Jinx' free cruise with no losses amongst the crew. The *K26* had returned home with the same crew she had departed with. The crew were granted Special leave and the boat went into dock for a refit.

On the 28th October 1925 the Admiralty published the news that all the remaining K" class submarines, except the *K26* were to be scrapped. The First submarine Flotilla was to be reconstituted with *K26* and four 'L' class submarines.

David Beatty who was to serve for an unprecedented 8-year term as the First Sea Lord envisaged the future capital ship as the submersible battlecruiser. The result of this fantasy was a second 'M' class submarine was authorised and to be commissioned during his tenure. On the 17th March 1926 while manoeuvring within Gibraltar's Admiralty harbour, the *K26* rammed the tug *Rambler.* Both were to suffer slight damaged.

THE TUG BOAT RAMBLER (1909-1953)

By early 1929, the First Submarine Flotilla had been deployed, with the last of the 'K' boats, the *K26*, to the Mediterranean. On the 13th December 1930 she was finally reduced to Material Reserve at Malta. Then after nine years of service, in 1931 the *K26* was decommissioned. Her demise was in part due to the London Naval Treaty, as her displacement now exceeded the limits set for submarine displacements.

> *"No submarine the standard displacement of which exceeds 2,000 tons (2,032 metric tons) or with a gun above 5.1-inch (130 mm.) calibre shall be acquired by or constructed by or for any of the High Contracting Parties".*

A possibly much relieved Admiralty, having been gifted a free 'get-out-of-jail' card by Washington could finally decommission the last 'K' boat with no loss of face. She was sold to be sold to Mamo Brothers in Malta, being broken up in March 1931. The K26 was to be the last steam-powered submarine built. Until 1954 when the first nuclear powered submarine, *USS Nautilus*.

CHAPTER THREE. K BOATS - A SUBMARINER REMEMBERS

I must confess that my imagination refuses to see any sort of submarine doing anything but suffocating its crew and floundering at sea.

H. G. Wells

From the Naval Review 1943 and posted on the World Naval Ships Forum by Bob Hoole Provided by Peter Schofield.

"*I yield to no man in my admiration of engineers," observed Eeyore Smith, for, without them there would be none of the amenities of life (and that reminds me to ask you to be more liberal with your steam on the baths, Chief) but I think that their attitude towards the internal combustion engine has always been tinged with conservatism." To the average 'plumber' the word engine is synonymous with steam. I remember as a midshipman once talking to a stoker who was feeling particularly proud of a set of picket-boat engines. 'Ah,' he said, 'if only George Washington could see this little lot!' and when I queried his remark he told me 'that that was the bloke wot invented steam.' So you see that even the humbler members of the profession associate the stuff with truth and possibly progress as well. "Speaking as one who has suffered to the full from the wiles and weaknesses of the diesel engine, I do feel that if it had not been looked on as the poor relation of all propelling machinery for a great many years we in submarines would not have passed through that strangely romantic period of the steam submarine." Just as it used to be said that no submariner could truly claim to be fully fledged until he experienced the worst that Mr. Shanks could do to him, so it can be asserted that those who have not served in K-boats missed an experience, unique (let us trust) in the annals of submarine history. It is not for me to cast aspersions on the wisdom of Those who decided to fit submarines with chimneys ; no doubt there were excellent reasons ; perhaps it was a little matter of rivalry with our gallant Allies, the French, who ran to a tasty line in kettle-fitted submersibles (longez! Plongez! Vite! pow la gloire de France) ; as has been suggested, perhaps it was the result of confusion in the drawing office whereby a destroyer was grafted on to a submarine - after all, there were such things a 'P' boats. It is sufficient to quote the Chinese proverb that A State of War is Conducive to Imaginative Effort. It may, however, be of interest to the present generation if I touch on some aspects of life in the K-boats in the years succeeding the Armistice; and here is a brief description of those weird vessels. Over three hundred feet in length,* herring-gutted so that their period of roll was the fastest ever, they took five minutes to submerge if it was a good day and fifteen if the Engineer Officer had been careless about his feed water. Once under water with no adverse reports coming from the boiler-room as to the efficacy of the funnel and intake covers, the trimming of such unwieldy craft was fraught with considerable interest. Visitors to the Firth of Forth (if there were such people who voluntarily went there) in the early twenties, would as a daily occurrence have observed parts of K-boat projecting above water. Sometimes it would be the stem with two propellers idly whizzing and sometimes a large sinister-looking bow could be seen projecting above the surface of the water like a basking whale. There were, of course, other occasions when one was thankful for the proximity of the sea bed; but it is better not to dwell on that point. "The essential difference between the K-boat Flotilla and the ordinary submarine flotilla was that the former were self contained that is to say that on return to harbour the crew continued to live on board and not to seek relaxation and comfort in some such handsomely furnished depot as has been described on another occasion; and, of course the officers did likewise. There was little in this to complain of from the point of view of the crew for they were spared many irksome routine matters and petty chores but to the officers, who were expected to appear in a variety of costumes ranging from football togs to mess dress, there were certain disadvantages. There was, too, the question of one's proximity to the captain. The K.R. and A.I. in their wisdom have ordained that for the sake of discipline and morale the Captain should as far as possible keep himself apart from his officers. In K-boats this was interpreted by the erection *of a matchboard partition which screened off a substantial portion of the wardroom and behind which the Captain was said to be in his cabin. The fact that he could hear everything just as well from behind his cribbed confines as if he were sitting in the mess was at times a trifle hedging for those junior officers who like to express themselves freely in their hours of ease. There was another member of the wardroom mess who was even more unpopular it was a large air-compressor. When it was running speech, though possible, was a waste of time and it also had the unpleasant habit of spattering the surroundings with fine drops of the very best mineral oil. "I need hardly say that this air-compressor was only used when its opposite number in the after-compartment fell sick, and when this was the case the Engineer Officer felt that he was persona non grata with his captain and messmates. The question of the stowage of our clothing was as nearly solved, in my case as it was ever likely to be by a truly miraculous drawer which, like an inverted widow's-cruse, never entirely filled. It was the simultaneous discovery of an assortment of garments in the bottle-well together with the fact that the drawer was without a back to it that did much to cause the eternal sourness of my present outlook. "Another interesting fitment was a pipe to the upper deck which was known as the six-inch hand-up. Its origin was traced to the early design of the K-boats, when an additional gun was mounted on the upper deck at a position which gave it 30 inches of free-board (the fact that the upper deck was only tenable when the sea was as calm as the Serpentine had escaped the notice of the designer but 'What the Hell Brother,' as our American Allies have been heard to remark). The existence of this hole in the roof was of great benefit, for a*

small intake fan was fitted to it and gave good supplies of fresh air to the captain's cabin. On one occasion it gave other service that was when a cheerful-
minded officer poured a sack of potatoes down the
ventilating cowl with the result that the captain's
bunk was filled with 'finely-divided particles of po-
tato which we call chips.' You will have observed,
my dear Chief, that the cramped physical conditions
in the Flotilla did not affect the high spirits of the
officers. They used to meet on board the good ship
Remarkable from time to time. This vessel was not
considered even officially to be worthy of the name
depot ship, but acted as a useful tavern and bathroom. It was aboard the Remarkable that the well-
known confraternity known as the Brighter K-boat
Society was founded and became an enormous success. Like all such societies, the objects were purely
convivial, and it added much to the merriment of all
concerned. In particular the steady flow of lam-
poons which found their way on to the screen on
cinema nights in the Remarkable was a most encouraging sign of the literary versatility of submarine officers. There are still many old-timers who
cherish the little badge which was worn on official
occasions, whilst to this day certain songs which
originated from the B.K.B.S. can be heard on Guest
Nights. For example:-

'Early in the morning the Inconstant hoists a signal

See the little K-boats all in a row

Man in the control-room pulls a lot of levers

Swoosh-Swish-Down we go.'

Neither my voice nor my memory, you will observe, have lost their timbre after all these years. But enough of such frivolities we learnt how easy station-keeping can become when you are supplied with a revolution telegraph and a couple of boilers full of steam; we learnt that after ringing down 'Dive' and pressing the hooter it was a good thing to walk along the casing and watch the clips secured on the funnel doors; we learnt that unwelcome visitors could be firmly dealt with by shutting down for diving and opening main vents as they stepped aboard and we learnt that the end of the world does not come when the boiler-room fills up by reason of heavy seas breaking over the funnel tops. "We learnt, too, to recognize by a preliminary flickering of the depth gauge needles the symptom that warned us that we were twenty tons bodily heavy, that it was a mistake to try and force a K-boat under by putting an angle on her bows and thus elevating the whizzers above the surface of the ocean, that ammunition hand-ups should be shut before diving and that cable locker doors which give access to the sea are best screwed on at night. "Those and many other useful lessons we learnt; but, above all, we found that even under the most uncomfortable and peculiar circumstances it is always possible to enjoy life. I will wager you a month's wine bill, Chief, that there is not one K-boat chap who does not look back on that curious era with a nostalgia that grows more poignant as the distance lends its increasing enchantment. Nevertheless, if any damned designer starts working again on steam-propelled submarines I for one am going to make an application for the Chiltern Hundreds."

G. H. J

PART FIVE. THE 'M' CLASS & GERMANY'S STEAM U-BOATS.

THE M2 RECOVERING HER PARNEL PETRO SEA PLANE

CHAPTER ONE. A BRIEF NOTE ON K18-21. (THE 'M' CLASS).

On the 5th August 1915 Admiral Fisher had proposed a 'Dreadnought-submarine' to be mounted with a single 12" gun, (whilst still retaining four of the traditional torpedo tubes), should be built. The Admiral believed that the vessel would be able to carry far more of the 12-inch 850 lb shells (50 in total) than the 2,100 lbs to 2,800 lb torpedoes. In addition, the Royal Navy had suffered a series of torpedo failures through the war with a poor track record for not running either smoothly or well. Fisher, the former First Sea Lord even made the offer to return for six months to serve in the lesser post of the Third Sea Lord to run the 'dreadnought submarine' project, but the First Lord of the Admiralty, Arthur Balfour, was not a fan of the former First Sea Lord and did not take up the offer. An undeterred Fisher next approached Sydney-Hall to present the idea to the Admiralties Submarine Development Committee. Fisher envisaged a (diesel powered) craft that would rise to the surface, her gun preloaded, aim the boat at the target, correct the barrel's elevation and having then fired one shell, would crash dive, all in the space of 45 seconds. The fact that the gun could only be loaded while surfaced was a problem Fisher resolved, by simply ignoring the flaw. In 1918 Admiral Fisher, by then retired, took his 'dreadnought submarine' project one stage further with a design for a submersible battlecruiser of 30,000 tons, with 18-inch or 20-inch guns and capable of 30 knots. But by this stage in time the war was won, and the 20-inch monster never progressed beyond Fishers futile imagination.

HMS M1

The 12-inch gunned Dreadnought-submarine was to be based on a keel of a 'K' class hull and in February 1916 the Admiralty ordered one prototype, using the *K18*, from which she would become the (non-steam powered) *HMS M1*. A few months later the Admirals ordered that the *K19* was to follow her sister and she too was earmarked for conversion and she would in turn become the *M2*. The Admiralty warming even more to the concept added the *K20* and *K21* to the growing list of suitable candidates. But Fisher now decided to start worrying that the Teutonic masters of submarine design, the Germans, might learn of his new dreadnought concept and reply with their own version, which would not be good for the British battle fleet. Fisher could easily envisage German submersible dreadnoughts hounding the Grand Fleet, popping up from the depths, firing a 12-inch shell at close range, then returning beneath the waves. As a result, all work on the *M1* project was stopped and a colossal tarpaulin was dragged over the incomplete hull to hide it from any prying eyes. In addition, the plans were hidden away, and the project went dark for a year. Then in the spring of 1918 the plans were brought out of a dark cupboard, dusted down, the tarpaulin lifted off and work was resumed once more. Some of those involved simply tutted, rolled their eyes and muttered "Fisher" before returning to a truly 'Jules Verne' concept.

The lone 12-inch gun had a weight of 60 tons which to many seemed insanity and they speculated that when she fired the entire hull would travel backwards. They also feared, given such a weight sat well above the waterline, she would capsize in any rough seas. But on her trials the *M1* was to confound her critics and made a respectable 15 knots surfaced and 10 knots whilst dived. Unlike her steam powered sisters, with no holes and vents to seal, she dived in 30 seconds. In addition, it was found that even after a week submerged with a shell stored in the breech, the gun was capable of being fired once the boat surfaced. The gun was relatively trouble-free, although on one occasion *M1's* hydraulically operated tampion which was designed to seal the barrel, allowed water to leak in ahead of the shell. When the gun was finally fired, the shell ripped off the muzzle, which flew away with the wire winding of the barrel trailing behind, like a giant fly-cast. Given her shape of her profile (caused by the silhouette of her big gun and its housing), her crew named the *M1* the "Mutton ship", resembling as she did a leg of the meat. The process of surfacing, firing and then diving became known amongst the crew as "dip-chick". By June 1918 she was ready for her commissioning and the dreadnought-submarine (or submarine monitor) was ordered to the Mediterranean where she was never to be in any real danger of coming face to face with the Germanic enemy.

On conception the gun had been designed to be used in bombardment against shore targets, but their use of the single barrel was changed even before they were laid down. Their new method was to engage any merchant ships while at periscope depth with the gun. It would in addition be able to surface to use the gun, instead of wasting torpedoes. Such weapons were considered by some at the time to be ineffective when used on moving warships more than 1000 yards away. The gun, when fired at a short range, would follow a flat trajectory which greatly simplified the aiming process and they expected most targets not to survive the shells impact.

The guns used were taken from the de-commissioned Formidable-Class pre-dreadnought which were no longer of use by the end of 1919. The barrels elevation could reach a maximum of 20 degrees and it could depress by 5 degrees and in addition train up to 15 degrees off the bow in port and starboard. The weapon was usually fired when the submarine was at periscope depth and this required the use of a simple bead sight at a range of approximately 1000 yards. A major disadvantage of the weapon was the fact the sub had to surface each time the gun required reloading, and this took 3 minutes with each reload.

In addition, the *M1* and *M2* submarines also had four 18-

inch torpedo tubes and the *M3* and *M4* had the newer 21 inches tubes, which resulted in the tubes being longer.

THE M2 LAUNCHING HER PARNEL PETRO SEA PLANE

The big gun submarines armament was to be impacted by the Washington Naval Conference in 1922 and as a result the *M2* and *M3* had their guns removed, undergoing drastic modifications. The *M2* was then adapted to carry a small seaplane and the *M3* was converted into a minelayer.

The *M1* was the only one of the 3 to be ready for service during World War 1, but hidden away in the Mediterranean, she saw no action (1). During her trials her captain was one of the submarine services best, Commanders Max Horton. Tragically on the 12th November 1924 she was to be lost, with all her crew members, while exercising in the English Channel. She collided with the Swedish collier, SS Vidar which struck the M1 whilst she was submerged. The former 'K' boat sank in 70 meters of water, the force of the impact ripping the gun from her hull and allowing water to flood into the boat.

The wreck of the *M1* was rediscovered by Innes McCartney and his diving team in 1999 at a depth of 239 feet 6 inches (73 mtrs). An examination of the wreck by the divers showed that the crew to have attempted to escape by flooding the interior of the boat and opening the escape hatch, but no bodies were ever to be found.

The *M2* conversion from a big-gun submarine into a seaplane carrier was in 1925. The modification saw the gun housing replaced with a hangar but sadly, like her sister, the *M2* was lost in service. On 26th January 1932 off the coast of Chesil Beach it appears that whilst the submarine was in the process of surfacing to launch her aircraft, the hanger door was opened before full buoyance had been achieved. Water flooded into the hanger and was able to pour into the submarine via the hanger access hatch which was also open. The submarine buoyancy was destroyed and the *M2* sank with the loss of all sixty crew members.

The wreck of the *M2* was located on 3rd February, 6 days after her accident. The salvager of Germany's scuttled fleet in Scapa Flow, Ernest Cox was called in to lead a salvage team working on the *M2*. The salvage task was to last almost a year and took 1,500 dives. Finally, on 8th December 1932, the M2 was raised to just 20 feet below the surface, but a gale sent her back to the seabed. Any thoughts of salvaging her were abandoned. The wreck of the *M2* sits today in waters of 104 feet 11 inches (32 mtrs) depth and at low tide her conning tower sits only 65 feet (20 mtrs) below the surface.

The *M3* was in turn converted into a minelayer in 1927 and was able to carry a cargo of 100 mines. The mines were transported along a conveyor system on her deck and then taken out through a door at her stern. A decision to scrap the *M3* was taken in 1933, but this was to happen sooner as unfavourable reports of her service were beginning to emerge. The *M3*, the final 'K' boat keel was scrapped in April 1932. Although the M3 was scrapped she had demonstrated that the minelaying system was a success. A similar system, capable of handling 50 mines, was fitted to the six smaller submarines of the 'Porpoise' class which saw service during WW2. The *M4* was never completed......

K18 (M1) Ordered 2/16 Laid down 7/16 Launched 9/7/17. completed 17-18/87/18 K20 (M2) Ordered 8/16 Laid down 12/16. Commissioned & renamed 16/03/20 . "handed over" 09/07/20. (SOURCE KEW FILES)

CHAPTER TWO. THE GERMAN STEAM SUBMARINE

F isher had been concerned that the Imperial German Navy would learn of the British Navy's 'K' and 'M' classes and decide to pursue the two concepts with their own versions. Whilst it is unclear if the Germans learnt of the British plans or if it was a matter of 'great minds thinking alike', the Imperial Navy did develop a steam powered big (but still smaller) gunned U-boat. One of the proposed class made it as far as the builder's yard. She was the 'UD 1'.

Following a series of boiler tests, the 'UD 1' was ordered from the Kiel Navy yards in February 1918, but hers was to be the only keel ordered and it was never to be laid down. By the time of the Armistice in November 1918 all work on the project had ceased. Unfortunately, the records concerning the class were to be lost in the post war chaos of 1946, so little more is known. But the little we know was the design was known as "Tauchschiff Projekt 50" and was to have originally been built with three 150 mm (5.9-inch) guns and two 88 mm (3.4-inch) AA guns. But the U-Boat Inspectorate demanded that four of the 150 mm weapons be worked into the design. *'UD1'* seems to have been armoured and un-like the 'K' class the solitary funnel was fixed in place. It was envisaged that the U-boat would have carried 10 torpedo tubes, in an era when 6 was considered possibly excessive for a submarine. Four tubes were mounted in the bow and two in stern tubes, with none mounted in the broadside. But *'UD1'* was only ever to be a paper submarine and was never to progress beyond that.

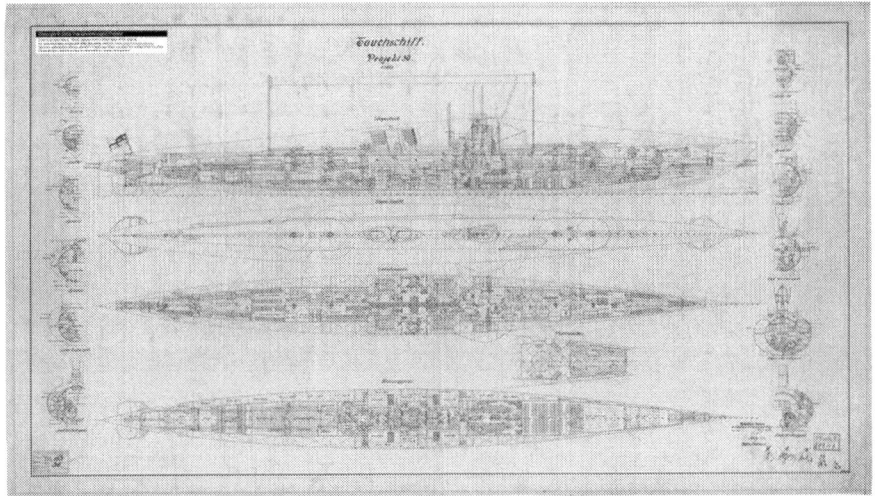

TO CONCLUDE.

Any conclusion or summary of the 'K' class has always to be unfortunately an incomplete task based on the limited amount of source material available currently. The Admiralty followed standard practice for all their ships and sealed the relevant files, but in this case, for the unusual length of seventy years. By the time some (and even today it remains as only some), of the files were opened, those persons in danger of red faces and awkward questions had died. Faces had been saved!

I have spent many hours reading files that relate to the 'K' class which are held in the National Archives. I read over 2000 pages, some that still bear the stains of being on board ship and (to probably my imagination), the smell of their past. The ship's logs (as logs so often can be), were limited in the information they contained. But the court of inquiry files were a treasure trove of first-hand information. A few books on the class had been written before the files were finally cracked opened. I have been more fortunate than my predecessors with a greater amount of source material available to me and I have been able to correct a few erroneous tales. For example, Benning and his map digesting mice!

The 'K' boats were (in my opinion) not a true submarine. A submersible is a vessel designed to be underwater with surface capabilities. The 'K' boats were (once again in my opinion) surface craft with the capacity to dive. They had the much often quoted turning circle of a battlecruiser, the size of a small cruiser, the speed of a dreadnought, but they dived like no submarine. Their surface propulsion apparatus (the funnels) had to be sealed and the copious holes the propulsion required sealed watertight. They dived with no apparent sign of speed or indecent haste. Almost a slow grace over a frantic panic...

They were conceived to operate between the Grand Fleets leading battle squadrons and the fleets outer screen. They were (in theory) part of the surface fleet. They were not to be found prowling the seas sinking lone warships or merchant craft. When they put to sea it was to serve and to support the Grand Fleet in some way. There were exceptions, for example operation 'B.B'. But the 'K' boats were not to be a success in that role. They were a creation of the surface admirals and not asked for or possibly even dreamt of by the submarine fleet. Before we move on, their slow diving times were never a real problem. These were the times before the air borne threat could at any moment drop from the sky and with their place within the Grand Fleet, they would always have ample warning that a dive was required.

The 'K' boats technology was if anything both bold and creative. Maybe it was foolish, dangerous and not thought through, but it was needed to meet the Admiralties goal for sufficient speed to maintain a position before the fleet. Steam was the only way to go, it was tried and tested, but only on surface bound vessels. The French had attempted to develop the propulsion method prior, but that was not to work with the success as they had envisaged. The evidence of unsuitability was visible for the Admiralty to see, but maybe it was a case of the belief that Nelson's Royal Navy could solve what the French Navy could not?

Putting a steam engine in a submersible craft was sadly never going to work given the technology of the time? The process needed to take air in, burn oil (in the process generating stifling heat and expelling smoke), necessitated holes, lots of them. But the goal of a submarines hull is to have as fewer holes as possible. Holes let water in! But the 'K' boats needed copious amounts of the holes and each additional one was an extra chance for disaster to strike the boat. It was a problem the 'can-do' attitude of the 'Victorian-Edwardian' engineer was always going to struggle with.

As we have made our way through the catalogue of 'disasters' an unusually high percentage were on boats that were both newly commissioned and with new (inexperience) crews. The $K5s$ final commission was a few years post her completion, but she had during that last flawed refit taken on, (officers aside), an all-new crew.

With the demands of a wartime expansion of the submarine service, new crews unfortunately equal inexperience and a high risk of errors. They also need ample time (and more) to fully master the skills of diving a 'K' boat with any degree of automated confidence.

Many 'K' captains were appointed for their experience of commanding of submarines, but the 'K' boat was never anything like the vessels the officers were used to. They were of a new level of complexity and little of their past experiences prepared then for service on a giant steam powered fleet submarine.

Next is their poor build quality as indicated by the number

of 'K' boats that had issues with their rivet quality. They were built as an emergency Wartime construction and the haste led to problems with rivets over the next few years. The *K26* was built at a slower peacetime process and seems to have escaped the issues? The K26 was also fortunate to have the experiences of group 1 to learn from and to have her design amended where needed.

From their keel laying and commissioning the 'K' boats were a work in process, adapting and being modified as problems and their potential solutions became apparent. The bows underwent a major redesign. The boiler room was unbearable to work in and fans were installed. The funnels were modified...

But at some stage between the *K13's* sinking in Gareloch and the *K15's* loss at Portsmouth the Admiralty wrote the group 1 boats off in their minds. Of the two boats *K15* was the least damaged by her experience, but it was the earlier K13 that was raised and refitted at great expense. At that time in Gareloch the Admirals still had hopes for the new bold, exciting steam propelled submarines. But by the time K15 was lost, those hopes and dreams had withered to reality and nightmares.

Finding crews in a volunteer service was to become problematic as the class suffered more and more 'incidents '. In the end the boats went into early reserve and decommissioning.

The Group 2 was in theory the answer to the earlier boats problems and were designed, adapted and built on the group 1 experiences. The lone Group 2 boat, K26 had an (apparently) trouble free time in commission. But I cannot help feeling by the time K26 hoisted her white ensign even the London bound admirals had decided the concept had run its course and failed.

So, to conclude:

Was the 'K' boat class a success? NO.

Was the 'K' boat class a good concept for the early twentieth century? NO.

But 100 years on the seed the 'K' boat planted (the fleet submarine), has germinated and bloomed. No modern naval fleet is complete without a submarine in support of it. The descendants of the 'K' class still prowl the seas under nuclear-steam power. The concept was a sound idea, it is just that the technology was not up to it in 1917.

On a personal note, do I believe the class was 'jinxed' or 'cursed'? NO. It was simply inexperienced crews trying to cope with a complex, new, and untried propulsion system. The use of the term 'Jinx' in the book is simply a handy coat peg on which to hang the series of disasters that permeated through the classes short lived careers. Jinxes do not exist, do they?

.

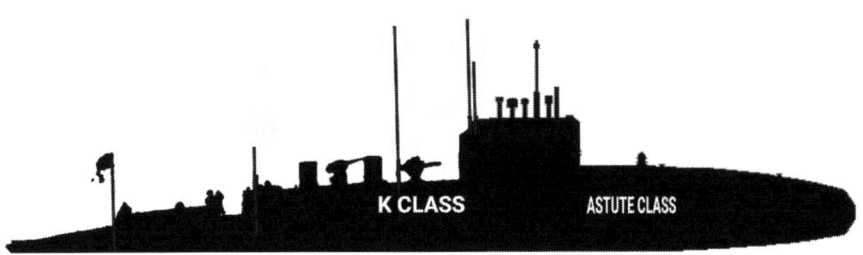

THE APPENDICES

APPENDIX A: LIEUTENANT-COMMANDER GODFREY HERBERT'S LETTER RECOUNTING THE K13'S SINKING IN THE WATERS OF GARELOCH.

Fairfield Yard
Govan

3rd February 1917

Sir,

In accordance with your orders I beg to submit the following, viz., Account of the accident to H.M. Submarine K13.

On Monday, the 29th January, I proceeded to the Tail of the Bank, after carrying out various trials on the surface proceeded up the Gare-Loch for Diving Trials. About noon I dived the boat to 80 feet for about 15 to 20 minutes to test the water-tightness of the hull; the After Beam tube in particular which was quite dry. On rising to the surface, Engineer Lieut. Lane reported that there was a small (leak?) in the Boiler Room but owing to the heat there he was unable to find out exactly the cause. Accordingly he asked me to dive again after he had ventilated the Boiler Room. This was done for half-an-hour during which time all hands went to dinner. About 3 p.m. I ordered Diving Stations, after remaining on the superstructure abaft, the Bridge Shelter until the funnel doors were clipped down, proceeded to the Conning Tower where I received the report from Lieut. Singer (1st Lieut.) that the Engine Room was shut off. I ordered flood all externals and headed the boat up the Gare-loch, as soon as she was steady ordered Dive to 20 feet. I watched the bows through the periscope, simultaneously with their going under water I received a message from the Engine Room from Eng. Lieut. Lane to come to the surface as the Boiler Room was flooding. I gave the order "Surface blow 2 & 3". There was by this time a very considerable rush of air from aft which indicated that there must be a large inrush of water so I ordered close W/T doors. The depth gauge showed 35 feet with a 40 inclination by the bow. I stopped both motors and proceeded to blow every tank possible but with no effect. Great difficulty was experienced in shutting off the Voice pipes through which large quantities of water were coming, the Main fuses blew in quick succession which indicated that the motor room was flooded.

The boat was quite tight everywhere except the Beam Tube Room made about 1 foot an hour which was easily kept down with Forward Pump. I consulted Mr. Hillhouse, Naval Architect, he gave me no hope of raising of the bow of the boat would bring us up even though every tank forward was empty. Cdr Goodhart and I were of the opinion that there was nothing to be done until the diver found us, then although getting air and food down nothing short of blowing off the after part of the boat would bring us up.

During the night we heard sounds as if someone was trying to locate the ship, with a grapnel, at about 6 or 7 a.m. we reported to the divers tapping, but could (make?) no sense with the Morse Code. During the forenoon I asked Commander Goodhart if he would try and get out at low water, 12.30 p.m. with the necessary instructions to those on top for giving us air and food.

Accordingly, after thinking things out, Commander Goodhart decided to try for it and I agreed that I should try and close the door after him. I arranged a code of signals to Lt. Singer in order that he could drain down the Conning Tower after Commander Goodhart had gone clear.

Commander Goodhart and I worked all forenoon taking away the projector compass to give headroom and also in connecting an H.P. valve to the whistle pipe to act as a blow. When everything was ready I charged the Conning Tower with air, to make sure the bottom door and glands through which electric cables passed were tight. After rectifying this, which took roughly an hour, we were ready.

A small tin cylinder about 8 x 2 ½ was then filled

with instructions to the people on the surface and Commander Goodhart putting this in his belt proceeded into the Conning Tower with me. His last words were Well if I dont get up the cylinder will. He opened the flooding valve (fuel vent disconnected) and when the water rose to our waists I turned on the H.P. Air. Commander Goodhart knocked off the clips of the Conning Tower. The Conning Tower lid began to let water in and was soon wide open. Commander Goodhart stood up in the dome, took a deep breath, then made his escape. We were both exceedingly out of breath at the time. Almost immediately, I put my hands up to feel for the lid but without knowing found myself carried through the opening into the shelter, the roof of which must have struck my head from the bruises and a cut I subsequently discovered.

All the time H.P. air was escaping fast from the Conning Tower and I attribute my escape entirely to this, for, without doing anything I found myself shooting through the square hatch in the top of the wheelhouse. I breathed hard all the way to the surface and fortunately, arrived between to craft, one of which hauled me aboard.

What followed is well known to you. Unless ordered to do so I do not propose to give an account of it here.

The ultimate escape of all those who were in the forward compartment is entirely due to the promptness with which the various craft assembled to the spot, I take this opportunity on behalf of my boats crew and myself to thank you and those under your orders for their timely assistance.

I have the honour to be,

Sir,

Your obedient Servant

Signed Godfrey Herbert Lieut. Commander

APPENDIX B: " ALIVE
TO TELL THE TALE"

Below is an excerpt from a Sydney Morning Herald article by Charles Freestone recounting his remarkable escape from death.

57 Hours in a Sunken Submarine.

REMARKABLE ESCAPE FROM DEATH!

By C. A. Freestone.

The K Boat.

.... I had been promoted to the dizzy height of a leading telegraphist and had the distinction of being the first leading telegraphist to be in charge of the wireless installation of a "K" class submarine K13 – which was being built, together with K14, by the Fairfield Shipbuilding and Engineering Co., of Govan, Scotland, and was officially known as H.M.S. No. 522.

The K boats were the very latest in under water construction, being over 300 feet long with a displacement of over 1,800 tons.

January 27, 1917, was the appointed day for K13 to undergo her final acceptance trials which, if successful, meant that she would be accepted by the Admiralty, and handed over to the captain by the contractors who built the boat. These trials were being carried out in the Gareloch, off the west coast of Scotland. Besides the crew who were to commission the boat, numerous Admiralty officials and representatives of the contractors were on board K13 for these important trials.

After successfully diving in the forenoon to a depth of approximately 100 feet, K13 was brought to the surface, and a small boat, the Comet, came alongside to enable everyone go to aboard her for lunch. Immediately after lunch K13 dived again. It proved to be one of the most eventful dives in submarine history, as never before or since have men submerged for 57 hours in one dive in a submarine and lived to "tell the tale." By a tragic oversight the boiler-room ventilators had been left open, and in a moment hundreds of tons of water flooded the after part of the boat, sweeping the entire engine-room staff into eternity. To prevent the complete flooding of the boat, bulkhead doors were immediately closed, and the remainder of the crew and the civilian authorities not in the engine-room found themselves trapped on the bottom of the sea in a half-flooded submarine, with half their mates killed.

Desperate Position.

Then began the longest 57 hours of my life. I do not believe that anyone expected to see Glasgow again, but there was not the slightest of panic, and a spirit of determination prevailed that every effort tried, however feeble, was better than no effort at all. Hour after hour of patient endeavour failed, but still the fight against overwhelming odds continued. Alter the first day we could hear surface craft sweeping for us above, and soon divers were sent and located our whereabouts. What a queer experience to be inside a sunken submarine and to hear divers walking about on the outside of the boat! One wondered what they were doing and whether they could possibly be of any assistance to us in time. It was at this juncture that Mr. Hillhouse, of the constructing firm, tore from his notebook a page with these words written on it: Can you fit seven-inch tube from officers vent to water surface for food and air?" This signal was made to the divers by myself by means of Morse code with a spanner on the hull of the boat. The message was repeated time after time.

Our position hourly was becoming more desperate. We were facing death by (1) starvation, there being no food whatsoever in the boat: (2) thirst, only a limited supply of water being on board: (3) suffocation, as the air was hourly getting worse and worse, and it hurt one to breathe; and (4) poisoning from chlorine gas when the salt water leaking from bulkhead reached the batteries. Only for the wonderfully patient way In which the representative of Messrs. Peter Brotherhood, of Peterborough, attended the pump for hours pumping out salt water bailed by us into a tank we would have been gassed long before. We knew, however, that the pump could not be driven when the battery failed, and that that was only a matter of a few hours.

A Bold Plan.

As the rescue workers were ignorant of the cause of our sinking, and therefore unable to put their maximum effort to practical use, our captain. Lieutenant-Commander Herbert, D.S.O., after conference with Commander Goodhart, D.S.O. (the captain to be of K14), decided on a bold plan. They were both to enter the conning tower, and after flooding the conning tower to obtain sufficient pressure to force open the lid Commander. Goodhart was to escape through the lld to thc surface, taking with him, in. the event of failure, a two gallon sealed tin, with the names of the living written therein, and also the best method to adopt to rescue them. Commander Herbert was immediately to close the lid after Goodhart had gone, drain the conning tower, and return to us in our compartment.

However, the pressure of air was too great; Commander Goodhart made the supreme sacrifice for his comrades, while Lieutenant Commander Herbert was blown up and reached the surface safely, and so was enabled to direct rescue operations with a first-hand knowledge ot the situation.

On the second day, the seven-inch tube was fitted and we were thus enabled to communicate with the surface. Immediately a flexible air hose was passed down the tube, so that the foul air in the boat could escape between the space surrounding the air hose. After this, a small bottle of brandy was lowered down the tube, the contents of which were issued out to each man in the top of a metal polish tin, holding approximately one tea-spoonful. An effort was made to lower a larger bottle down the tube, but it became jammed, and a leadline was lowered to break the bottle. That also became Jammed, and so the tube had to be disconnected, and we once again lost touch with the outside world.

Divers At Work.

Meanwhile, the divers had begun their colossal task, working continuously like Trojans in a bed of mud, as our stern was rapidly becoming more and more embedded in the mud, and hourly the task of raising the nose of the boat became more difficult.

On Wednesday night, after having been down since Monday afternoon, we could feel the boat beginning to adopt an angle. The nose was pointing upwards. Was the weight of the flooded stern dragging us down slowly and surely into deeper water? No; the work of the rescuers was bearing fruit; our nose was being lifted to the water line, our stern remaining on the bottom. Then came a sudden hiss and sparks, the flame of an oxy- acetylene blow pipe burning a hole in the boat, sufficient for the entombed crew to crawl through into the night. Wonderful fresh air and freedom after being prisoners for 57 hours at the bottom of the sea with half of the crew killed! We were then taken to the Shandon Hydropathic Hotel to sleep in a real feather bed, to bathe, and to drink soup-our first food since

Monday. The cables lifting the boat parted soon after we were rescued, and she sank again....

SOURCE:
PARRAMATTA MAN ALIVE TO TELL THE TALE. (1938, DECEMBER 31). THE SYDNEY MORNING HERALD P. 9. HTTP://NLA.GOV.AU/ NLA.NEWS-ARTICLE27975407

APPENDIX D: HMS 13 GARELOCH CASUALTIES AND SURVIVORS.

ROLL OF HONOUR

NAME   RANK/TITLE   AGE
Bevis, George William   Stoker   35
Bradley, Tom   Engine Room Artificer 3rd Class 24
Clark, Stephen Clutson Acting Leading Stoke   25
Cornish, Herbert Stoker   22
Dickinson, John   Stoker   24
Dymond, Ridgeway Stoker   23
Fenson, Walter Abraham   Chief stoker   34
Fieldwick, George William   Stoker Petty Officer 35
Goddard, Henry Charles   Stoker   22
Goodhart, Francis Herbert Heaveningham (DSO)   Commander 32
Hallihan, Timothy   Stoker   24
Hole, Frederick Stephen   Civilian: Admiralty Overseers Assistant
Hooper, Richard   Stoker   24
Howard, Frederick James   Leading Stoker   24
Kirk, James   Civilian: Fairfield Engine Department
Lane, Arthur Ernest   Engineer Lieutenant
Lewis, William John Civilian: Fairfield Engine Department

Mitchell, Thomas   Leading stoker   36
Neate, Frank Thomas   Civilian: Fairfield Foreman Electrician
Porter, Frederick Raymond (DSM)   Petty Officer   39

Pratt, Herbert Bosun   33
Roberts, John Arthur, (Born Perth, Western Australia 15/12/1887) Engine Room Artificer 2nd Class 29
Roberts, William Stoker   26
Scarlett, Alfred   Stoker   23
Simpson, Horace Stoker   25
Smith, Frederick William George   Chief Engine Room Artificer   38
Smith, William Chalmers   Civilian: Fairfield Engine Department
Steel, John P   Civilian: Fairfield Engine Department

Strachan, William Alfred   Civilian: Fairfield Engine Department
White, Leonard   26
Williams, Robert William Able seaman   25
Williamson, George Jenkins   Stoker Petty Officer 29

THE SURVIVORS

OFFICERS
Commander Godfrey Herbert
Lieutenant Paris Graham Singer
Lieutenant (Engineering) Leonard Chichester Rideal

RATINGS

Chief Petty Officer Reginald Atkinson O/N
Chief Petty Officer Robert Oscar Moth
Chief Petty Officer Robert William Nicholls

Chief Petty Officer Stanley Albert White
Leading Seaman Charles Frederick Osborne
Leading Seaman Robert Henry Hudd
Leading Seaman Arthur Travers
Able Seaman James Patrick ORegan
Able Seaman Frank Harry Byrnes
Able Seaman Albert Knight
Able Seaman Arthur Henry Kirk
Able Seaman Henry John George Akers
Able Seaman Ernest Edward Stevens
Able Seaman Henry William Frederick Mackrell
Able Seaman Richard John Pring Wattley
Able Seaman Robert Young
Able Seaman Thomas Arnold Guthrie
Able Seaman George Edmondson O/N
Leading Signalman Arthur Reginald Riley
Leading Telegraphist Charles Albert Harry Freestone
Boy Telegraphist Joseph Swift
Engine Room Artificer Owen Charles Lewis
Chief Engine Room Artificer Albert Denne
Store Petty Officer Charles Smith
Stoker Ernest Alfred Smith
Stoker George Baker O/N

Civilians

Frederick W Searle, Admiralty Ship Overseer
Edward Hepworth, Admiralty Overseer (Boilers)
William Hancock, Admiralty Overseer
Robert Lake, Brotherhoods Ltd
Frederick C Cocks, RCNC
Prof. Percy Hillhouse, Fairfield Chief Engineer
Edward Skinner, Fairfield Electrical Department
William Mclean, Fairfield

Donald Hood, Fairfield
Frank Bullen, Fairfield
John Green, Fairfield Mechanical Foreman
Henry Kerr, Fairfield
William Struthers, Fairfield
Edward Powney, Chadburns of Liverpool
Donald Renfrew Kelvin, Bottomley & Baird
Sidney Black Kelvin, Bottomley & Baird
William Williams, Brown Brothers (Boilers)
Captain Joseph Duncan, Clyde Pilot.

APPENDIX E: K13
SALVAGE LIST

DURING THE PROCESS OF REFLOATING HMS K13/22
A SIGNIFICANT AMOUNT OF EQUIPMENT WAS TO BE
LOST. WITHIN THE KEW FILES ARE A SHORT SERIES
OF LISTS DETAILING THE LOSSES INCURRED:
ENGINEER LIST

STORES WANTED TO REPLACE THOSE USED
AT THE CASE OF OF THE "K22"

1 length 50 ft armoured hose ¾". (carried away when vessel lifted).

4 length 50 ft plain ¾" hose. (carried away when vessel lifted).

1 length 15 ft 2 ½" Flex Steam. (carried away when vessel lifted).

4 dozen ¾" leather washers. (air hoses etc).

2 dozen ½ " leather washer. (air hoses etc).

6 Sherman ¾" clips. (for air hoses).

2 Pneumatic Diamond point chisels. (lost on case).

1 50 c.p 65 V lamp sub: light. (Broken).

1 Well Globe and rubber for same. (Broken).

1 Tin Aeroline Grease (used on case).

1 Tin Aeroline oil. (used on case).

1 4 volt lamp for sub: hand lamp (Broken).

1 length chisel steel 3 ft long. (punch to centre drill).

4 steel wedges. 1"x4" long. (Used on doors).

50 ft strip rubber for 12" pipes. (Renewing joints).

3 dozen hacksaw blades 9". (Used for joints).
1 blank flange 7" x ½" (covering apertures).
1 blank flange 6" x ½" (covering apertures).
1 blank flange 10" x 3/8" (covering apertures).
1 blank flange 7" x 3/8" (covering apertures).
2 2" Flanges screws 6" dia (covering apertures).
1 piece 2" piping 3 ft long. (Water discharge).
1 piece 2" piping 18" long. (Water discharge).
1 piece 2 ½" piping 3"ft long. (Water discharge).
2 piece 2" piping 3 ft long. (Water discharge).
3 1" to ¾" Reducing couplings. (Air pipes).
2 ¾" to ½" reducing couplings (? Air pipes).
6 ½" iron nipples. (air connections).
3 ½" to 3/8" brass nipples. (air connections).
1 1" couplings gs iron nipples. (air connections)
1 ¾" [?] iron nipples. (air connections).
4 ¼" to ½" brass nipples. (air connections).
3 ¾" gas plugs. (Plugging air and water holes).
3 ¾" iron couplings. (air connections).
4 ¾ Elbows. (air connections).
1 2ft of 2" angle iron. (Securing manhole doors).
1 ½"? Air cock. (Drilling stand).
1 7/8" x 2'6" hock bolts. (Shoring hatches).
1 6" round 5/8" brass (stud). (fastening down suction pipes to food pipe).
1 length 5/8" rd brass. 2 ft long. (fastening down suction pipes to food pipe).
3 sq 1/8" insertion. (Jointing doors).
4 [?] Flat iron ¼" x 2? (Washer plates).
20 galls. Engine oil. (Large steam compressor).
4 galls . Cylinder oil. (Large steam compressor).
60 pairs carbons. (arc lights).
1 doz 1" sq plate washers. (securing doors etc).
1 doz 5/8" x 6" bolts and nuts. (securing doors etc).
1 5/8 x 2½" set bolt. (securing doors etc).
1 doz 5/8 x 2½" bolts and nuts. (securing doors etc).

1 doz ½" x 1 ½" set bolts. (securing doors etc).
2 doz 4" x ½" bolts and nuts. (securing doors etc).
1 doz ½" x 2 ½" bolts and nuts. (securing doors etc).
1 5/8 "26" bolts and nuts. (securing doors etc).
? 7/8" nuts. (securing doors etc).
3 doz 1" round washers. (securing doors etc).

--*--

CARPENTER'S LIST
STORES WANTED TO REPLACE THOSE USED
AT THE CASE OF OF THE "K22"

2 Sheets hair pelt. (Used in shoring hatches).
7Ibs 6" wire nails. (Various). [70 nails approx]
8 Anchor rings ¼ iron. (For submarine).
12 Anchor Forelocks.(For submarine).
3 Doz. Hard wood wedges.(For shoring etc).
3 Doz soft wood rivet plugs. (For shoring etc).

(Sgd.) Frederick Newton. Master.

--*--

BOATSWAINS LIST
SS RANGER
12.3.17
STORES WANTED TO REPLACE THOSE USED
AT THE CASE OF OF THE "K22"

3 barrels paraffin oil (cleaning gear "Koh-I-Noor").
1cwt waste (cleaning screws on lighters).
3 Galls Colza oil. (Cleaning gear).
1 sheet yellow metal (used on case. Various).
200 feet canvas hose 3". (Burst on case).
7Ibs mineral grease (screws on lighters).
1Ib 3/4 copper tacks. (used on sundry jobs).

1 Marline spike (lost overboard).

1 L.V Fid 1w" long x 3 ½" (lost on case).

2 steel heel wedges. (lost on case).

2 cold chisels. (lost on case).

1 7/8 sweep shackle (lost on lighter).

1 4 feet chisel bar. (Broken).

1 2" wire thimbles.(hydroplane fender).

1 packet grass eyelets (belts for bodies).

6 hank boat lancings & signal halyards (soundings and depth marks).

3 coils 6" Manila (1 returned well worn out. Others fairley used not returned).

2 coils 3" Manila (foot rips. whips etc used for supporting 12" pump suction).

2 coils pointline. (Sundry use).

3 coins tagline.(Sundry use).

1 bolt canvas. (Sundry use),

14Ibs seizing wire. (Lashings etc).

1 coil 1 1/2 target wire steel. (Lashings buoy ropes.

1 doz seaming twine.(Sundry use).

1 pad spun yarn.(Sundry use).

10 fathoms 8 coir.(for clamps on lighter).

1 1 1/4 x 9 ft nipper. (Broken).

1 7/8 x 9 feet nipper. (Broken).

1 2" screw sharks. (Broken).

1 1 1/4 screw shanks.

1 1/2" x 14 ft chain sling 2 rings.

--*--

MOTOR ENGINEERING LIST
STORES WANTED TO REPLACE THOSE USED
AT THE CASE OF OF THE "K22"

1 no 6 shifting spanner (lost overboard by diver).

1 heavy T screw driver.

1 hand slide set.

1 round nose chisel.

1 15 ft length hand pump hose (Burst with pressure).

5 Doz Hand pump washers (leather). (On hand pump hose).

1 6ft lengths 3/4" Iron Gas Pipe. (Cut & adapted for suction & blower pipes)

2 4 ft lengths 3/4" Iron Gas Pipe. (Cut & adapted for suction & blower pipes)

1 2 ft lengths 3/4" Iron Gas Pipe. (Cut & adapted for suction & blower pipes)

1 3/4" gas spanner. (Cut & adapted for suction & blower pipes)

1 10 ft length flex pipe. (Cut & adapted for suction & blower pipes)

2 1/2 doz 9" hacksaw blades. (Used for connection).

2Ibs soft solder. (Used for connection).

1 small tin fluxite. (Used for connection).

1/2 cwt white waste. (Cleaning gear etc).

1 small gauge 260Ibs for oxygen bottles. (Broken).

1 5/16 twist drill. (Broken).

1 3/32 twist drill. (Broken).

1 1/16 twist drill. (Broken).

2 hand flat chisels. (Lost overboard workmen).

1 hand hammer. (Lost overboard workmen).

1 no 4 shifting spanner. (Broken).

1 sheet 1/8 rubber insertion. (Used for joints etc).

1/2" sheet 1/16". (Used for joints etc).

2 Doz assorted Emery cloths. (Used for joints etc).

6 5/8" brass nuts. (Used for joints etc).

APPENDIX F:
OPERATION
E.C.1 PLANS

All images in this chapter are sourced from the official court of enquiry file from the National Archives and are copywrited as such. They may not to be reproduced without consent.

No.... 012/33.

MEMORANDUM.

"BARHAM"
30th January 1918.

OPERATION R.C.1.

With reference to H.F. 0037/113 of 28th January 1918, the following information relative to the movements, etc., of the 5th Battle Squadron is promulgated for information.

2. "Barham" will pass the North Bridge Gate at 1730 and proceed to the outer channel light vessel at 12 knots, passing the light vessel at 1810 when speed will be increased to 16 knots.

3. "Barham" will communicate time she actually passes May Island by W/T buzzer to all ships in company.

4. After passing through the latest swept area, course will be shaped for a position latitude 56°38' N, longitude 0° 25' W, and on reaching this point course will be altered to 038°. Speed of advance 16 knots.

5. Ships in company are to conform to these movements so as to be in the positions, relative to "Barham", assigned them by Commander-in-chief's memorandum, paragraph 4(b), at daylight.

6. It is requested that the Vice Admiral, Light-cruiser Force, will arrange for the Battle-cruiser Force to leave so that the 2nd Battle-cruiser Squadron will be ten miles ahead of the 5th Battle Squadron when "Barham" passes the outer channel light vessel. The 13th Submarine Flotilla will follow "Courageous"; while the 12th Submarine Flotilla will proceed so as to be five miles astern of the 2nd Battle-cruiser Squadron and five miles aahead of the 5th Battle Squadron.

7. P.V's are to be got out after passing outer channel buoy and before reaching the outer channel light vessel.

HUGH EVAN-THOMAS

Vice Admiral.

The Commanding Officers of ships of 5th B.S. ...... 4 copies.
The Rear Admiral Commanding and 4 ships of 2nd B.C.S....5 copies
The Vice Admiral, Light-cruiser Force and "Courageous"..2 copies
The Commodore Commanding and 4 ships of 1st L.C.S.......5 copies.
The Rear Admiral Commanding and 4 ships of 3rd L.C.S....5 copies.
The Commodore Commanding and 6 ships of 4th L.C.S.......7 copies.
"Fearless", "Ithuriel", submarines of 12th & 13th Flot..13 copies.
Captains (D), 13th and 14th Flotillas ....3 copies.
"Woolwich" and "Gabriel" ....2 copies.
The Commander-in-chief, Coast of Scotland...............1 copy.

SECRET

"COURAGEOUS",
30 January 1918

No.335
MEMORANDUM.

SUPPLEMENTARY ORDERS FOR BATTLE CRUISER FORCE.

1. In "leaving harbour" (B.C.S.O.No.14) :-
4th L.C.S. will take the place of 6th L.C.S.;
"ITHURIEL" and 13th S/M Flotilla will follow
"COURAGEOUS", as "by day";
Destroyers may be required to screen before dark,
and later if moon is bright;
"ITHURIEL" and 13th S/M Flotilla will move down to
Burntisland Roads before B.C.F. leaves harbour;
Battle cruisers will unmoor by signal from Senior
Officer of Squadron;
Speed after Outer Channel Light Vessel will be the
speed ordered by Vice Admiral Commanding, Fifth
Battle Squadron;
Distances will be adjusted from "COURAGEOUS", who
will signal time of passing May Island.

2. When clear of swept channel, course and speed of each
squadron will be adjusted by Senior Officer of Squadron so
as to be in their L.S.1 positions at 0700, except that each
light cruiser squadron will remain intact as a squadron and
gain visual touch at daylight before spreading to positions
on A - K line.
Distances for L.S.1 will be adjusted from "BARHAM", who
will signal time of passing May Island.

3. Positions on the A - K line as follows :-

A.	B.	C.	D.
"CALLIOPE".	"CAMBRIAN".	"CONSTANCE".	"CHATHAM"
"CAROLINE".	"CORDELIA".	"COMUS"	"BIRKENHEAD".
Cordelia	Caroline		

F.	G.	H.	K.
"CHESTER".	"YARMOUTH".	"PHAETON".	"CALEDON".
		"INCONSTANT".	"ROYALIST".

The Flag Officers and Commodores
Commanding 2nd Battle Cruiser
Squadron and 1st, 3rd and 4th
Light Cruiser Squadrons; the
Commander (S), "ITHURIEL"; and
Commanding Officer, "GABRIEL."
(Copy to Vice Admiral Commanding,
5th Battle Squadron)

T. D. W. NAPIER

VICE ADMIRAL.

M E M O R A N D U M.

OPERATION "E.C.1".

1. __Object__: (a) To exercise cruiser reports.
              (b) To practise deployments.

2. __Squadrons and Flotillas taking part__:

(a) __SCAPA FORCE__: "Queen Elizabeth".
                1st Division of Battlefleet, 4 ships.
                    (This division will rendezvous with Scapa
                    Force as ordered below.)
                2nd Division of Battlefleet, 4 ships.
                3rd   "   "   "   3 ships.
                4th   "   "   "   3 ships.
                5th   "   "   "   4 ships.
                6th   "   "   "   4 ships.
                8th   "   "   "   4 ships.
                Attached cruisers "Blonde","Boadicea","King Orry".
                "Lion" and 1st B.C.S. ... 5 ships.
                6th Light Cruiser Squadron...4 ships.
                "Castor", "Champion", and destroyers.

   Note:— Orders as to whether "Campania" and "Pegasus" will take
           part will be given by signal.

(b) __ROSYTH FORCE__: 7th Division of Battlefleet, 3 ships.
                "Blanche".   ...   ...   1 ship.
                2nd Battle Cruiser Squadron..4 ships.
                "Courageous" ...   ...   1 ship.
                4th Light Cruiser Squadron...6 ships.
                3rd Light Cruiser Squadron...4 ships.
                1st Light Cruiser Squadron...4 ships.
                "Fearless" and 12th Submarine Flotilla.
                "Ithuriel" and 13th Submarine Flotilla.
                Destroyers from Rosyth.

   Note:— "Nairana" will not take part in these exercises.

3. __British Intelligence__: The 1st Division of the Battlefleet, 2nd
Light Cruiser Squadron and screening destroyers will be supporting a
convoy which leaves Methil at about 0900, 30th January and proceeds
through Lat. 56°50' N., 1°30' W., Lat. 57°40' N., Long.0°15' E., Lat.
59°20' N., Long. 3°25' E., Lat. 60°08' N., Long.5°00' E., speed about
7½ knots.
     The 1st Division will rendezvous with the Scapa Force at 0800,
1st February.   The 2nd Light Cruiser Squadron and three destroyers
will continue to support the convoy.

4. __Movements__:
     (a) __Scapa Force__: The Scapa Force, including the 1st division of
the Battlefleet, will rendezvous in position Lat. 59°30' N., Long.
3°30' E. at 0800, 1st February.
            (Special orders as to leaving Scapa, and the disposition to
be assumed at daylight, 1st February, will be issued to the Scapa Force
only as an addendum to this Operation order.)

                                                       The...

(Memorandum H.F.0037/113, of 28 January,1918,-Operation "E.C.1")

The Scapa Force will steer from the 0800 position towards position 'ZZ', Lat. 58°50' N., Long. 2°48' E. The advanced light cruiser line are not to approach within 10 miles of the position 'ZZ' before 0900, 1st February.

(b) Rosyth Force: The Rosyth force is to leave Rosyth as ordered by the Vice-Admiral Commanding 5th Battle Squadron. Modified Cruising Disposition No. 1 is to be assumed at daylight, 1st Feby.

5th Battle Squadron to represent a battlefleet of three squadrons at 'V'.
"Fearless" and 12th Submarine Flotilla five miles ahead of 5th Battle Squadron.
2nd Battle Cruiser Squadron five miles ahead of "Fearless".
"Courageous", "Ithuriel" and 13th Submarine Flotilla five miles ahead of 2nd Battle Cruiser Squadron.
'U', on line A – K, five miles ahead of "Courageous".
Distance of line U – V to be 20 miles.

The whole force is to approach the position 'ZZ', Lat.58°50' N., Long. 2°48' E., from a South-westerly direction. The line A – K is not to be within 10 miles or at a greater distance than 20 miles from the position 'ZZ' at 0900, 1st February.

5.   Special Orders for the Exercises:

Exercise I.:-
      Position of Heligoland ...   ...   Fair Island.
      'Red Fleet'   ...   Scapa Force – see para.2 above.
      'Blue Fleet'   ...   Rosyth Force – see para. 2 above.

Note:-   The three ships of the 5th Battle Squadron are to represent the German 1st, 3rd and 4th Squadrons. Their distance apart on approach and deployment is to be arranged accordingly.

Speeds.   Vessels may proceed at any speed up to full speed. All vessels are to have steam for full speed by 0800, 1st February.

- - - - - - -

Exercise II and subsequent exercises – as ordered by signal.

- - - - - -

6.   General Orders.
      (a). Destroyer Screening groups are to screen their column on both sides throughout the exercise unless special orders are received.
      If conditions admit, the Commander-in-Chief may order a division, half flotilla or flotilla on each side to carry out torpedo attacks.   Destroyers detailed are to hoist their recognition sails point down.
      (b). Smoke screens can be used by each side when opportunity occurs, but with discretion.
      (c). Records.   The instructions contained in Grand Fleet Gunnery and Torpedo Order No.189 are to be complied with.

For Exercise I.

483

(Memorandum H.F.0037/113 of 28 Jan. 1918 - Operation 'Z.C.1')

Address:

Admiral, Second in Command	2 copies.
8 ships of 1st Battle Squadron and "Blonde".	9 copies.
Vice-Admiral Commanding, 2nd Battle Squadron ...	2 copies.
6 ships of 2nd Battle Squadron.	6 copies.
Admiral Commanding, 4th Battle Squadron	2 copies.
8 ships of 4th Battle Squadron, "Boadicea" and "King Orry"...	10 copies.
Vice-Admiral Commanding, 5th Battle Squadron ...	2 copies.
3 ships of 5th Battle Squadron, and "Blanche".	4 copies.
Rear-Admiral Commanding, 6th Battle Squadron .	2 copies.
4 ships of 6th Battle Squadron...	4 copies.
"Queen Elizabeth"	1 copy.
Vice-Admiral Commanding, Battle-Cruiser Force ... and "Lion".	3 copies.
Rear-Admiral and 4 ships of 1st Battle-Cruiser Sq.	5 copies.
Rear-Admiral and 4 ships of 2nd Battle-Cruiser Sq.	5 copies.
Vice-Admiral, Light-Cruiser Force, & "Courageous".	2 copies.
Commodore Commanding First Light-Cruiser Squadron.	1 copy.
4 ships of First Light-Cruiser Squadron ...	4 copies.
Rear-Admiral Commanding, 2nd Light-Cruiser Sqdrn.	1 copy.
Rear-Admiral Commanding, 3rd Light-Cruiser Sqdrn.	1 copy.
4 ships of Third Light-Cruiser Squadron ...	4 copies.
Rear-Admiral Commanding, 6th Light-Cruiser Sqdrn.	1 copy.
4 ships of 6th Light-Cruiser Squadron ...	4 copies.
Commodore Commanding 4th Light-Cruiser Squadron.	1 copy.
6 ships of Fourth Light-Cruiser Squadron ...	6 copies.
"Fearless", and for distribution to submarines of 12th Submarine Flotilla, "Ithuriel", and 13th Submarine Flotilla	13 copies.
"Castor", and for distribution to Captains (D) and half leaders of 11th, 12th and 15th Destroyer Flotillas and "Anzac"..	7 copies.
Captain (D), 14th Destroyer Flotilla	1 copy.
Captain (D), 13th Destroyer Flotilla.	2 copies.
"Woolwich	1 copy.
"Gabriel"	1 copy.
"Campania"	1 copy.
"Pegasus'	1 copy.
"Oak"	1 copy.

(Copies to: Admiralty	4 copies.
Commander-in-Chief, Coast of Scotland.	1 copy.
Admiral Commanding, Orkneys and Shetlands.	1 copy.
Rear-Admiral, Scapa.	1 copy.

COPY OF TELEGRAM

FROM ... THE COMMANDER-IN-CHIEF, GRAND FLEET.

TO ...... THE VICE ADMIRAL COMMANDING 5th BATTLE SQUADRON.

Date ... 29th January 1918.

With reference to Operation E.C.1, orders for which will reach you to-night Tuesday, the speeds of the three ships of the 5th Battle Squadron are to be limited to 19.5, 20.5 and 21 knots respectively, representing the speeds of the German 1st Battle Squadron,   3rd Battle Squadron, and 4th Battle Squadron. The Rosyth light-cruisers are to spread and are to act as British light-cruisers in accordance with the Battle Orders. Only the four ships of the 6th Light-cruiser Squadron will be available as light-cruisers of the Scapa force. Each light-cruiser of the Scapa force will represent a unit of three light-cruisers.

(1216).

No.... 012/32.

For information.

HUGH EVAN-THOMAS

"BARHAM"
30th January 1918.   VICE ADMIRAL.

The Commanding Officers of ships of the
   5th Battle Squadron... ... ... 4 copies.
The Rear Admiral and four ships of the
   2nd Battle-cruiser Squadron   ... ... 5 copies
The Vice Admiral, Light-cruiser Force and
   "Courageous"   ... ... 2 copies
The Commodore Commanding and four ships
   of 1st Light-cruiser Squadron ... ... 5 copies.
The Rear Admiral Commanding and four ships
   of 3rd Light-cruiser Squadron ... ... 5 copies.
The Commodore Commanding and six ships
   of 4th Light-cruiser Squadron ... ... 7 copies
"Fearless" and "Ithuriel" and submarines
   of 12th and 13th Submarine Flotillas ...13 copies
Captain (D), 14th Destroyer Flotilla ... ... 1 copy
Captain (D), 13th Destroyer Flotilla ... ... 2 copies
"Woolwich"   ... ... 1 copy
"Gabriel"   ... ... 1 copy
The Commander-in-chief, Coast of Scotland ... 1 copy

SECRET

3 Ships
Blanche
6

Page 6.

Appendix No.2 to Memorandum M.D.0037/113 of 28 January, 1918).

OPERATION 'E.C.1'.

(Note. Appendix No.1, page 5, paragraphs 10-12, issued to ships at Scapa only).

13. After Exercise I. a distribution of gun and torpedo fire exercise will be carried out. For this purpose the Battle-cruiser Force, consisting of :-

1st and 2nd Battle-cruiser Squadrons 9,
"Courageous" 1,
1st, 3rd and 6th Light-cruiser Squadrons.... 12,
                                            ―――
                                             22,

will form the target squadron.

A position 'ZZ' and course will be given, and the two fleets will approach and deploy as in action. The Vice-admiral Commanding, Battle-cruiser Force, is to manoeuvre his force so as to test the fire discipline of the battlefleet. He should also exercise casualties. The instructions in Grand Fleet Battle Orders, sections XIV., IV. and XXa. will then be practiced.

14. During this exercise ships are to practise zig-zagging independently to avoid enemy's fire.

15. Each battleship and battle-cruiser is to send in subsequently, through her divisional commander, a record showing, for first opening fire and for each occasion target was shifted :-

(a). G.M.T.
(b). Fire discipline signal received from divisional commr.
(c). True bearing of target actually engaged, with name, or description, of ship.
(d). Range.

16. Flag officers commanding battle squadrons and V.A.B.C.F. are requested to summarise these reports so as to show in diagrammatic form the section of the enemy ordered to be engaged, and actually engaged, by their squadrons, with the fire discipline signals made and received by divisional commanders, and approximate ranges.

17. It is particularly required to establish the time lag between the transmission of a fire discipline signal by Commander-in-chief and divisional commanders respectively and its execution by the fleet as a whole.

18. In order to analyse the torpedo fire developed, tracings are to be forwarded by divisional commanders of the battlefleet to the Commander-in-chief, showing the bearing and distance at intervals of units of the target squadron.

Similarly tracings are to be forwarded by the senior officers of battle-cruiser and light-cruiser squadrons to the V.A.B.C.F., who is requested to forward to the Commander-in-chief a tracing showing the movements of the target squadron, with the bearing and distance at intervals of units of the battlefleet.

19. A blue print showing the combined movements of both sides will be issued from the fleet flagship as soon as possible, on receipt of which senior officers of squadrons are requested to plot and analyse the results of torpedo fire, and subsequently to forward the results with any recommendations to the Commander-in-chief.

29 January, 1918.

APPENDIX G: SIGNAL LOG FOR THE BATTLE OF MAY ISLAND

The following are a combination of two signal lists published within the court of enquiries pages. One set is the signals sent to the senior officer commanding the 5th Battle Squadron and the other the signals to HMS Fearless. Both list have a number of differing abbreviations for either the sender or recipient and i have attempted to translate the more obscure ones, marking them [ ]. Some it seems have more than one abbreviation which makes the task even harder and some are lost within the spinal binding of the book holding the pages. But I have tried my best.

Also please note the time stamps. The first listed is the time sent and the second time received, if received. The symbol '-' denoted an unreadable entry.

.

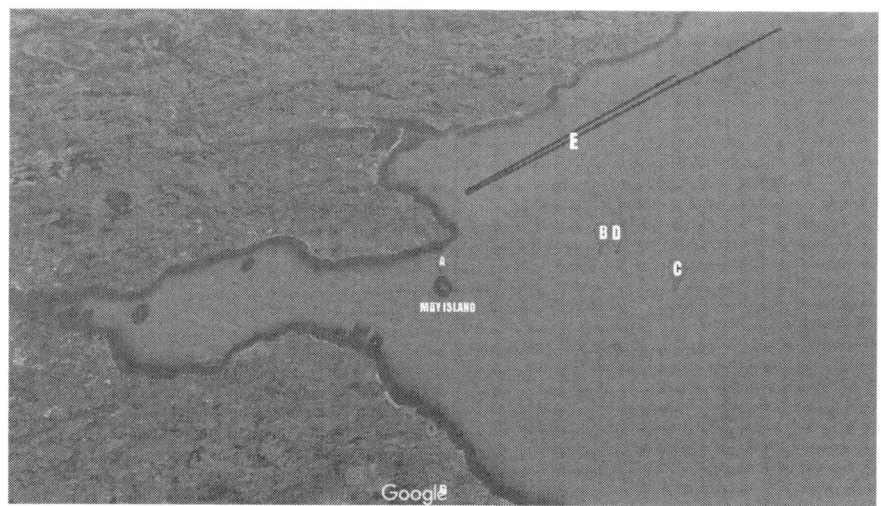

THE BATTLE GROUND

PREVIOUS PAGE: THE POSITIONS MARKED 'A' TO 'D'
ARE LOCATIONS NOTED WITHIN THE SIGNALS BELOW.
POSITION 'E' APPROXIMATES THE TB BOATS COURSE THAT
NIGHT. (ALL POSITIONS ARE APPROXIMATE)

ABBREVIATIONS

A.C.5 = ADMIRAL COMMANDING 5TH B.S [?]

S.N.O.A = ?

CAPTAIN S12 = COMMANDER OF 12TH FLOTILLA,

CAPTAIN CHARLES J. C. LITTLE,

CAPTAIN S13 = (ITHURIEL) COMMANDER ERNEST W LEIR

C-IN-C = ADMIRAL JELLICOE

D14 = CAPTAIN (D) AFLOAT 14TH DESTROYER FLOTILLA CAPTAIN HARRY R GODFRE

S.O 5TH BS = REAR ADMIRAL SIR ARTHUR LEVESON

S. O 2ND BCS VICE ADMIRAL SIR REGINALD G.O. TUPPER

SO, 1ST LCS VICE ADMIRAL TREVYLYAN D.W. NAPIER

SO, 3RD LCS REAR ADMIRAL ALLEN T HUNT

SO, 4TH LCS REAR ADMIRAL ALLAN EVERETT

S.O.L.C.S = SENIOR OFFICER LIGHT CRUISER SQUADRON VICE ADMIRAL TREVYLYAN D.W. NAPIER?

V.A.L.C. F LCS VICE ADMIRAL TREVYLYAN D.W. NAPIER

C OF S = CAPTAIN OF SUBMARINES = CAPTAIN CHARLES J. C. LITTLE & COMMANDER ERNEST W LEIR [?]

THE SIGNALS

14:45-15:15
NAIRANA* TO S.N.O.A
(SEMAPHORE)
SEAPLANE N.1665 REPORTS ENEMY SUBMARINE 5 MILES
S.E FROM MAY ISLAND. SUBMARINE SUBMERGED IMMEDI-
ATELY. REQUEST C-IN-C, C OF S, AND N.C BE INFORMED.
TIME OF SIGHTING 14:40.
(C-IN-C INFORMED BY TELEPHONE)

(* HMS NAIRANA WAS A PASSENGER FERRY THAT WAS RE-
QUISITIONED BY THE ROYAL NAVY (RN) AS A SEAPLANE
CARRIER IN 1917)

15:02-15:25
- TO BARHAM
(5TH BS FLAGSHIP)
(TELEPHONE)
E.D.O REPORTS SEAPLANE IS BEING SENT FORM DUN-
DEE TO POSITION 5 MILES E.S.E FROM FIFENESS WHERE
ENEMIES SUBMARINE WAS SIGHTED BY SEAPLANE FROM
NAIRANA AT 14:40 (COURAGEOUS AND AUSTRALIA IN-
FORMED)

B.C.5 TO SHIPS OF 5TH B.S, BLANCHE*, D.14 FOR INFO
(SEMAPHORE)

RAISE STEAM FOR 15 KNOTS BY 17:20. STEAM FOR 18 KNOTS BY 19:00, STEAM FOR 22 KNOTS BY 19:30. SQUADRON WILL WEIGH AT 17:20 AND WILL PROCEED AT 21 KNOTS FOR ONE HOUR WHEN MAY ISLAND IS ABEAM OF BARHAM, THEN 16 KNOTS.

(*ATTACHED TO 5TH BS AS SCOUT CRUISER)

15:35-15:49
[?] TO GENERAL
(SEMAPHORE)
SWEEPERS ARE COMPLETING SEARCH OF NORTHERN HALF OF CHANNELS SWEPT THIS MORNING.

15:50-16:00
5TH BS TO NAIRANA
(SEMAPHORE)
REPEAT BEARING AND DISTANCE FROM MAY ISLAND OF SUBMARINE REPORTED IN YOUR 14:46. E.D.O STATES THAT NAIRANA REPORTED SUBMARINE 5 MILES E.S.E OF FIFENESS.

15:55-16.14
NAIRANA TO AC5*, NC
(TELEPHONE)
CORRECTION. SEAPLANE N.1665 REPORTED SUBMARINE 5 MILES E.S.E OF FIFENESS AT 14:40 SUBMERGED IMMEDIATELY.
[* ADMIRAL COMMANDING 5TH BS?]

16:10-16:18
[?]. O. A* TO GENERAL
(SEMAPHORE)
MAY ISLAND LIGHT HAS BEEN ASKED FOR DARK TO 20:30
[*SENIOR OFFICER ASHORE = ADMIRAL SUPERINTENDENT
[ROSYTH] REAR ADMIRAL SIR HENRY H BRUCE?]

15:52- 16:20
B.C.5 TO S12, FEARLESS, S13 ITHURIEL, S.O.L.C.S, FOR INFO
(W/T)
DEPARTURE OF ALL UNITS IS PUT BACK 20 MINUTES.
SPEED FROM MAY ISLAND WILL BE 21 KNOTS FOR ONE
HOUR THEN 16 KNOTS.

16:35-16:45
B.S 5TH TO: SHIPS OF 5TH BS. D14. S12
(SEMAPHORE)
ENEMY SUBMARINE REPORTED BY SEAPLANE AT 1420
TODAY THURSDAY 5 MILES E.S. OF FIFENESS
(PASSED TO FEARLESS BY W/T 17:13)

17:05-17:30
S.O.5TH BS TO S.O.L.C.S, S.O.2, BC.S.A, S.O.1, L.C.S, S.O.3, L.C.S
S.O.4, L.C.S, D13, D14, FEARLESS & ITHURIEL
(W/T)
KEEP IN SOUTHERN HALF OF AREA 1010 10 MIDDLE.

19:06-1914
L.C.F* TO BARHAM
(W/T)
MAY ISLAND BEARING 180 DEGREES

[* LIGHT CRUISER FORCE?]

19:15-19:42
K22 TO ITHURIEL
(W/T)
--------SUBMARINE K12 BOTH SHIPS ARE FLOODED FOR-
WARD

19:45- 1955
SO 5BS TO WAKEFUL
(W/T)

PRIORITY. KEEP CLEAR OF AREA 10 MIDDLE, UNTIL FLEET
HAVE PASSES OUT. LAST SQUADRON PASSES MAY ISLAND
20:15 COURSE 075 DEGREES

19:44-19:46
INCHKEITH TO TB25,23 &32
(W/T)
SUBMARINE K14 IN COLLISION ABOUT 3 MILES NORTH OF
MAY ISLAND. RENDER ASSISTANCE IMMEDIATELY

19:40-19:55
K14 TO ITHURIEL
(W/T)
HAVE BEEN IN COLLISION IN NEED IF IMMEDIATE ASSIST-
ANCE.

19:40-19:55
(W/T)
S.O 2ND BCS TO S.O 5TH BS
VESSELS IN DISTRESS IN PATH OF FLEET DUE NORTH OF
MAY ISLAND DESTROYER STANDING BY

19:44-19:47
INCHKEITH TO TB 25
(W/T)
PRIORITY. INCHKEITH TO TB'S 25,26,32. STAND BY K14 IN
COLLISION ABOUT 3 MILES NORTH OF MAY ISLAND REN-
DER ASSISTANCE IMMEDIATELY.

19:44 TO 21:10
WARSPITE TO S.O.5TH BS
(W/T)
INCHKEITH TO SYLVIA, T.B 25 AND RAINBOW. SUBMARINE
K.14 IN COLLISION ABOUT 3 MILES NORTH OF MAY ISLAND
RENDER ASSISTANCE.

19:48-20:00
K.14 TO CAPTAIN(S)12
(W/T)
PASS FOLLOWING. SUBMARINE K.14 TO ITHURIEL. HAVE
BEEN IN COLLISION REQUIRE IMMEDIATE ASSISTANCE .56
DEGREES 12' N 2 DEGREES 34'N
(A)

19:48-20:15
K14 TO ITHURIEL VIA FEARLESS
HAVE BEEN IN COLLISION IN NEED OF IMMEDIATE ASSIST-
ANCE MY POSITION 56 DEGREES 12' N 2 DEGREES 34'W

(A)

19:55
CAPTAIN S12 TO 12TH FLOTILLA
(LAMP)
SPEED 12 KNOTS, EXECUTE.

19:56-20:17
2 BCS – SO 5BS (W/T)
PRIORITY. INFLEXIBLE TO AUSTRALIA. HAVE BEEN IN COL-
LISION WITH SUBMARINE K22. SHE NEEDS ASSISTANCE
(ALSO INTERCEPTED BY AUX. INFLEXIBLE TO AUSTRALIA
20:07)

20:00-20:05
CAPTAIN S12 TO 12TH FLOTILLA
(LAMP)
K14 HAS BEEN IN COLLISION WITH -------- REMAINDER UN-
INTELLIGIBLE

5TH B.S TO 5TH BS
RECEIVED 20:09
(SEARCH LIGHT)
COURSE 075 DEGREES SPEED 21 KNOTS

20:04-20:12
INFLEXIBLE TO AUSTRALIA
(W/T)
MY POSITION COURSE AND SPEED AT 20:15 56 DEGREE 18
' N 2 DEGREE 15' W, N E, SPEED 21 ½ KNOTS.

(B)

20:05-20:28
GRANTON SHORE BASE TO SHEMARA*
(W/T)
PROCEED IMMEDIATE TO ASSISTANCE OF SUBMARINE K.14
POSITION 3 MILES NORTH OF MAY ISLAND.
(*SHEMARA (EX-VICTORIA), HIRED YACHT,)

20:15-22:28
K3 TO C-IN-C, C-O-S
PREPARATORY SIGNAL FOR ENTERING FIRTH OF FORTH BY
NORTH CHANNEL LEADING SHIP ARRIVES WITHIN GUN
RANGE INCHKEITH AT 00:30 TWO SUBMARINES. PROPOSE
ANCHORING BURNTISLAND UNTIL DAYLIGHT.

20:15-21:30
K7 TO CAPTAIN S12
(LAMP)
DOCTOR IS REMAINING ONBOARD. ALL SURVIVORS
TURNED IN SHALL I SEND BACK WHALER. (REPLY: YES)

20:17-21:37
S.O 5TH B.S TO FEARLESS, ITHURIEL, S.O 2ND BCS, S.O 1ST,
3RD & 4TH L.C.S. V.A L.C.F
MAY ISLAND ABEAM AT 2009.

20:22-20:40
FEARLESS TO S.O.5.B.S
URGENT HAVE BEEN I COLLISON WITH SUBMARINE K17,
56.17 N 2.9 W

(c)

20:25-20:33
2ND BC.S. TO A.C.5
(W/T)
PRIORITY. HAVE JUST PASSED ITHURIEL AND THREE SUB-
MARINES INWARD BOUND.

20:26-20:39
2 B.C.S TO A.C.5
(W/T)
HMS INFLEXIBLE NOT IN COMPANY.

20:27-20:55
S.O 5TH BS TO WAKEFUL
(W/T)
PROCEED TO POSITION 56.12N 2.34 W TO SUBMARINE IN
COLLISION

(A)

20:30-20:38
K6 CAPTAIN TO S12
(W/T)
AM IN COLLISION IN NEED OF IMMEDIATE ASSISTANCE.

20:30-20:30
CAPTAIN S12 TO 12TH FLOTILLA
(W/T)
SHOW NAVIGATION STERN LIGHT ONLY

20:30
CAPTAIN S12 TO 12TH FLOTILLA
(LAMP)
SHOW NAVIGATION LIGHTS

20:33
CAPTAIN S12 TO 12TH FLOTILLA
(LAMP)
STOP ENGINES

20:34

CAPTAIN S12 TO 12TH FLOTILLA
STOP ENGINES (TO BE FOLLOWED BY EXECUTE)

20:32-20:38
FEARLESS TO S12 AC5
(W/T)
HAVE BEEN IN COLLISON WITH K17. MY POSITION 56.15N
2.9. W

(A)

20:30-20:34
CAPTAIN S12 TO 12TH FLOTILLA
(W/T)
EXECUTE

20:25-20:34
SO, 2ND BCS, SO 5TH BS
(W/T)
HAVE JUST PASSED HMS ITHURIEL AND THREE SUB-
MARINES ----- INBOUND.

20:36
K6 CAPTAIN S12
(LAMP)
AM IN COLLISION WITH K BOAT REQUIRE IMMEDIATE AS-
SISTANCE. (REPLY: BOAT SENT)

20:40-20:56
ITHURIEL TO V.A.L.C.F
(W/T CYPHER)
SUBMARINE K12 & K22 HAVE BEEN IN COLLISON AND ARE
HOLED FORWARD. I AM PROCEEDING TO THEIR ASSIST-
ANCE. 13TH SUBMARINE FLOTILLA POSITION 1`8 MILES

EASTWARD MAGNETIC FROM MAY ISLAND

20:40
K6 CAPTAIN TO S12
(LAMP)
HAVE BEEN IN COLLISION WITH K3 WHICH IS SUNK

20:40
CAPTAIN TO S12 & S.O.5TH B.S
(W/T)
HAVE YOU RECEIVED SIGNAL 1945 FROM K14 TO ITHUR-
IEL. URGENT,

20:42
K7 CAPTAIN TO S12
(LAMP)
HAVE JUST PASSED OVER SINKING SUBMARINE

20:45
K7?
MADE DEMAND TO DESTROYER OFF PORT BOW. (REPLY: 6
PTS 56 PEYTON [DESTROYER])
("5TH BS PASSED CLOSE TO THE NORTHWARD OF FEAR-
LESS")

21:00, A.D.E DEMAND TO SUBS ON PORT BOW. K 12 & K3.

21:02-21:09
K12 ITHURIEL
(W/T)
I AM WITH 12TH SUBMARINE FLOTILLA
(PASSED ON S. WAVE AT 21:25 TO FEARLESS)

21:10
K7 CAPTAIN TO S12
(LAMP)
WE HAVE 7 SURVIVORS. ONE APPARENTLY LIFELESS AND
3 REQUIRING MEDICAL ASSISTANCE. I WENT RIGHT OVER
SINKING SUBMARINE.

21:15-19:41
K22 TO ITHURIEL
(W/T)
PRIORITY (HAVE BEEN IN COLLISION WITH) SUBMARINE
K12. BOTH SHIPS ARE FLOODED FORWARDS.
(NOTE: GROUP IN BRACKETS WAS NOT DECODED UNTIL
SOME HOURS LATER AS IT WAS CODED FROM NEW GEN-
ERAL SIGNAL BOOK NOT YET IN FORCE)

21:20
CAPTAIN S12 TO K3
(LAMP)
RETURN TO BASE MAKE YOUR OWN ARRANGEMENTS FOR
LIGHTS. ARE ANY OF OUR BOATS NEAR YOU (REPLY: NO)

SENT:21:24
S.O 5TH BS TO CAPTAIN S12
(WT)
SIGNAL 1948 K14 TO ITHURIEL RECEIVED.

21:24
CAPTAIN S12 TO K12
(LAMP)
PROCEED INTO HARBOR WITH K3
21:25-21:45

CAPTAIN S12 TO K3
(LAMP)
TAKE K12 WITH YOU

21:40-21:49
CAPTAIN S12 TO K7
(LAMP)
I AM GOING TO RETURN TO HARBOR STERN FIRST AT SLOW
SPEED. KEEP ME.

21:43-22:27
CAPTAIN S12 TO C-IN-C, C OF SUB.
(W/T CYPHER)
FEARLESS IN COLLISION WITH SUBMARINE K7. LAT 56.15N
LONG 2.9. W (FULL STOP) K17 SANK (FULL STOP) K6
IN COLLISION WITH ANOTHER SUBMARINE PROBABLY K4
WHICH HAS ALSO SUNK (FULL STOP). AM ORDERING ALL
SUBMARINES TO RETURN TO BASE (FULL STOP) FEAR-
LESS AND K6 DAMAGE FORWARD FEARLESS SERIOUSLY RE-
QUIRES DOCKING.

(A)

21:45-21:45
CAPTAIN S12 TO K6
(LAMP)
WHAT COMPARTMENTS HAVE YOU FLOODED. ARE YOU IN
DANGER.

0:35-20-45

WAKEFUL TO S.N.O.A, D13, INCHKEITH
(W/T)
STRIKING FORCE PROCEEDING ASSISTANCE SUBMARINE
K14

20:27-20:50
A.C.5 TO WAKEFUL
(W/T)
PROCEED IMMEDIATELY TO 56 DEGREES 12' N 2 DEGREES
34' W TO RENDER ASSISTANCE TIO SUBMARINE IN COLLI-
SION

(B)

20:40 TO 20:59
ITHURIEL TO V.A.L.C.F. & A.C.5
(W/T)
SUBMARINES K12 AND 22 HAVE BEEN IN COLLISION AND
ARE HOLED FORWARD. I AM PROCEEDING TO THEIR ASSIST-
ANCE WITH 13TH SUBMARINE FLOTILLA POSITION 18
MILES E.MAG FROM MAY ISLAND.

21:00-21:12
CAPTAIN(S) K12 TO ITHURIEL
W/T)
SUBMARINE K.12 TO ITHURIEL.AM WITH 12TH SUBMAR-
INE FLOTILLA

RECEIVED 21:05
A.C.5 TO 5.B.S

(SEARCH LIGHT)
COURSE 069 DEGREES, SPEED 16 KNOTS.

21:10-22:20
WARSPITE TO S.O.5
SHEMARA TO S.N.O GRANTON. DESTROYERS STANDING BY
SUBMARINE, NO FURTHER ASSISTANCE NEEDED.

21:19-21:46
WARSPITE TO S.O.5TH BS
(W/T)

VENETIA TO D13, C-IN-C, C OF SUB & INCHKEITH. HAVE
TAKEN K14 IN TOW, HAVE SOME OF HER CREW ON BOARD
REMAINDER IN BOAT. SHE APPEARS SERIOUSLY DAMAGED
FORWARD. ARRANGE TO INFORM S.O.2 B.C.S. REQUEST MAY
ISLAND LIGHT.

21:50-21:50
CAPTAIN S12 TO K6
(LAMP)
NO COMPARTMENTS FLOODED. AM LEAKING SLIGHTLY
FORWARD.

21:55-22:57
CAPTAIN S12 TO K6
(LAMP)
DID YOU SEE THE SUBMARINE SINK. (REPLY: LAST SAW
BOWS ABOVE WATER. I HAVE SEEN NOTHING SINCE)

21:59-21:59

CAPTAIN S12 TO K6
(LAMP)
AT WHAT ANGLE WITH THE VERTICAL WAS THE SUBMAR-
INE AT WHEN YOU LAST SAW HER (REPLY: AT ABOUT 60
DEGREES APPARENTLY K7 PASSED OVER HER)

22:00-22:10
K3 TO C-IN-C, C OF SUB
(WT)
REQUEST LIGHTS IN GROUP 4 BE SHOWN FROM 21:30 TILL
MIDNIGHT,

22:00-22:10
WAKEFUL TO CAPTAIN S12, INCHKEITH, C OF SUB.
(W/T)
STRIKING FORCE (FULL STOP) ITHURIEL REQUIRES NO
FURTHER ASSISTANCE WITH SUBMARINE.

22:00-22:15
WAKEFUL TO INCHKEITH, D13, S.N.O.A
STRIKING FORCE PROCEEDING TO OIL, ITHURIEL REQUIRES
NO FURTHER ASSISTANCE WITH SUBMARINES.

22:03-22:41
INCHKEITH TO K12
(WT)
PLEASE REPORT NAME OF DESTROYER THAT HAS YOU IN
TOW.

22:22-22:34
CAPTAIN S12 TO K6 & 7
(LAMP)

AM GOING AHEAD 4 KNOTS S.86 W IN SINGLE LINE. K6 K7

22:34-22:50
CAPTAIN S12 TO K7
(LAMP)

WHAT WAS THE LAST YOU SAW OF THE SUBMARINE OVER. (REPLY) APPARENTLY, SHE WAS BROADSIDE TO ME AND I WENT OVER BETWEEN THE BOW AND THE PERISCOPES. SHE WAS SINKING SO RAPIDLY THAT I SCARCELY TOUCHED HER ONLY A BUMP NOT AS MUCH AS ONE FEELS WHEN SWINGING AT A BUOY SOMETIMES. SHE APPARENTLY SANK BY THE STERN K6 WAS VERY CLOSE TO HER.

22:55-23:05
CAPTAIN S12 TO C OF SUB. C-IN-C
(W/T)
REQUEST LIGHTS IN GROUP 4 MAY BE SHOWN FROM MID-NIGHT UNTIL 02:00 TOMORROW FRIDAY.

22:45-23:13
CAPTAIN S12 TO C OF SUB C-IN-C
(WT)
MY POSITION 56.18N 2.12W COURSE 242 DEGREES SPEED 4 KNOTS SUBMARINES K6 AND K7 IN COMPANY.

(D)

23:00-23:00
CAPTAIN S12 TO K6 & K7
(LAMP)

DIM YOUR LIGHTS

23:22-23:30
CAPTAIN S12 TO K6
(LAMP)
PROCEED INTO HARBOR WITH K7 MAKING YOUR OWN AR-
RANGEMENTS FOR LIGHTS.

23:25-23:57
-CARABORO TO CYCLOPS*
FOLLOWING FROM VENETIA. HAVE TAKEN SUBMARINE
K14 IN TOW, SOME OF HER CREW ON BOARD. REMINDER IN
BOAT. SUBMARINES SERIOUSLY DAMAGED FORWARD.

(* HMS Cyclops was a submarine repair and depot ship of the
Royal Navy.)

23:25-23:40
FEARLESS TO C IN SUB, C-IN-C
(WT)
REQUEST A VESSEL MAY BE SENT TO ESCORT ME SO THAT I
CAN SEND K6 & 7 INTO HARBOR. 23:50
WHAT WAS VESSEL YOU PASSED. (REPLY SMALL MER-
CHANT MAN).

23:31-01:26
INCHKEITH TO ITHURIEL
REPORT SUBMARINE IN COLLISION, ESTIMATED TIME OF
ARRIVAL AND WHETHER ANY FURTHER ASSISTANCE RE-
QUIRED. RESCUE TUG WRESTLER HAS BEEN SENT.

CAPTAIN OF S12 K6
(LAMP)
MAY ISLAND BEARS 231 DEGREES AT 23:42 USE SOUTH
CHANNEL MAKE YOUR OWN ARRANGEMENTS.

00:10-00:17
ITHURIEL
AM IN COMPANY WITH VENETIA AND SUBMARINE K14
BEARING 113 DEGREES FROM MAY ISLAND. MY SPEED 4
KNOTS, HAS K22 PASSED IN?

01:00-01:28
CAPTAIN(S)12 TO C-IN-C, C OF SUB
SUBMARINES K6 AND 7 PROCEEDING TO HARBOR.

01:58
ITHURIEL TO INCHKEITH
ASSISTANCE NOT REQUIRED. ARRIVE ROSYTH BETWEEN
08:00 AND 10:00. SUBMARINE K14 AND 22 IN COLLISION.
DAMAGE TO LATTER NOT KNOWN.

02:08-03:23
INCHKEITH TO WAKEFUL
279 OF TODAY FRIDAY FORCE PROCEED AT ONCE AND ES-
CORT FEARLESS WHO IS DAMAGED IN COLLISION. POSI-
TION APPROXIMATELY 8 MILES EAST OF MAY ISLAND.

APPENDIX H: BATTLE OF MAY ISLAND CASUALTY LIST.

K.4'S Fifty Five Dead

ADAMS, Leonard, Chief Engine Room Artificer, M 324 (Po)
ADAMS, Percy W, Stoker Petty Officer, 306739 (Ch)
APPS, John S, Engine Room Artificer 1c, RNVR, Clyde 3/1892
ARMSTRONG, James, Able Seaman, J 32585 (Po)
BALDWIN, George H, Petty Officer Telegraphist, J 10360 (Dev)
BEER, Frank J, Chief Stoker, 298980 (Ch)
BLAKE, Stanley H, Able Seaman (RFR B 5018), 211925 (Po)
BOUNDS, Horace, Stoker 1c, "K" 14491 (Ch)
BROWN, Charles E, Stoker 1c, "K" 22591 (Ch)
BURGESS, Albert C, Stoker 1c, "K" 9375 (Po)
BURT, Ernest S, Able Seaman, J 9569 (Ch)
CARTER, Charles, Leading Signalman, 236423 (Dev)
CHURCH, William, Leading Stoker, "K" 9438 (Po)
COCKERILL, Percival, Stoker 1c, "K" 21001 (Dev)
CORFIELD, Alfred A B, Petty Officer, 232865 (Ch)
CRAWFORTH, Harry W, Stoker 1c, SS 115298 (Po)
DANGERFIELD, William G, Able Seaman, J 17629 (Dev)
DUGGAN, Alan M, Able Seaman, J 16974 (Ch)
FENNER, Athelstan A L, Lieutenant Commander

GODDARD, Charles W H, Able Seaman, J 2150 (Ch)

GODDARD, Henry T, Engine Room Artificer 4c, M 11218 (Dev)

GOODSALL, John H, Leading Stoker, "K" 12209 (Ch)

GRANT, Patrick, Stoker 1c, "K" 20768 (Ch)

HAMMOND, John W, Gunner

HANKS, Frederick F, Stoker 1c, "K" 16885 (Po)

HAYES, Joseph C, Stoker 1c, "K" 19004 (Ch)

HAYMAN, William H, Leading Stoker, 305390 (Dev)

HILL, Ralph R, Chief Engine Room Artificer 2c, 270525 (Po)

HOGG, Albert E, Leading Seaman, J 9082 (Ch)

IRON, James T, Leading Stoker, "K" 11011 (Ch)

JACKSON, Thomas W, Able Seaman, 215195 (Po)

LEEDER, Edward B, Able Seaman, SS 5311 (Po)

MARTIN, Herbert E, Stoker 1c, "K" 10876 (Ch)

MOCKFORD, Fred, Able Seaman, J 9223 (Po)

PEARSON, Alfred E, Leading Seaman (RFR B 10623), 206490 (Ch)

PUDDIFOOT, Ernest J, Able Seaman, J 46875 (Ch)

RIVETT, Leonard W, Able Seaman, J 18186 (Ch)

ROWLEY, William, Petty Officer, 215872 (Po)

SELLICK, Sydney J, Stoker 1c, "K" 12966 (Ch)

SHEATH, Harry, Stoker Petty Officer, 355913 (Po)

SPICE, Albert, Able Seaman, 239765 (Ch)

SPICE, John, Able Seaman, 219424 (Ch)

STOCKS, David De B, Commander

TREDGETT, James H, Stoker 1c, "K" 22822 (Ch)

VAREY, Alan, Engine Room Artificer 4c, M 21630 (Ch)

WALKER, Frederick, Leading Telegraphist, J 25725 (Dev)

WATKINS, Malcolm P, Signalman, J 19411 (Po)

WATTERSON, Thomas A, Lieutenant, RNR

WELLESLEY, Claud M A, Lieutenant

WINDIBANK, Albert C, Able Seaman, J 18037 (Ch)

WOOD, Thomas S, Leading Stoker, "K" 12229 (Ch)

WOODS, George O C, Leading Stoker, M 2250 (Po)

WYATT, William T, Stoker Petty Officer, 308247 (Po)

YOUDALE, Harold W, Officer's Steward, L 3820 (Po)
YOUNG, Thomas S, Able Seaman, J 16770 (Ch)

HMS K4'S DEAD

BOWELL, Walter J, Able Seaman, J 15186 (see HM Depot Ship
Crescent above)
SCOTT, Alexander, Leading Seaman, 232696

HMS K17 DEAD

ADAMS, Albert V, Engine Room Artificer 3c, M 632 (Dev)
AGNEW, William, Able Seaman, SS 2844 (Dev)
ANTRAM, Herbert W, Ty/Lieutenant, RNR
BERRIMAN, Thomas H, Able Seaman, 213863 (Dev)
BINNINGTON, Charles E, Stoker 1c, "K" 18963 (Ch)
BLACKMAN, James, Stoker 1c, "K" 13078 (Po)
BROWN, Jack G, Engine Room Artificer 4c, M 8692 (Ch)
CARESS, Henry A, Stoker 1c, SS 115673 (Ch)
CARTER, William J F, Stoker 1c, "K" 17477 (Ch)
CASE, Charles, Chief Petty Officer, 186086 (Po)
COOK, William J, Leading Stoker, "K" 6363 (Ch)
COOLEY, William C, Petty Officer, 227154 (Po)
COOPER, William W, Leading Signalman, 239571 (Ch)
CUNNINGHAM, Ernest S, Midshipman, RAN
De BANK, Arthur G D, Stoker 1c, J 22444 (Ch)
DRAKE, Arthur R, Able Seaman, 238786 (Ch)
FINCH, William, Leading Seaman, J 1069 (Po)
GALE, William J, Leading Stoker, "K" 11623 (Dev)
GIBBS, John, Able Seaman, J 10934 (Dev)
GIBSON, Isaac, Chief Engine Room Artificer 2c, 270632 (Dev)
GILL, Robert, Leading Seaman, 211672 (Po)
HAMMOND, Francis, Able Seaman, J 9547 (Dev)
HEARN, Henry J, Lieutenant Commander
HERRING, Harold L, Engine Room Artificer 4c, M 13296 (Ch)
HOSKING, Cecil J, Leading Seaman, J 16056 (Dev)
JONES, Edward, Stoker 1c, "K" 20796 (Po)
KNIGHT, George A, Leading Telegraphist, J 8438 (Ch)
KNOWLES, James E, Stoker 1c, SS 115292 (Dev)
LIGHTBODY, Henry G, Able Seaman, J 24810 (Ch)

LORD, Frederick E, Telegraphist, J 55202 (Po)
MCDONALD, John R, Stoker 1c, SS 114477 (Ch)
MEADMORE, Edward J, Leading Seaman, 223356 (Ch)
MONTGOMERY, Joseph R, Able Seaman, J 12871 (Dev)
MORRIS, Ernest, Stoker Petty Officer, 309458 (Ch)
MYOTT, Dominick, Engine Room Artificer 3c, M 7565 (Po)
NETTLETON, Harold, Able Seaman, J 20766 (Ch)
NOLAN, Patrick, Stoker Petty Officer, 284013 (Dev)
RICKETTS, Henry L, Stoker 1c, "K" 27466 (Dev)
SAMUEL, Frederick, Able Seaman, J 10440 (Ch)
SANGSTER, Leo F M, Stoker 1c, "K" 22599 (Ch)
SAVAGE, Charles H, Officer's Steward, L 2005 (Po)
SAVAGE, Charles K, Stoker Petty Officer, 311292 (Po)
SINFIELD, Albert E (real name, but served as Albert E Simpson), Leading Seaman, J 1181 (Ch)
TILLEY, Edmund, Leading Stoker, "K" 10609 (Po)
TYRELL, Hugo W L, Lieutenant
WARDE, Cecil, Lieutenant
WHEBLE, Henry H, Able Seaman, 225581 (Po)
WHITE, Alfred, Able Seaman, J 6137 (Dev.
Those fortunate to survive on from the K17 were:
Lieutenant Gerald Edward Armitage Jackson
L/Sea Anthony Westbrook
AB (SG) Joseph Clark
Sig George Thomas William Kimbell
SPO James Stewart, RAN
Sto1 Henry Fulcher
Sto1 Albert Dowding
Sto1 Kenneth Vass

APPENDIX I: COXSWAIN OSCAR MOTH, AN AUTOBIOGRAPHY.

C oxswain Oscar Moth, Survivor of the K13 has left us a biography of his service. Its has been quoted in the main body of the book, but the full account affords us a fascinating insight and career of a man who served on the "K"s, twice:

> *"It must "be clearly understood, by all those who read my War Experiences, that, they were only written under pressure from my relatives and also the Friends I made during the Great War. They all tell me that my experiences are so varied that they deem it my duty that I should try and write them in Book Form. I think myself that my effort should prove*

very interesting to everyone and instructive to the younger generation.

Before I commence my experiences and so that everyone will understand what they are reading, it will be necessary for me to point out that at the outbreak of war, I had over twelve years' service in HM Navy. Over five years of this I had spent in the Submarine Service, in which I had served from an Able Seaman in A5, rising to a Petty Officer and serving as Coxswain of A12 and latterly as Coxswain of C24.

In those days, five years was the limit of service allowed in the Submarine Service and accordingly after five years of peace time experience I went back to 'Sea', that is, the Navy proper. At the outbreak of war I was serving in HMS Attentive, that ship being stationed at Dover and it is from this Ship that my story must start. I may not be able to make a great deal of HMS Attentive but I ask my readers to bear with me until I re-enter the Submarine Service, when I know they will be interested to read how our brave boys fought in those Ships who really went out and under in more senses than one.

August the fourth was the fateful date and the sixth Flotilla of Destroyers were anchored in Dover Harbour. The Navy had just finished playing at war and had demobilized, only to mobilise again and prepare for War in earnest.

Germany had declared war on France and had over run Belgium in their eagerness to get to Paris and the whole world was watching Britain and we in the Navy were only too eager to get the chance of a bump at Germany.

There was a great deal of activity in the Light Cruisers and also the Torpedo Boat Destroyers which were attached to the sixth Flotilla.

I was serving in HMS Attentive and we were the senior officer at Dover, as we carried the Captain "D" of the Flotilla. We were preparing for War. Many a time had I done this before, but then only for drill, but now this was in earnest. From time to time you could hear the Question, "Do you think we shall go to war?" but nobody cared to chance their arm with a 'Yes' or 'No'. At four o'clock we made the signal for the fleet to get underway and we all put to sea to await the Government's decision whether we should, or should not, go to War.

Out through the breakwater at half speed and into the Straits of Dover. On our way we were cheered by the Forts on either side and it could easily be seen that the army was just as enthusiastic as we were. And now we made straight for the French Squadron which was patrolling the Straits and there was a great deal more cheering.

We straight away took on this Patrol and transferred one of our Officers to the French Flag Ship, who transferred one of her officers to us. We then steamed round the French Squadron and cheered to our hearts' content, after which we officially took on the Patrol, the French Squadron going further west.

It will now be seen that we had taken over the Straits of Dover, some hours before the declaration of War, but we were there all ready and waiting for the fateful signal "Commence Hostilities".

At 11pm the signal was received and we were at war with Germany. We were very much on the alert for we all knew well that our patrol was very important, in fact was really "the Key" to the situation.

Day after day, we were searching merchant ships of all nations and quite several prizes were sent into Dover or the Downs to anchor.

Watch keeping in two watches is very monotonous and especially as we had a very young Ships Company, so that as the days wore on it was jolly hard to keep some of the younger ones awake. You can guess we wore fed up with this waiting business and everyone was wishing that the Germans would come out and give us a chance to get it over.

Every third day we went into Dover to "Coal Ship" but there was no leave. It was simply "Coal Ship", "Clean Ship" and really before we had a chance to clean ship we were out again on our Patrol.

We weren't being cheered up with news, for things were looking rather black in France and we were getting bad news from everywhere.

At last we got something to look for, for we received the news that the TBDs had been torpedoed by a German submarine, so we knew we had at last got something to get on with. Special submarine "Look Outs" were posted and everyone was backing our chances of seeing a German submarine off. We didn't have long to wait for the chance, but in any case, I think his chance was a better one than ours.

It was the Sunday after the Pathfinder was sunk

that we nearly "got it". It was in the afternoon and the watch below were sleeping. I myself was sleeping in my mess, when I heard a hell of a scuffle and a tremendous amount of rushing about. I rushed on deck just as the bugle sounded "Action". I could hear men saying "Didn't you see her?" I went to my station which was in the Conning Tower, at the helm and then I found out that we had been attacked by a German submarine who had come up on our port bow and had fired a torpedo at us but had missed by mere inches.

There is no doubt whatever that the torpedo must have hit us, but for the sharp look out which was kept, for as the torpedo was fired, it was sighted and our helm was put hard over and we managed to just evade the deadly missile by going "Full Speed Ahead" on our engines.
I now had a very dizzy two hours at the helm for the submarine was sighted many times and the helm was swung from one side to the other, so as always to keep the submarine on our stern and then we would be a small target as well as a running target. I supposed by now that we had at least a dozen TBDs in the Straits and they were all steaming at full speed and darting all over the place, in the off chance of ramming the submarine.

During the whole of the two hours I was at the helm I saw nothing and I even went so far as to say that I didn't believe we had been attacked although I had heard continually the cry "There she is".

At last, as she had not been seen for some time, we dispersed from Action Stations and the pipe called the watch to Defence Station, so now I got a chance to speak to someone who knew as much as I did about submarines. This was our Torpedo Gunner's Mate and he had served with me for a good many years in the Submarine Service and after this incident served again with me in L6.'

After leaving the helm I strolled aft to where he was and greeted him in this fashion, "Well Buck, (all Taylor's are called Buck in the Navy and this man's name was Taylor) what do you think about it? Have you seen her?" "No and I don't believe for one minute that there is a submarine anywhere near us", was his answer. Just at that, time both of us Disbelievers were very quickly converted to Believers, for up she came out of the water about 200 yards off our Port Beam and clearly showed 2 feet of periscope.

"Hard a Port" came the order from the Bridge to the Conning Tower and we swung round very quickly to Starboard and once again put the Submarine on our stern. I am fully convinced that we missed a splendid opportunity, as I consider we were in a good position to have turned to Port and rammed her, as I am sure she only came up to see for her own safety. That was the last we saw of her, but by this time we had about 20 TBDs and four cruisers belting about the Straits of Dover in the hope of ramming the submarine.

We had attached to us 12 submarines of the B and C Class but we had ordered them into harbour and they had to remain in until the next day. This spasm caused us to do much more harbour time and I am inclined to think that, that German submarine did us a good turn, anyhow the patrol was now kept up by Severn and submarines who were considered to stand a better chance if attacked by enemy sub-

marines.

Our next bit of real excitement came on a Saturday afternoon near the end of the month of October. We had had a very busy week, our Ships Company being employed in loading the Mine Layers with mines and as things had slackened down we were looking forward to an afternoon off or what in termed "A Make and Mend". Our luck was certainly out for at 1.15 the pipe went, "Out Pipes", "Hands Fall In". Soon the "Buss" went round that there was something doing, for we were employed in getting the Ship ready for sea and you could see that the remainder of the Flotilla was doing the same.

At four o'clock we slipped our mooring and proceeded to sea with the whole of the sixth Destroyer Flotilla and we were also accompanied by the Monitors "Severn", "Humber" and "Mersey". These Monitors had recently been commandeered as they were built in England for a foreign state and they proved to be very useful indeed.

No one seemed to know what our mission was but after a bit we found out that our destination was the Belgium coast, where at that time we were getting a lot of bad news. We put into Dunkirk and there we saw a ship which had on board the remnants of the Marines who had so gallantly defended Antwerp. We steamed quite near to her and there was a good deal of shouting, "Are we downhearted?" and the answer which was shouted back was always "No".

While we were at Dunkirk we received a wireless message from the Admiralty to the effect that all the cruisers were to go back to Dover, as hostile submarines were out and it was not considered advis-

able to use the cruisers for bombarding.

This was bad news for us, for we wished to be in it and it came as "Good News" to us when Admiral Hood who was flying his Flag on board, the Attentive, said he would keep us and. send the remainder back.

An Officer and two Signalmen were landed from the Flotilla and they were to go up into the lines and give us information by signal when and how to conduct the bombardment.

We now steamed up the coast and waited for the signals. We were due to start the bombardment at 2 am but we had received no signal, so could not start, as we had no knowledge which were our men and which were the enemies. It was nine o'clock when we "commenced firing" into vast masses of German troops. This was the signal for the whole of the Flotilla to start and we simply played havoc with them.

I would like here to pass a few remarks concerning the first shot that was fired on the Belgium coast. I have heard a good many arguments concerning this and quite a few ships claim this distinction, but I have no hesitation in saying that the first round was fired from the forecastle 4" Gun Starboard, of HMS Attentive and the Gun layer who fired the first round was Petty Officer F Kelly. Things now began to get a bit hot, as our bombardment was being answered from the shore by big guns, but the only ammunition that was fired was shrapnel. This of course was no good for fighting ships, although it caused quite a number of casualties in the Flotilla.

The ship who was hardest hit by casualties was the

TBD Viking. She had got in rather close and received, a direct hit on the muzzle of the forecastle 4" gun just as it was in the act of being fired. This caused a very big explosion, which laid out the whole of the gun's crew as well as all the Officers and men who were on the Navigating Bridge, as well as the men who were "handing up ammunition".

At noon the "Cease Fire" was sounded and the "Attentive" steamed back to Dunkirk. We had no idea what was going to happen but on arrival at Dunkirk a boat was lowered and sent into shore. Two military officers came off in this boat with plans of the district and we steamed back along the coast again. One of these officers was "Colonel Bridges" but I have forgotten who the other was but anyhow he was an Artillery Officer and under their guidance, the bombardment was re-opened. This was carried on until darkness set in and we then withdrew. That evening, the Admiral transferred his Flag to one of the TBDs and we had orders to collect the casualties from all the Flotilla and return to Dover.

The effect of this bombardment - which was only a prelude to many others - had the desired objective and checked the German advance along the coast line and for a good many miles in land. The advance had begun to be very serious and a good many of us are of the opinion that our Flotilla saved Calais, for at the rate the advance was going it would have only meant another day before they would have been before Calais. We in England all know what that would have meant, so this is one of the things that all Britishers should warmly thank the Navy for having accomplished successfully.

We arrived back in Dover at midnight and there was

quite a stir there when we arrived for the news that we had arrived with casualties spread like wild fire. These we soon landed and now we found out that we were not to go back, as the Admiral had asked for old ships who were of no material consequence and yet could do the bombarding more effectively.

Another period of monotony followed and I was just about fed up when I found that they were asking for volunteers with submarine experience to re-enter the Submarine Service. Thinking that this would prove a far more exciting job than the one I already had, I immediately offered my services, which were straight away accepted.

I now had to await a relief and it was some weeks before this arrived. We were employed as "Working Parties" loading up ships with ammunition for the ships who were carrying on the bombardment of the Belgium coast. This didn't at all suit me and I renewed my application for further service in submarines, but my Captain told me I would have to wait until my relief arrived, in fact he tried hard to keep me, but at last my perseverance was rewarded.

On December the 23rd we left Dover, all in a hurry not knowing what was happening, but the next day (Christmas Eve) we found ourselves in Southampton. We arrived at noon and by two o'clock we had half of our Ships Company on seven days leave. We were to be refitted by the firm of H

I went to Portsmouth for my leave and I visited Fort Blockhouse (the submarine depot) where I saw the Drafting Officer and as we had served together before, he told me he would do what he could for me.

Accordingly, on January the 10th a relief arrived for me and on the 11th of January I proceeded to Portsmouth and joined the submarine depot. I will here point out that the Petty Officer who relieved me was killed some two months afterwards in the "Attentive" by a bomb dropped by a Taube.

I now underwent a course of instruction in later boats than I had already been in. It must be understood that the Submarine Service had advanced by leaps and bounds and we had submarines of all classes building, all over the country, as well as boats building for us in Canada. It necessarily follows, I had a good deal to pick up as my experience only took me as far as C Boats and they were fast becoming obsolete.

I remained in the depot until early in April when I was told off, as Coxswain of H1, which boat was built in Montreal, Canada. We left on April the 8th with four Boats crews H1, H2, H3 and H4 and we were to tackle the Atlantic for the first time in the annals of submarine history.

We travelled by train to Liverpool and from that port we embarked in "SS Misanibie" a GPA Line and we had a real good trip across the Atlantic to Halifax. We made lots of friends on the passage for the passengers and crew knew on what errand, we were bent and. they were not slow in showing their appreciation. They were very open in telling us that they didn't envy us our job and quite a number of the crew told us they wouldn't tackle the Atlantic in a submarine at any price.

On our way out our crew with the assistance of a

few of the passengers gave a concert in the Saloon, on behalf of the Mercantile Marine Orphanage and it proved a great success and from a financial point of view it was even a greater success. On our arrival at Halifax we disembarked end proceeded by train to Montreal. So, we said "Good Bye" to the many friends we had made, who wished us "God Speed" and the best of luck in our trip across the Atlantic.

On our arrival at Montreal, which happened on a Sunday evening, we were met by some of the advance party who had been out for some two months. They told us that as far as could be judged, the boats were going to be good ones, -and they also told us that HM Submarine H1 had been launched that day.

All our party now dispersed to look for lodgings, as we were put on what is termed in the Navy "Lodging and Compensation", which is of course money with which to provide for yourself, instead of being provided by the Navy, everything in the way of accommodation and food. We all found lodgings in the vicinity of Vickers Yard, where 10 H Boats were being built. We were all very lucky with lodgings as in most cases we lived with people who had emigrated from the Old Country and deemed it a duty to look after the Boys in Navy Blue.

The next morning found us all eager to see our boats and we were early at the yard, but found the gates closed on us and we were not allowed inside until our Officers arrived and vouched, for us. I was struck by the way the secrets of the yard were kept for anyone would have thought that our uniform would have been sufficient guarantee, but after this we were all given a card, without which it was im-

possible to get in. There were sentries all over the yard and at night searchlights were burnt by Boy Scouts who belonged to the firm.

When we got inside we found H1 in the water and nine other H Boats building on the slip. They were literally swarming with workmen who in the majority were Yanks, but were going full pelt at their work, all with one object in view, '"The Almighty Dollar.

During our stay at Montreal we had a right royal time, everybody treating us with the greatest respect, in fact we all made good friends, of whom we talked about for years afterward. Our greatest pals were the 42nd Canadian Highlanders and we spent many a happy hour in their messes. I am very sorry to say a great many of these paid for their Patriotism dearly, for the best part of them made the great sacrifice in France. I remember one incident quite well, .it was a recruiting march and the Colonel of the Regiment thought a Naval Brigade would form an added attraction. He approached our Captain "Lieutenant Pirie" on this subject, who was quite agreeable. Accordingly, we formed a Brigade and marched with the Regiment. We took the place of honour, behind the Pipe Band and the whole thing proved a great success. On our return to the Drill Hall we were inspected by the Commanding Officer of the Regiment who congratulated the Officers on having such a fine body of men to commission their submarine with. On Sunday the 9th of May, we left, I mean H1, Montreal for Murray Bay to do our trials. We had a good run down the St Lawrence and arrived at Murray Bay, which is below Quebec, on Monday afternoon. Our trials proved very successful and everybody was very pleased indeed with our boat, so on the 18th inst. we left for Quebec.

How happened our first bit of bad luck, for on the way up it began to blow and rain and it was anything but comfortable. At about 9pm we were, in collision with "SS Christine" who was damaged so badly that she sank in 3 minutes, in fact the propeller was still going around when she made her final dive. It was very rough by now and a great deal of difficulty was experienced in rescuing the lives of those that were floating. A very brave bit of work was done by one of our Able Seamen, he went overboard and was instrumental in saving the lives, of the Captain of the "Christine" an RNR Lieutenant and that of the Signalman. The Captain's leg was broken and he really must have had a very bad time. In all we saved ten of the crew, but I never found out how many were lost.

The ABs name was "Moyes" and he was congratulated by everyone on his good work and sometime afterwards he received the Humane Society's Silver Medal. He also was the recipient of a silver wrist watch from the Captain whose life he had saved. This was suitably engraved and I know that he was very proud of it. Poor fellow, he made the supreme sacrifice some two years after for the E boat in which he was then serving went to sea and never returned. She was only one of our boats who went out and was never heard of again.

Ever since the H1 had left Montreal she had been in charge of a 'Yankie' crew and the boat was piloted by a French pilot. As soon as the collision occurred, our own Captain, Lieutenant W Pirie RN took charge and gave the necessary orders while the rescue work was going on, he then navigated H1 to Quebec where he reported the circumstances of the accident.

Of course, we had damaged our bows pretty badly and it was necessary to go back to Montreal for repairs. On the next day, we embarked a new Pilot and proceeded to Montreal. By the look of the damage we had sustained, I really thought we were in for at least another fortnight at Montreal, but owing to the smart way in which the work was taken in hand we were ready to leave again in three days.

On Monday the 24th of May we finally left Montreal, it was a great day and there were swarms of people on either bank of the river to see us off and we had a very hearty "send-off" from the many friends we had made in our short stay in Montreal. We now proceeded to a spot just outside of Quebec where we were to do our final trial. This was a dive of 200 feet. I hardly believed it when I was told, for although I had had considerably over five years' experience in submarines I had never heard of a boat going that depth.
I would like to point out that the pressure on the hull of a boat when she is submerged is roughly half the pressure per square inch that the depth of water is, so it will be seen that at 200 square feet, we nearly have 100 pounds per square inch.

Anyhow our deep trial came off successfully for, to use a Navy expression, the boat was as "Tight as a Drum". Everyone being well satisfied with the boat we now put into Quebec, where we made fast in the outer basin, there to get the boat "Ship Shape" and to wait for H2, H3 and H4 who were to cross with us.

We officially commissioned the boat as UK Submarine H1 on the 26th of May 1915 and now we simply had to make her look something like a British, Man of War. The other boats arrived in good time and on the 2nd of June, we were all inspected by the Duke of Connaught who was accompanied by Princess Patricia). They seemed delighted to think such nice boats were built in Canada and they expressed the opinion that they were sure we should manage the Atlantic.

We were now employed in talking in provisions and water and then we filled our tanks with fuel and lastly took our torpedoes on board, so now it will be seen we were ready for action at a minute's notice. By the 10th of June we left Quebec in company with H2, H3 and H4 and we were escorted by a gunboat called the "Canada", but we (H1) were very unfortunate for we damaged our port propeller so badly that we had to return to Quebec and go alongside the "SS Glenalmond" who was carrying all the spare gear.

I must point out, as some of my readers are not aware that it is possible by flooding tanks at either end of a submarine to do what we call "Trim Down" either by the stern or by the bow. In this case we had to "Trim Down" by the bow and get our stern out of water, we then shipped a new propeller and got ready to leave again*

That evening we left in company with the "SS Glenalmond" and shaped our course for Newfoundland. The weather was fine and we were making a good speed in fact we had to go slower than we needed, so as to keep in touch with the "Glenalmond". Things continued to go very smoothly until the afternoon of the 12th inst. when it came on to blow hard. Soon there was a very big sea running and it was any-

thing but comfortable. The boat proved a very good "Sea Boat" and she rode the big waves finely, in fact she made less of the weather than the Glenalmond. All day the 13th it blew great guns and we had to go dead slow, but on the morning of the 14th the weather eased up. At about 9.0 in the forenoon we sighted a very large ship which proved to be the "Calgarian" an armed liner - who toward the end of the War fell a victim to a German U Boat. We closed on her and she told us that she had met the "Canada" with H2 and H3 but she was looking for H4 and as we could give her no information, she left us and continued her search.

At 7am the next morning we sighted a ship lying at anchor under the lee of an island. We ran in to see who it was and it proved to be the "Canada" and with her was H2 and H3. We also anchored to wait for the weather to moderate altogether.

By noon we considered it was fine enough so we all got underway and once more shaped our course for St Johns, Newfoundland. On the next morning at daylight we could see a number of icebergs and the weather turned very cold and then it turned to fog, so we had to keep a good look out in case of running into one of those lumps of ice. At last we sighted St Johns and we ran in and moored to the jetty at 12:30 on the 15th of June. On the jetty were thousands of people who had come to see the first submarines that had ever come to Newfoundland. They simply gazed at us in awe and it was a long time before we could entice them to come anywhere near where we were laying.

Our only worry now was for H4 for she had not

yet joined us and we were really beginning to believe that something very wrong had happened to her. It was a. great load off our minds when she arrived on the 17th. She reported that she was unable to stick the rough weather and had turned and. run with it and had eventually anchored under the lee of an island.

We were now employed in getting our boat ready for the Atlantic and there was a very strong buzz that we were booked for the Dardanelles. We were to stop four days at St Johns and during that time we made a number of friends, who were all on the jetty to see us leave on Saturday morning the 19th of June.

Our escort now was to be the "Calgarian" who made a signal to say we were to be ready to leave by 10am, but soon after, this was cancelled, as the fog was so thick outside the harbour, that it was considered unsafe to make a start. Accordingly, orders were given that we should not leave until 10am on Sunday so we had another day with our friends.

The Calgarian had on board a contingent of Newfoundland soldiers and we left sharp to time on Sunday morning. We had a good send off and as we got near to the Calgarian we got a rousing cheer from the soldiers who I should say were in high spirits, for they were singing all the patriotic songs. When clear of the harbour the "Calgarian" made the signal "Destination Gibraltar" so that now we were almost certain that we should eventually reach the Dardanelles. We now took up our stations, 2 boats on either quarter of the "Calgarian" and the "Glenalmond" astern. The speeds were 11 knots and we made a jolly good start.

Fog was to be a very great hindrance to us for after about three hours run, we ran into a very thick bank and we had to reduce our speed to nine knots and afterwards to seven knots. The next day was very foggy and to make things worse H3 reported to the "Calgarian" that she had damaged one of her propellers and she had to be taken in tow. This was rotten luck for she proved to be a source of trouble practically the whole way over. The next day the weather cleared and we were able to increase our speed, but we couldn't do any more than 10 knots as the "Calgarian" was afraid of the tow parting, as I have already said H3 was being towed. Anyhow ten knots proved too fast for at about 11 am the tow parted and we all-had to "Lay To" while another line was being passed to H3. This proved a very difficult job for it must be remembered that we were well into the Atlantic and even in fair weather there is a very big swell, especially for boats as small as we were.

Eventually after losing about two hours of very valuable time H3 was taken in tow and we proceeded at nine knots, but ill luck was up against us again, we soon after ran into another fog and we had to reduce our speed the remainder of the day and the whole of that night to seven knots. All that night the fog was absolutely black and we could see nothing, but at intervals we could hear the mournful wail of the "Calgarian's" siren followed by the screech of the air whistles of the submarines and then another wail from the "Glenalmond" so we knew that we were all in company.

The next day the sun came out in all its glory and the sea was a flat calm. A happy idea struck one of our crew and with a piece of canvas and a couple of hours work, we converted our Flat haversack into a canvas bath. This we rigged on our upper deck and we ran a hose from the pump below into the bath and so filled it with salt water. We now bathed to our hearts content, for it was possible for four of us to bathe at the same time. I expect a good many of my readers have seen the photograph of the bath, for it was published in the "Daily Mirror".

The weather now remained fine until Saturday but H3 was absolutely a nuisance so the Captain of the "Calgarian" made a signal to alter course far the "Azores" as he intended to get under the lee of one of the islands, to allow H3 to go alongside the "Glenalmond" and ship a new propeller. At 3pm the Glenalmond and H3 parted company and ran in under the lee of the Azores and the remainder of us had to "Lay To". The Captain of the "Calgarian" now signalled to us to know if we wanted anything, so we took the opportunity and went alongside her, where we replenished our fresh water and also got some bread and beef. H3 succeeded in shipping her new propeller, but it was nearly 10pm before we got under way again. H3 was again taken in tow, but as she could use her own engines, we made ten knots our speed.

Nothing happened now out of the ordinary, except that H3 still gave trouble, until Tuesday at midnight when our engines stopped altogether, I mean H1. This caused the whole of the convoy to "Lay To" and we found that our engine was sucking on a tank that was found to be full of water instead of fuel. These tanks were all supposed to have been filled up, but we can easily say we were browned off by the Yanks, who had filled one of the tanks with water. This was soon remedied as we only had to put the engines on another tank and then we all proceeded at ten knots. The weather remained delightful and we kept up a steady ten knots, which caused us to wash down, for the rollers of the Atlantic are, after all, a trifle too big for a small submarine.

On Thursday evening, our starboard engine gave us a lot of trouble, but we managed to keep up with the remainder, as our port engine was running grand. Now came the worse port of our trip for early on Friday morning it came on to blow and soon there was a big sea running. We could make very little headway at all and we were washing down "Fore and Aft". All day Friday and all Friday night it continued to blow great guns and I can assure you it was anything but comfortable, especially as we were doing our best with one engine. The "Calgarian" gave us as much lee as she could and she wanted to take us in tow, but our Captain wouldn't hear of it, we had come so far on our power and he said he meant to finish, so we jogged along until Saturday morning when the weather showed a decided improvement.

At 6am we sighted land and everyone seemed quite pleased. I myself was shaking hands with myself, for I knew we were the first submarines to ever attempt to cross the Atlantic and here we were within a stone's throw of our journey's end. At 8 o'clock we sighted the rock of Gibraltar and now the weather had eased right down and we were making good progress. At 10:25 we secured to the mole, so it will be seen that we had taken thirteen clays and 25 mins in the passage and I consider we only earned the congratulations which we got from everyone at Gibraltar.

I had a very pleasant surprise awaiting me, for waiting on the Mole, was my brother who was attached to the RNAS and you can bet that our boats were soon over-run with ratings that belonged to that service. What struck me about these men, was their willingness to go up in aeroplanes or seaplanes, but with a few exceptions, they said they "Barred going down in one of those things". I would like to point out the splendid condition of our boats after this long run and also the great radius of action they had. There were only a few minor defects in either of them end we all had plenty enough oil fuel to take us back across the Atlantic if it was so wished. This was a surprise for most people, who thought the radius of action for a submarine was only a few hundred miles.

During our stay at Gib. which lasted ten days, we were docked for examination and we also filled up with oil fuel. We took on board eight of the latest torpedoes and then we reported ready to proceed. We left for Malta on the 12th of July and I think we had pretty well all the "Naval Air Service" down to see us off. There was a great deal of hand shaking and wishes of "Jolly Good luck", for in ten days we had made good friends of them. We had received orders to proceed to Malta to be fitted with a gun and also a wireless set, without which they would not let us take on the "Sea of Marmora" job. We cast off at 6pm and we were in company with H2, H3 and H4 and, also, Monitor M15. The latter was to be our escort and we had received orders to keep a sharp "Look Out" for a strange vessel who had been reported and was thought to be an enemy's submarine parent ship.

H4 Brindisi 1916

It was lovely weather and we easily proceeded at twelve knots, the Monitor leading with two boats on either quarter. Just as dawn was breaking we observed a steamer who was carrying no lights and seeing that no one else had noticed her, we altered course and challenged her with our Cruisers Arc Lamp. She took no notice of our challenge, so we turned away from the remainder and gave chase. We increased our speed to just over 14 knots which was about our limit, but the ship increased her speed and soon out-distanced us, so we had to give up the chase and returned to our convoy.

Our Captain was very angry to think that no one else had seen the ship and he demanded that we should put into "Algiers" to report the occurrence. This we did and I have been led to believe that this was the ship we were looking for and she was afterwards destroyed. On our arrival at "Algiers" we secured, stern to the jetty and that night we gave leave, so I had what we call in the Navy "A Dicky Run", which means I went ashore for a couple of hours.

The next morning, we proceeded to "Algiers Bay" in company with H4, where we dived and carried out experiments with our submarine sound signalling gear. At 2pm, Monitor M15 with H2 and H3 arrived and we all proceeded, shaping our course for Malta.

Nothing of any importance happened during the remainder of our trip and on Sunday morning at 8am we arrived at Malta and secured to E11 and heard great tales of her doings in the "Sea of Marmora". There was a great deal of speculation among the E Boats whether we would be allowed to do the Marmora job, they said we weren't big enough, but we just told them to wait and see.

We had a good spell in Malta and during the time we were there, we had a six-pounder gun put in, wireless fitted and we also had "Knife Edges" fitted to our bow and big jumping wires fitted which went from our bows, over the periscope and finished on the stern. This was to enable us to dive through the net which we knew was placed across the Dardanelles. After these jobs were completed, we went to sea for trials, which proved to be very successful and then we returned to Malta. All we had to do now was to await an escort to take us on to Mudros.

The escort proved unavailable for some time and at last came a message to say we were urgently required, so we proceeded to sea with no escort and shaped our course for Mudros. We had fairly decent weather and we proceeded at twelve knots leaving Malta on Thursday the 2nd of September. Nothing of any note happened until the afternoon of Saturday the 4th when we met HMS Cornwall, who gave us orders to proceed to Mudros. At 5pm the same afternoon we met HMS "Anemone" and she escorted us the remainder of the journey. We anchored that night outside Mudros and awaited orders to enter. At 7am on Sunday we weighed anchor and proceeded into Mudros. I had no idea how important this place was but there must have been hundreds of ships of all classes and sizes, belonging to all the allied countries. We proceeded past these ships and secured to

HMS "Adamant" who was to be our parent ship.

We now had to prove to the "Powers that be" that our boat was suitable for the Dardanelles, so from time to time we took different officers out and dived the boat for their opinions. We also did a lot of running purpose to get the crew as well as the boat in an efficient state for the dangerous job we were going to undertake. All the reports were in favour of the boat being suitable and on the 28th of September we took in thirty days provisions in excess to a week emergency rations which we always carried.

The Dardanelles & The Sea Of Marmara

On the 29th we proceeded to sea, our destination being "Kephala", which is very near the mouth of Dardanelles and at 2pm, we secured to HMS Cornwall, there to await a favourable opportunity to force the Dardanelles.

I would here like to point out that our crew were simply elated to think we were going to be given a chance and if we had asked for volunteers to man the boat, every man jack of the crew would have willingly volunteered.

Our Captain had to report to the Commander in Chief, who ordered that he was to go to one of the destroyers who were patrolling the mouth of the Dardanelles and he was given an order to go up as far as she could so that our Captain would have a fair chance of seeing where we were to start our dive.

On Thursday, the 30th September, we cast off from the Cornwall and had a short dive, getting a good trim. I might say our final trim before making the dash. We then secured again to the Cornwall and waited for our time to make the final effort.

A Month In The Sea Of Marmora

Now commences the story of the most exciting time of my life. A whole month and our nerves on edge the whole of the time. A whole month with nothing but excitement and something doing all the time. I don't want to make too much of it, as I have a long way to go yet, so I will be as brief as I can and stick to the facts which were outlined in the official report which our Captain sent to the Admiralty.

At 2:45 am on the 2nd of October we cast off from the "Cornwall" after receiving the best wishes of the whole of her ships company. We ran on our engines until we got Cape Helles abeam which was at 4:35 am.

We now stopped our engines and ran on our electric motors keeping a good look out. At 4:50 we observed a collision between one of our TBDs and a collier, but as we were working on time we could not stop to see the amount of damage done.

At 5:15 we commenced our dive and shaped our course up the Dardanelles, our speed being six knots. At 6:10 we altered our course to pass "Kilid Bahr" and found our compass was showing a difference of six degrees to the adjustments that were made the day before.

This was very bad for us as we were absolutely dependant on our magnetic compass and I might here point out that we were the only boat who had tackled this job, without having a gyro compass fitted. These compasses are electrically driven and it is impossible for them to be affected by electricity or metals as ours had been. This in a great measure was responsible for us grounding which nearly proved our undoing.

We now dived to eighty feet, this was to enable us to pass the mine fields and also so that no trace of us could be seen. We remained at this depth until 7.20 when we came up for an observation. We found that we had "Kilid Bahr" abeam, so we altered course and dived again to eighty feet.

Soon after altering course we grounded very heavily and we were thrown up right out of the water our depth gauge only reading 15 feet. This meant that the top of our Conning Tower was out of water and that we were really in a very serious plight. There was a great deal of excitement, but our Captain grasped the situation very coolly and calmly. "Hard a Port", "Stop Port" and "Full Speed Starboard" were his orders and luck being on our side, we gradually slipped off into deep water.

This was certainly a very bad start, for we had absolutely given ourselves away. Why the Turks didn't fire at us while we were aground I don't know, my opinion is that they thought they had captured us, anyhow they now knew we were there and we were continually harassed by a motor boat, who followed us until long after we were in the "Sea of Marmora".

We now dived to eighty feet again but we could distinctly hear the swish of the motor boats propeller and we knew we were being followed,
At 8:30 we came up to see if we could get an observation of the Net and we found we were in a very good position. A Lighter was moored over the Net and men could be seen distinctly, working about the Net. Our Captain decided to dive under the lighter, so we set our course and then dived to eighty feet. When we reached eighty feet, our motors were put Full Speed Ahead and we crashed into the net at a speed of about eleven knots.

It was at 8:44 we struck the Net and it certainly did seem to hold us for a bit, but we pushed through it and we heard a terrible grating noise as we tore it. Eventually it dropped clear of our stern and we knew we had got through the worst part of our journey up.

We remained down at eighty feet until 9am when we had to come up for an observation, but as soon as our periscope broke surface we were fired at. We could plainly hear the noise of bursting shell, so after getting a very quick observation, we dived to fifty feet and as we could hear the propeller of the motor boat and also the noise of bursting shell we deemed it advisable to remain at fifty feet for some time.

At 9:30 we stopped and turned out our forward hydroplane, as up to the present we had been diving with our after rudders only. This was to enable us to make as small resistance as possible and it will be easily seen, it was far easier to tear our way through the net, only having to make a small hole at first. Of course, it is far more difficult to dive a boat with only one set of rudders, but as I had experience in A class of submarines who only have the "after rudders", I managed quite well.

I suppose the motor boat could follow our trail for sometimes we could hear her quite plainly, at other times only faintly. Anyhow she made things very awkward for us, for it was impossible for us to come up to get a decent observation.

At last we knew we must be somewhere near Gallipoli, so we eased down and listened. We could not hear the boat, so we came up rapidly to get a look. We immediately heard the boat again but we got a rough observation before we dived again to fifty feet. In this short look we found out that Gallipoli was abeam and it only remained for us to shake off this boat and we should be able to come to the surface.

At 4:20pm having not heard the boat for some time we came up, but this time we found an enemies TBD waiting for us. This was worse than ever and we quickly got down to eighty feet. Our Captain then decided to dive on and we set our course to pass Marmora Island.

At 5pm we came up and found everything clear, so we decided to charge our batteries. We blew our tanks to enable us to get on the upper deck and then we mounted our gun. We also put our clocks on 1½ hours so it will be seen that we started "Daylight Savings" a long while before the country decided to have "Summer Time".

We also made a signal by wireless to our Flag Ship to let her know we had got through. This signal was never received and in our parent ship, the "Adamant", they gave us up for lost. They got no news of us until a week or so later and then E12 communicated by wireless in a code we had taken up with us so then they presumed we were safe. The signal put on the notice board was "As a signal has been received from E12 in a code taken to "The Sea of Marmora" by H1, it is presumed that the latter boat is safe".

It will be seen by comparing our time of diving and our time of coming to the surface that our trip had lasted nearly twelve hours. It was a very strenuous time for us, for our nerves were strained to the utmost the whole of the time, knowing full well that we were "Forcing the Dardanelles" which was one of the most, if not the most difficult task ever undertaken by a submarine of any nation. This will easily be verified if we remember that this task was undertaken by as many French submarines as English submarines and yet only one of then "the Turquoise" was successful in getting up and even then she was captured on the way back.

Our batteries were nearly run down on the voyage up, so it took us nearly four hours to charge them up. At 9pm we dived and set our course up the Sea of Marmora and we did not break surface again until 7am the next day.

We already had one boat ("E12") up here and we had orders to find her out and work in conjunction with her. We knew she was doing good work up here and we were very eager to meet her, for we had decided ourselves that she was to be our "Chummy Boat". Accordingly, we set our course for the rendezvous and when we arrived there we waited on the surface for her.

We remained on the surface until 9.15pm and then as there was no sign of E12 we decided to dive for the night. I want here to explain that the "Sea of Marmora" was a very convenient place for diving, for as we all know the "Black Sea" runs through the "Bosphorus" into it. This gives us what we call in the submarine service a Patch. It is the salt water floating on the fresh water before it has got time to mix. What we used to do was simply trim our boat a trifle heavy and just let her sink very gradually. Of course, according to the state of the weather and the chance of mixing the water had, so we stopped at different depths. Of course, the boat continues to sink until she picks up this patch and then she would gradually stop. Our depth gauge generally told us we were somewhere near sixty feet, although once I remember we went down to over a hundred feet and couldn't find the patch, this of course was after some very rough weather and that night we simply kept underway on one motor, diving in a circle, but to get on with my story.

We remained submerged until 7am the next morning but still there was no sign of E12, so sooner than waste time our Captain decided to dive into Pandermo Harbour. This we did and we sighted a small steamer but she took jolly good care to hug the coast and keep under the cover of the guns, so of course we could not get a pop at her. We dived right into the harbour but as there was nothing there we dived out and came to the surface at 3:30pm.

Soon after we sighted a small Dhow and made her
"heave to". She was a very small thing and carried no
boat, so after examining her, our Captain decided to
let her go. She had two Turks aboard her and I can
picture them now calling down blessings on us for
letting them go.

At 7:30 we sighted a submarine which proved to be
E12 and she told us afterwards that she had a round
in her gun, all ready for us, as she thought we were
an enemy. She told us that she had been expecting us
for days and had given us up for lost. Anyhow we
were very pleased to see each other and at 8pm we
dived for the night.
We came to the surface at 700 the next morning and
parted company with E12. At about 8am we sighted
two lots of smoke so dived and went toward it. The
smoke proved to be two enemies TBDs but they were
too far away for us to get a shot at them and I believe they went into "Pandermo". That afternoon we
chased two Dhows and drove them ashore and afterward we destroyed two more by gunfire. At 8pm we
dived for the night.

We were up early the next morning at about 6am
which really was 4:30am and we ran on the surface
for some time charging our batteries. In the forenoon we decided to try a dive into Mudania just to
see if there was any luck. We dived right up the river
and at 1:30pm we sighted a steamer moored to a
jetty. We got a torpedo ready and got a good attack in,
although when our periscope came out of the water
we were fired at. This happened continually until
2:50 when we fired our first torpedo.
The torpedo ran straight for the target and registered

a Hit. There was a loud explosion but it was not near so loud as I thought the explosion of a torpedo would have been. Anyhow this was very satisfactory, as this was the first torpedo fired by us and we had got a "Bullseye".

We now decided to dive on and see if there was anything in "Glenilik" but although we dived right up we saw nothing but small boats, so we turned and dived out. On our way back, we had to pass Mudania again and we could see the steamers sunk by the Stern. We were fired at again, so we decided to dive deep and get away out of it. At 6:30 we came up and saw a TB. She saw us as well and started to zig zag. She was an impossible shot so we dived deep and came up an hour later. After charging our batteries we dived for the night.

The next day we broke surface at 7am and went toward the rendezvous to meet E12. We destroyed two Dhows during the forenoon and at noon we met E12. We decided now to steam in company toward the east and when we got in the centre of the "Sea" we stopped and the hands were allowed to bathe over the side. Of course, a good "look out" was kept while we were bathing. Afterwards we parted company with E12 and remained on the surface charging our batteries, at 9pm we dived for the night.

We did not come up until 8am the next morning and then we decided to have a go at "San Stephano". We ran on the surface until 2:30pm when we dived and ran in toward the shore. About 3pm we sighted smoke and altered our course to see what it was. It proved to be a TB. and we tried very hard to get an attack in on her. She was steaming very fast and she *passed us at a range of about 1,200 yards and as she was so small we considered her too bad a target, in fact she was what we call an "impossible shot".*

We now altered course again and ran in toward "San Stephano" and when we got in close, we could discern what appeared to us to be a big new factory or perhaps a munition shop and it was about two miles west of San Stephano. Soon after this we saw a "Steam Tug" towing two Lighters and as we thought they must be ammunition lighters, we altered course to try and head them off. We certainly thought we would be able to do this but soon after altering our course, we grounded very heavily at thirty feet. This of course made us turn and come out a bit, but we examined our charts and we found that at the spot where we grounded, it was marked 15 fathoms. This of course made our task all the more difficult, for we knew we couldn't trust to our charts.

Soon after this in the failing light we sighted a steamer and tried hard to attack her. In this we were again unsuccessful for the light became so bad that we couldn't see through the periscope and we had to give her up. At 4:30pm we came to the surface and charged our batteries.

The examination of this place was with a view to a future bombardment of the railway bridges, but we didn't consider it was worth risking, as we only had a six pounder and we didn't think we could get in close enough to do any real material, damage. At 9 o'clock our batteries being fully charged we dived for the night.
The next day we broke surface at 7am and immedi-

ately saw a Dhow. We gave chase on our engines and when close enough, put a shot across her bows. She immediately "Hove to" and we ran up along with her. She had a crew of eight men but she carried no boat. On examination we found her to be empty, so as we dare not risk having so many prisoners as eight we decided to let her go. At 8:20 we met E12, she had had no luck since we last met, so she told us she was going- to dive into "Mudania". We waited outside on the surface and at 3:30pm she returned but told us that there was nothing at all inside. Soon after this we sighted a sail so we set a course to head her off. She appeared to be a very large yacht, so we dived and thought we would approach her without being seen. Then we at last got close enough to make her out we found she was flying the "Red Cross", so not wishing to put ourselves away, we dived away from her. Soon after we came up to charge our batteries and at 8pm we dived for the night.

The next morning, we came up at 8am but found, the weather very rough indeed. At 11am it was so bad that we dived to dodge the weather. There was a good motion at thirty feet so we set a course for "Chekmedyah" .and dived to fifty feet where we found it quite comfortable. It was 4:30pm. before we got very near and then we found several Dhows. At 7pm we sighted a big sail and we came to the surface quite close to her. She was a two master and she also carried two boats, so we put a shot across her bow and made her "heave to". We now made them take to their boats and to make certain there was no one left we put a round into her. The weather was too bad for us to go alongside without damaging ourselves so we rammed her on both sides. She was nearly cut in half and then we gave her four rounds from the six pounder to polish her off. We then ran out a bit and charged our batteries and at 9pm we dived for the night.

The next day was a day of "Ill Luck", for on coming to the surface at 6am, we heard water moving in the Forward Battery Tank. We immediately got busy to find out what this was and on examination we found about three feet of salt water in our Battery Tank which must have leaked from No 2 Main Ballast Tank. This was very bad news for it meant continual work or we should get salt water in our batteries which would mean disaster to us as chlorine gas is caused by salt water meeting electrolyte. We decided to run out into the centre of the "Sea" and make a thorough examination. We opened up No 2 MBT and our Chief ERA got inside and found that one of the seams was leaking badly. This he managed to overcome t+o a certain extent but the leak continued so we had to have the pump on this tank each day. This of course had been caused by a pressure being on the tank so long as we dived with our Kingston valves open, we now always closed them as soon as our tanks were full.

Our next misfortune was our Main Fresh Water Tank, for our Captain gave me order to try the water in it. On examination we found out that the Kingston valve had leaked and the water in the tank was as salt as the water over the side. This was a very serious blow to us for we had only half a ton of water in our ready use tank and we yet had another twenty-day trip to do. Our Captain was very disappointed and he worked out the amount of water per man he could allow us. He told us that we could have three cups of water a day but that must be for cooking as well as drinking and we could have no water at all to wash with. He asked us if we would stick this as he wanted to make our trip successful and. every man Jack readily assented. Three cups of water a day may seem a good allowance, but when you take cooking water out of it, it doesn't leave over much and I can assure you there was a good many times when I felt down right thirsty as well as filthy. This happened on the 11th of October find we came back on the 31st so you can guess we were all in a decent pickle when we did get back. The weather now came on very bad so at 7pm we dived for the night.

The next morning, we wore up at 7am and as the weather was still very bad we decided to run into the Gulf of Ismud. We saw several Dhows but they all took pretty good care to keep near the shore and under the guns. In the afternoon we sighted a large steamer and got a very good attack in on her. We were standing by to fire a torpedo when it came on to rain a perfect deluge. It was impossible to see through the periscope and this proved her salvation. It's a good job for her but the rain lasted an half hour and when it did clear off she was nowhere to be seen. We saw her afterwards but she was under cover of the guns and it was impossible to get at her. We came up soon afterwards to charge and then as it was still very rough we decided to dive until the next morning.

The next morning, we broke surface at 7am but we found the weather very bad indeed. In fact, the sea was (as sailors term it) running mountains high and we thought it only a waste of time to stay on the surface as it would have been impossible for us to do anything, so we decided to dive and dodge the *weather. We picked the patch up at sixty-three feet but we had a distinct motion so we knew it must have been very bad on the surface. We stayed down all that day and did not come up until 8am the next morning.*

We found a decided improvement in the weather so we ran along on our engines charging our batteries as we were doing so. At 10am we destroyed a Dhow which was on the beach by gunfire, but soon after the weather came on worse than ever and at 1pm we decided to dive again. This time there was a decided motion at eighty feet so you can bet is must have been very rough indeed up top.

During the night the weather eased right down and we came up at 7:30 the next morning, we ran on our engines toward the rendezvous and at 10am we met the E12. We told her the bad news about our fresh water and being "Chummy" she gave us about sixty gallons. This was a "Godsend" and that day we managed an extra, cup of water each. We ran out into the centre of the "Sea" and that afternoon we bathed, one boat looking out all the time the other was bathing. At 7:15, after making arrangements for the next day we separated and dived.

The next day was Sunday, the 17th of October and it -proved a real exciting Sunday. At 7am we signalled E12 on the submarine sounder and we both came to the surface. Our Captains had a short conference and decided to steam toward Constantinople. At 9am smoke was reported on the horizon and soon we could discern two distinct lots of smoke, so we steamed towards them. Soon we could make out two ships and, after a few minutes we could see through our glasses a large steamer being escorted by a gunboat. We immediately dived and cut the gunboat off but the steamer was too swift for us and she turned and ran for Constant. E12 was now on the surface but we were trying hard to get an attack in so that we might be able to fire a torpedo at the gunboat. She was zig sagging a great deal, but at 9:20 we got within range and fired a torpedo at her. She must have seen the torpedo fired for she altered her course immediately and it missed.

E12 was now on her engines and started to chase her on the surface, she had a four-inch gun and of course was more of a match for the gunboat, than we were with our little six pounder. Anyhow, not to be outdone, we came to the surface and joined in the chase. At about 10 o'clock E12 opened fire and those of us who were on our bridge saw her get a couple of good hits. This of course made the gunboat turn and she made direct for us, so thinking that "Discretion was the better part of valour", we immediately made ourselves scarce and dived to thirty feet. We heard the swish of her propellers and knew she had gone nearly over the top of us, so soon after we came up to look through our periscope. Now our Captain could see E12 in action with her and soon he told us that she was badly on fire and was running toward Mudania. He ran in on one side of the "Island of Kalamino" but we came up and ran in the other side to try and. cut her off. As soon as we sighted her again we altered in close to the land, but immediately two guns opened fire from the shore. This caused us to open out again, but for all that we were successful in cutting her off, for she turned again and started to run for "Pandermo". We had not seen E12 for some time now so thought she must be div-

ing and decided to signal the gunboats position on the submarine sounder.

We were quite right for E12 received our signal and started to fire as soon as she was in range. The gunboat was now burning very badly and both E12 and ourselves tried hard to cut her off from Pandermo but in this we were unsuccessful for she got inside and ran herself high and dry on the beach. E12 remained outside but we dived right into Pandermo but we couldn't get anywhere near the gunboat. We now decided to run further in and soon we saw a very large steamer that we found was moored on the inside of a stone jetty and it was almost an impossibility to get at her, anyhow the light was getting very bad so we dived out. We could not see E12 and at 9:30 we dived for the night.

We were on the surface the next morning at 7 o'clock but there was no sign of E12. Our Captain said she must have gone into Pandermo, so we didn't signal as we thought it would give her away, so we decided to wait outside for her. At half past nine we sighted a large sail, so we got underway on our engines immediately and gave chase. As soon as we were within range we put a round, across her bow, so she lowered her sails and "Hove to". She proved to be a pretty large Dhow with two masts and as she carried a boat we told her crew to lower it and get in it. We then ran alongside her and searched her. She carried a general cargo, so acting on orders we destroyed her. We made a fire in her forecastle and also in her after cabin and soon she was a blaze of fire fore and aft. It was rather a cheeky thing to do as we were we'll in sight of Pandermo but I think everyone must have had the "wind up" for no one came after us. We took some photos of the burning Dhow and then left her and we could see her crew well inside the mouth of Pandermo Harbour. At 11am we met E12 but she said she had been to the rendezvous and. not inside Pandermo. Soon after this we saw two TBDs coming out of Pandermo, but I think they sighted us, anyhow we didn't get a

chance to attack them, for they ran in again.

We now arranged with E12 that she should dive into Pandermo and try to torpedo the steamer we had seen secured to the jetty the night before. We were to run in on the surface as far as was deemed, safe and we were to watch and wait to see the effect of the explosion if their torpedo hit. Accordingly, we both ran in and I consider we were very cheeky indeed to go in as far as we did on the surface. We watched and waited but no explosion happened and soon we saw E12 dive out, as she told us afterward she could not get a shot in. We ran out on the surface and although we were quite close to the shore and must have been seen, no one interfered, with us, so I am certain that everyone in Pandermo that day must have been on the "All is Lost" side. At 9:15 we signalled our position to E12 and then we dived for the night. These last two days had been very exciting but we were beginning to get fed up for we really hadn't done anything great yet and we were howling for the lack of targets, but we had better times to come.

Operations In The Marmara

The next morning, we broke surface at 7am and went to meet E12. We met her and decided to separate and go to each end of the sea and give Pandermo a spell. We accordingly parted company, she going toward Constantinople and us toward the Marmora Channel. At noon smoke was reported and we ran towards it. It proved to be an enemy's gun boat, no we dived immediately and got a torpedo ready. We got a beautiful attack in and we certainly weren't seen. When we got within eight hundred yards we fired a torpedo and our Captain watched its course through the periscope. It ran straight for her and appeared to hit her amidships but there was no explosion, so we knew she must have been a very shallow draught vessel for our torpedo must have run under her. This was very disappointing for us, but I suppose they were entitled to as much luck as we were. Anyhow they carried on and as far as we know they never knew they had been attacked. To use our own Captain's words in his official report "It was a good attack and with a little luck we should have hit her". Nothing more of importance happened that day, so at 7pm we dived for the night. Our crew were very disappointed for up to the present we had fired three torpedoes and had only got one hit but the next day was to prove a great day for us and were given a chance to retrieve our fortunes.

We broke surface at 7am and found that the weather was rather rough and we decided to run into San Kioi to see if there was anything worth having a pop at. We dived well inside and found a glorious chance waiting for us for there were three steamers lying at anchor close into the shore and near the town. We only had one torpedo ready, so our Captain selected the biggest of the three ships for our first shot. She was a pretty big ship of about three thousand tons and she was quite a good target. She had three masts and from each there flew a Turkish flag, so we concluded that she must have had someone belonging to the Staff aboard her. Anyhow we took it that the flags meant she was carrying someone "pretty big". We get in a splendid attack on her and as we were not fired at until we had fired our first torpedo I should say that we weren't seen. At 11:40 we fired the torpedo and it ran straight and registered a "Hit amidships". Then followed a tremendous explosion, which blew us right up out of the water and shook the boat from stern to stern. As I have already said we had already had a hit when we fired a torpedo in Mudania, but the explosion was nothing to compare with this.

What made it worse was that we were not prepared for this tremendous upheaval, but anyhow we soon got the boat down to thirty feet and commenced to dive out. Our Captain's idea was that the ship must have been full up with explosives and that they were detonated by our torpedo. Anyhow she settled straight down and we were very busy getting another torpedo ready.

At 12:40 we returned, all ready for another splash and this time our Captain selected the next biggest ship. This ship was about two thousand tons and was quite a good target, but this attack was much more difficult for every time our periscope came out of the water for the Captain to get a look, we were fired at from the shore. At 1:30 being in a good position we fired another torpedo and this also registered a "Hit". This time we were more prepared for the shock of the explosion, but although this was a very heavy shock it was nothing to compare with the first one. We believe that this ship as well must have had a tremendous amount of explosive aboard, as the explosion was also very much heavier than the "Mudania" explosion. The shore batteries were continually firing at us now, but our Captain gave everyone a chance to see through the periscope, the amount of damage we had done. We could see the second ship settling down very rapidly, but all we could see of the first one was the tops of her mast from which still flew the Turkish flag.

We now dived out and got another torpedo ready after which we came in to look for more blood. The third ship was a much smaller ship than either of the others and our Captain said he thought she was a very doubtful shot. He said she must be very shallow draughted and he hardly thought her worth a torpedo. I don't think he would have fired only for the prompting of our second officer who said that three hits in one day would be worth blowing about. Anyhow we got a good attack in and fired from about six hundred yards range. Again, the torpedo ran straight, but this time there was no explosion, so we knew it was as the Captain had said she was very shallow draughted and our torpedo had run underneath her. Things were getting very hot now and we were continually fired at so we now decided to let "Well be" so we dived right out clear of "San Kioi". We then came to the surface and charged our batteries and at 7:30 we dived for the night. It was a far different crew that dived this boat that night than that which dived her the night before. Everyone seemed contented and we really were on jolly good terms with ourselves for our percentage of hits had gone up with a bang. We had a bit of a sing song that night and we came to the surface at 7:30 the next morning.

We were now out for more blood and we decided to dive into Karabuga Bay to see if there was anything worth looking at here. We dived right inside but we saw absolutely nothing, so we turned and ran out again. We came to the surface soon after noon and we could discern several Dhows but they all kept well into the land and well under the guns, so we could riot possibly get at them. We now ran on our engines toward Marmora Island, charging our batteries as we went and at 3:30 we dived and remained submerged until we were well through the Marmora Channel. We came up to charge at 6:30 and at 9 our batteries being right up we dived for the night. The next morning, we came up at 8 but we found the weather very rough again, so thinking it much more comfortable, we dived and shaped our course for the rendezvous. At 11 we signalled E12 on the submarine sounder and we learnt afterwards that she read us very easily. At noon we broke surface and after being on the surface for some time we sighted a submarine. At first, we thought this would be E12 but after a bit we could see she was a foreign looking boat and we dived in care she might be a "Fritz". Presently as we got nearer to her we could make her out to be a "Frenchman" and that she was one of the "Gem Class" so we rapidly came to the surface and made ourselves known.

This submarine turned out to be the "Turquoise" and she. was the first and I might say, the only French boat who successfully attempted the Dardanelles, end even then she was unfortunate enough to get caught in the Net on the way back on the day after we successfully passed down. We were very surprised to see her and we gave her our hearty congratulations for we were really very pleased to, at last see a French boat, for they had paid very dearly up to the present, with no success at all. At 4pm we met E12 she was also very surprised to see the "Turquoise". Soon after it began to blow up, so all three of us dived for the night.

The next morning, we were up at 8am and met E12 but we saw nothing of the "Turquoise". Our Captain now decided that we should go to the "Gallipoli" end of the Sea of Marmora and try to communicate with our Fleet. Accordingly, we got underway on our engines and ran in company, but at 10am we sighted two submarines on the horizon. This appeared very strange and thinking they may be enemies we both dived and ran toward them. Soon we could distinguish that the first of these strangers was an E boat and then we could see that the other was the "Turquoise". Not knowing whether E12 had also recognized these two boats and thinking that perhaps she would fire a torpedo at one of them we decided to signal on the submarine sounder and the signal we made was "H1 coming to the surface". We then came to the surface very rapidly and E12 having received our signal also came up. The E boat proved to be E20 and she had been sent up to relieve E12 who had already been in the "Sea of Marmora" considerably over a month. I would like to point out that, both of the new comers were very unlucky for they were both captured or rather sunk by the enemy. E20 in the "Sea of Marmora" and the "Turquoise" on her return down the Dardanelles. Both E12 and ourselves proved successful although E12 had about the worst

trip any
boat had who did not get captured.

E20 Was Fitted With A 6 Inch Gun

E12 went alongside E20 and after that she got ready
to go back. We ran with her to the Gallipoli end and
there she got in communication with our Fleet. Here
was a chance for us to send letters so we all got busy
and we passed our letters to E12 by means of a bottle
made fast to an heaving line. Anyhow although our
letters had a rotten trip E12 had the satisfaction of
delivering them alright. We were well in the centre
of a signal from the Fleet when we saw smoke ap-
proaching very rapidly and not wanting to give E12
away we both dived and as it was getting dark we de-
cided to remain down until the next morning.

We came up at 7:30 and E12 again got into commu-
nication and we received a signal to say that we were
at war with Bulgaria and that our Fleet had played
up havoc and had bombarded Dedeagach. Soon after
this we said "Good bye" to our "Chummy Boat" and
left her to make the dash. As I have already men-
tioned this proved an awful time for her, for al-
though she eventually did get through it was only
"just". What really happened to her was, she fouled
one of the upright wires of the net which dragged
her to over two hundred feet. The wire was jammed
between her forward hydroplane and the hull of the
boat, which made it impossible for the hydro-planes
to be used. She at last broke away by blowing water
from her tanks and going full speed ahead but she
simply dragged one of the mooring anchors with her

until she reached shallower water. The anchor took on the bottom again and once more she was dragged down and they thought she had fouled another net. Eventually she got away again and arrived at Cape Helles, but when she came to the surface she had used all her compressed air and the electric batteries were run down so low that her lights only just flickered.

After leaving E12 our Captain decided to find a quiet spot where we could open up our hatches and ventilate the boat, so we ran into "Artaki". There was nothing in there and after placing good "Look Outs" we opened our hatches and started both engines. This of course dragged fresh air down as the engine sucked the foul air out. We carried on this for about an hour and the boat new being quite fresh we decided to have a long night. As we were in shallow water we went to the bottom and this was the only occasion we rested on the bottom during the trip.

We came on the surface at 7:30 the next morning and had a good look round "Artaki" but there was nothing there, so we decided to dive into "San Kioi" again to see if there was any more luck. We dived in about 10 o'clock but there was nothing fresh. We could see the ships we had sunk on the 20th, the second ship having her funnels and superstructure showing, but the first ship only had three masts. As there was nothing to do here we dived out at noon and came to the surface when we were well clear of the land. At 1:30 smoke was reported so we dived again and steered towards it. Soon we could make out a large steamer, but as she got closer we could distinguish by her markings that she was a hospital ship.

She was a fine big ship, but we remained submerged until she was out of sight for we thought she might give us away. At 2:30 we sighted a fine Dhow and we came to the surface very close to her. Her only occupants proved to be a grey headed old. Turk and. a small boy of about seven years. The old man was in a terrible panic and. the boy cried pitifully. I can assure you I had a big lump in my throat when I saw the boy's tears and we did our best to quiet his fears. Of course, we let them go and the youngster soon dried his tears. The old man called down blessings on us and. hoisting his sail he waved his hand to us, as he sailed away. We talked a good deal about this in-cident, for the best part of us were married and the youngster's tears had touched our hearts. We now ran on the surface toward the rendezvous but as there was no sign of E20 we dived for the night.

We came up at 7:30 the next morning and at about 10.0 we sighted a sail. There was a good breeze and he was going very fast and we had to go "all out" on both engines to get onshore near her. As soon as we were within range we fired a round across her bow and she "Hove to". When we got close to her we could see there was a great deal of panic going on and presently we were close enough to see that she car-ried a whole crowd of women. The only male aboard was an old man who was at the helm. We hailed her but the women absolutely got in a state of terror and our Captain decided not to go too close to her for he thought they would have jumped overboard. We did our best to quiet them and told the old man that he could get underway again. We took photos of her and. I can picture those women blessing us now. They were a bit too previous with the blessings for just as they were getting underway up bobbed the "Turquoise". All the yelling end crying was now renewed, I think that they just have thought that the sea was infested with submarines. We told the "Turquoise" to let her go and they once more started to bless us. I believe that these women were refugees running from Constant and, I believe at the time the Turks wore nearly down and out. We now closed on the Turquoise, who told us in broken English that E20 had been shelled by a sailing ship, who was armed, with two guns. We knew now we must be very careful of these Dhows and we always gave them a round before we went alongside then. We left the Turquoise soon after and dived inside of the "Island of Kalamino. We saw nothing, so we dived out and. came to charge. When our batteries were fully charged we dived for the night.

We broke surface at 7am the next day which was the 27th, but soon after dived and set our course to pass through the "Marmora Channel". At 8am we sighted smoke and presently we could distinguish a large steamer being escorted by a gunboat. The gunboat was zig zagging and. covering the steamer, but we could see that they were both making for Pandermo.

We were a long way away from them and it was going to be a difficult job to intercept them, so we dived to fifty feet and increased our speed to "Full" which would be just over eleven knots. We carried on this speed until 9am and then we came up for a look we found the gunboat only three hundred yards away and she was making straight for us. We dived very quickly to forty feet and heard her pass over us and then we came up for another look. We found the steamer very close into shore and the gunboat about six hundred yards away. She altered course just then and as she passed our bow we fired a torpedo. We could not get a look to see how the torpedo ran but *we listened to hear if there was an explosion and, as there wasn't, we knew it must have missed. We kept on with the off chance of cutting either of them off and also with the hope of getting another shot. In this we were unsuccessful for they both managed to get into Pandermo. Our Captain said in his report that the gunboat was doing a "Splendid zig zag" and that it was a very difficult attack. We dived into "Pandermo", but we found the steamer had gone inside the Mole and it was nearly impossible to get at her. We now tried another attack on the gunboat, but she kept up this "Splendid zig zag" and as we had the sun in our eyes we had to give her up. Our Captain was very disappointed as he said the steamer was a very large one and would probably be about 5,000 tons. We now proceeded to the rendezvous and met E20, we told her what had happened since we last met and then dived for the night.*

We came up at 7 in the morning and as the weather was very fine, we went alongside E20. They told us that they had taken in a signal which we had made on the submarine sounder to E12 before she went down, although E20 must have been at least forty-five miles away. We hardly believed this but sometime after she read a signal distinctly thirty miles away.
We suggested to E20 that she should dive into Pandermo to see if it was possible for her to have a shot at the steamer with her beam tubes. We were not fitted with beam tubes, or we should have had another go ourselves. She dived in about 9am but at 11:30 she came out again and told us it was impossible to get close enough in and there was no earthly chance of torpedoing her.

The Captain was not to be put off though and he decided to hang around until she did come cut. She certainly had outwitted us and had got in alright, but we were still after her blood. We parted company with E20 end after she was gone, our Captain thought we would go into Pandermo. Accordingly, we dived in and we could, easily see the steamer who was being loaded alongside the Mole. The Turks had made a very effective screen for her, for they had moored an Hospital Ship to her and we could see them unloading wounded from her. Our Captain said it was of no use trying to get her unless they shifted the Hospital Ship so we dived out again. After charging our batteries we dived for the night.

That night the Captain told me that he had worked a scheme out by which we should be able to dive in and torpedo the steamer, but he said there was a possible chance that it would fail. He said if it did fail he didn't intend to fire, because we had only one torpedo left and he meant to get a hit with this. He said if the plan failed, he meant to come out and go in on the surface at night and then torpedo her and chance being able to dive out. I am pleased to say the first scheme worked and we didn't have to go in on the surface. I am afraid we would have had a jolly rough time if we had.

We cane up at 7:30 in the morning and soon after we dived into "Pandermo". We saw the Hospital Ship coming out and we kept well clear of her. We found our charts very incorrect and we touched bottom several times when we oughtn't but by skirting the seven-fathom line we managed to get in a. very good position. We touched bottom at thirty feet and at once came up. We fired our last torpedo and it ran straight for the mark, hitting the steamer on the starboard bow. We immediately altered course and dived into deep water, but only just in time for with thirty-five feet showing on the depth gauge we heard a TBD pass over the top of us. There proved to be the two of them and they were certainly after our blood for they continually passed backwards and forwards over the top of us. It was some time before we could get rid of them, but at last we managed it and feeling very pleased with ourselves we dived out. In the Captain's report he said we were continually harassed by smaller boats and it was a very difficult attack. The steamer war: a large one, probably five thousand tons but we did not get the chance to find out the exact amount of damage done as she was lying in shallow water. We had now got rid of all of our torpedoes and we thought we hadn't done badly by getting half of them to hit.

Now we set to work to get our boat ready for the trip back. Before we dived that night, we signalled E20 on the submarine sounder and told her our good luck in Pandermo. She was over thirty miles away but she read quite easily and the next day when we met her, she gave it to us by semaphore, so we could no longer doubt that it was possible to signal so many miles with the submarine sounder. In each case when long distance signals were read both boats were at sixty feet, so that proved a good conductor for sound.
We came to the surface at 7:45 the next morning and ran on our engines toward the rendezvous to meet E20. At about 9 we sighted a sail and had to put on to Full Speed to intercept her. When we got her within range we fired a shot across her bow, but we were very surprised to see her crew lower a boat

and abandon their ship without taking in sail. You can easily guess that we had some job to get alongside her and she repeatedly ran off on different tacks as though there was someone at her helm. Eventually we managed to get our bow very near her and a couple of our crew jumped aboard her.

These men cut the halyards which kept the sails up and down the sails came with a run. She now of course "Hove to" and we ran alongside her. She was a. pretty large Dhow and she was loaded with a general cargo of merchandise. Her crew, as I have already said, had abandoned her so we set fire to her, both ends and she made a good bonfire. We were now employed in getting ready for the trip back and at about 11 we met E20. We told her that we had expended all our "Tin fish" and that we proposed to go back so she came with us to the Gallipoli end of the sea, so that she could, communicate with the Fleet and let them know we were coming down. On our run down the Sea of Marmora we saw nothing, so we stopped off San Kioi and E20 got up her wireless mast and got through to our guard ship. She told, our Admiral that we proposed coming down the next day and we got an answer to say that E12 had had a great deal of trouble - which I have already outlined - and our best way back was fifty yards from the shore. This didn't appear to be right at all, so our Captain consulted his charts and said he would, use his own discretion, as to the course he would go down on.

Soon after this we sighted an aeroplane coming straight for us, so not knowing whether she was a friend or an enemy we decided to dive. E20 didn't dive, but perhaps it was a good job that either she was not sighted, which wouldn't have been very probably, or else the plane was one of our own.

Anyhow as there was a good setting sun, our Captain decided to swing our compass on the courses which we would, be steering the next day on our passage through the Dardanelles.
While we were doing this, we got about a couple of miles away from E20, so that when we came to the surface we didn't think it worthwhile to close her. Now we were very surprised to see E20 flashing to us by means of her cruiser arc lamp and she made a signal to us which read "Good bye and God Luck". Our Captain was very angry about this for we were very near the shore and he said that he gave the Turks enough "Common Sense" to have been able to read, the signal as well as us. He also said, that he wouldn't have gone down the next day only for the fact that, the Fleet had been informed and an escort would, be bound to have been told off to meet us. That night we dived, at 8pm.

We only came up for an half hour or so the next morning and. then started our return dive shortly after 6. This trip did not prove quite so exciting as our trip up, but for all that, it proved exciting enough.

At 7:20 we could see the day breaking and it looked as though it was going to be an ideal day for our trip, as there was just a slight ripple on the water and this is just what is required when coming up for a look through the periscope.

Soon after this we sighted the Eski Tamar Burmi light and we eased our speed to four knots. At 8pm we sighted a gunboat, but being that we were not out for blood this time, we avoided her and at 8:30 we sighted Gallipoli. Lying close into the shore we could see another gunboat and also some small sailing ships but still we were not seen.

At 8:44 we got a good bearing of the Chardap Burmi Light and saw three more sailing ships which we successfully avoided.

Things now went on very nicely until 10:20 when we had trouble with our port motor, so we decided to stop it until we reached the net, when we would use it if required. Accordingly, we continued the run on our Starboard motor, but this made a lot of difference to our steering and sometimes we had.to have our helm "Hard Over" to keep the boat on her course. At 11:09 we came up for an observation and saw a large Hospital Steamer so we dived very quickly to forty feet.

At 11:23 we came up to fix our position and also to try and get an observation of the net, but as soon as our periscope cane out of the water, I received the order to dive as quickly as possible to forty feet. What was the matter, was that a TBD had been waiting for us in a position where she knew we would have to come up for an observation and it has always been in my mind, that the reason she was there was because E20's Good Bye signal had been read ashore. As soon as I received the order to dive quickly, I gave the boat "Hard to Dive" helm and we simply shot down, but only just in time for the TBD passed, over us with only twenty-five feet showing on our depth gauge, so it is a "dead cert" that if she had passed directly over our "Conning Tower" that she would have hit us.

This was a very bad stroke of luck for us for we didn't get the necessary observation and we had to chance to luck, when and how, we were going to hit the net. Luck must have been with us this time for at 11.36 we struck the net at eighty feet and easily went through it. Our First Lieutenant was in the Conning Tower looking through the port holes and he said he could see the net quite easily. His account of the net was that it was made of steel hawsers (wire), those running up and down being six inches and those running across three inches. This you will see was a very formidable obstruction and being that we had only one motor and our speed was only seven knots, I think we did very well to make such a light job of it. As soon as we were through we came up for a look knowing that the TBD would be on the other side of the net.

We fixed our position and dived to eight feet again. We now dived at various depths, coming up occasionally to have a look, at other times diving deep to avoid the minefields and also say other obstruction that may have been placed for us. At 2:30 we came up and found Siddul Bahr on our starboard bow and we could easily make out our destroyer patrol, which was kept at the mouth of the Dardanelles.

Soon after this we came to the surface very rapidly, blowing all our tanks and coming right up out of the water. We quickly hoisted the "White Ensign" and turned to round Cape Helles. We were immediately sighted, by a French TBD who thinking we were an enemy come straight for us. She soon saw the "White Ensign" and we could hear orders being given on board her and soon after the whole crew came on deck and cheered lustily.

We stopped quite close to the wreck of the "Majestic", but we were fired at by the enemy from the Asiatic side, so we shifted our position another half a mile away.

We got tons of congratulations from our TBDs on patrol, who were very curious to know what our "Bag" was. One of them lowered a boat and sent us some fresh bread and also a ham, which you can easily guess was very acceptable.

At 3:30 the destroyer "Basilisk" arrived to escort us to "Kephalo" and it was about 4.0 o'clock when we arrived there. We had a very hearty welcome and every ship from the largest battleship to the smallest TBs and Monitors gave us three (I think it must have been thirty-three) cheers.

We now went alongside the "Triad" who was flying the flag of the Commander in Chief, Admiral de Robeck.

I believe every ship in the harbour sent signals of congratulations and also asked if they could in any possible way do anything for the comfort of our Crew. To these signals we replied, thanking them but telling them also that the "Triad" was doing all the feeding and also the washing. As soon as our boat was secured, we went on board the "Triad." and enjoyed a hot bath and when it is remembered that we hadn't even washed for about three weeks, you will easily see it was a luxury. I must say when we went into the ship we looked an awful mob, but in a couple of hours, after the water and razors had been to work, there was a. real transformation.

We now sat down to a square meal and enjoyed it, for we had been on tinned food for over a north and it was a real treat to get our teeth into something fresh and you can bet it was even better to be able to drink as much as you wanted and only think of the three cupful's we had been having.

Out of all the congratulations we received I think the crew appreciated the Admiral's most, for it was accompanied by a bottle of beer for each man.

Pathfinder Back To Malta And A Return To Uk

Our return trip through the Dardanelles took place on Sunday the 31st of October, 1915, by this you will see that we did practically the whole of the month of October 1915 in the "Sea of Marmora", a worthy feat for such a. small boat as an 'H' boat.

In the Captain's official report, he says "The boat dived admirably throughout, but owing to her being only on one motor, "Full Helm" had often to be used to keep the boat on her course in "current Eddies". No obstruction other than the net was felt, but to give us as much chance as possible, the "Forward Hydroplanes" were kept turned in the whole of the passage and the boat was dived only by her "After Rudders".

Then followed the Captains recommendation for the different members of the crew, but his final recommendation said. "The whole of the crew behaved admirably although at times in a queer fix and it was only because of their splendid behaviour that such a successful trip was made".

For work done in connection with our month in the "Sea of Marmora", the Captain was decorated with the Distinguished Service Order and myself with the Distinguished Service Medal, but I consider that we only wear the decorations that rightly belong to the whole crew.

The next day we left "Kephalo" escorted by the destroyer "Scourge" and proceeded to Mudros. We arrived in the afternoon and had another hearty welcome. We secured to the "Adamant" our parent ship about 2:50 and we got the good news, we were leaving for Malta the next day, if our Captain could finish his report. It meant him working the best part of the night to finish this but he managed it and we left on the 3rd. of November in company with E14 and the SS Florian. We took the best part of four days getting to Malta as we encountered rough weather, but we arrived at daybreak on the 7th of November.

During our stay at Malta there is very little of interest worth recording, but needless to say we had a good time. All our defects were made good, which meant that our forward battery had to come out of the boat, to enable the dockyard workmen to repair our battery tank. We had a new set of wireless gear fitted and early in December we went to sea to enable us to carry out trials. We then returned to Malta and we spent Christmas and the New Year there.

On Sunday, 2nd January 1916, we again left Malta. This time we were in company with the "SS Homer City". I don't know for certain whether she was escorting us, or whether we were escorting her. I should think it would be the latter for she wasn't armed in any way and all she was carrying was the Christmas mail for the Fleet. In her holds were hundreds of bags of parcels and being that people at home would insist on sending such things as oranges and apples, to the Mediterranean, you can guess that by this time some of them had begun to smell high. It would have been another fortnight or so before they would be delivered, so goodness only knows what they would be like when they were delivered.

We were now, all looking forward, to another trip in the "Marmora" but it was not to be, for although we were fitted up much better, we didn't get the chance, for the Dardanelles job was packed up before we arrived there, in fact we didn't get as far as Mudros.

The day after leaving Malta, the weather changed and it blew up very rough. We eased down to "Dead Slow", but even then it was so bad that we bad to batten down and. navigate the boat from below. This business is anything but comfortable, for with the engine running and only a small ventilator to supply the air, we soon got a very foul atmosphere and besides this we have to stick being thrown about a good deal. It takes a good sailor to stick this and some of the younger members of the crew suffered very badly from seasickness. The next morning the weather eased up a great deal and we were very pleased to be able to open up the Conning Tower Hatch. We now navigated the boat from the bridge and we were able to proceed a bit faster. Things went on alright until the morning of the 5th of January and then it began to blow up again, by noon it had got very bad indeed and we had to abandon the bridge once more, but only after having our bridge screen torn to ribbons and the bridge stantions bent up very badly. We had to ease right down again and the most we could do was five knots

During the night it eased down again and we once more went up on the bridge and at 3 o'clock in the morning watch, we met the light cruiser "Foresight". She told us that we were not to go to Mudros, but that we were to go into Milos and await an escort to take us to a new patrol but where this was to be we didn't know.

We altered course and at 10am we arrived at Milos. We were very surprised to find that the harbour had been netted in and that the French had established quite a big naval base. We anchored quite near to the French flagship and waited to see what news we could get.

We got no real news until January 12th when a small ship named the "Folkestone" arrived. She told us that she had been sent as an escort for us and that our new patrol was to be the "Adriatic". She also told us that, we had evacuated the Peninsular, very successfully, but that we had given the "Sea of Marmora" job up. This wasn't very good news for us, for we all thought that our fleet would have been able to force the Dardanelles and we were also looking forward to another trip up ourselves.

We had orders to remain at "Milos" until the 14th and on that date we left at 7am with our escort. As soon as we were clear of the land the weather came on rough again, but this time we were far better off than our "Escort" for she made very bad work of it, in fact she made such bad weather of it that we ran for "Cape Matapan" and got right in under the lee of the land.

We made four attempts to leave but it was not until 8pm that we were really got underway again. Anyhow we had a jolly rotten night but managed to stick it and in. the morning it cleared off. We arrived at Gallipoli "Italy", the next afternoon at 2pm.

There were several. Italian TBs in here and we secured alongside one of these. We filled up with fresh water and also provisions and left the next day with another escort, this time an Italian TB, for Brindisi at 6pm. We found lots of French and Italian ships and also submarines and we found that we were to run patrols with those.

I won't burden you with the details of the patrols we were put on, but we did plenty of sea time and only on one occasion did we see anything like an enemy. We did eight; or nine days on patrol, but in the middle we used to run into Barletta for one night. Soon after vie arrived in the Adriatic, other British submarines arrived and afterward the "Adamant" arrived.

I will relate the incident in which we did see an enemy, to the best of my ability. It was at the time that we were evacuating "Durazzo" and we were sent over to see if anything was being transported by water. We left Brindisi on the 20th February and at about 10am we dived. We dived toward "Durazzo" and. at noon we sighted an enemy's submarine. I didn't know what it was- that we had sighted, but I knew by the way our Captain was working the periscope that he had something in line. It was just after noon and I had been relieved by the second Coxswain at the diving wheel, but hearing the periscope going up and down, I again went in the control room. I then asked the Captain if there was something doing and he replied "Yes, I think: you had better get the crew to action stations". This I did as soon as possible and soon the order came to flood the torpedo tubes. I asked the Captain whether I should take her down after he had fired, but he said "No, I think we will come on the surface, that is if the torpedo runs alright". We get in a splendid attack and we got right in to eight hundred yards range and still we were not seen. "Stand By", "Fire" came the orders in quick succession and seeing that the torpedo was running straight, the captain now gave the order, "Blow 3 and 4", "Surface". We came up very quickly and our Captain watched his torpedo run straight for the submarine.

It appeared to hit just before the conning tower under her gun but there was no explosion. "Flood 3 and 4", "take her down" and this we did as quickly as possible. We were very lucky to get down as quick as we did for the submarine fired a torpedo at us but in this case it whizzed over the top of us. You will see that we were very lucky and they were very lucky also, for his torpedo had run over us and ours had run under them due in neither case to us who had fired. It was a bit of bad luck us missing as we did, but still I suppose they were entitled to as much luck as we were. Our captain says it was a "boat a good deal larger than us and she was laying on the surface, not moving at all, the reason he came on the surface was that he saw his torpedo was going to hit *and he thought he would, save as much life as he could. The captain was very disappointed as he said if he had known the torpedo was going to miss he could have rammed her quite easily. We now came up to look but the enemy had dived and. as we didn't think it wise to hang around here we made our way back to Brindisi and reported the occurrence. It was a very disappointed crew that took H1 back to Brindisi for we knew it was absolute bad luck which caused us not to have another hit to our credit.*

Some days after this, H4 returned from patrol end reported firing two torpedoes at an enemy's submarine but in both cases the torpedo ran underneath. This led to experiments being carried out at Malta by H2 who happened to be there. These experiments proved our statements to be correct, for each torpedo fired, when picked up again was found to have had its balance chamber blown in by the force of the air discharge which is used to expel the torpedo. This caused an order to be sent round to say that all torpedoes of that mark, were to be returned to have their balance chambers strengthened.

Soon after this H3 was lost with all hands. How she was lost I don't suppose we ever shall find out, but she left to go on patrol and did not return to harbour. I lost some of my best pals in this boat for it will be remembered she was the boat which gave us all the trouble in crossing the Atlantic.

On returning from patrol on the 29th March, I found a relief had been sent out from England for me and that I was to go home for a bigger boat of which there was plenty building. I didn't leave Brindisi until the 10th of April and then I travelled over land through Italy and France arriving at Fort Blockhouse on the 14th of April 1916.

The next few months passed with no items of interest which are worth recording. I was employed as an instructor in submarine work, to the new ratings who were joining the Submarine Service, to make good the loss of the brave lads who had already given their lives for King
and Country.

Back In England

In October, I was drafted to "HMS Vernon" the torpedo school at Portsmouth, where I underwent a course of instructions for the rank of "Torpedo Coxswain". The reason I had to do this course was, because I had been selected as a suitable man for a "K" Class of submarine. As these boats were to be "Self-Contained" it was necessary to have a Torpedo Coxswain, who being qualified in Ship's Steward's work, would be able to victual his crew without assistance from a parent ship

The Loss Of K13

I joined K13 in December and she was being completed at the Fairfield Shipbuilding Company, Govan, Glasgow. She was a fine big boat, being 340 feet long and 26 feet in the beam. Her gun armament was two four-inch guns and one three-inch anti-aircraft gun. Her torpedo armament was four bow tubes and four beam tubes, all submerged and two upper deck beam tubes. These tubes were all for eighteen-inch torpedo of which we would carry twenty

She was a departure from any boat I had already been in, for she was driven by steam when on the surface. This of course has its disadvantages as well as its advantages, as it is necessary to have large air intakes to the boiler room and, also funnels. These have to be shut and as it is a pretty big job. It takes some time and the quickest time I have known a "K" Boat to dive in is four minutes

On the surface her turbines would be used and they were capable of driving her at twenty-five knots, while submerged she would be driven by electric motors, which were capable of propelling her at ten knots. Her submerged displacement was over two thousand tons, so you will see by this description that she was a very powerful boat. Her crew consisted of fiftyseven and she was commanded by one of our most distinguished and experienced officers, Lieutenant Commander Godfrey Herbert DSO

The end of December saw the crew all up and we were on trials and the whole of the month of January, we were employed doing trials of some sort. All our trials so far went off splendidly and we were very pleased with our boat

January the 29th was the day selected for us to leave the Fairfield Yard to do our Acceptance Trials and it proved a fatal one. We started very badly for just after leaving the Yard, our steering gear gave out and. we ran high and dry on the banks of the

Clyde. We soon had two powerful tugs alongside us and with their assistance, we managed to get off although we had to be towed stern first until we got to a wider spot where it was possible to turn round. We now continued our journey down the Clyde and at 10am we entered the "Gare-Loch"

The "Gare-Loch" had been selected as a suitable spot for submarines to do their trials and it really was a good place, for there was no traffic of any sort and yet there was plenty of water to dive in

On our arrival we "Shut off for Diving" and we now did our Acceptance Trials. Things went off very well indeed, so at 12 o'clock we came up for dinner

Our captain being quite satisfied with the boat now took her over and the Fairfield Manager was put ashore at "Shandon"

We now had our dinner in a small steamer called the "Comet" end while we were at dinner our captain decided to have another dive during the afternoon. As the boilers had been lit up by the firm's people, our captain sent orders that everything was to be shut off and everything was to be got ready for diving as soon as the dinner hour was over

Now comes the darkest hours of my life, for although the incident has been written about by a good many writers, I have never read a good description. Nobody really understands what happened and I consider it impossible to write a real account of a thing unless you were there and being that I was unfortunate enough to be there, I am to my best ability going to describe it. I am going to give my opinion and my own version of the affair and, in no way am

I going to exaggerate so if you can picture something worse than you are reading, you may in some way understand what the poor fellows who came out of K13 suffered

As near as I can remember it was about 2 o'clock on the afternoon of Monday, the 29th of January 1917, when we did the fatal dive. Quite in the ordinary way the order had been passed, "Hands to diving stations" and everyone had been at their allotted stations. I should say at least ten minutes before any orders were given for flooding tanks or working the electric motors

Before the "Comet" had cast off she had taken on board every one of the firm's people who had nothing special to do and so that afternoon we dived with a great many less that we did in the forenoon

Everything had been reported "Shut Off". All the hatches had been reported closed and the electric indicator in the Control Room, which is switched on from the Engine Room was illuminated and the words "Engine Room Shut Off" could be read distinctly

At last came the fatal orders for diving. They were simply "Half speed, ahead both" and "Flood all externals". The motors were started and the vents for the ballast tanks were opened and then the order was given "Take her down". The necessary helm was given on the hydroplane and the after diving rudders and she started to go very slowly

I was watching the bubble which tells the inclination of the boat, so I can hardly be certain what the gauge read, but I believe it was eleven feet when we got a terrible pressure on our ears. From experience we know that something very large had been left open and that water must be coming in very quickly

Our captain realized this instantly and gave the orders, "Blow all external tanks", "Close water tight doors", "Hard to rise", "Try to fetch her to the surface"

These orders were carried, out as quickly as possible. Air from our High-Pressure System was put on the Ballast Tanks.

The water tight doors were closed and our helms were put over to rise, but all to no avail, instead of coming to the surface K13 sank to the bottom of the Gare-Loch like a stone and the pointers of our depth gauges were pointing to seventy-eight feet

In the corner of the Control Room, near the Switchboard, is a group of voice pipes running to all the compartments aft and water simply rushed through these as though from a fire hydrant, so we know that she must be flooded from the beam tube room to the stern, which would be roughly two thirds of the boat

We worked the telegraphs which led from the control room to the motor room and also the engine room, but we got no answer and we knew that everybody abaft the beam tube room must be drowned.

What made things a great deal worse, was the water pouring over the switchboard. As the switchboard was alive with electricity, the salt water caused fire, gas and smoke and we were nearly choked before we could stop the water and put the fire out

The scene is very hard to describe and nobody can imagine what it really was like. My description is that it was like an inferno, with men fighting for their lives, battling with the water and trying to beat out the flames with pieces of sacking which had been torn up from the battery boards. At last success attended our efforts and the water was stopped are the fire put out, but you can guess what the air was like. We had the full pressure of air from the flooded compartments, which of course had come in before we could get the water tight doors closed and besides this the air was very foul with smoke and gas which had come from the switch-board

The excitement had now died down and it can easily be seen that we were in a very sorry plight indeed. There was not a bit of panic and everyone was taking things as coolly as the circumstances could warrant, but for all that, I am afraid there was some very heavy hearts among us, for it certainly did look like death

Everything was now as quiet as the grave and we simply looked at one another and then we began to look around to see if there was any chance or any possible means to escape from this "Death Trap". There certainly seemed to be very little cause for hope and in our own hearts each man knew, in all probability, that "K13" would be our tomb

I will now leave K13 on the bottom of the Gare-Loch and relate what I have since found out, happened on the surface

There were two other submarines of the E Class, E50 and E51, doing trials on the Gare-Loch and the captain of one of these, "Lieutenant Michell", was watching us dive. He knew by the way we went down and also by the way the volumes of air came out of us, that something very wrong had happened. He waited a few minutes to see if we should come to the surface and then as we didn't he anchored his submarine and decided to look for us. Accordingly, he got a small pulling boat and went to the spot where he saw us disappear and with the help of a "Lead and Line", he sounded for us and found us

The next thing to do was to get help, so he immediately went back to his boat and by wireless sent messages to the Senior Naval Officers of the Clyde district for help. It so happened that a salvage steamer was at Greenock and she was despatched with two hoppers to the spot to render assistance

Captain Barttelot was the SNO of the Clyde and he was very quickly on the spot to take charge. As soon as possible divers were sent down and on Tuesday morning we in the boat knew help was at hand, for we could hear a diver walking about on the hull of the boat. You can guess we were very much relieved to know that we had been found and we were now wondering what they would do. We knew what a big job they would have especially as they didn't know under what circumstances we were, neither did they know how much of the boat was flooded. Our only chance was to get into some kind of communication with then and. this we tried to do by making signals in the "Morse" code, which we did by tapping the hull of the boat. We got no answers and afterwards I found out that although the diver could easily hear the tapping he had no knowledge of the "Morse" code and could not receive our signals. Anyhow, those who were working on us knew that there were men alive inside the boat and this of course made them put every ounce of energy into their task

Eventually the difficulty in getting signals through was overcome, to a certain extent. The method now employed was, a signalman with a lead line in a small boat. He simply made the signals by raising and lowering the lead and a diver was employed below just guiding it. The way our signals were received was by means of a hydrophone. Of course, this was a very crude method, but although it took hours to get a signal through it certainly relieved the situation a bit

It will be seen that the task of raising K13 was going to be a very difficult one and Captain Barttelot decided that the first thing to try and do, was to save the crew, or rather those of the crew who were still alive in K13
He therefore decided to give us air. Not air to breathe but to blow our ballast tanks with. He gave orders for one of the E Boats to be moored, very close to us and she was to be employed running her air compressor and give us air into our H.P. system. A flexible pipe was taken from her compressor and the diver connected this to our forward four-inch Gun connection, which was already connected to our High Pressure System. It was some time before the diver succeeded, but at last it was finished and the E boat started to pump air into us.

I expect a good many of my readers will be asking why the air wasn't pumped, into the boat to breathe?

Well the reason is this, inside the boat we already had a tremendous amount of pressure, but there was no means of telling the amount, as we had no barometer to measure it. We ran our low-pressure compressorfrom time to time to take air out of the boat, but after a bit we considered it unwise, for the simple reason we didn't know whether we had taken the pressure down to normal or not. Of course, we found afterwards that there was still a tremendous pressure, but we thought it wise to leave things as they were, for the present at any rate.

Another reason we didn't use the LP compressor is, that it is run by the same motor which runs the Ballast pump and we needed the pump very badly. This motor can either be clutched into the compressor or the pump, but only one thing can be run at a time and as the pump was most needed, we kept it clutched in, the best part of the time

Our biggest trouble was the watertight bulkhead between the boiler room and the beam tube room. This was leaking very badly and it will easily be seen why it did leak. This was only a collision bulkhead and was tested to a pressure of fifteen pounds and as we were below seventy feet, the pressure on the bulkhead would be thirtyfive pounds, so we must think ourselves very lucky it held as well as it did

We knew this water must be kept down and the only way to do this was by keeping the pump running continually. If this water could not be kept down it meant flooding the control room, where our electric batteries were and if salt water reached these batteries, it would immediately cause chlorine gas and this would have suffocated us all in a few minutes

It was on Tuesday morning that our Captain, after

a discussion with Commander Goodhart, the Captain of K14, decided that if we were to be saved it was necessary for someone to get out of the boat and let those who were working on the surface, know exactly how things were inside the boat and, also, to let them know exactly what we wanted them to do

To make myself more clear I had better point out the reason that Commander Goodhart, was on board of K13. He was the captain of K14 and that boat was under construction at Fairfield's Yard, where K13 had been built and he, with his engineer, had decided to do a run in K13 to pick up anything in the way of information, which would afterward be of use to them in their own boat. K14 was to be exactly the same as K13 so you will see that these two officers, did a wise thing in having a run in a sister boat. Commander Goodhart had very recently come home from the Baltic where he had been in command of an E boat and had done particularly good work, for which he had been decorated with the Distinguished Service Order, he had also received The Order of St George
from the Russian government.

K13 The Rescue Part 1

Now to get on with my story. These two brave officers (Godfrey & Goodhart) decided that one of them must get out of the boat and they also decided that no one should risk themselves in any way for them-

selves. They worked, out their own scheme, which was to go out through the Conning Tower and they did the bulk of the work themselves also. Inside the Conning Tower is the magnetic compass and this is inside a large metal dome. This is what they proposed to use as on airlock as it was plenty big enough for two men to get under. The magnetic compass was taken down and all the electric leads running through the conning tower were taken down also. When the holes through which these leads had been taken were plugged with small wooden plugs so that the tower was again made water tight. The next thing to do was to run a length of copper pipe from the "Whistle Pipe", which came off the HP system and fit valves to it. These were taken down from another part of the boat and the reason they were fitted was so that they could control their own air.

It took me hours to complete the work but, at last, it was finished to their own satisfaction and now I will relate as far as possible what this scheme was.

They were both to go into the conning tower, which is fitted with a hatch at the bottom as well as the top. We were then to close the lower lid and await four taps. Herbert was then to open the top lid of the Conning Tower, sufficient to allow water to come in slowly. He was then to go under the airlock with Goodhart and wait until the tower was flooded. He was then to go out into the water and throw back the lid and then get back into the airlock. They were to mutually arrange a time, when Herbert would open the air valve and allow a volume to come out and Goodhart was to try and go out in the bubble. This, of course, would be a far more difficult task in a "K" Boat than any other submarine, as they have *wheelhouses built over the Conning Tower and it would mean that he would have to get out of one of the doors, which were not direct above the conning tower but in the after end of the wheelhouse. After Goodhart had gone, Herbert was then to close the top lid and get back under the airlock, he would then give us the four taps which I have already spoken about and we would drain the conning tower down into the bilges. When the tower was dry we would open the lower lid and Herbert would come back into the boat again.*

This, of course, was what was really meant to happen, but what did happen I will try to explain, using the Captain's own version of the trying ordeal as well as what I saw happen myself.

Both men were ready and I can picture now as I am writing this, these two brave officers. Two of the bravest men it is possible to meet. What a picture, Goodhart was dressed, in his shirt, pants and sea boots and Herbert was dressed in his shirt, cap and sea boots. The sea boots were worn on my advice, knowing that he was to come back into the boat and also knowing how difficult it is for one to keep his feet when standing in water, unless he is weighted, at the feet. Goodhart carried in his hand a sealed tin tube, in which was a message, saying how we were placed and also saying what we wanted. The last thing we heart Goodhart say was, "If I don't get up this tin tube ought to".

Herbert now said, "I think everything is ready now", "I think we will try". He then took off his wrist watch which he handed to the second coxswain, at the same time making this remark, "I might ask you for that later on".

These two brave officers now went into the conning tower and we closed the lower lid.

That was the last I ever saw of Goodhart. Poor fellow he was killed while doing his very utmost to save our lives. Herbert, I am pleased to say, was more fortunate, although he must have had a terrible time, anyhow, I am of the opinion that he saved my life and also the lives of everyone who came out of K13. My reason for saying this is, the knowledge that he had of the interior as well as the exterior of the boat, made it possible for the salvage people to get to work in the proper way and they were successful in raising the boat sufficient for us to get out.

I will now relate what happened after the lower lid was closed. They were both in the airlock and after satisfying themselves that all was ready and according to scheme, Herbert stepped out and knocked the clips off the upper hatch. He then opened it sufficient to allow water to come in very slowly and then stepped back in the air lock. Soon they could tell the tower was full although they were only up to their waist in water the tower had finished venting.

Of course, you will understand now, that although the upper parts of their bodies were not in water they were subject to a big pressure, I should say they must have had thirtyfive pounds pressure on their bodies, whether they were in the water or not.

Now came the time for the final attempt and Goodhart's last words were "Goodbye, Herbert, I'll try now". He then stooped out of the airlock into the tower and at the same time, Herbert turned on the air from the high pressure system. What happened now is very hard to tell, for Herbert does not know exactly himself and this he told me himself, when he was speaking to me on the Thursday morning.

What he does know is this, when he turned the air on, the force caused him to lose grip of the valve and he did a complete double somersault and found himself out of the airlock, but in an enclosed place. This must have been the wheelhouse for he groped about and it was some time before he got out. He felt the tremendous pressure on his body and he thought he would lost consciousness when he found a hole (which I think was the side door) and got through it. He then found himself rapidly coming to the surface and, just as he was losing consciousness, he broke surface and was immediately dragged by willing hands into a boat.

Herbert now wanted to explain, but they made him wrap up in a blanket for an hour before they would listen to him and then he jolly soon got them busy. He worked himself from this time onward until the last man came out of the boat. What happened to Goodhart is, that he was blown out by the volume of air at a terrific rate and stuck to the roof of the wheelhouse. He must have been killed instantly, for the divers found him in the wheelhouse with his neck broken. Poor fellow he was killed, whilst endeavouring; to get to the surface and had given his life to try and save ours while Herbert who had meant to come back in the boat was now safely on the surface.

I have always been of the opinion that the sea boots

which Herbert wore, must have been of great as-sistance to him when he was groping about in the wheelhouse, for they certainly would help him to keep his feet. Besides that, being weighted at the feet, he would not have come out of the tower with nearly the force that Goodhart did.

Anyhow, it was a jolly good job for us that one of them got safely up, for I am led to believe, by the men who were working; there, that Herbert after having the hours rest which they forced him to have, took on (not exactly the salving of the boat) the salving of the crew and he carried on until the last man came out of her. There were plenty of voluntary helpers and I know quite a few of the Gare-Loch side people who were there and they are loud in Herbert's praise. They say he worked like a Trojan and they also say that it was entirely due to his untiring efforts, that at last the job of getting us out was accomplished. He was then so completely dead beat that he had to turn the job over to somebody else. I must now leave them working on the surface and return to the inside of K13 and I will explain how things were going on there.

After we had closed the lower lid we simply lis-tened and waited very anxiously. At last we heard the noise of the clips being knocked off the upper hatch and then we heard a rush of water and knew the tower was being flooded. Minutes seemed hours to us, but at last the rush of water stopped and we know the tower must be full. There was a dead si-lence now and we looked at one another not daring to speak and. then we heard the noise of the upper lid being thrown right back and from this we knew everything had gone off according to plan.

It was some minutes before we heard anymore. I suppose this was the time when Goodhart said his last farewell. At last we heard a tremendous rush of air and by looking at our high-pressure gauge we could see two thousand pounds of air disappear very rapidly. We knew in our own mind that this shouldn't have happened, but knowing that they had a valve in the conning tower, we didn't think it was right for us to interfere with the air from below.

As soon as the rush of air had finished, it was all still again and we were beginning to wonder if success had crowned their efforts. We now waited to hear the noise of the upper lid closing and the signal to drain the conning tower, but none came. A dead silence reigned every-where and we simply looked at one another not daring to voice an opinion, although I am sure we all had aching hearts for we thought the whole enterprise had failed and. that both of these brave men had lost their lives.

I think myself that at this time things absolutely looked their blackest, for we had lost what I consider the brains of the boat and I was wondering who we would have to take their places.

I am very pleased to say there were more brains left in the boat. I consider that the Admiralty Overseer, also the Boat Manager and his Assistant, ably assisted by members of the crew came up to scratch in a most remarkable manner. We simply worked together with these civilians as I have never seen Service men and civilians ever work together before. He were all brothers in distress and we all did our very best to help those up top who were trying to save us.

I have only mentioned three civilians because they were the outstanding, ones, but the whole of the civilians worked the same as the Service men did. We will now return to the surface of the Loch and see what was happening there. With the news that Herbert had brought with him, it was decided that they really must find some means to supply air, food and water to the men imprisoned below, as at present there was no water to drink, the food was of course a very secondary consideration.

It was also decided that some kind of communication must be rigged and being guided by Herbert the four-inch ammunition uptake was chosen as the place where this should be rigged. This uptake was a seven-inch hole and. its real use was to supply the forward four-inch gun with ammunition, it was just big enough to hand a four-inch shell from below to the gun.

Accordingly, the Fairfield Shipbuilding Yard, were expending every ounce of energy and skill in the making of a flexible pipe, which was to be used for this purpose. They were also making at "Full Speed" a large tube which was to be the life-saving tube. The idea, this tube was being made for, was to fix it over the beam torpedo hatch, this was to be pumped out and then we would be able to raise the hatch from inside and be pulled up through the tube.

I don't think this tube would have been any good, but still it was never completed for Herbert told Captain Barttelot that the imprisoned men would never be able to fight the water inside the boat, long enough for them to be saved in this manner.

Herbert's idea was that the boat must be lifted and dragged toward the shore until her bow could be got out of water. To do this it was necessary to give K13 air to blow her ballast tanks and she must help herself to lift her bow, so that the salvage lighter could do the rest and get the bow out of the water.

His advice was taken and now every ounce of human strength and skill was devoted to the one task, that of raising her bow and towing her toward the shore. Divers set to work to pass steel hawsers round her bow and when at last this was completed, the task and lifting and towing was begun.

Inside the boat were exhausted men, some working in spells and some working all the time. They were fighting the water which was pouring through the bulkhead and which threatened to reach our batteries, which if it had done would soon have suffocated us.
How some of these men worked and how exhausted they got. I can picture them now, as they packed up work and lay on the deck, gasping for breath, struggling for air and knowing they must work again for the water must be kept down or their chance of salvation was gone.

With the air which was being put into our high-pressure system, we commenced to blow our ballast tanks and also our oil fuel tanks. We started forward and we worked on tank after tank, until at last we had blown every tank dry, it was possible to get at and we now had a rather unpleasant angle on the boat.

The salvage craft now also started to lift and tow us

nearer the shore and the angle go so bad that we had "Lost the bubble" - that is the bubble had gone so far forward, that we could, not tell what our angle was. I know this that it was like climbing a steep hill to try and walk from aft to forward, but we didn't mind this so much because we knew we must be nearer the surface because the depth gauge only read fifty-four feet.

Now we had another very anxious time for our pump lost its suction and refused to pump water from the beam tube room. This was very serious indeed, for the water began to gain rapidly. Our hearts began to sink once more and we had to pass water in buckets forward to a place where the angle of the boat helped the pump and, at last we got it to suck again. I can picture the exhausted men passing these buckets of water, for what in normal times would have been, an easy task, now was a very heavy one and it was as much as a man could do to lift a small bucket of water.

Outside the boat the workers were having an anxious time as well and it's a good job that us inside of K13 didn't know the difficulties that they were experiencing outside. They had lifted and towed, but she had slipped back from her hawsers until her stern brought up in the mud at the bottom of the Gare-Loch.

At last the flexible tube arrived and the divers were taken off the other jobs and were given the task of rigging it. This proved a very difficult job and, although they worked their hardest, it was a very long time before the tube was secured and the joint made watertight.

At last the tube was secured and. signals wore made in "Morse" for us to unscrew the watertight cap at the bottom of the intake. Of course, we in the boat didn't know what the divers were doing and when we got this signal we could not understand it and were very loath to open it, for we thought the signal must have been taken in incorrectly.

Anyhow the signal was repeated and we thought that we had better do as we were asked, so we started to unscrew the cap. We all looked at this very anxiously and quite a few have since told me they expected to get water in when, the cap was taken off. Very gradually we unscrewed the clips that held the cap and very gradually we opened it.

We soon found out that no water would come in, in fact just the opposite happened and we could now tell what a tremendous pressure we must have had in the boat. The air simply rushed out through the tube end we had an awful drag on our ears. This continued for some time and I can tell you, we were all jolly glad, when the air inside levelled off to the atmospheric pressure outside the boat.

Of course, you will understand it is impossible for me to remember the time of all these incidents but to the best of my belief, the tube was opened at about 8am on Wednesday the 31st of January and at that time we had been imprisoned for about fortytwo hours.

The pressure being now out of the boat we could breathe more freely, although, Herbert told me afterwards that there was an awful smell coming up and he said it was a marvel how men could live in the air that was corning up.

Herbert was the first man to speak down the tube and McLean, the Boat's Manager and one of the Fairfield firm was the first man to speak up the tube. What a load was taken off our minds when we heard Herbert's voice, for we had long since given him up for dead and you can guess our hearts leapt with joy to hear his voice. He told us to keep our peckers up for he meant to get us out.

We now all expected to hear Goodhart speak and as we heard nothing we began to ask one another questions, but nobody seemed to have the courage to ask anything about him through the tube.

After a time I thought I would ask, so I went to the bottom of the tube end spoke up. Herbert answered and I asked if Goodhart was safe". His answer was, "I am afraid not for we have seen nothing of him". He then outlined the scheme he had under way and he told us to keep our heads and keep the water down, as he thought it would be hours yet before we could be got out. He told us how hard everyone was working outside the boat and he also told us that we must do the same inside.

K13 The Rescue Part II

Soon after this they told us to close down the intake again, as they were going to start towing again and they didn't care to risk getting water down the tube. We closed this up end once more we were out off from the outside world, although we were nowhere near as bad as we were before as we had got the pressure off our lungs.

At last after what seemed ages we discerned a flicker on the eyepiece of the forward periscope. This periscope dips at thirty-one feet so we knew that our bow must be out for we had a terrible angle on. I jumped to see if I could see anything and I could easily see the bow of K13 sticking up between the stems of two hoppers.

We could now see what was going on but nobody inside the boat would believe me when I said her bows were out, so they all came along, one at a time and convinced themselves by looking through the periscope.

Soon after this we saw a small boat come toward the periscope and one of the men in her held a small card with some writing to the window of the periscope. It was very difficult to read but at last we managed to pick out the words "Open the flap at the bottom of tube". You can guess we weren't very long doing this and once more we were in communication with those working on us.

We could easily see through the periscope (the) men working on the salvage lighters. They were a great many of them - volunteers who did exactly as they were told. They knew not what they were doing, but I am told, that if they were asked to pull on a rope they did it and did it with all their might. At last the darkness came on and we could no longer see through the periscope, except a light here and there.

We now had an accident with our switchboard and we were put in total darkness, until at last one of the electricians managed to rig one light direct to the battery. This was taken forward where the exhausted men now lay huddled together trying to keep warm.

Stone bottles filled with soups and milk, were now lowered through the tube and afterwards' chocolates were dropped down. These were a real "God Send" for it must be remembered that we had been considerably over forty hours without food and water, besides living in such a rotten atmosphere and having no sleep. Eventually one of these bottles broke in the tube, so that it was decided to send no more down in case the tube should get choked.

It was now decided, by the people at the top of the tube, that we must have our air refreshed, for the smell that was coming up was awful. Accordingly, one of the E Boats rigged an air lead which was passed down the tube. The compressor was then started and we simply took the air lead and squirted fresh air all over the boat. This was very beneficial to everyone and. we felt a great deal better and our hopes of escape looked better each hour.

Hour after hour passed and we knew that outside they were experiencing some difficulties which they hadn't expected and to make matters worse we got a very big set back inside as well. Our ballast pump gave out and try as we would, we couldn't get it to heave. This was very serious indeed for it simply meant that the water would gain on us and reach the batteries. We could all then be suffocated and the good work which had already been done, would have all been done in vain. I think the reason the pump would not heave, was because of the extra pull it would require to overcome the tremendous angle which the boat had now developed. Anyhow she had absolutely "Chucked her hand in" and we couldn't get her to heave, but some other method would have to be found to keep the water down.

At last a happy thought struck one of the company, I believe it was Mr Bullen the Second Manager. Anyhow I believe the credit belongs to him and Searle, the Admiralty Overseer and, of course, those members of the crew who were only too willing to help the scheme to work.

The scheme was this. Underneath the beam tube room, that is the room where the water was gaining so rapidly, were our oil fuel tanks. These tanks had already been blown empty and we were to get the water into these. To do this we should require (to get) a man hole door off the top of one of the tanks and then of course the water would run in. When these tanks were full, we simply would have to put back the door and blow the tank empty, with air from our high-pressure system. We would then be able to take the door off and repeat the operation. The scheme certainly sounded alright, but it entailed a. great deal of -work, as the manhole door was covered by about three feet of water. You can easily see it was no easy job to work in three-foot of water - especially as we were stone cold already and working in water up to the waist on the 31st of January is anything but pleasant. Anyhow it had to be done and willing hands started the job which, although it proved very difficult, was eventually done. As soon as the door was got off, the water simply rushed into the tanks in tons and we soon had the beam tube room clearer of water than at any time during our imprisonment. What a load was taken off our minds for we know now that the great-est danger was over for we had found a method, whereby we could get rid of the water as fast (or even faster) than it came in.

With very little work to do now, you can guess a period of very anxious waiting followed. We were continually asking one another the question "I wonder when they are going to start to cut the hole?" At last, after what seemed ages, we got a message to say they had started and our hopes were raised high for we knew, if things went alright, that we should very soon be out of our prison.

From time to time we received messages down the tube and invariably these messages were to say that things were going on alright. Somehow, I seemed to think that there was a certain amount of "Spruce" in them and they were keeping something away from us and then the message came to say that they had cut a hole into the outside lining of the boat that is into the external tanks which surround a "K" Boat. Here they were hung up for they found the tank into which they had cut, full up with water. They could not proceed until they had got a salvage pump but that was soon forthcoming. When this pump was rigged it was started and it hove water alright, but as quick as the water was pumped out, it ran in again and the pump had no effect.

Herbert then spoke down the tube and told us to make certain that the flooding valves of those tanks were closed. The order was passed, forward and soon the answer came book "they were closed" tight. This answer was sent up and Herbert told us he was very disappointed as he was sure that water was; coming in through these valves, but he would have to send divers down to cover them, this he said would take some time.

Time was now beginning to play havoc with our nerves for we thought that we would have been rescued long before this. I went forward and everyone was asking, "Have they started the other hole?" I told them how we were placed, but I told them exactly what Herbert had said. There was no grumbling, everyone seemed resigned and they huddled up to try and keep warm.

Whilst I was forward I heard someone shouting up the tube to say there was chlorine gas in the boat, as I didn't think this was right, I rushed aft and I found out that someone had passed a message to say salt water was getting to the battery and that we were getting chlorine gas. I immediately asked one of the firm's representatives to come with me into the control room. All was pitch black, but luckily this man had a small electric torch and with this we made a thorough examination.

I climbed under the switchboards and looked into all the "bottle wells" and also all the bilges, which were in the vicinity of the battery, but found, no salt water, in fact they wore quite dry. This told me for certain that we were not getting chlorine gas and I hurried back to the tube to inform those who were working up top.
I shouted up and asked that Herbert might speak to me and when he came he asked who was speaking. I said, "The Coxswain" and then I told, him that I had had a thorough examination and that the boat was absolutely free from gases of any kind.

His answer was a simple "Thank God" but I have since found out why he said this. On the Thursday when he was talking to me he told me that when the message about chlorine came up, they were in an awful stew. They knew that something must be done, for we would all have to be out of the boat within half an hour or we should be suffocated. Knowing this it was decided that they should again try and lift the boat, this time until the top bow torpedo tubes came out of water. They immediately got under way with this.

Their idea was that we would come out through the torpedo tube and to do this she would have to be raised at least another dozen feet. It was a forlorn hope and Herbert said he thought the hawsers wouldn't stick it and that she would, again slip back and all the work would have been in vain. You can easily see now, why Herbert said "Thank God" for he knew that they could continue to work on the water and cut the hole into the boat as was originally suggested.

The divers now reported that the "valves" on the tank were not closed but were wide open, so I went forward to have a look. I found this to be correct for all the valves to A1 and B1 were jammed wide open, although they had the appearance of being jammed closed. I immediately got them closed and went to the tube and told them what had happened and soon we had the good news passed clown to say that the water was being pumped out.

The pump was now making great strides and the messages we were getting now were very cheery in-

deed. At last came the message to say that the water was clear of the hull of the boat and that they had started to cut the hole.

Cutting the hole was not a hard job but it took some little time, which to us seemed hours but at last it was done and a lump of plate big enough for a man to get through was removed. I was standing near the tube when I heard a tremendous cheer, how my heart leaped with joy for I know the first man must be out of the boat.
How those outside who had been working on us cheered. Cheered because they knew their untiring efforts had been rewarded. As each man came out so there was a fresh cheer and us near the tube could easily tell when another man got out.

There was no panic and not a great deal of hurry. Each man irrespective of rank, whether civilian or service man all waited their turn. I have been led to believe, but I do not know for certain, that the pilot whoso name was Duncan, was the first man out of the boat, but I do know for certain that the First Lieutenant was the last man and myself the last but one.

You can guess that everyone was in a very weak and exhausted condition and had to be helped into the boats who were to take us ashore. What a. feeling of satisfaction Herbert must have had, for he stood at the top hole and helped every man out, those men whose lives he had assuredly saved.

What a beautiful night it was and what a treat it was to breathe the fresh air once more. There was not a breath of wind and the water was a calm as a mill pond. Everywhere there was a blaze of electric light and we could see the small rowing boots taking the men ashore.

I am sure there was an extra cheer for me as I came out of the hole, for I was very well known to the whole of the crews of E50 and E51, in fact quite a few of these men I had put through their course of submarine training. The Coxswain of E51 was one time my Second Coxswain when I was Coxswain of C24, so you can guess he was especially pleased to see me. He told me he thought I must have been one of the unlucky ones, when so many come out and yet I hadn't made my appearance.

I was now helped into a boat and was taken ashore and then we were all helped to walk to Shandon Hydro where we spent the night and best part of the next day. Everything that was possible for human hands to do, was done for us and after having a bath and a cup of beef tea, I went to bed and slept.

I think everyone slept the sleep of the just that night, I myself can remember nothing from the time my head touched the pillow until I was awakened by a pleasant faced maid. The sun was streaming in on me and I had to shake my scattered brains together before I could remember what had happened. She told me that there was hot water for my use, but they were waiting below for breakfast.

I hurriedly dressed and went below where I found the best part of the survivors having breakfast and they didn't look much the worse for their trying experience, except that our clothes which we had worn in the boat were all we had and you can guess it was *in a pretty pickle.*

The staff at the Hydro did their best for us and borrowed clothes and we didn't look much like "Navy Men" after they had finished with us. I had some very pleasant memories of kindnesses which I received from time to time from the staff at "Shandon Hydro", as well as from the good folk who live on the Gare-Loch side. I did the trials of two boats in the Gare-Loch at later dates, so you can guess I became a well-known figure there.

There is not a great deal more to relate about the sinking of K13 and the saving of those who come out of her, but later on in my story I shall have a great deal to say, for she was eventually salved and I commissioned her as K22 only to meet more trouble. The morning after we came out of her the ill-fated vessel slipped back out of the hawsers which were holding her and once more she went to the bottom of the Gare-Loch. This time she filled right up, for there was no one inside her to fight the water, so the job was made more difficult and it was some five weeks before she was eventually salved.

Commander Goodhart's body was found by the divers and buried at "Faslane Cemetery", a pretty spot on the Gare-Loch side. The remainder were not got out until she was raised and then they were also buried there.

After breakfast was over I was employed, with the Captain and we were very busy letting the Admiralty and also our Depot know, who were lost and who were saved. I had quite a long yarn with the Captain and he told me, that we would all have to go south to Fort Blockhouse. It was decided that I should take the crew back to Glasgow that afternoon and get things squared up there so that we could go on leave on the Friday night.

We left Shandon by train and there was a great many of the staff of the Hydro to see us off. When we got to Helensburgh there was some very distressing scenes for the news had spread like wildfire and some of the relatives of the deceased men met us. I was very pleased to get in the train again and I must say I heaved a sigh of relief when I got to my lodgings at Govan.

The next morning, we were employed in getting the effects of the unfortunate men together, as well as our own and this was then despatched to the Submarine Depot at Gosport. That night we were sent on ten days leave, at the expiration of which we were to return to our Depot.

Before going on leave, Herbert (our Captain), had the whole of the survivors of the crew mustered and he read a telegram of congratulations from the King, who had also sent a telegram of thanks and congratulations to the men who had worked so hard and had helped to save our lives.

A Court of Inquiry was held a fortnight after and I had to attend as a witness. The finding of the court was never published, as it was war time, hut I don't think any blame could possibly be put on anyone, as in all our evidences, there wasn't a shadow of doubt but that the Indicator was showing Engine Room Shut Off.

When the boat was raised the four air intakes to the

boiler room were all open and the boiler room door burst open, so this was the cause of the whole of the boat from the beam tube to the stern being flooded.

The 29 bodies were found in different parts of the boat, but there is no doubt, but that these poor fellows were drowned very quickly. Sadly 10 of the men were unable to be identified sk badly were there remains damaged.When they were taken out for burial, it was found that two were missing and these proved to be Engineer Lieutenant Lane - the boat's Engineer and Mr Steele - the Firm's Engineer. One of the after hatches were found open and it is presumed that they tried to escape from the boat through this hatch. The evidence that implied the two mens fate was:

(1)Eng. Lieutenant Lane was last seen in the engine room

(2)Mr. Steel was, in all probability, also in the engine room (where he was seen just before the accident)

(3)No bodies were found in the engine room, but Eng. Lieut Lane's coat was found there.

(4)The clips of the engine room hatch were open. It is therefore possible that the two attempted to escape through the engine room hatch and were drowned.

Lane's body was found floating on the Gare-Loch about four months afterward, but up to the time of my writing this, Steele's body has never been found and I daresay it lies at the bottom of the Gare-Loch until the present day.

This finishes my narrative of K13, but my readers must bear in mind that I didn't write this until years after the incident and the times may not be absolutely correct, but the incidents outlined in my story are true.

I would like to pass a few comments on the recognition which Commander Goodhart and Lieutenant Commander Herbert got over this affair. Nothing was heard of the affair until eighteen months after and then the posthumous award of the Gold Albert Medal was made to Goodhart. It took all this time for Goodhart's brave action to receive recognition, but nothing at all was done for Herbert. I am voicing the opinion of all my Boat's crew - who volunteered to serve with Herbert again - when I say, that the highest award possible should have been made to both of these brave officers. I suppose that this is only one case, of which there must be many, where a brave deed has counted for nothing and must be turned down, because the public must not know. This deed was not done on the spur of the moment with red in their eyes, it was done after reviewing the aspect of things for hours. Both of these brave men knew, they were risking their lives, in what I should say at least a hundred to one chance and they were doing this to try and save the lives of others, a good many of them practically strangers.

K22

On my return from leave to Fort Blockhouse, I was again put on the staff as an Instructor for new ratings joining the submarines, but I afterwards found out that this was only something for me to do, while K13 was being salved and afterwards overhauled. Of course, I didn't think for one minute that I should commission her again and when I was "told off" I was greatly surprised as well as were a good many more.

Anyhow one evening; after tea I was sent for by the Drafting Officer, who I might remark was my captain in H1 (Lt Wilfrid Pirie). He asked if I would go to K22 as a volunteer. At first my answer was "No" and I said I didn't think it was right to expect me to go back to a boat in which I had seen such awful sights. Anyhow after a bit I decided I would go; I think it was so that no-one could accuse me of having cold feet. Accordingly, I once more left the Depot and travelled to Govan where the boat was being re-fitted and soon I was installed as Coxswain of K22.

It was a surprise packet for the men at Fairfield's Yard to see me come up again for this boat and I soon had the civilians who were down in her with ne, around to see me. They one and all told me I was a fool to tempt providence in her again and one of them told me he wouldn't go to her if he was dragged.

I simply laughed at them and told them I had just as well be at sea in this boat as any other and I also told then I considered she was a jolly fine boat. I also told them that they would soon hear about her, as I felt sure she would do something. I was quite right about this, but they heard of her in a far different way to that which I meant them to. Our crew came up in September and in October we were once more on the Gare-Loch doing trials. I shan't forget the day we first went inside the Gare-Loch for we anchored

611

of Shandon in the exact spot where our accident had happened. Neither shall I forget the first dive I had in her as K22. I can assure you I had a jolly good look round myself this time, but it was next to impossible for the same accident to happen.

Whereas in K13 we had only had electric indicators in K22 we had both electrical and mechanical indicators and it was a dead cert that the intakes, which were the cause of the disaster, must be closed before the indicators showed it. Our trials went off very well but when we dived there was no firm's people aboard. I can honestly say I was the only one who had been down in her that dived in her this time.

Well, as I said before, the trials went off alright and we commissioned the boat as K22 during the last week in October 1917. We remained in the Gare-Loch for about a fortnight and each day we were exercising, the idea of this was, so that the boat and the boat's crew could be worked up to an efficient state. During this time, I spent my evenings ashore and renewed, my acquaintance with the staff of Shandon Hydro as well as the people on the Gare-Loch side, who were all very pleased to see me, I also had an opportunity to see the graves of my late boat mates as well as the civilians who lost their lives in K13

One of the Sundays we laid off Shandon, we decorated the boat and threw her open for the people on the Gare-Loch side. We had a very big crowd aboard and they marvelled to think so large a boat could be so easily handled. There were two other boats on the Gare-Loch also exercising, they were K17 and N1 so before we left to join up with the grand fleet, the staff at the Hydro gave us a farewell dinner and dance. It was a really good show and I think everyone enjoyed themselves immensely. I am very sorry to say that a good many of the brave lads who were enjoying themselves, were "Down Under" within four months for K17 was lost with nearly all hands. We continued exercising until our Captain was satisfied with his boat and crew and then he reported fit for sea. We left the Clyde soon after and proceeded to Scapa Flow and joined the Grand Fleet.

We were now employed with the fleet and although we did a good deal of running it was far different work to what I had been used to, for in this case we did all surface work, early in December we shifted our base south to Rosyth. Our "stunts" now consisted of work with the mine layers and mine sweepers. We used to go to sea with them and. after they had done their work over the "other side", we were used to cover their retreat. We saw nothing during these escapades, but we were always on the "Top Line" in case we were wanted to dive and attack anything. There was not a great deal of work to do and. I would have far sooner been in a boat to do submarine patrols, but still we were kept with the fleet and had to put up with it. Christmas came with the usual jollifications and by this time we had settled down and I prided myself on having one of the best and I am sure the happiest boat, in the Flotilla.

We went to sea with the mine layers and sweepers on the 29th of December and we returned on New Year's Eve. We secured to K5 in the pens at Rosyth at about 11.40pm so we were in for the usual sixteen bells at midnight. My crew were very lively and we sang the old year out and the New Year in and our greatest wish was that this year would see the trouble all over. January passed along with nothing of unusual interest until the night of the 31st. I must here say that I had watched the anniversary of K13s fatal dive and I was very pleased we were in harbour for the 20th and 30th. On the evening of the 31st we had orders for sea and as we were leaving the "pens" we could see that the whole of the fleet were preparing for sea. Both the "K" Boat flotillas with their leaders "HMS Ithuriel" and HMS Fearless" were anchored off the Inland of Inchkeith and awaited the hours of darkness.

At 5pm we weighed anchor and proceed to sea.
It was very dark, but it was a fine night. We had no idea what we were going to sea for, but we could easily see it was to do with the whole of the fleet. Everyone was asking the question "I wonder what is doing?" is it one of Beatty's stunts, or is there really something doing? I never found out what really was doing that night but one thing I do know and that was it was a very unfortunate "stunt" for our boats, for we lost two "K" Boats with practically all hands and beside;"' that we had three other "K" Boats put out of action as well as the light cruiser "Fearless". As near as I can remember it would be about 7pm and as it was the last day of the month, I was very busy with my Paymaster's accounts. I thought being that we were at sea on the last day of the month that I should be able to finish the accounts and have them all ready to send to our parent ship on our return to harbour. I was sitting in my mess and only one other Petty Officer was there with me, when I suddenly thought this was the anniversary of the night I came out of "K13". I looked up from my work one remarked this fact to this Petty Officer and his an-

swer was, I hope we shan't have to come out of her the same way. I said "No. I hope we shan't and then I went on to outline what had happened on that night. All of a sudden, we got a terrible crash and it was like running bang into a stone wall and I knew in a minute that we were in collision with something and whatever that something was we had run into her and not her into us'

I threw my books across the table and yelled "Close Watertight Door" and I rushed into the control room. I was going farther forward but I net a Leading Seaman who was rushing aft. "What's the damage I said?" and he told me that we were holed very badly, but that he had closed the forward bulkhead door. He said water was rushing in very quickly and he was only just in time. I went forward and found the bulkhead was standing alright, so I got the crew underway to shore the bulkhead with beams of wood. Our Navigator who was in charge of the bridge, had sent below for our captain, but he didn't want sending for, for he was up there like a shot. He found out that we had rammed another submarine, but we didn't know for some time which it was. We soon found out that we were very badly damaged forward, but there was no danger of sinking. The boat we had. rammed was damaged a great deal more than we were and she lay on the surface in a very dangerous predicament with her stern sticking out of the water and her nose well down into it.

The boat we had been in collision with proved to be K14 our sister boat and now made a signal to us, asking us to stand by her as she was in danger of sinking. In fact, it was a miracle that she didn't sink for she had two compartments flooded forward and *she had a very big angle on and looked though she would make the fatal dive at any minute. As she had asked us to stand by her, our Captain decided to send a wireless signal to say what had happened'. This we did and our two leaders the "Fearless" and the "Ithuriel", who of course were always listening on our wireless wave, received the signal and immediately gave orders for the flotilla to turn. I consider this was only making things worse, as the whole of the fleet were leaving the Firth of Forth, at frequent intervals.*

I will now try and explain what was happening in K22, we had already shored up the bulkhead between the forward torpedo room which was flooded and the wardroom and we found this to be holding alright. We were a good bit down by the bows, so we blew the water out of the forward ballast tanks and also the fuel from the forward group of fuel tanks and this brought us right up out of the water and we could see that there was no danger at all of us sinking. I now thought I would go on deck to look at the damage and when I got up there I found our bows had been pushed back and squashed in just like a concertina. We could do nothing now but sit and see what was to happen to K14. She still had a very big angle on, but we could do nothing, unless they decided to abandon her, in which case we could have taken her crew on board us.

Now occurred another collision, far worse than the one we already had had and this time we thought that we were doomed. I was still on the upper deck, when I heard a cry from someone who was aft. Everyone on the bridge turned and we could easily see the hull of a very big ship looming out of the darkness. She was making straight for our Conning Tower at a great speed, but I think she must have seen us about the same time as we saw her, for we could see she was altering course. I am sure everyone must have held their breath for although she was altering her course, we could all see that it would be impossible for her to avoid us. We put our telegraphs to full speed astern, but all to no use, for she crashed into us at a terrific rate, the blow simply heeled us ever to a very bad angle and tore away our bow and pushed it around to port, for we had been struck on the starboard side. I think myself the ship must have been carrying extreme helm, for as she passed her stern swung in on top of us. Her port propeller or her rudder tore our external tanks all along the starboard side and she also shoved us down in the water until the water was only a few inches from our conning tower and the boiler room intakes, which were of course wide open. I really thought it was all up this time for I thought it would be impossible for the boat to float after being so severely damaged.

But no! Up she came again and she put me in the mind of a living thing; who did not intend to give up so easily. As the stern of the ship swung by us, it was possible for us to make out part of her name and we found her to be HMS Inflexible. We immediately signalled her, told her we were in a sinking condition and asked her to stand by us, but she didn't even answer us. I don't suppose she dared to risk turning back for she would most probably have had more trouble with the other ships who were now leaving the Firth of Forth. As we could see that we were going to get no help from anyone else, we set to work to do our utmost to keep the beat afloat. We blew all the fuel from the tanks leaving sufficient only to get us back. This brought us up in the water and we could see now, that we weren't going to sink.

Now followed a period of anxious waiting, for we still had to stand by K14. We could see how badly we were damaged, in fact the whole of the fore-end of the boat looked like a scrap heap and the whole of the externals on the starboard side were very much damaged as well. We were lying on an even keel for our bows being pushed round to port, compensated for the water we had taken into our starboard exter-nals. We had some very narrow escapes from more collisions that night, for ships of all kinds were con-tinually passing us. At one time I thought it was all up, for a battleship passed us going full speed and I am sure could only have missed us by inches.

At last a trawler arrived on the scene to help K14 and our captain decided to get underway on our own power and try to get back to Rosyth. Accord-ingly, this was done end our engines were worked up until we were doing revolutions for eighteen knots but, owing to the tremendous amount of resistance which our damaged bow got, we only made about two and a half knots through the water. This was jolly slow work, but at any rate we knew we were not going to sink, so we didn't mind taking a long time to get in. I can remember well taking the boat under the Forth Bridge. Many a time I had been under this bridge, but it was always about twenty knots but this time it was two, in fact it seemed to me that we were never going to get under it. We arrived in Rosyth at 7am on the 1st of February and we were immediately put inside the Basin. Later or in the forenoon K14 arrived, she had been towed in stern first. It was absolutely a marvel how this boat had been floated, as she was flooded internally a great deal more than we were. She was berthed alongside of us and that evening we were both put in dry dock. "Didn't we look a lovely pair" two sister boats and what had been two good boats now looked like two heaps of scrap iron.

Now came the worse part of the lot, for we got the news to say that other boats of our flotilla had been in trouble and they weren't as fortunate as us. At first the news came in what is called "busses" but at last we got the official news to say that K4 and K17 had been sunk: K4 with all hands and K17 all hands except six. This was awful news to us and soon we came to find out how it had happened. K4 had been sunk by K6 and K17 had been sunk by HMS Fearless. What a pot mess this had left our flotillas in. The complete list of damage was K4 and K17 sunk, K6, K14 and K22 damaged and HMS Fearless, one of our parent ships also damaged and. put out of action. K6 and. the "Fearless" were ready for sea again in about a month, but K14 and K22 were so badly damaged that they were put out of commission and it took nine months to repair the damage.

K4

What a gloom this cast over our flotilla. It is bad enough to know that a boat has been sunk by the enemy, but to know our own ships had done this was terrible. I lost a great many friends in those boats and as I have already said, the boys who were dancing with us a few months before at Shandon had now made the supreme sacrifice. Of course, this had to be kept quiet as it was War Time but in the "K" Boat flotillas I have often heard this incident spoken of as "The Battle of May Island". I think it is a very good name for it, anyhow I expect if the Germans had heard of it, they would have had a good chuckle. We now waited for the Admiralty to decide what was to happen to us and when the news came, it was to say that K22 and K14 were to be paid off and put out of commission until they were thoroughly overhauled and the damage made good. My captain was now appointed to K16, which boat was completing at Beardmores Shipbuilding Yard, Dalmuir. The reason he was appointed here was because the Captain who had been standing by her, was unfortunate enough to be out in K4 and so lost his life. I don't think my captain was very pleased when he got his appointment, for he told me he had hoped to get an L Boat, as there were a good many of this class of boat building.

He sent for me and asked me if I would serve with him again, but when I found out he was going to a K, I thanked him very much, but said I considered I had had quite enough of Ks. I don't think any of my readers will accuse me of having cold feet, but my experiences in "K13/K22" had certainly made me think and I didn't intend to tempt providence for a third time in a K. I was also asked to stand by K22 and this meant a quiet time for nine months, but knowing if I stood by her, I should be expected to commission her, I refused. Accordingly, I paid off K22 on February 20th and proceeded on leave and again joined Fort Blockhouse on the 6th of March. Here I was again asked to go to K16 in fact my rating of torpedo coxswain was pointed out to me. The Drafting Officer said I was only allowed in the com-

plement of "K" Boats, but he said he could ask the Commodore of the submarine service, if he could send me to an L Boat. I told him that I would revert to the General Service if I was again told off for a "K" so at last consent was given for me to go to an L Boat commissioning.

The month of March saw me doing my old job as instructor, but early in April I once more found myself on the move. I was told off as Coxswain of "L6" and this boat was building at Beardmore's, Dalmiuir. She was commanded by Lieutenant Commander C O Regnart, who was a very experienced and capable submarine officer and I spent the reminder of my war time in this boat. I again made my acquaintance with the Gare-Loch, for after we were completed, we went there to do trials, I went ashore and visited the friends I had made on the Gare-Loch side and once more I visited the graves of my late boat mates in "K13". "L6" proved to be a good boat and to use a navy slang term "I would sooner have served in an L Boat on one meal a day than go to a "K" Boat on full rations." Our trials prove successful but one afternoon when diving across the loch, we hit the bottom very badly. We immediately blew our ballast tanks and came to the surface to see what was the extent of damage done.

L6

We found the bow shutters of the torpedo tubes were badly buckled and. it would, be necessary to go into dry dock for repairs. Our captain informed "Commodore (S)" and we received instructions to go to Govan and wait for a vacancy for docking. This only hindered us for a few days; and we then went back to the Gare-Loch to complete our trials. Everything proved successful and our captain reported. "Ready for Sea." A destroyer was told off to escort us and we left the Clyde, the last week of April. This escort took us as far as Milford Haven and then another escort took us to Plymouth. Here we picked up a Destroyer who escorted us to Portsmouth. We were now attached to HMS Ambrose and this ship was lying in Portsmouth. She had a flotilla of eight L Boats attached, to her and their job was to clear the channel of German U Boats.

Captain Nasmith VC of E11 fame was Captain of our parent ship and he organised a system of patrols, which proved very successful. Our patrols were kept continually going and I think every one of our flotilla at some time had a scrap with a U boat. Up till the arrival of the "Ambrose" and her flotilla of L Boats, the patrols in the Channel had been kept up by some of our older class of submarines. These were no good where the U boat war concerned. And, consequently, the English Channel was the "Happy Hunting Ground" of the U boats. Ships were being sunk quite near to Portsmouth and it was on this account our flotilla was based there. We had a very strenuous time, for three patrols had to be kept going and our sea time proved to be much longer than our time in harbour. Our Eastern patrol extended as for as Dover and our Western as far as the Scilly Inlands while our Middle Patrol was centred about the Isle of Wight.

I think every boat at some time fired torpedoes at U boats, but they were all unlucky and missed. We ourselves, came up and had a bump at one on the surface with our gun but she dived and got away. We had heard her all day on our hydroplanes and I don't doubt but that she heard us as well, but we saw nothing. We came to the surface that night to charge our batteries and we weren't up very long before the order was passed down "Surface Action Stations". The guns crew immediately manned their gun end a couple of rounds were fired. I think she must have thought of the old proverb "He who fights and runs away lives to fight another day", anyhow; as I said before, she dived end got away end we got no more trouble from her .I think that the U boat Commander now began to find out that they were up against something quite as good as themselves and they wisely cleared out of the Channel. No ships were being sunk at all and this caused us to shift our base farther west.

Before leaving Portsmouth, the Commander-in-Chief issued a memorandum to each L Boat attached to the "Ambrose" and in it he acknowledged the good work which the flotilla had done and in fact gave us the credit of clearing the Channel. He asked the Admiralty to allow us to keep the same patrols going, but the powers that be said there was no more work for us to do. Early in October we left Portsmouth and made our headquarters at Plymouth. Our patrol was the northern end of the Bay of Biscay and you can guess we got some awful weather there. I had often crossed the Bay in a Ship, but I never thought it would come to my lot to patrol the Bay in a submarine. L2 and L3 were the first boats on this patrol and they experienced very heavy weather indeed. It was so rough that they had to do their patrol on the surface, for it was impossible to dive. When they returned to Plymouth they were so badly damaged that they had to spend a month in dock being repaired. Rough weather or no, we had to keep this patrol up. Day after day we sighted convoys and our hardest job was to keep out of the way of our own ships who were acting as escorts for these convoys.

One day we dropped across four Yankee destroyers escorting one of our large merchant men and it was hours before we could get away from them. Eventually we dived very deep and remained down for a couple of hours and when we came up again the coast was clear. I don't think that any of us were a little bit sorry when we were recalled from patrol, pending the armistice being signed. I can picture my crew that night, hanging round the wireless cabinet, for good news followed good news and then we were ordered to return to Plymouth. It was a very happy boats crew that brought L6 back from her last "War Patrol". I can picture the lads now, having a sing song on the mess deck. They sang and sang, nobody wanted to sleep and all was excitement.

We arrived back in Plymouth two days prior to the signing: of the armistice and we had the distinction of being last boat of our flotilla to do a "War Stunt". I think the morning the Armistice was signed was a day of all days for our flotilla. Our First Lieutenant made out a "Noise Station" bill and in it every man was allocated to some job which made a noise. The "siren", "ships bell", "telegraphs" and "whistles" were the chief things and those who had no job simply yelled themselves hoarse. 11am was the official time and there is no mistake we "let her go". How elated we all were for we knew that the terrible War was over and that we were the victors. We also knew that the very large sacrifice our Submarine Service had made had not been made for nothing. I think my boats crew were the noisiest of the flotilla. Long after the others had packed up, my crew grouped around the gun and sang the "Boats Crew's War Cry! (The Governor of Malaya) and finished up with cheers for the boats officers and officers of our parent ship.

I think my story is practically finished, for after giving leave to our crews, the flotilla soon settled down to peace routine. "For a few months we carried out exercises outside of Plymouth and then we learnt that the "Ambrose" and her flotilla was booked for China. They were all put into dockyard hands to have cooling apparatus put in them and they left for China in June 1919. Myself I didn't go for I left L6 in April and once more came back to Fort Blockhouse where I was lucky enough to be when peace was signed. This concludes my little effort and if it is only read by a few and they appreciate the acts of the brave men of Submarine Service, I shall feel this effort was not made in vain.

Robert Oscar Moth, DSM
O/N 220366 (Po)

A5 & A12 Able Seaman to Chief Petty Officer Coxswain 31st January 1909 to 26th March 1914

C24 Coxswain 12th January 1915 to 30th January 1921

H1 Coxswain 8th April 1915 to 10th April 1916 at the Darda-

nelles

K13 Coxswain 14th April 1916 to 30th January 1917

K22 Coxswain 20th October 1917 to 11th February 1918

L6 Coxswain 11th July 1918 to 9th May 1919

APPENDIX J: THE FLEET FROM WITHIN. BEING THE IMPRESSIONS OF A R.N.V.R OFFICER [ON BOARD K12]

"CHAPTER XX

WITH A SUBMARINE CRUISER AT SEA

The most thrilling moments of war are those when a submarine, having spotted the enemy, dives, and makes ready to fire. War, on sea perhaps more than on land, is not half so exciting as the layman imagines. Excitement is spasmodic and rare. A battle certainly offers a thrill when men at a given word leap from their trenches and charge with the bayonet. Such a charge, however, comes after a prolonged period of monotonous inactivity, and the order to charge is in the nature of a relief to men weary with waiting. As regards flying in a warplane, the only thrill is the mad rush forward — on terra - firma ! — before the machine has risen. After that — when you have soared high enough — it soon settles down to a noisy sameness.

An airship is the most monotonous, if pleasant Est, of all, like its younger brother the kite balloon. This does not mean there is no danger — the airship I went up in came to grief just a week later — only the danger during the flying is not apparent.

In the submarine, however, there are always possibilities of the unexpected. Anything may happen, and this constant feeling dispels all monotony. The great tension when diving and during firing operations lends sufficient excitement to the life in a submarine to last during the entire journey.

The ship in which I went down is a super-submarine, one of the latest types — the K class. Beside her the submarine of yesterday is a mere toy. In construction, and in possibility, she is as different from the famous E-boats as a ship of the first line in Nelson's time is from a modern Dreadnought. The K boat has a displacement of 2,000 tons on the surface and 2,700 tons submerged. Its length is 340 feet, with a beam of 26 feet — a veritable submarine cruiser ! It has a surface speed of 24 knots and a submerged speed of 10 knots an hour. It is self-contained. On the surface it is driven by steam.

It is not easy, if you are not of the submarine personnel, to get aboard these huge vessels. They possess secrets which the Germans would have dearly liked to get hold

*of, and the Commander in command of the
flotilla does not encourage '* visitors." In
my instance, however, the barrier was raised,
although he wasn't particularly keen about
it.*

*"I've fixed you up, Moseley" he said one
day. "K12 goes out tomorrow. . . . Here,
signalman ! " Commander (S.) to Captain
K12. He writes out a signal saying he is
sending me aboard." That's all right.
Half-past six to-morrow
morning."*

*"Good," I say. ... He stops at the door
of the cabin as if something more were wanting.*

*"I hope you damn well get drowned,"
he says as a kind of a cheerio.*

*"Well," says I, "the conditions are all in
your favour, sir. To-morrow is Friday and
the 13th!"*

*"By jingo," says he, "that makes it certain. #
You'll never come back."*

*A very excellent submarine officer,
Commander (S.), but a trifle indifferent in the
choice of sweet words.*

*Not everybody of the old school, quite
naturally, fully trusts these "new-fangled"
giants, and certainly nobody trusts Friday —
or the 13th.*

"I hope to go down in K12," says an old lieutenant, "but I'll see her — when she's in dock". "Friday"! Good Lord! You're not going out on a Friday?"

Oh, a cheerful lot of knaves!

Superstition dies hard. It is believed that the Admiralty actually issued an order giving captains the option of altering any vessel numbered 13 to any other number not on the pennant board.

I discover, too, that the submarine I am going down in is sister to the one which sank on her trials. ^The story is most tragic and thrilling. The K13 had over seventy persons aboard, including the naval constructors and builders. It proceeded to Gareloch, near the Clyde when the order was given for her to dive. When she was below, the surface water began to pour into the ventilating shafts astern which had been accidentally left open. Thirty-one persons who were in the compartments aft were drowned. The fore compartments, with forty-two persons, were fortunately shut off. The Admiralty Salvage Department soon sent divers down to investigate. These discovered that the stern of the vessel was embedded in many feet of mud. It seemed a hopeless task, but, strangely enough, replies to their tapping were heard. What happened next can only be conjectured. It would seem that Captain Goodhart, D.S.O., who was one of those entombed in the submarine, decided to

*escape by using the high-pressure air bottles.
With the aid of these contrivances, he was
to be projected through the conning tower
and shot into the water, hoping to reach the
surface and give help and information to the
rescue party. The brave attempt failed,
however. Captain Goodhart was hurled with
terrific force against a support in the conning
tower and was immediately killed. For his
brave attempt he was posthumously awarded
the Albert Medal in gold. Another effort
to escape by a commander was more successful.
The officer was fortunate enough
to reach the surface and was caught and
saved by the rescue party. The information
he was able to give the salvage men helped
considerably the work of rescue. Divers
were able to get into communication with
those imprisoned in the submarine by means
of the Morse Code. Working in conjunction
with the imprisoned men, the engineers were
able to insert a flexible hose through a water-
flop which was momentarily opened from the
inside. Through this, not only fresh air,
but meat extract, chocolate, and other food
were pumped into the entombed men.*

*The chances of rescue were still slender,
but the imprisoned men were always full of
heart and asked for cards to be pumped
down in order "to beguile the tedium of
waiting". By the aid of the air bottles — for
which they now had no need — they blew out
the oil fuel stowed forward. This resulted,
eventually, in the submarine rising at a high
speed by the bows in a perpendicular position.*

The salvage party at once made a big hole in
her with acetylene burners, and the forty-
two men were rescued by midnight and conveyed
to a neighbouring hospital. The escape
was timely, for before long the vessel settled
down again and was seen no more. Altogether
the rescued men had been entombed in the deep
for fifty-seven hours.

. . .

Sharp at 6.30 on a grey, uninviting morning
I am conveyed alongside K12, which has
been lying about a mile south of us. The
slip rope is rove and she is ready to proceed.
There is no time to lose, and as soon as we
draw alongside one must board her. But
how on earth am I to get aboard this elongated
ball? You simply have to make a
jump for it, and as you slip back — catch
hold! That's all. It is of no use waiting
aboard the picket boat all the morning. A
civilian can demur ; an officer must go
ahead as if he were used to this sort of
gymnastics and had been for years!

I jumped, slipped, caught hold and hung
on. Then I tried to walk the slippery round
deck to a hole which led to the "wardroom".
A wardroom in a submarine!)The hole, to do it
justice, is no smaller, if no bigger, than the
"holes" on board battleships. So, I squeezed
me down and found myself in a square, comfy
cabin,
chockful of domestic comforts and ship's gear, and
dis-

covered that this was the wardroom, from
the table which was laid for a certain number
of officers. The captain's cabin was opposite.

This wardroom, mess-room, bedroom, and
storeroom all in one strikes you as a trifle
stuffy first thing in the morning but you
soon get to know it as a veritable haven.
Especially when the bunks are pushed back
into their lockers — like a chest of drawers —
leaving no sign of beds. There are cosy arm-
chairs, a huge gramophone, a settee, ventilation
fans, or a fire if necessary ! After a
couple of hours on the bridge, later on, I
was very glad to come down here, throw
myself in a cosy chair and drink from one of
the numerous treasures hidden away in the
"wine-cellar!" Aye, life in a submarine
might be worse. . . . The Captain pokes his
head out of his portable cubicle and, as he
straightens his tie, calls out to me, "We
shall slip in three minutes !"

"Today is Friday," says I inconsequently.

"Lord I hate it ! Something always
goes wrong on a Friday !" he replies seriously.

The 'First' intervenes.

"Yes, last time I was out in a submarine
on a Friday the 13th we had a fortnight in
dock!"

Another cheering set of mortals, to be sure !
And they are not even pulling my leg !

We clamber up the long, narrow ladder of steel to the bridge, by way of the conning tower.

"Make ready there! Stand by forward!"

A signalman is busily hoisting flags or making semaphore. The engines faintly throb and K12 gently glides away from the buoy.

From the time we start till she picks up the buoy again the air vibrates with the voluminous orders from the Captain. Not even the captain of a battleship has so much to do. There are no flies, to be sure, on the Captain — and no hair either! I noticed that most of the submarine captains I have met are almost bald. The job is enough to do it. Some manage to retain a lock or two which stand out in isolated glory, and it is, I am told, from the manner of these well-cared-for tributaries that the barometer of the Captain's temperature is ascertained by his staff. "When the wisp stands perpendicular all is well. When it veers to the north there's a squall a-coming."

"Revolution for 16 on," calls the Captain.
"Revolution for 16 on," comes the reply.
"Signalman, hoist G12."
"G12, sir," he repeats, and disappears.
Back he comes shortly.

"Gates open, sir".

"Revolution for 15 on."

*The crew aboard is a mixed one. We
have about a dozen men from another boat
of this class training with us "taking the
dive" they call it.*

*The Engineer-Lieutenant is a laughing-
faced youngster in oilskins, bustling about
when necessary but always grinning.*

*"Come and I'll show you my engine-
room," he says.*

*The boat is well under way, and I slip
along from fore to aft pretending to like it,
but holding on to the slack rail like grim
death.*

*Down another hole, down, down, down!
(These flat-bodied submarines are not so flat
as I thought!) The engine-room isn't so
bad. It is hot, as indeed most engine-rooms
are but this is neat and spacious. Here, as
in the other compartments, a tall man can
walk upright with care. There are more
"clocks" (indicators) than I can count.
"Come in here."
He opens an airtight compartment, we
crush in (it is just large enough to hold us
both), and the draught of air beats hard
against my eardrums.*

*He opens another airtight door which re-
leases us from our cramped prison. This*

instruments which simply baffles description.
It takes an engineer expert to appreciate all
this use of modern science ; it is just enough
to awe the layman. Who would think in
looking at the exterior of a submarine that
she was so chokeful of such ingenious contriv-
ances ?

The boat is now going at sixteen knots
when I join the Captain on the bridge. He
is still shouting orders.

"Executive ! What's the bearing — what !
what ?" . . .

We are now well out in the open sea, and,
failing the kindly promise of support by a
German vessel, we have to fall back upon
one of our destroyers for torpedo practice.
(How our submarine personnel envy the
U-boats !) We are to lire a real torpedo at
her — with a dummy head on.

It is, of course, not quite the same target,
firing at an expectant destroyer, as at a
surprised enemy.

We prepare to dive. On the bridge all
scuttles or hatches are firmly screwed down,
but the gun remains as it is — the breech alone
protected from the water. From the bridge
one sees, fore and aft, the smooth, elongated
body of the submarine "closed up" like a
show taken down for the night. Somebody

*shouts to me a piece of advice one has
received more than once: "Don't get left
behind."*

*It doesn't often happen, but sometimes
men through their own fault, are 'left aloft
somewhere in one of the stowing's and
consequently, are washed out.*

*On my return from the engine-room (I had
come away without my engineer friend), I
felt a momentary sensation of what it is to
be left behind. Nobody was about, and
I knew we were about to submerge, and I
had to hurry along the slippery deck from
aft to the bridge gangway. It seemed a
great distance. As it was, I got below none
too soon, for the watertight door clanged
down almost directly after.*

"All correct for diving?"

"All correct, sir."

"Dive!"

*I stood below in the control-room and
watched the tense faces of the crew, and
I wondered whether this was the only ordeal which despite repetition never quite
palled.*

*The men at the hydroplanes were busy
turning wheels and shouting results to the
Captain, who now stood on a platform, eyes
glued to the periscope.*

"Ten feet, sir."

*A young seaman stands by, taking down the
records shouted out to him by the Captain.
a curly-haired Scotch lieutenant — the 'First'
is at the chart making calculations, other
hands are at the tanks, my oilskinned friend
from the engine-room has reappeared still
smiling — to him there is nothing doing till
we emerge again — and another lieutenant —
a good-looking, kindly-natured boy — is
standing by, ready to take charge of the torpedo
firing.*

"What angle is she ? "

*The Captain is still shouting questions and
orders, and puts fire, by the manner of his
words, into the men.*

"One degree, sir."
"Fifteen feet."

*The air is fairly good, just the warmth one
would expect in a small compartment holding
a number of busy men. There is a rumbling
noise of bolts being shut, of machines running,
of a million voices being in conflict.*

And above all I hear :

"Dive 25 feet ! ... open external ... !"
*The rest of the command is drowned. Voices
repeat the order, and the diving gauge duly
registers 17, 19, 20, 23, 25 feet.*

"One-and-a-half degrees, sir."

"Are hydroplanes correct?" the Captain demands.

"Hydroplanes correct, sir," comes the reply after a brief pause.

Then another order, which produces a miraculous change. All engines cease to throb, voices cease to shout, and there is an intense and strange silence. The crew at their stations stand by, looking strained and expectant at the Captain, whose eye-balls — which reflect a ghostly green — are still glued to the periscope which revolves as he himself moves round the platform.

"Keep an eye on destroyer bearing 30 red," he breaks the silence with.

The activity begins afresh. At a motion from the Captain, I mount the foremost periscope and try to pick up the "enemy." The atmosphere above the water is still hazy, and at first all I can see is a blur. For a moment I look to see whether I can adjust the lens to suit my sight! But as I move round, the unmistakable outlines of a destroyer come into focus until one can almost make out her number. But she moves rapidly out of the picture, and you have to follow her hurriedly. She seems to be going at a terrific speed, but a mere turn of the periscope defeats all her splendid efforts to get away.

*The Captain on the after-periscope shouts
out an order hurriedly and excitedly. He is
body and soul in his work and the men seem
to catch his whole-hearted enthusiasm.*

*"Immediate action ! Down foremost
periscope ! "*

*The order rings out like a siren, and at
once all becomes bustle bordering on pandemonium.
In the midst of this hubbub I
clear off at the run to the torpedo-room, for
I am hungry to see everything. This torpedo
quarter at the nose of the submarine is cool
and well stored with ammunition. The great
shining torpedoes are nicely shelved; but
one shelf is empty. The torpedo which was
there is now in Tube No.1 and the operator
is anxiously standing by till the word (or
signal) comes to fire it by electricity — or if
that happen to fail, as the lieutenant warns
him, to fire her by hand. The glass screen
is lighted up in red from the control top.
It reads, "Flood Tube No.1 "*

*A seaman sits aloft on the tube ready to
open the valve when the torpedo is fired, in
order to balance the half-ton deficiency by
an inrush of water. He must count 1-2,
and not hurry.*

*The screen lights up with the words "Stand
by." The operator's hand twitches eagerly.*

"Fire!"

*He pulls a lever : an immense sizzle, a
tremendous splash, and a deafening bang, as
if all the noises in the heavens were belched
forth, a great number of new orders, and the
torpedo is on the way to her new billet. . . .*

*The problems that now worry the Captain
are :"Is she going true?" and "Have I
estimated the right deflection ? "*

*When I rush back to the control-room, I
find the crew a-sweating and the Captain
still gazing anxiously through the periscope,
trying to pick up the torpedo by her wake,
but this morning there is little wake. The
kind of torpedo we use nowadays leaves little
wake. He now gives the order "Surface!"*

*The clanging, which one has got used to,
is succeeded by a new sort of noise. The
indicator, from showing a depth of 34 feet,
now gradually drops 30 — 28 — 27 — down to
10. Hatches are opened, and the Captain
and I quickly climb aloft into the fresh cool
air. The boat is still half submerged, for
hundreds of tons of water have to be blown
from her tanks. The gun is dripping, and
soon the men are at work on her "putting
her to rights again."*

*"An exciting ten minutes, sir" I say to
the Captain.*

He turns on me. "Ten minutes ! Why,

we were submerged forty-three minutes!"

The Captain, in the middle of talking to
me, is still giving orders, and he hears with a
sigh of obvious relief that the "mouldy" or
"fish" or torpedo has gone true.

It is no easy matter firing at a target 4,000
yards away, coming at the rate of 20 knots
toward you, and conscious, as our destroyer
was conscious, of our presence and whereabouts. To make an appointment with a
vessel with the avowed object of torpedoing
her is like an angler making a "date" with
a fish.

And now the electric motors are being
recharged, her funnels are up, and as the
tanks are blown one by one we emerge fully
and are steaming along, cutting gracefully
through the waters, at a speed of 20 knots.

There is much a layman learns in such a
voyage. To him the submarine was a great
shell, with hardly anything inside except two
levers, one which made the boat submerge
and the other which brought it to the surface
again.

As a fact the ship is full from stem to stern
with the most ingenious contrivances ever invented by man, and to say that the Germans
could turn out a submarine in a week is sheer
idiocy after even a cursory glance at a submarine from within.

*"More like a year," I estimate, and the
Captain echoes :*

"Hardly less."

*Another item which surprised me was the
great preparations necessary before the boat
can dive, and, vice versa, before it is ready
to proceed on its surface engine. It is not,
as one fondly imagines, a matter of rushing
below and pressing a button.*

*Finally, the torpedo does not fly from a
submarine and, in a jiffy, reach its object.
Ours took five minutes.*

*The class of boat I have been describing
was still in its experimental stage, and this
particular boat had been as yet upon few
voyages. While she has, as I have said, revolution-
ised submarine construction, there is no doubt she
only represents a step towards even
more startling changes. Already, I understand, advances have been made on her, and
in the next flotilla we shall have vessels which
can hardly have been in the conception of
engineers a year ago. I do not profess to
speak as an expert, but from what I have
recently seen I should think that if ever war
comes again it will be fought exclusively under
the sea and in the air".*

SOURCE: THE FLEET FROM WITHIN. BEING THE
IMPRESSIONS OF A R. N. V. R. OFFICER.

APPENDIX K: THE K7 TANKS.

EXTERNAL, BALLAST, FUEL...
(P: PORT, S: STARBOARD, ML: MIDDLE LINE)

Main Ballast Tanks

- 'A' FRAME POSITION 40-43 CAPACITY (CUBIC FT): 298.46
- 'B' FRAME POSITION 59-65 CAPACITY (CUBIC FT): 527.90
- 'C' FRAME POSITION 65-73 CAPACITY (CUBIC FT): 847.24
- 'D' FRAME POSITION 73-80 CAPACITY (CUBIC FT): 848.04
- 'Q' FRAME POSITION 158-163 CAPACITY (CUBIC FT): 377.40
- 'X' FRAME POSITION 163-169 CAPACITY (CUBIC FT): 423.30
- 'Y' FRAME POSITION 169-176 CAPACITY (CUBIC FT): 381.84
- 'Z' FRAME POSITION 206-218 CAPACITY (CUBIC FT): 657.34

External Main Ballast Tanks

- NO 1 S FRAME POSITION: 37-53 CAPACITY (CUBIC FT): 677.85
- NO 1 P FRAME POSITION: 37-53 CAPACITY (CUBIC FT): 701.07
- NO 2 S FRAME POSITION: 53-66 CAPACITY (CUBIC FT): 743.61
- NO 2 P FRAME POSITION: 53-66 CAPACITY (CUBIC FT): 743.24
- NO 3 S FRAME POSITION: 65-83 CAPACITY (CUBIC FT): 1172.83
- NO 3 P FRAME POSITION: 65-83 CAPACITY (CUBIC FT): 1167.14
- NO 4 S FRAME POSITION: 83-98 CAPACITY (CUBIC FT): 1060.17
- NO 4 P FRAME POSITION: 83-98 CAPACITY (CUBIC FT): 1110.84
- NO 5 S FRAME POSITION: 98-113 CAPACITY (CUBIC FT): 1034.41
- NO 5 P FRAME POSITION: 98-113 CAPACITY (CUBIC FT): 1065.09
- NO 6 S FRAME POSITION: 112-127 CAPACITY (CUBIC FT): 1052.38
- NO 6 P FRAME POSITION: 112-127 CAPACITY (CUBIC FT): 1046.24
- NO 7 S FRAME POSITION: 126-141 CAPACITY (CUBIC FT): 987.84
- NO 7 P FRAME POSITION: 127-141 CAPACITY (CUBIC FT): 982.61
- NO 8 S FRAME POSITION: 141-154 CAPACITY (CUBIC FT): 863.10
- NO 8 P FRAME POSITION: 141-154 CAPACITY (CUBIC FT): 858.99
- NO 9 S FRAME POSITION: 154-165 CAPACITY (CUBIC FT): 682.67
- NO 9 P FRAME POSITION: 154-165 CAPACITY (CUBIC FT): 682.97

- NO 10 S FRAME POSITION: 165-178 CAPACITY (CUBIC FT): 730.55
- NO 10 P FRAME POSITION: 165-178 CAPACITY (CUBIC FT): 723.44

Auxiliary Ballast Tanks

- NO 1 ML FRAME POSITION: 37-40 CAPACITY (CUBIC FT): 84.72
- ML FRAME POSITION: 9-16 CAPACITY (CUBIC FT): 409.75
- 2 P FRAME POSITION: 97-101 CAPACITY (CUBIC FT): 291.72
- 2 S FRAME POSITION: 97-101 CAPACITY (CUBIC FT): 291.72
- 3 ML FRAME POSITION: 101-107 CAPACITY (CUBIC FT): 294.45
- 4 ML FRAME POSITION: 120-125 CAPACITY (CUBIC FT): 249.00
- 5 S FRAME POSITION: 133-141 CAPACITY (CUBIC FT): 116.81
- 6 P FRAME POSITION: 133-141 CAPACITY (CUBIC FT): 296,53
- 7 S FRAME POSITION: 141-148 CAPACITY (CUBIC FT): 305.36
- 8 P FRAME POSITION: 141-148 CAPACITY (CUBIC FT): 232.99
- COMPENSATING TANKS NO 1 ML FRAME POSITION: 32-37 CAPACITY (CUBIC FT): 279.20
- COMPENSATING TANKS NO 2 ML FRAME POSITION:194-199 CAPACITY (CUBIC FT): 143.13
- TRIMMING TANK FORWARD ML FRAME POSITION: 14-22 CAPACITY (CUBIC FT): 160.14
- TRIMMING TANK AFT FRAME POSITION: 206-212 CAP-

ACITY (CUBIC FT): 358.47

• RESERVE FEED TANK FRAME POSITION: 107-114 CAPACITY (CUBIC FT): 307.78

• RESERVE FEED TANK FRAME POSITION: 114-120 CAPACITY (CUBIC FT): 126.78

• FRESH WATER TANK ML FRAME POSITION: 26-30 CAPACITY (CUBIC FT): 116.33

• FRESH WATER TANK ML FRAME POSITION: 199-202 CAPACITY (CUBIC FT): 26.39

• W.R.T: TANK P FRAME POSITION: 22-24 CAPACITY (CUBIC FT): 26.39

• W.R.T: S FRAME POSITION: 22-24 CAPACITY (CUBIC FT): 26.39

• W.R.T: P FRAME POSITION: 24-26 CAPACITY (CUBIC FT): 26.79

• W.R.T: S FRAME POSITION: 24-26 CAPACITY (CUBIC FT): 26.79

• W.R.T: INNER P FRAME POSITION: 97-101 CAPACITY (CUBIC FT): 29.70

• W.R.T: INNER S FRAME POSITION: 97-101 CAPACITY (CUBIC FT): 29.54

• W.R.T: OUTER P FRAME POSITION: 97-101 CAPACITY (CUBIC FT): 33.54

• W.R.T: OUTER S FRAME POSITION: 97-101 CAPACITY (CUBIC FT): 33.54

• OIL FUEL TANK ML FRAME POSITION: 43-48 CAPACITY (CUBIC FT): 545.57

• OIL FUEL TANK ML FRAME POSITION: 48-53 CAPACITY (CUBIC FT): 234.43

• OIL FUEL TANK ML FRAME NUMBER 52-56 CAPACITY (CUBIC FT): 264.60

• OIL FUEL TANK ML FRAME NUMBER 56-59 CAPACITY (CUBIC FT): 228.37

• OIL FUEL TANK P FRAME NUMBER 80-85 CAPACITY (CUBIC FT): 622.59

• OIL FUEL TANK S FRAME NUMBER 80-85 CAPACITY

(CUBIC FT): 623.07
- OIL FUEL TANK ML FRAME POSITION: 85-88 CAPACITY (CUBIC FT): 481.76
- OIL FUEL TANK ML FRAME POSITION: 88-91 CAPACITY (CUBIC FT): 516.37
- OIL FUEL TANK ML FRAME POSITION: 91-94 CAPACITY (CUBIC FT): 519.25
- OIL FUEL TANK ML FRAME POSITION: 94-97 CAPACITY (CUBIC FT): 527.26
- OIL FUEL TANK P FRAME POSITION: 125-133 CAPACITY (CUBIC FT): 155.97
- OIL FUEL TANK S FRAME POSITION: 125-133 CAPACITY (CUBIC FT): 155.97
- OIL FUEL TANK ML FRAME POSITION: 148-153 CAPACITY (CUBIC FT): 314.35
- OIL FUEL TANK ML FRAME POSITION: 153-158 CAPACITY (CUBIC FT): 455.39
- OIL FUEL TANK P FRAME POSITION: 178-185 CAPACITY (CUBIC FT): 435.65
- OIL FUEL TANK S FRAME POSITION: 178-153 CAPACITY (CUBIC FT): 435.65
- OIL FUEL TANK ML FRAME POSITION: 185-190 CAPACITY (CUBIC FT): 489.08

APPENDIX L: K BOAT CAPTAINS (WHERE KNOWN).

HMS K1

Commander Charles S. Benning, December 1916 to 30 November 1917 (Benning was to be her only commander, as she was lost while under his command).

HMS K2

Commander Noel F. Laurence, 12 November 1916 to 9 September. 1918.
Lieutenant-Commander Reginald B. Darke, 9 September 1918 to 7 May 1919.
Lieutenant-Commander Victor E. Ward, 23 June 1919 to 27 October 1919.
Commander John F. Hutchings, 26 April 1920 to 14 February 1921 (and in command of "K" 10) . Lieutenant-Commander Frederick H. Taylor, 8 March 1921 to 18 December 1922,
Lieutenant-Commander Henry G. Higgins, 18 December 1922 to 15 August 1923.
Lieutenant-Commander Cyril G. B. Coltart, 15 August 1923 to 16 April 1925.
Lieutenant-Commander Claud B. Barry, March 1925 to 13 November 1925.

HMS K3

Commander Ernest W. Leir, 6 April 1916 – 22 April 1917. Lieutenant-Commander Herbert W. Shove, 22 April 1917 to 11 September 1919.

HMS K4

Commander David de B. Stocks, October 1916 to 31 January 1918 (died when vessel was lost under his command).

HMS K5

Commander David de B. Stocks, October 1916 to 31 January 1918 (died when vessel was lost under his command).

HMS K6

Lieutenant-Commander Robert R. Turner, 29 August 1916 to 18 September 1916.

Commander Geoffrey Layton, 8 December 1916 to January 1918.

Commander William R. D. Crowther, January 1918 to 7 March 1919.

Lieutenant-Commander Frederick C. C. Kennedy, 7 March 1919 to October 1919 (and in charge of a group of G and "K" class submarines in reserve).

Commander Hubert Vaughan-Jones, 30 December 1919 to 10 December 1920.

Commander Charles de Burgh, 10 December 1920 to February 1922.

Lieutenant-Commander Christopher P. Satow, 30 January 1922 to 25 September 1922.

Lieutenant-Commander Oswald E. Hallifax, 25 September 1922 to 16 September 1924.

Commander Alexander B. Greig, 14 September 1924 to 13 November 1925.

HMS K7

Lieutenant-Commander Geoffrey Layton, 15 November 1916 to 8 December 1916.
Commander Gilbert H. Kellet, 8 December 1916 to 14 November 1917.
Lieutenant in Command Samuel M. G. Gravener, 14 November 1917 (left upon sub paying off, then went to "K" 16).

HMS K8

Commander Robert R. Turner, 18 September 1916 to 14 November 1918.
Lieutenant-Commander Colin Cantlie, 14 November 1918 to 30 December 1920
Lieutenant-Commander Alfred G. Hine, 7 May 1920 to 26 July 1920.
Lieutenant-Commander Hugh R. Marrack, December 1920 to 10 June 1921.

HMS K9

Lieutenant-Commander Brownlow V. Layard, 1 January 1917 to February 1919.
Commander Henry H. G. D. Stoker, 10 February 1919 to 30 January 1920/
Lieutenant-Commander Geoffrey R. S. Watkins, 30 January 1920 to 9 August 1920.
Lieutenant-Commander Alfred G. Hine, 9 August 1920 to 2 July 1921.

HMS K10

Commander Claude C. Dobson, 5 March 1917 to 5 August 1918.

Lieutenant-Commander Donald I. McGillewie, 15 August 1918 to October 1919.
Commander John F. Hutchings, 26 April 1920 to 14 February 1921 (and in command of "K" 2).

HMS K11

Lieutenant-Commander Thomas F. P. Calvert, 18 September 1916 to 9 September 1918.
Lieutenant-Commander (I) George P. Thomson, 9 September 1918 to 22 July 1919.
Lieutenant-Commander (I, Fr.) George P. Thomson, 27 October 1919 to 27 September 1920 Lieutenant-Commander Frederick H. Taylor, 27 September 1920 to 8 March 1921.

HMS K12

Lieutenant-Commander John R. A. Codrington, 6 June 1917 to 8 June 1917.
Lieutenant-Commander John G. Bower, 12 June 1917 to 25 November 1918.
Lieutenant-Commander Godfrey Herbert, 1 January 1919 to February 1919.
Lieutenant-Commander (emergency) Gilbert E. Venning, 25 February 1919 to 12 July 1919. Lieutenant-Commander Victor E. Ward, 27 October 1919 to 22 October 1921.
Lieutenant-Commander William R. Richardson, 22 October 1921 to 15 November 1923.
Lieutenant-Commander Christopher P. Satow, 15 November 1923 to 27 July 1924.
Lieutenant-Commander Guy D'Oyly-Hughes, 27 July 1924.

HMS 13/22

Lieutenant-Commander Godfrey Herbert, 11 October 1916 to 29 January 1917 (sub sunk under his command, later to

return to service as "K" 22),
Lieutenant-Commander Charles de Burgh, 18 July 1917 to 13 February 1918.
Commander Fitzroy H. D. Byron, 12 August 1918 to.
24 May 1919 Lieutenant-Commander Allan Poland, 27 October 1919 to 1 July 1922.
Lieutenant-Commander Ronald W. Blacklock, August 1921 to February 1923.
Lieutenant-Commander Ronald A. Trevor, 3 February 1923 to 23 February 1925.
Lieutenant-Commander Frank P. Busbridge, 13 January 1925 to 13 November 1925.

HMS K14

Lieutenant-Commander John R. A. Codrington, 8 June 1917 to 14 September 1917.
Commander John B. Glencross, 19 August 1918 to October 1919.
Lieutenant Harry Percy Kendall Oram, April 1920 (also in command of "K" 16.
Lieutenant William Ibbett, 20 November 1920 (also in command of "K" 16).
Commander John F. Hutchings, 14 February 1921 to 22 May 1922.
Lieutenant-Commander Henry G. Higgins 6 May 1922 to 18 December 1922
Lieutenant-Commander James L. Boyd, 14 September 1924 to 13 November 1925.

HMS K15

Commander Hubert Vaughan-Jones, 15 January 1918 to 30 December 1919.
Commander Geoffrey R. S. Watkins, 9 August 1920 to 6 February 1921,

Commander George F. Bradshaw, 6 February 1921 to 5 August 1921 (sub sank at dockside under his command).

HMS K16

Lieutenant-Commander Charles de Burgh, 13 February 1918 to 13 September 1918.

Lieutenant-Commander Colin Cantlie, 13 September 1918 to October 1918.

Commander Charles G. Brodie, October 1918 to 22 July 1919.

Lieutenant-Commander George P. Thomson, 27 July 1919 to 27 October 1919 (temporary). Lieutenant-Commander Samuel M. G. Gravener, October, 1919 (joined after "K" 7 paid off). Lieutenant Harry P. K. Oram, April 1920[14] (also in command of "K" 14).

Lieutenant William Ibbett, 20 November 1920 (also in command of "K" 14)

HMS K17

Lieutenant-Commander Henry J. Hearn, 9 July 1917 – 31 January 1918 (killed when sub was lost under his command.

HMS K26

Commander Allan Poland, 22 November 1922 to 29 October 1923.

Commander (I Fr., Gr.) George P. Thomson, 29 October 1923 to 12 September 1924.

Commander Anthony B. Lockhart, 12 September 1924 to 1925.

Commander Alexander B. Greig, 13 November 1925 to 19 July 1926.

Commander Claud B. Barry, 22 November 1926 to 31 December 1926.

Commander (I Sp.) Gerald A. Garnons-Williams, 6 August 1928 to 25 August 1930.

APPENDIX M: HMS K5 ROLL OF HONOUR.

1. A BURROW, CECIL FREDERICK JOHN (28), Able Seaman (no. J/4284), HMS K-5, Royal Navy, 04/04/1892 ~ 20/01/1921, Son of Albert and the late Annie A Burrow, of Riverside House, Redhill, Surrey; husband of Rose Evelyn A Burrow, of 25, Crellin St., Barrow-in-Furness, Joined boat 22/4/20.

2. ANDREWS, HERBERT GARNHAM (27), Petty Officer (no. J/5147), HMS K-5, Royal Navy, 20/01/1921, Son of James A. Andrews; husband of Gertrude L. Andrews, of Newland St., Eynsham, Oxon, Joined boat 24/11/20 as 2nd Coxswain.

3. BACKHOUSE, ALBERT EDWARD (26), Stoker 1st Class (no. K/21000), HMS K-5, Royal Navy, 20/01/1921, Son of Mr. and Mrs. Herbert Backhouse, of Kelsaie, Saxmundham, Suffolk; husband of the late May A. E. Backhouse, Joined boat 19/08/19

4. BAKER, GEORGE WILLIAM (32), Acting Engineer Lieutenant, HMS K-5, Royal Navy, 20/01/1921, Son of George William and Nellie Baker; husband of Ethel Baker, of 8, Gordon Terrace, Rochester, Kent, was relieving Eng. Lieut Bowles.

5.   BEAUMONT, GEORGE LANGWELL (36), Chief Engine Room Artificer 2nd Class (no. 272157), HMS K-5, Royal Navy, 20/01/1921, Husband of Alice Maud Beaumont, of 208, Shearer Rd., Portsmouth, Joined boat 04/02/19

6. BOWLES, EDWARD JOHN (34), Engineer Lieutenant, HMS K-5, Royal Navy, 04/03/1887 ~ 20/01/1921, Son of Mr. and Mrs. E. J. Bowles, of 67, Lambeth Palace Rd., London; husband

of Violet Bowles, of 6, Station Rd., Dovercourt, Essex,

7. BURNS, JOHN (26), Stoker 1st Class (no. K/17609), HMS K-5, Royal Navy, 08/03/1894 ~ 20/01/1921, Son of John and Rose Burns, of Lewisham, London; husband of Ethel Lydia Burns, of 22, Chaplin St., Forest Hill, London,   Joined Boat 10/02/19

8. BUTLAND, RICHARD WILLIAM HENRY (21), Officer's Steward 3rd Class (no. L/9741), HMS K-5, Royal Navy, 20/01/1921, Son of Mr. J. R. and Mrs. J. F. Butland, of 25, Lyndurst Rd., Chichester, Sussex, Joined boat 02/05/20

9. CHARMAN, WILLIAM JAMES (23), Leading Telegraphist (no. J/31517), HMS K-5, Royal Navy, 20/01/1921, Son of James William and Kathleen Charman; husband of Hannah Charman, of 26, Plessey St., Netherton Colliery, Nedderton, Newcastle-on-Tyne, Joined boat 08/02/20.

10.   CHASE, FREDERICK WALTER (30), Leading Stoker (no. K/3799), D S M, HMS K-5, Royal Navy, 20/01/1921, Son of James and Sarah Chase, of Portsmouth; husband of Florence Elizabeth Chase, of 46, Malthouse Rd., Portsmouth,   Joined boat 16/01/20.

11.   CLARKE, BENJAMIN JACOB (35), Lieutenant, HMS K-5, Royal Navy, 20/01/1921, Son of Benjamin Jacob and Lucy Clarke, of Hackney, London; husband of Ellen Mary Clarke, of 26, Kent Rd., Ford, Devonport,

12.   CLARKE, CECIL FREDERICK (22), Able Seaman (no. J/32900), HMS K-5, Royal Navy, 20/01/1921, Son of Charles William Clarke, of 48, Heron Rd., Herne Hill, London, Joined boat 16/01/20.

13.   CLOWES, JOHN HENRY THOMAS (25), Able Seaman (no. J/25668), HMS K-5, Royal Navy, 08/10/1895 ~ 20/01/1921, Joined boat 24/10/19.

14.   CORNISH, PERCY WILLIAM (25), Able Seaman (no.

J/11540), HMS K-5, Royal Navy, 05/02/1895 ~ 20/01/1921, Son of George Cornish, of Pilgrims Hatch, South Weald, Brentwood, Joined boat 08/02/20.

15.   COX, JOHN WILLIAM (20), Telegraphist (no. J/49821), HMS K-5, Royal Navy, 20/01/1921, Son of Mrs. K. A. Cox, of Portsmouth, Joined boat 16/01/20.

16.   CUDDEFORD, FREDERICK WILLIAM FRANCIS (26), Lieutenant, HMS K-5, Royal Navy, 20/01/1921, Son of William and Mary Cecilia Cuddeford, of Sunnybank, Mortimer Common, Berks. Native of Chester. Present at Battle of Falkland Islands, Dec. 1914 (H.M.S. Carnarvon),at the attack on Kronstadt; joined H.M. Submarines in 1917 and saw service in C4, D4, L9, E40, KII,K5,

17.   DONOVAN, MICHAEL (25), Able Seaman (no. J/18322), HMS K-5, Royal Navy, 20/01/1921, Son of Michael and Sarah Donovan, of Croydon; husband of Mrs. Donovan, of 12, North Rd., Hersham, Walton-on-Thames, Joined boat 28/04/20.

18.   EDMONDS, CHARLES (28), Leading Seaman (no. J/2996), HMS K-5, Royal Navy, 20/01/1921, Husband of Agnes Mary Edmonds, of 9, Park Side, Chingford Lane, Woodford Green, Essex, Joined boat 28/09/20.

19.   ELLIS, CHARLES ALFRED (19), Stoker 1st Class (no. SS/124701), HMS K-5, Royal Navy, 20/01/1921, Son of Charles Ellis, of Ponders End; husband of Catherine Rose Ellis, of 9, Nelson Rd., Ponders End. Middx, Joined boat 26/02/18.

20.   EVANS, JOHN HORACE (25), Able Seaman (no. J/14734), HMS K-5, Royal Navy, 20/01/1921, Son of Joseph and Ann Hicken Evans, of West Bromwich, Birmingham; husband of Florence May Evans, of 11, Great Arthur St., Smeth-

wick, Birmingham, Joined boat 15/02/19.

21.   FRENCH, ALFRED FREDERICK (35), Petty Officer (no. 214229), HMS K-5, Royal Navy, 20/01/1921, Son of William and Mercia French, of Hailsham, Sussex; husband of Ethel E. French, of 53, Paulsgrove Rd., North End, Portsmouth, Joined boat 01/09/20 as Coxswain.

22.   GAIMES, JOHN AUSTIN (34), Lieut-Commander, D S O, HMS K-5, Royal Navy, 20/01/1921, Son of Ada Bancroft Gaimes, of Randtville, Tonbridge, Kent,the late Henry Austin Gaimes,

23.   GEORGE, WALTER (24), Able Seaman (no. J/17015), HMS K-5, Royal Navy, 20/01/1921, Son of Frederick and Rosetta E. George, of 3, Clausentum Rd., St. Cross, Winchester, Hants, Joined boat 28/04/20.

24.   GILLETT, VICTOR ALLEN (20), Able Seaman (no. J/24980), HMS K-5, Royal Navy, 26/01/1898 ~ 20/01/1921, Joined boat 11/11/18 (Day of Armistice!)

25.   HESTER, WILLIAM JAMES (26), Engine Room Artificer 3rd Class (no. M/1516), HMS K-5, Royal Navy, 08/06/1894 ~ 20/01/1921, Son of William and Minnie Hester, of 78, Festing Grove, Southsea, Portsmouth, Joined boat 10/12/20.
26.   HICKLIN, WILLIAM OSBORNE (28), Leading Stoker (no. K/12306), HMS K-5, Royal Navy, 24/10/1892 ~ 20/01/1921, Joined Boat 16/11/20.

27.   HUTCHENCE, HARRY (24), Stoker 1st Class (no. K/22154), HMS K-5, Royal Navy, 14/02/1896 ~ 20/01/1921, Son of Ernest Hutchence, of Whitchurch, Hants; husband of Beatrice Annie Hutchence, of I, Hawthorne Villa, Balfour St., Holderness Rd., Hull, Joined boat 29/04/20 .

28.   INIGHT, WALTER (25), Leading Seaman (no. J/10959), HMS K-5, Royal Navy, 20/01/1921, Son of Alfred and Norah Inight, of 12, Lansdowne St., Worcester. Wounded in Dardanelles on H.M.S. Amethyst., Joined boat 16/04/18.

29.   KENDALL, JOHN GILMOUR (25), Stoker 1st Class (no. K/24052), HMS K-5, Royal Navy, 20/01/1921, Son of William and Jessie Kendall, of 112, Canon Gate, Edinburgh, Joined boat 14/04/20.

30.   LAMPARD, THOMAS FREDERICK (26), Leading Seaman (no. J/12698), HMS K-5, Royal Navy, 20/01/1921, Son of the late Thomas and Sarah Lampard, of Portsmouth; husband of Lizzie Lampard, of 101A, High St., Aldershot,   Joined boat 28/04/20.

31.   LAMPORT, ALBERT JOHN (26), Leading Seaman (no. J/6059), HMS K-5, Royal Navy, 26/05/1894 ~ 20/01/1921, Son of Alfred Lamport, of Southampton; husband of Jean Lamport, of 50, North Junction St., Leith,   Joined boat 01/09/20.

32.   LASHMAR, BERTRAM ARTHUR (31), Engine Room Artificer 2nd Class (no. M/4306), HMS K-5, Royal Navy, 20/01/1921, Son of William John and Kathleen Lashmar, of Cowes, Isle of Wight; husband of Constance Daisy Lashmar, of 3, Bath Rd., Southsea, Portsmouth, Joined boat 15/04/2.

33.   LAWRENCE, JAMES CRORDON (24), Leading Seaman (no. J/26878), HMS K-5, Royal Navy, 12/07/1896 ~ 20/01/1921, Medal for Valour 2nd Class (Romania). Son of Helen Inglis Lawrence, of 14, Jeffreys Rd., Clapham, London, the late James Lawrence. Native of Aberdeen,   Joined boat 01/05/20.

34.   LAWRENCE, STANFIELD (30), Stoker 1st Class (no.

K/24155), HMS K-5, Royal Navy, 17/10/1890 ~ 20/01/1921, Son of Mary Ann Lawrence, of 23, New Rd. East, Copnor, Portsmouth, Joined boat 01/05/20.

35.   MACGREGOR, ROBERT JAMES RUSSELL (35), Stoker 1st Class (no. K/19376), HMS K-5, Royal Navy, 20/01/1921, Husband of Mary Isabel Macgregor, of Dalhowan St., Crosshill, Ayrshire,   Joined boat 16/06/20.

36.   MALE, BERT EDWARD (36), Chief Stoker (no. 302183), HMS K-5, Royal Navy, 27/01/1884 ~ 20/01/1921, Son of Andrew and Elizabeth Male; husband of Polly Male, of 37, Osborne St., Southsea, Portsmouth, Joined boat 24/04/20.

37.   MANSFIELD, RICHARD ALBERT (28), Able Seaman (no. J/2617), HMS K-5, Royal Navy, 16/08/1892 ~ 20/01/1921, Joined boat 26/07/19.

38.   METCALFE, FRED (25), Able Seaman (no. SS/8401), HMS K-5, Royal Navy, 20/01/1921, Son of Albert and Emily Metcalfe, of Tockwith, York. Joined boat 25/07/20.

39.   MIDDLEMOST, ROBERT JAMES   Royal Navy, 20/01/1921, Son of Milly Annette Crump (formerly Middlemost), of 2, Furneaux Villas, Paignton, Devon, the late Capt. James Menteith Middlemist (Seaforth Highlanders),

40.   MOULD, WILLIAM (28), Petty Officer (no. J/7392), HMS K-5, Royal Navy 20/01/1921, Son of Amos and Mary Ann Mould; husband of Amy Bedtrice Mould, of 49, White St., Analby Rd., Hull, Joined boat 02/01/18.

41.   PAGE, ALFRED GEORGE (34), Petty Officer Stoker (no. 229695), HMS K-5, Royal Navy, 20/01/1921, Husband of Esther Mary Marion Page, of 50, Shakespeare Rd., Portsmouth,

42.   PARR, FREDERICK (25), Stoker 1st Class (no. K/20815), HMS K-5, Royal Navy 20/01/1921, Son of William and Ellen Louise Parr, of Park Cottage, Swallowfield St., Reading, Joined boat 15/01/20.

43.   PARRY, JAMES FREDERICK (26), Stoker 1st Class (no. K/17768), HMS K-5, Royal Navy, 20/01/1921, Husband of E. M. Parry, of 40, Hampshire St., Gipsyville, Hull. Native of Bromley, Kent, Joined boat 01/01/18

44.   POLLARD, GEORGE (29), Engine Room Artificer 3rd Class (no. M/10901), HMS K-5, Royal Navy, 21/01/1891 ~ 20/01/1921, Husband of Eva Pollard, of 152, Liverpool Rd., Cadishead, Manchester, Joined boat 17/07/19

45.   PURKIS, FREDERICK WALTER (28), Stoker 1st Class (no. K/19579), HMS K-5, Royal Navy, 20/01/1921, Son of John Purkis, of Hornchurch; husband of Gladys Emma Purkis, of Hill Farm Cottage, Hacton Lane, Hornchurch, Joined boat 01/01/18

46.   RAGGETT, ALFRED DAVID (23), Stoker 1st Class (no. K/26671), HMS K-5, Royal Navy, 20/01/1921, Son of David and Eliza Raggett, of Stakes Corner, Littleton, Guildford, Surrey, Joined boat 01/05/20

47.   RILEY, HERBERT , Engine Room Artificer 2nd Class (no. M/4194), HMS K-5, Royal Navy, 20/01/1921, Joined boat 16/01/20

48.   SEYMOUR, GEORGE (26), Stoker 1st Class (no. K/24204), HMS K-5, Royal Navy, 30/01/1894 ~ 20/01/1921, Nephew of Mrs. P. Fairow, of Thornden Farm, Headcorn, Ashford, Kent, Joined boat 01/05/20

49.   SHEPPARD, WILLIAM CYRIL (27), Petty Officer (no. J/5572), HMS K-5, Royal Navy, 20/01/1921, Husband of Mar-

garet May Sheppard, of 92, Clarence St., Landport, Portsmouth, joined boat 01/09/20.

50.   SMITH, FREDERICK JOHN (42), Petty Officer Stoker (no. 299134), HMS K-5, Royal Navy, 16/11/1878 ~ 20/01/1921, Long Service and GHod Conduct Medal. Son of William Smith, of Bignor, Pulborough, Sussex, the late Mary Smith; husband of Rosie Longhurst (formerly Smith), of 6, Council Cottages, Burpham, Guildford. Present at the raid on Zeebrugge. Awarded Africa General Service Medal (Somaliland Clasp), Joined boat 16/01/20.

51.   SMITH, WILLIAM BALFOUR (25), Stoker 1st Class (no. K/19915), HMS K-5, Royal Navy, 05/07/1895 ~ 20/01/1921, Son of David and Elizabeth Smith; husband of Daisy Caroline Smith, of 98, st Thomas's St., Portsmouth, Joined boat 16/01/20.

52.   SMITH, WILLIAM CARRINGTON (26), Able Seaman (no. J/6219), HMS K-5, Royal Navy 20/01/1921, Son of Abraham Smith of High St., Wrotham, Kent, the late Jane Smith, Joined boat 01/09/20.

53.   TANNER, WILLIAM JAMES (23), Signalman (no. J/21454), HMS K-5, Royal Navy, 19/09/1897 ~ 20/01/1921, Son of Edward and Elizabeth Ann Tanner, of Forest Rd., Crowthorne, Berks, Joined boat 22/05/20.

54.   WARD, HORACE WILLIAM (21), Able Seaman (no. SS/8464), HMS K-5, Royal Navy, 20/01/1921, Son of Mr. and Mrs. William James Ward, of 22, Peach St., Luton, Beds, Joined boat 05/07/19.

55.   WEST, LEWIS HERBERT (31), Stoker 1st Class (no. K/20832), HMS K-5, Royal Navy, 06/08/1889 ~ 20/01/1921, Son of Fanny West, of Bridge Villa, Runcton, Chichester, Sus-

sex, Joined boat 16/01/20.

56.   WILTSHIRE, RICHARD (22), Signalman (no. J/31907), HMS K-5, Royal Navy, 20/01/1921, Son of the late Mr. A. Wiltshire, of 376, Moseley Rd., Birmingham,

57.   WOOTTON, WILLIAM (29), Petty Officer Stoker (no. K/2665), HMS K-5, Royal Navy, 20/01/1921, Son of William Wootton, of 18, Frederick St., Latchford, Warrington, Joined boat 14/01/20.

APPENDIX N:
CREW FIGURES

Within the Kew file is a page that provides a numerical comparison of the Royal Navy's submarine crew numbers. The original unfortunate does not reproduce to a quality that is readable, so the following is a translation to a tabular form.

Source: K2 ships book, National Archives	R CLASS	M CLASS	L5 CLASS	L CLASS	K CLASS	H CLASS	E&S CLASS
COMMANDER	-	0	0	0	1	0	0
LIEUT CMDR OR LIEUT	1	2 (B)	1 (B)	1(B)	1	1	1
LIEUTENANT (G)	0	1	0	0	0	0	0
LIEUTENANT (N)	0	1	0	0	1	0	0
LIEUT SUB-LIEUT, MATE & WARRANT OFFICER	2	1	2	2	1	2	2
WARRANT OFFICER	0	0	1	1	0	0	0
PETTY OFFICER	2	5 (A)	4(A)	3(A)	3(A)	2	3
LEADING SEAMAN	2	6	3	3	4	2	2
A.B OR ORD SEAMAN	6	25	8	8	13	4	5
P.O TELEGRAPHIST	0	1	1	1	1	1	0
?DG TELEGRAPHIST	0	0	1	1	1	1	1
TELEGRAPHIST	1	1	0	1	1	0	0
YEOMAN OF SIGNALS	0	0	1	1	0	0	0
?DG SIGNALMAN	0	0	-	-	1	1	1
SIGNALMAN	1	1	-	-	-	-	-
INCLUDED IN THE ABOVE							
G.M, G.L.1ST CL	-	1	-	-	-	-	-
G.L 1ST CL	-	1	-	-	-	-	-
G.L 2ND CL	-	2	2	1(C)	2(D)	-	-
RANGE TAKER 3RD CL	-	1	-	-	1	-	-
S.G	-	20	2	2(C)	4(4)	1	1
Q.O	-	1	-	-	-	-	-
T.G.M	1	1	1	1	1	1	1
T.C	-	1	-	-	1	-	-
SUB COXSWAIN	1	1	1	1	-	1	1
L.T.O	2	3	2	3	2	2	2
S.T	6	6	7	6	9	4	6
ENGR LIEUT. LIEUT OR	-	-	-	-	1	-	-
CMDR OR W.T ENGR	-	1	1	1	-	-	-
CHIEF E.R.A	-	1	-	-	1	1	1
E.R.A	2	3	4	4	5	2	3
CHIEF STOKER	-	1	1	-	1	-	-
STOKER P.O	1	1	1	1	3	1	1
LEADING SEAMAN	2	4	3	4	3	2	3
STOKER	2	8	9	9	13	3	6
ORDNANCE ARTIFICER	-	2(F)	-	-		-	-
ELECTRICAL ARTIFICER	-	1	1	-		-	-
OFF. STD. 2ND CL	-	1(E)	-	-		-	-
TOTAL	22	67	42	39	57	23	30

SOURCES

THE NATIONAL ARCHIVES, LONDON

LOSS OF H.M. SUBMARINE K.5 - COURT OF ENQUIRYADM 116/2125

LOSS OF HM SUBMARINE K5. STATEMENT BY LIEUT. G WHITFIELD. QUESTION OF SEAGOING.ADM 1/8599/23

SINKING OF HM SUBMARINES G9 AND K1; LOSS OF HM SUBMARINES C16, C34 AND E47 ADM 137/3709

COLLISIONS INVOLVING HM SHIPS INFLEXIBLE AND FEARLESS, HM SUBMARINES K14, K22, K17, K4.ADM 156/86

SHIP: H.M. SUBMARINES K.1, K.2, K.3, K.4, K.5, K.6 AND K.7. REMARKS: OPERATIONAL STEAM   ADM 136/12

STRANDING OF HM SUBMARINE K1 CDR C S BENNING D S O, R N HMS FEARLESS ADM 156/83

K3 LOG (UNCONTROLLED DIVE KING ONBOARD)   DECEMBER 1916 ADM173/6093

K3 LOG (TRIALS) ADM173/6094

K3 LOG (K1 LOST)   18.11.17 ADM 173/6099

K3 LOG (UNCONTROLLED DIVE) 09.01.17 ADM173/6104

K7 LOG (ATTACK U-BOAT)16.06.17   ADM173/6267

K9 LOG (K1 LOST)   18.11.17 ADM173/6270

K9 LOG (K5 LOST) 19.01.21   ADM173/6380

K15 LOG   (SUNK) 25.06.21ADM173/6658

MODIFIED 'K' CLASS SUBMARINE: QUESTION OF SUBMERGED EXPERIMENTS   ADM 226/21/34

MODIFIED 'K' CLASS SUBMARINES: LARGE SCALE BRIDGE SCREENS ADM 226/22/5

MODIFIED 'K' CLASS SUBMARINES: SUBMERGED AND FURTHER SURFACE EXPERIMENTS   ADM 226/23/11

MODIFIED 'K' CLASS SUBMARINES: PRELIMINARY REPORT OF SURFACE EXPERIMENTS WITH STERED BOW ADM 226/22/33

(AUTHORS TITLES FOR CONVENIENCE. ADM=KEW REF)

THE ROYAL ARCHIVE, WINDSOR CASTLE.

Admiralty Salvage in Peace and War 1906 - 2006: Grope, Grub and Tremble

Admiralty Salvage in Peace and War 1906 - 2006: Grope, Grub and Tremble

An Index to British Warships 1914-1919" by F J Dittmar & J J Colledge.

Barrow Built Ships by John Watts

Dock Book, June 1909, published by the British Admiralty "For the Information of Officers in H. M. Service Only.

HMS K5, Grand Fleet. Voices from the Front: An Oral History of the Great War by Peter Hart

John Watts "Barrow Built Ships"

K26 - Barrow Submariners Association

K Boat Catastrophe: Eight Ships and Five Collisions by N.S. Nash

Katastrophe Edward C. Whitman

Report of a deep dive by submarine K.3 by Lt. Cdr. Shove.

The British submarine. Liscombe

The K boats. Don Everitt

www.janmeecham.wordpress

www.interactive-learning.com.au

www.gracesguide.co.uk www.warshipsresearch

www.britsub

www.merriam-webster.com

www.wrecksite.eu

www.oceanservice.noaa.gov

BOOKS BY THIS AUTHOR

H.m.a.s Sydney: A Chronological History. Volume1. (The Pre-War Year 1913-14)

HMAS Sydney is famed for destroying the Sydney. But there was much more to here tale. The 13 months of peace time service, the capture of Germany's pacific colonies, service in the Atlantic hunting the great tran-atlantic liner and commerce raider the, Kronprinz Wilhelm and over two years as part of the Royal Navy's Grand Fleet.The first volume in this series tells the story of those first 13 months when she visited South Africa, toured eastern Australia and escorted the two submarines AE1&2 from Singapore to Sydney.The narrative draws on the ship's log, crew members journals and the local Australian newspaper achieves. It tells the tale of the ship but also the story of those crew men who served in her. Who in volume two will face the Emden and the First World War.

Follow The Author

Andy South
✓ Following

Hmas Sydney : The South Pacific & Emden Campaigns. (Vol 2)

This, the second volume of a planned three, tells tale of the first five months of the light cruiser HMAS Sydney's war time service. In those first few months she was to be present as Australia and New Zealand wrestled the German Kaisers Pacific islands away from his colonial forces. Then she was called on to escort one of the biggest convoys of the war, as the ANZAC's made their passage to Egypt. But on route destiny was to bring her to the remote Coco Island's and a ship-to-ship battle with Germany's most successful light cruiser of both wars, SMS Emden. The narrative leaves her laying alongside in Gibraltar, where the forthcoming volume III will accompany her as she hunts the Kaiser's remaining warships in the Atlantic, before she is called on for Grand Fleet service and aeronautical adventures.

The first volume told her pre-war tale and gave an indepth study of her technical aspects.

Together the three volumes when complete will tell the in depth tale of one of the most famous cruisers of both World Wars.

The volumes draw on the ship's log book as well as her crew members journals, official post war accounts and volumes of secondary sources. Its heavily illustrated throughout, something only possible with the help and support of the Australian War Memorial and the countries archives.

The Tegetthoff Class: Austria-Hungary's Dreadnoughts (1909-1925)

For less than 5 years, (1913-1918) the Austria-Hungarian Empire had a navy that was in part comprised of all big gun dreadnoughts, (or battleships). They were in their short lifetime to see 4 years of war and by the time the guns fell silent across the battlefields of Europe, 50% of that new dreadnought force lay on the seabed. Aside from a bombardment of the Italian mainland, they were never to fire their powerful main armament in anger. They were to be lost not to a blow by blow exchange of fire with their peers, but to Italian torpedoes and limpet mines carried into battle by fast torpedo boats and frogmen.

Of all the battleships that were created in the years prior to the First World War, the four ships of the Tegetthoff class, were probably the most flawed, born from a designer with failing eyesight and a growing deafness, who refused to take sage advice from the German Admiralty in ship design. They were conceived through a process that saw political scheming and 'untruths' told. But for all these flaws and the life's they were to cost, the Tegetthoff class is one of the most fascinating in a genre of warship that has been lost to technological advancement in naval design.

In conjunction with Andrew Wilkie's stunning computerized images, that bring the class back to life, in a way no other battleship of the era has been so blessed, this 'E' book tells the story of the 4 dreadnoughts, from conception, to their ultimate demise. The book holds over 300 photographs and plans, having been heavily researched and drawing on a wide range of sources and experts.

This the second edition of the book has been expanded prodigiously beyond the scope of its earlier predecessor, covering topics that the first publication only touched on. The final product is an in-depth study of the class that will hopefully appeal to a wide cross section of readers.

On a final note, this volume is the second addition and the textual errors that were prevalent in its predecessor have been amended. This edition has been proofread by three separate persons and corrections made. For th
ose who brought the original edition I apologize, and I have learnt much from the mistakes within that first book I had

penned. This new edition is only based on the foundation of what went before and is a different creature altogether. Its subject matter is deeper, wider and draws from sources that span the globe.

Printed in Great Britain
by Amazon

55844048R00404